NEUROPSYCHOLOGY for the ATTORNEY

NEUROPSYCHOLOGY for the ATTORNEY

Robert J. Sbordone, Ph.D.

Diplomate, American Board of Clinical Neuropsychology
Diplomate, American Board of Professional Neuropsychology
Fellow, National Academy of Neuropsychology

Orange County Neuropsychology Group
Irvine, California

GR/St. Lucie Press
Delray Beach, Florida

1996 printing by GR/St. Lucie Press

Printed and bound in the U.S.A. Printed on acid-free paper.
10 9 8 7 6 5 4 3

ISBN 1-878205-26-9
Library of Congress Card Catalog Number: 91-070189

Direct all inquires to:
GR/St. Lucie Press
100 E. Linton Blvd., Suite 403B
Delray Beach, FL 33483
Phone: (561) 274-9906
Fax (561) 274-9927
Email: information@slpress.com
Web site address: http://www.slpress.com

Dedication

To Frank R. Ervin, M.D., for encouraging me to enter the field of neuropsychology. To Drs. G. Marsh, L. Majovski, E. Kaplan, W. Lynch, A. Purisch, and the late N. Geschwind, who have been my teachers and provided me with their wisdom and encouragement.

Acknowledgements

I wish to express my gratitude to my associate, Dr. Arnold Purisch, for his advice, friendship, and support in the preparation of this book. I also wish to thank many of the attorneys with whom I have had the privilege of working with in the past. They have provided an education on medicolegal issues, in which clinical psychologists and neuropsychologists receive virtually no formal training. I also want to acknowledge Andrew C. Siegel, Ph.D., who critically reviewed the manuscript and made a number of excellent suggestions to improve the manuscript from the perspective of a neuropsychologist. I also wish to acknowledge George Knopfler, Esq., who provided many sound suggestions from an attorney's viewpoint. I recognize the generous assistance of my typists, Kathleen Ramdwar and Arlene Somerville, who worked so diligently on this manuscript with painstaking effort and care. I also acknowledge the generosity of Matthew Bender for granting permission to use illustrations from its *Trauma* series.

Introduction

by Kenneth I. Kolpan

As a trial attorney who has handled many cases involving brain injury, I am familiar with the difficulty in presenting these cases before a jury, judge, or claims adjuster. Though these clients have sustained serious injuries and have cognitive and intellectual deficits, the problems are difficult to demonstrate. The client with a brain injury walks into the courtroom and, often times, appears physically intact. In such a structured setting where questions are directed to the injured party, he or she may be focused enough to answer the simplest questions which do not tax their cognitive abilities. It is the attorney's job to present evidence that establishes the serious nature of this injury.

The person with a brain injury has significant problems which affect their activities of daily living, relations with others, and employment. If the client is fortunate, they have been evaluated by a competent neuropsychologist. Neuropsychological testing will typically demonstrate the areas of diminished capacity, provide data invaluable to the client's rehabilitation, and provide objective evidence which demonstrates the numerous manifestations of the client's brain injury.

The role of the neuropsychologist in brain injury litigation cannot be overstated. The neuropsychologist provides the fact finders, judges, and claims adjusters the objective data of the plaintiff's impairment. Presenting the neuropsychologist and this information in the courtroom in a comprehensible and persuasive fashion is essential to the successful completion of a personal injury case involving a brain injury.

Dr. Sbordone's book provides the trial attorney with essential information regarding the background of neuropsychology, the relevant training and experience of a neuropsychologist, and provides a clear description of the various tests utilized by neuropsychologists, particularly their strengths and limitations, in a manner readily presented before a jury on direct examination. His explanation of neuroanatomy, brain function, behavioral neurology, and testing give the trial attorney an outline for direct and cross examination of this expert testimony.

For those attorneys who know little or nothing about brain injury, this book will be a crucial part of his or her library. For the experienced personal injury attorney, Dr. Sbordone's book and his expertise and trial experience, will better assist them and all other advocates on the behalf of persons with brain injury.

The ultimate beneficiaries of Dr. Sbordone's book will not only be the attorneys who read it, but their clients as well.

Kenneth I. Kolpan is a plaintiff's trial injury attorney who has handled numerous cases involving brain injury. Mr. Kolpan practices in Boston, Massachusetts and concentrates on plaintiff's personal injury cases.

Mr. Kolpan is also an Associate Professor of Medicine in the Department of Rehabilitation Medicine, Tufts University School of Medicine, Boston, Massachusetts and Medical-Legal Editor for the *Journal of Head Trauma Rehabilitation*, one of the nation's leading medical journals on head trauma.

Preface

by Robert J. Sbordone, Ph. D.

Neuropsychology for the Attorney was written for attorneys who deal with personal injury, disability, criminal law, family law, and other cases involving brain damage or post-traumatic stress disorders. The purpose of this book is to provide information about the field of neuropsychology, including its origins and historical development, its purpose, use, and theoretical foundations, in order for attorneys to properly use neuropsychologists as experts and as treatment specialists. The book also contains an overview of neuroanatomy, as well as a description of the cognitive, behavioral, emotional, and social manifestations of neurological injuries and disorders which affect the brain. The book provides a systematic approach to the process of neuropsychological assessment, beginning with the patient's chief complaints; interviews with the patient's families and/or significant others; a chronological history of the patient's injuries and symptoms from the accident until the present; the patient's developmental, educational, family, employment, legal, military, medical, neurological, and psychiatric history; a review of the patient's educational, vocational, medical, and psychiatric records; and the administration, scoring, and interpretation of neuropsychological test data. The book also discusses many of the more commonly used neuropsychological tests and reviews their strengths and limitations.

The author has tried to remain as impartial as possible, in that approximately 50% of his practice consists of medicolegal work, of which half of all his referrals are from the plaintiff's attorney, with the remaining half being referred from attorneys representing the defendant. Realizing the problems that many people have in understanding psychological, medical, and neurological terminology and concepts, the author has made a deliberate effort to describe this material as simply as possible. Numerous case studies are utilized, based on the author's experience and that of other neuropsychologists to illustrate the points made in the text. The author presents two actual reports based on cases which have since settled, in which the author served as an expert witness. *Neuropsychology for the Attorney* also provides some useful guidelines to select or depose a neuropsychological expert, as well to detect malingering. Finally, the book tries to illustrate how attorneys can utilize the services of a neuropsychologist as an expert and as a treatment specialist.

Contents

		PAGE
	Dedication	v
	Acknowledgements	vii
	Introduction	ix
	Preface	xi
	List of Tables and Figures	xv
Chapter 1	Clinical Neuropsychology: Definition	1
Chapter 2	The Neuropsychologist: Education and Training	15
Chapter 3	Clinical Neuropsychology: Comparision to Other Specialties	23
Chapter 4	Neuroanatomy	31
Chapter 5	Neuropathological Aspects of Neurobehavioral Disorders	45
Chapter 6	Neuropsychological Assessment	67
Chapter 7	Neuropsychological Testing	103
Chapter 8	Neuropsychological Test Scoring and Analysis	177
Chapter 9	Test Interpretation	185
Chapter 10	Reaching Conclusions Regarding Brain Damage and/or Cognitive Impairment	197
Chapter 11	Determining the Prognosis of the Patient's Impairments Following Brain Damage	215
Chapter 12	Determining the Type of Treatment and/or Rehabilitation Services Needed for the Brain-damaged Patient	221
Chapter 13	Sample Neuropsychological Reports	229
Chapter 14	How to Select a Neuropsychological Expert	263
Chapter 15	How to Utilize the Services of a Neuropsychologist	267
Chapter 16	How to Depose a Neuropsychologist	271
Chapter 17	Malingering	289
Appendix A	Diplomates of The American Board of Clinical Neuropsychology	297
Appendix B	Glossary of Neurological and Neuropsychological Terms	313
Bibliography		347
Index		359

List of Tables and Figures

TABLES

		PAGE
Table 1.	American Board of Clinical Neuropsychology, Inc. Eligibility Requirements	21
Table 2.	Comparison of Clinical Psychology and Clinical Neuropsychology	25
Table 3.	Comparison of Psychiatry and Clinical Neuropsychology	27
Table 4.	Comparison of Neurology and Clinical Neuropsychology	30
Table 5.	Patient History	76
Table 6.	Behavioral Observations	99
Table 7.	Neuropsychological Tests Often Used to Assess the Brain-injured Patient	131
Table 8.	Strengths and Limitations of Neuropsychological Tests	159
Table 9.	Stages of Recovery in Traumatic Brain Injury	216

FIGURES

Fig. 1.	Major Regions of the Adult Brain as Seen in a Lateral View	32
Fig. 2.	Functional "Road Map" of the Brain	33
Fig. 3.	Schematic Drawing of Motor and Somesthetic Areas	34
Fig. 4.	Schematic Drawing of Medial Aspect of Hemisphere of Brain	37
Fig. 5.	Structures Located on "Underneath" Surfaces of Brain	38
Fig. 6.	Schematic Drawing of Vital Cerebral Arteries	40
Fig. 7.	Schematic Drawing of Arteries on Underside of Brain	41

Chapter 1

Clinical Neuropsychology: Definition

Clinical neuropsychology is an applied science which is concerned with the relationship between the brain and behavior. It integrates the fields of clinical psychology and behavioral neurology and attempts to evaluate individuals suspected of having sustained focal or diffuse brain dysfunction, as well as to provide psychological treatment and/or cognitive rehabilitation of such individuals. It primarily utilizes tests that have been specifically designed to evaluate a wide variety of cognitive functions and behaviors, which are dependent on the structural and functional integrity of the brain. It also utilizes background information obtained directly from the patient and significant others and relies on the patient's academic, vocational, medical, and psychiatric records to establish the premorbid level of functioning and abilities of the patient, to establish a baseline to determine what changes have been brought about by a specific accident or brain insult. Given this information, the clinical neuropsychologist attempts to formulate a clear picture of how the patient's personality, cognitive functioning, social, and emotional behavior have been altered. The effects which these changes have had on the patient's everyday functioning, ability to work, achieve specific academic or vocational goals, and to enjoy life are similarly assessed.

Purpose

Clinical neuropsychology can identify the particular "changes" that have been caused by a brain injury even though the effects of this injury may not have been previously recognized by the plaintiff's attorney, or have been undetected by skull x-rays, medical, psychiatric, or neurological examinations, or even by so-called "objective" neurodiagnostic tests such as an electroencephalogram (EEG), computerized tomography (CT) scan, or magnetic resonance imaging (MRI) studies. Thus, neuropsychological assessment can provide the plaintiff's attorney with a comprehensive and realistic assessment of their client's "damages" expressed as neuropsychological impairments, their relative severity, and the effect that such impairments are likely to have on their client's ability to work, live in society, and enjoy life. From the defense attorney's perspective, the neuropsychological assessment may identify non-neurological or pre-existing causes for the plaintiff's symptoms or neuropsychological impairments based on the plaintiff's history. Because of the comprehensive and rigorous nature of the neuropsychological assessment process, the neuropsychologist can ferret out "organic" from "functional" causes of the patient's symptoms or complaints which may be the result of pre-existing, situational, emotional, or motivational factors which are not directly related to a specific injury or accident.

Some Misconceptions of Neuropsychology

Many attorneys hold the belief that neuropsychology simply involves "testing for organicity or brain damage." Consistent with this assumption is the belief that the psychologist's role is simply to bring the patient who has sustained an alleged brain injury into his or her office, administer a battery of psychological tests, and upon scoring them determine whether the test scores corroborate the plaintiff or plaintiff's attorney's allegations that a specific event caused brain damage. In actuality, the practice of clinical neuropsychology is far more complicated. A similar analogy would be a plaintiff walking into an attorney's office, asking the attorney to file a personal injury lawsuit for a specific injury and expecting that the demand letter written by the attorney produce a check for the entire amount of the alleged damages within 10 days if the plaintiff can produce a bona fide police or accident report.

Sense of Frustration for the Attorney

As a result of some widely held misconceptions about clinical neuropsychology, many plaintiff attorneys may experience a sense of frustration, disappointment, and sometimes even anger, when the neuropsychologist requests to see the plaintiff's prior medical, academic, criminal, vocational, and psychiatric records. The neuropsychologist may also request that the plaintiff be referred to a neurologist or medical specialist for further testing or may even request that the plaintiff be referred to a rehabilitation program after completing his or her report, so that the plaintiff's cognitive and behavioral problems can be treated. Attorneys are often frustrated at the additional case costs associated with obtaining records and for medical evaluation and treatment referrals. Attorneys may also feel a sense of frustration when they are told that the patient's brain injury has not significantly altered the plaintiff's IQ, but instead has produced a number of subtle problems in behavioral and emotional regulation. Finally, the neuropsychologist's conclusions about the presence of brain damage may be inconsistent with the plaintiff's neurological examination including the results of computerized tomography (CT) scans, electroencephalography (EEG), or magnetic resonance imaging (MRI) scan. The plaintiff's attorney may similarly feel singularly betrayed when the neuropsychologist uncovers a pre-existing condition.

The Practice of Neuropsychology

The practice of neuropsychology can be broken down into five major areas: assessment/ diagnosis, treatment/rehabilitation, teaching, consultation, and research.

1. Assessment/Diagnosis

Patients are typically referred for assessment to determine their residual neuropsychological functioning following brain trauma, surgery, treatment, or rehabilitation; to determine whether the etiology of the patient's complaints are neurologic or functional, the degree of functional overlay in the patient's complaints following a specific injury, the degree of recovery the patient will make, the patient's future needs (which might include life-long treatment), their likelihood of returning to work or being able to work in the competitive labor market, competence, and need for hospitalization or treatment (this may also include an estimate of the cost of such treatment).

ASSESSMENT OF BRAIN DAMAGE

While studies have shown that the two most widely used standardized neuropsychological test batteries—the Luria-Nebraska and Halstead-Reitan—have demonstrated over 90% accuracy in discriminating the performance of brain-damaged and nonbrain-damaged patient groups (Golden, Hammeke, and Purisch, 1978; Wheeler and Reitan, 1974), it should be recognized that neuropsychological tests are best utilized in providing information about the behavioral impairments resulting from brain dysfunction, since a variety of neurological tests such as topographical brain mapping, MRI and CT scans, have lessened the need for neuropsychological assessment to localize the site of brain injury. Unfortunately, these neurological tests do not tell us about the cognitive, behavioral, and emotional impairments which typically result from brain trauma. Thus, it is the neuropsychologist who, because of his or her expertise, training, and experience, is able to provide a comprehensive description of the impairments resulting from brain trauma and their effects on the patient. While diagnosis of brain injury is not the primary role of the clinical neuropsychologist, it is not uncommon for the neuropsychologist to detect a pattern of cognitive impairments during neuropsychological assessment that is consistent with brain damage. For example, the neuropsychologist may find a pattern of impairments consistent with right frontotemporal lobe damage, even though the patient's neurological examination, including an EEG and MRI scan, was normal.

DETERMINATION OF BEHAVIORAL ALTERATIONS DUE TO BRAIN INJURY

Neuropsychological assessment examines the patient's intellectual functioning, language processing skills, perceptual skills, higher motor functions, attention and concentration skills, judgement, reasoning skills, mental flexibility, memory, constructional skills, abstract thinking and conceptualization skills, problem solving skills, behavioral regulation, personality alterations, and emotional functioning. Since the brain is the organ of behavior, any insult, however small, is capable of producing an alteration in one or more of these areas. Thus, the neuropsychologist's task is to carefully evaluate each of these areas and determine whether or not any significant alterations have occurred and the degree to which such alterations are indicative of brain injury and the degree to which they affect the patient's life and significant others. The neuropsychologist, by virtue of his or her training and expertise, is capable of fully evaluating each of these areas in considerable specificity, as well as determine the severity of these impairments. The neuropsychologist can also provide specific reports and testimony on the relationship between brain injury and altered behavior and how such behavioral alterations are manifested.

CASE STUDY

A 27-year-old school teacher was involved in a motor vehicle accident which was the fault of the other party. He struck his head on the steering wheel and was briefly rendered unconscious. When the paramedics arrived, he was awake, but appeared mildly confused and irritable. He was taken to the emergency room of a nearby hospital, where x-rays were found to be negative. He was discharged later that same day. He stayed out of school for one week because of severe aches and pains in his upper back and neck, for which he was prescribed pain medications and muscle relaxants. After returning to work, his students, family, and fellow teachers observed a dramatic change in his personality. While he had always been an easy-going and calm person, he was now impatient and showed a poor frustration tolerance to any type of stress or pressure. He began using foul language in his classroom, which upset his students. He would often appear confused and repeat the same material over and over again with little or no awareness. When his students pointed this out to him, he denied this problem and became extremely angry with them. He would often forget his lesson plans or fail to collect his students' homework. On several occasions, he arrived nearly two hours late for school and appeared unshaven and exhibited poor hygiene. When he was called in to meet with his principal, he denied these problems and indicated that he felt "great." He was referred to a psychiatrist by his principal, however, he failed to show up for his scheduled appointment. Later, he was taken to the appointment by his wife, who indicated to the psychiatrist that they had had no sexual contact since his accident two months ago. She observed that her husband was frequently angry, appeared fatigued, forgot conversations and appointments, and was no longer the intelligent, calm man she had once married. She also mentioned that on one occasion, her husband walked outside to fetch the newspaper with only his underwear on. She mentioned that he did not appear upset or embarrassed by this incident, even though it embarrassed several of their neighbors. The psychiatric examination revealed no family history of psychiatric or emotional problems. The patient did not appear depressed and exhibited no clear indication of psychiatric illness during the clinical interview. The psychiatrist diagnosed the patient as having an Adjustment Disorder and placed him on tranquilizers.

These medications, however, had little effect on the patient's cognitive and behavioral problems. When he was seen again by the psychiatrist, he denied any problems or difficulties. This contradicted conversations with the patient's wife and principal. He was referred for neurological examination that included an EEG and CT scan studies, which were all entirely within normal limits. The patient was referred for psychological testing and was found to have an IQ of 124, which placed him at the 95th percentile with respect to persons his age. He was also administered the Bender-Gestalt Test, which revealed no evidence of "organicity." He was also administered the Minnesota Multiphasic Personality Inventory (MMPI), which revealed no indication of psychopathology or personality disorders.

The patient continued working as a school teacher, however his continued use of foul language within the classroom and temper tantrums had enraged the parents of his students who demanded that he be terminated. His principal, bowing to the pressure of his students and their parents, was forced to place the patient on medical leave to save him from termination. The patient was seen again by a second neurologist, whose neurological examination and neurodiagnostic examinations were interpreted as normal. The neurologist, however, decided to refer the schoolteacher for neuropsychological assessment.

Neuropsychological assessment, on the other hand, demonstrated clear evidence of impaired judgement, reasoning, problem solving skills, cognitive flexibility, and memory, along with poor frustration tolerance, and an inability to regulate his emotions or behavior. These findings were consistent with bilateral frontal lobe damage, in the opinion of the neuropsychologist, and based on reviewing the patient's medical, academic, and vocational records, interviewing the patient and significant others, and finding no evidence that this patient had ever previously had these problems. Thus, it was possible to attribute these problems directly to his motor vehicle accident.

2. Psychological Treatment/Cognitive Rehabilitation

BEHAVIORAL AND COGNITIVE PROBLEMS OF BRAIN-DAMAGED PATIENTS

Within the past 10 years, there has been a growing realization that the emotional and behavioral problems that accompany traumatic brain injury are more disabling than the cognitive problems that are produced (Lezak, 1987; Sbordone, 1990). Patients with traumatic brain injuries are likely to exhibit significant emotional and personality changes consisting of either euphoria, apathy, emotional lability, irritability, changes in libido, poor frustration tolerance, impatience, and rapid mood swings. Additionally, the sensitivity of the brain-injured to the needs and feelings of others is frequently dramatically altered. This typically results in significant interpersonal difficulties, loss of friends, marital problems, divorce, and alienation of one's family. In addition to these problems, patients with brain injuries also exhibit impaired social judgement and planning skills, diminished self-control, impulsivity, poor self-evaluation skills, pathological egocentricity, increased dependency, diminished initiative and motivation, and inability to regulate their own behavior and their emotional reactions to others. These problems can be evaluated by the neuropsychologist and can add significantly to damages in personal injury cases.

EFFECT ON FAMILY

The family of the traumatically brain-injured patient undergoes extremely severe psychological stress as a result of disruption of the normal family interaction patterns, coping with a brain-injured patient's altered cognitive and behavioral functioning, trying to control or monitor the patient's behavior, and often must struggle with enormous financial responsibilities. However, the family of the brain-injured patient frequently exhibit what has been described as a "command performance syndrome" (Sbordone et al., 1984), in that they appear relatively "normal" and typically mask their emotional problems and create the erroneous impression that they are doing well and do not require psychological or psychiatric intervention. As a result of coping with the impact of a traumatic brain injury, families are likely to display a variety of pathological behaviors and psychiatric problems which require psychological or psychiatric treatment.

TYPES OF PSYCHOLOGICAL TREATMENT

Patients who sustain traumatic brain injuries are likely to receive either psychotherapy, behavior modification, or cognitive rehabilitation, depending on the severity of their cognitive, behavioral, or emotional problems and the time since injury. During the early stages, however, environmental modification may be necessary to minimize some of the patient's cognitive difficulties, as well as to maximize their functioning. Environmental modifications would include eliminating environmental precipitants such as pain, a full bladder or bowels, unfamiliar surroundings, or insensitive or authoritative handling of the patient (Eames, 1988). Other investigators have shown that placing the brain-injured patient in a highly structured environment and strict routine can significantly reduce their cognitive confusion and anxiety (Howard, 1988). As the patient's cognitive functioning improves, cognitive rehabilitation, which also includes computer-assistative cognitive rehabilitation, has been shown to improve the social and emotional functioning of the brain-injured patient (Rimmele and Hester, 1987), although it may be less than adequate in producing significant behavioral, social, and emotional changes (Sbordone, 1990). More recently, behavior modification techniques have been utilized with patients who have sustained traumatic brain injury. These approaches have been used during the early and late stages of recovery and are effective in reducing disruptive social behaviors and improve the patient's motivation, initiative, cognitive functioning, and socialization skills.

Individual psychotherapy is often difficult because of the brain-injured patient's poor self-awareness, memory difficulties, impaired conceptual skills, and problem solving abilities, and failure to follow through on recommended tasks. However, Sbordone (1990) has recommended that this form of psychological treatment be reserved for brain-injured patients who are several years post-injury.

Family therapy is extremely important, since many family members possess serious misconceptions about brain injuries and frequently entertain a number of misconceptions and fantasies. These beliefs create serious emotional problems and may cause frustrations and anger toward the patient and the patient's treating professionals. The family will then establish unrealistic goals for the patient which are likely to result in serious failures and precipitate serious emotional problems for both the patient and themselves. The need for psychological treatment and counseling for family members of traumatically brain-injured patients has been stressed by Lezak (1978) and Sbordone (1987, 1988, 1990).

CASE STUDY

The patient is a 19-year-old, right-handed male who sustained a severe brain injury three years ago when his best friend received a new motorcycle for his birthday and asked him to go for a ride. His friend lost control of the motorcycle, causing it to go over into a ravine. His friend sustained relatively minor injuries while the patient/victim sustained massive brain injuries and went into a coma, which lasted 14 days. Prior to his accident, he had been a straight A student, had been named valedictorian of his high school class, and had been awarded an academic scholarship to attend Harvard University that fall. His older brother had also been a straight A student and was attending Princeton, where he had made the Dean's list. His 12-year-old brother was also a straight A student. The patient's mother was a high school principal, while his father was an air force career officer. When the patient was seen at one year post-injury for neuropsychological assessment, he exhibited evidence of severe cognitive impairments, particularly on tasks involving recent memory. For example, the patient could not recall what he had done earlier in the morning and could not even recall this examiner who walked out of the room and returned five minutes later. One year later, the neuropsychologist received a phone call from the patient's mother requesting help for her oldest son, who had dropped out of Princeton and was recently arrested for public intoxication. She also mentioned that her 12-year-old son had been expelled from school for excessive absences and that she had been terminated from her job as a principal. The patient's father was interviewed and admitted that he had been considering retiring from the military and had recently been harshly criticized by his superiors for his inefficiency despite an excellent service record. A family meeting was held, at which time each family member admitted to feeling guilty and responsible for the brain injury that had occurred two years earlier. As a consequence of their severe guilt, each family member began acting in self-destructive ways and admitted that they had each given serious thought to committing suicide. Each of them confessed that they blamed themselves for the patient's brain injury and expressed the need to be punished.

The family was seen for therapy on a weekly basis for approximately one year. During this period, they expressed considerable animosity toward the patient for having done such a "stupid thing," but admitted they turned their anger toward themselves because of their pity and sorrow for the patient's condition. They also admitted that their dreams had been shattered by the patient's injury, and they could no longer lead normal lives again. Family therapy was generally successful in that the older brother began attending a nearby university, while the patient's younger brother began attending classes regularly. The patient's mother decided to change fields and expressed a strong interest in entering the rehabilitation field. His father managed to salvage his air force career and decided against early retirement. The patient continues to live at home and negatively affect the behavior of other family members.

3. Teaching

Many neuropsychologists hold faculty and clinical teaching appointments at universities or medical schools. They are frequently asked to provide lectures on the neurobehavioral consequences of brain disorders and trauma, neuropsychological assessment techniques, brain-behavior relationships, and the psychological treatment of the brain-damaged patient. Such lectures are frequently given to medical students and at neurology-neurosurgery grand rounds for residents. As a consequence, neuropsychologists must stay abreast of the professional literature and latest research findings on these topics.

4. Consultation with Other Professionals

Neuropsychologists are frequently referred patients from physicians, attorneys, insurance carriers, the court, rehabilitation nurses, and other professionals. Often, the neuropsychologist is asked to serve as a consultant to the referral source, which requires answering specific referral questions. For example, a physician may ask the neuropsychologist to "rule out dementia" or "organicity." The neuropsychologist may also be asked to assess the patient's cognitive functioning and to determine his or her ability to return to work or school. In other cases, the patient may be referred following a neurosurgical procedure (e.g., placement of ventroperitoneal shunt), to determine what specific changes have occurred in the patient's functioning as a result of a surgical procedure or medical treatment. The effect of specific medications may also be assessed by the neuropsychologist to provide feedback to the physician who is interested in changes in the patient's cognitive functioning.

Referrals from attorneys are typically concerned with the issues of damages/disability (or absence thereof). The determination of causation, prognosis, and the ability of the patient to return to work or school, and the need for future psychological care or rehabilitation the patient requires in the future are also questions asked of the neuropsychologist by the attorney. In many instances, the neuropsychologist will be asked to review the records of another neuropsychologist to determine if he or she agrees with the opinions or conclusions reached by that individual. While in other cases, the neuropsychologist may serve as an advocate for the patient and coordinate the patient's treatment and rehabilitation.

On many occasions, the neuropsychologist may serve as an educator/consultant to attorneys who have had minimal experience with such cases. In such cases, the role of the neuropsychologist is to educate the attorney about brain injury, its manifestations, and its effect on the plaintiff's life, ability to work, family, relationships with others, ability to function in society, and enjoy a rewarding and fulfilling life. The neuropsychologist may also educate the attorney as to the proper type of treatment the plaintiff requires, and the types of problems this individual is likely to have for the remainder of his or her life. The neuropsychologist can also serve as an expert witness and educate jurors in brain injury and how neuropsychological examination provides the most comprehensive assessment of the plaintiff's cognitive, behavioral, and emotional functioning.

The neuropsychologist may also serve as a consultant to a number of community agencies which specialize in treating patients with neurological disorders, brain injuries, and developmental disabilities. In this capacity, the neuropsychologist may be asked to provide in-service seminars to the treatment staff, as well as directly consult on various treatment and rehabilitation issues.

5. Research

Many neuropsychologists are actively involved in research studies within their field of expertise or interest. Since neuropsychological assessment has been utilized to study brain-behavior relationships, it is frequently utilized to investigate the specific cognitive and behavioral manifestations of specific brain disorders, behavioral disabilities, neurological disorders, psychiatric illness, and many medical illnesses and disorders. The precision and quantitative nature of many of the commonly used neuropsychological test instruments make them extremely useful for many types of research studies. As a consequence, many subtle and often clinically unrecognizable alterations in behavior and cognitive functioning may be recognized through neuropsychological investigations. As a result of these investigations, we have learned a great deal more about how the brain functions and its role in behavior. Such research may either directly or indirectly affect clinical practice and result in improved treatments and better recovery. Such research may also uncover problems that have not been previously recognized by physicians or may challenge many of the widely held beliefs of our medical colleagues.

Historical Development

Man's interest in the relationship between the brain and behavior extends back at least 2,500 years, when Pythagoras argued that the brain was the site of human reasoning. Approximately 100 years later, Hippocrates claimed that the brain was the organ of the intellect and recognized that a depressed skull fracture on the right side of the head could produce motor paralysis on the left side of the body. Galen, in approximately 170 A.D., was able to map out many of the major brain structures and argued that the frontal lobes were the seat of our mental abilities. Galen's hypothesis was discarded in favor of the belief that reasoning and intelligence were a product of the ventricles of the brain (areas which contain and manufacture the cerebrospinal fluid that covers the brain and spinal cord). It was not until 15 centuries later, that Galen's views of the relationship between the cortex and intelligence were taken seriously, when Vesalius reported an anatomical relationship between the brain and intellectual functioning. He argued that humans are more intelligent than animals, because humans had larger brains. However, it was not until the 19th century, that our present views on brain-behavior relationships began to take form. For example, Franz Gall, a French neuroanatomist, formulated a theory of phrenology which postulated that each area of the brain was responsible for a specific function or ability. Gall postulated a phrenological map of the brain, which identified each of these areas. He claimed that a person's character could be determined by examining the skull. However, Gall's views, which at one time were quite popular, were eventually discarded (Boring, 1950).

Later, Paul Broca, a neurologist, postulated that the area of the brain responsible for motor (expressive) speech, was located in the left posterior frontal lobe. Broca based this on approximately 10 patients who had suffered a loss of speech (expressive aphasia) and were found, on postmortem inspection, to have lesions in this region. Approximately 10 years later, another neurologist, Wernicke, found that damage to the posterior portion of the superior temporal lobe produced another type of disturbance in language processing. The patients could speak fluently, but could not understand what was being said. This was described as a receptive aphasia. During this period of time, Fritsch and Hitzig reported that the posterior region of the frontal lobes controlled the movement of the various muscles located throughout the entire body and that the most anterior (toward the front of the head) portion of the parietal lobes contained the major area of the brain responsible for sensation throughout the entire body. Specific areas of frontal cortex were identified as controlling the behavior of specific muscle groups. Thus, the functions of specific brain regions began to be delineated and the expected effects of injury to specific parts of the brain became more gradually understood (Walsh, 1978).

Another school of neurologic thought regarding brain-behavior relationships developed during the 19th century. This school argued that specific behaviors were not entirely controlled by specific parts of the brain, but were, in fact, controlled by the entire brain. They also asserted that loss of a particular behavior or function was determined by the extent or amount of brain damage, not by the location of the specific area damaged. They argued that the entire brain was "equipotential," which meant that if one part of the brain is damaged, the remaining brain tissue will take over its functioning. The debate between the conflicting views of the "localizationist" who argued that specific behaviors are controlled by specific parts of the brain and the equipotentialist resulted in numerous research studies, which have considerably enhanced our understanding of brain-behavior relationships, specifically the relationship between brain damage and behavior.

Essentially, our understanding today is that while sensory and motor functions are highly localized in specific areas of the brain, more complex behaviors—planning, judgement, reasoning, calculations, etc., involve the conjoint participation of many diverse and interacting areas of the brain (Luria, 1966). This more integrative school of thought arose during the latter half of the 19th century and has continued to gain popularity over the past 30 years. This school, which does not have a name, has been identified with a number of great neurologists, including the neurologist and neuropsychologist, Alexander Luria. Luria argued that while behavior reflects the functioning of the entire brain, each area of the brain plays a specific role in behavior. Luria was able to analyze what appeared to be relatively simple behaviors, such as catching a ball, into a series of complex behaviors which involved specific areas of the brain working in coordination with each other. For example, the individual must see and identify the object as a ball. This involves the visual cortex and its adjacent association areas also located in the occipital lobes. This information must be relayed to the frontal lobes which directs the motor activities of the body, thus causing the person to move their hands to the area in which the ball would be expected. As the ball is moving toward the gloved hand, the frontal lobe must make a number of fine adjustments, involving the parietal lobes, which determine the proper spatial coordinates for the placement of the glove in space and to time the sequence of movements to mesh with the position of the ball in space. As soon as the ball strikes the glove, this tactile information must be relayed to the parietal lobe indicating that the ball has been caught and is now secure. This information is sent to the temporal lobes which store this information in memory for future use, i.e., that the ball has been caught. The frontal lobes now discontinue catching activities and re-direct the player's attention to the next step in the sequence—throwing. A series of judgements are made: Throw? Yes? No? If so, to whom? This information is then processed by the frontal lobes of the brain, which direct the throwing hand to grasp the ball and also sends this information back to the parietal lobes so that the hand can be properly positioned based on the sensory (kinesthetic) feedback from touching the ball. The frontal lobes again must assess information stored in the temporal lobes to recall what action is required based on past experience. This information is then utilized by the frontal lobes which then directs the occipital lobes to search out where the ball should be thrown.

As you can see from the above example, the relatively simple task of catching a ball involves all four lobes of the brain, while portions of each lobe serve a different purpose in allowing the activity to be successfully completed. Luria emphasized the importance of what he described as functional systems, each responsible for specific behaviors, so that a pattern of interaction between various parts of the brain is necessary for a specific behavioral act to be completed. The disruption of one or more of these functional systems during any stage of the complex act is sufficient to produce any of a variety of alterations of the act. For example, if the individual sustained an injury to his frontal lobes, his ability to direct and coordinate the activities of the different functional areas of his brain would be impaired. For example, he may begin moving toward the ball too late or too early, which could result in dropping the ball. A lesion in the occipital lobes could prevent him from recognizing that the object traveling toward him was in fact a ball, rather than a bird, or some other object. Damage in the frontal lobes could also result in his inability to execute the proper sequence of movements, resulting in the ball going past him or throwing to the catcher after all runners are "in." A lesion in the parietal lobes could result in the inaccurate positioning of his gloved hand to catch the ball, while a lesion in his temporal lobes might leave him wondering what to do next after he caught the ball, since he may not recall whether he was playing a game of catch or a varsity game. Thus, you can see how injuries to various specific areas of the brain can influence the performance of a given task, such as catching a ball.

If you wanted to determine how a brain injury affects a person's performance on a task, such as catching a ball, you would most likely approach this task in several different ways. First, you might want to observe how this person catches a ball. You might note the percentages of errors made, given the number of balls thrown. This would serve as a "quantitative" approach. You might then compare this to his performance prior to brain injury, if that were possible. In the absence of such pre-existing data, you might interview people who may have played catch with him in the past. If each of these persons interviewed described him as a good catcher, then you would expect that he rarely made errors. If you wanted to be more precise, you might pool them and find that they consistently agreed that he missed catching the ball only one percent of the time. However, now you find that he misses the ball 10 percent of the time. The issue, of course, which arises is, "Does this really make a difference?" In other words, "Is this difference significant?" This is obviously a difficult question. However, if this individual earned his livelihood from playing baseball, then it might seriously jeopardize his ability to play the game at a professional level. On the other hand, if this was an activity that he occasionally engaged in with his 10-year-old son, one might not take this very seriously. However, the effects of this brain injury may cause problems in other areas in his life. For example, if he were an artist, surveyor, traffic cop, baseball umpire, or in any profession which placed heavy emphasis on intact visual-perceptual functioning, his ability to perform as he had done prior to his injury would most likely be significantly compromised.

Neuropsychological Assessment

HISTORICAL DEVELOPMENT

Neuropsychological assessment relies heavily on the use of specific tests to investigate brain-behavior relationships. The use of psychological tests to investigate the behavioral consequences of brain damage was first utilized approximately 55 years ago, in the United States. For example, a number of publications appeared during the 1930s and '40s, which described the effects of frontal lobe lesions on intelligence and other functions, visual spatial impairments following right frontal lobe lesions, the effect of brain damage on abstract thinking, and memory impairments following focal brain lesions (Jones and Butters, 1983). In the Soviet Union, during this same time, was Luria, who utilized psychological tests to investigate the effects of brain trauma and disease.

The first neuropsychological laboratory in the United States, was set up by Ward C. Halstead, in 1935. He utilized neuropsychological tests to study the effects of brain damage on a wide range of cognitive, perceptual, and sensory motor functions. Prior to utilizing psychological tests, he spent a great deal of time observing brain-damaged patients in a variety of work and social settings, to familiarize himself with the types of problems which they experienced. He then put together a battery, or collection, of tests, which he administered to these patients. Based on the results of his findings, he assembled a battery consisting of 10 psychological tests. In 1951, Halstead collaborated with his former student, Ralph M. Reitan, who established a neuropsychology laboratory at Indiana University Medical Center. Reitan (1955) modified Halstead's neuropsychological battery and created what is now described as the "Halstead-Reitan Battery." Reitan administered this battery to a number of patients with documented focal and diffuse brain damage, as well as to a group of hospitalized control patients, presumably free of brain disease. Scores obtained by the brain-damaged group were contrasted with scores of the controls to develop a set of test norms. He also developed indices of brain damage, based on the patient's scores and performance patterns. These indices allowed him to localize which areas of the brain had been damaged, as well as infer the cause of the neurological injury (e.g., whether it was due to a brain tumor, stroke, or traumatic brain injury).

Reitan and his collaborators have utilized the Halstead-Reitan Battery in numerous studies to identify specific areas of the brain which have been damaged, to determine if an acute or chronic condition is present and to predict a specific diagnosis (e.g., type of tumor, cerebrovascular, hypoxic insult, etc.). Reitan also provided numerous seminars, in which he attempted to teach psychologists how to utilize his comprehensive test battery to evaluate patients who are suspected of having focal or diffuse brain damage. It is still considered the most widely used neuropsychological battery in the United States.

Brenda Milner and her colleagues at the Montreal Neurological Institute and at McGill University have utilized neuropsychological assessment techniques to evaluate behavioral changes in patients who have undergone the surgical removal of portions of their temporal lobes, which were felt to induce uncontrollable seizures. Milner and her students studied the behavior of these patients both before and after neurosurgical intervention. She described the relationships between verbal and nonverbal learning following temporal lobe lesions. For example, she found that patients whose surgery involved the left temporal lobe, had impaired verbal learning skills, while the patients who underwent right temporal lobe surgery, had impaired visual learning skills (Milner, 1970). She also found that bilateral removal of the hippocampi (which is located in the medial temporal lobes of both hemispheres) produced a severe and permanent impairment in the ability to learn new information. On the basis of the research studies of Milner and her colleagues, a number of neuropsychological tests were developed, which were particularly sensitive to damage to specific areas of the brain.

Hans-Lukas Teuber, at the Massachusetts Institute of Technology, used neuropsychological tests to study the effects of local brain damage on a variety of visual and spatial skills. He studied World War II veterans, who had sustained penetrating missile wounds to the brain. Teuber and his colleagues identified the importance of the parietal lobes in spatial relations and the role of the frontal lobes in problem solving. These studies led to the development of several psychological tests, which were found to be highly sensitive to specific brain lesions to and the functions served by these regions (Teuber, 1972).

The Boston V.A. Medical Center, under the leadership of Harold Goodglass, Edith Kaplan, and Nelson Butters, has been responsible for the development of a number of neuropsychological tests based upon their numerous research studies, which were conducted over nearly 30 years. These investigators focused on an assessment of patients with aphasia (disorders of language processing secondary to brain damage), amnesia (disorders of learning and memory secondary to brain damage), and dementia (a global loss of cognitive functioning secondary to a neurologic disease process). These investigators also developed "qualitative" methods of analyzing the various psychological and behavioral manifestations and damage to specific parts of the brain. They developed a "process" approach to neuropsychological assessment, which relied heavily on their behavioral observations of the patient's performance on a particular test or task. Their approach has provided clinical neuropsychologists with a greater appreciation of the specific effects that brain damage can have on the individual. For example, they found that patients who had sustained damage to the right parietal lobe, often lost their ability to draw or place objects together according to its "Gestalt" (overall configuration or shape). Patients who sustained left parietal lobe damage generally maintained this ability, but the internal details of their drawings were severely distorted while the outer shape remained intact. Thus, the Boston group has strongly maintained that without behavioral observations, or the use of a "process" (qualitative) approach during neuropsychological assessment, much important information can be lost which may be crucial in determining whether an individual can return to work, school, or remain within a specific profession. Thus, neuropsychologists trained in this approach tend to test their own patients rather than rely upon numeric scores generated by testing technicians (Jones and Butters, 1983).

Arthur Benton, at the University of Iowa, developed a number of neuropsychological tests over the past 45 years and made a number of important contributions to clinical neuropsychology. He has studied a wide variety of cognitive impairments following brain damage utilizing the tests he created. He has also been responsible for training many distinguished neuropsychologists and has played a prominent role in the development of this field.

The work of Alexander Luria, who was initially trained as a cognitive psychologist and then later as a physician and neurologist, spent over 40 years studying the behavioral and psychological impairments of head-injured war victims, neurological, and neurosurgical patients. Luria developed numerous neuropsychological tests, which could be administered at the patient's bedside. They permitted Luria and his colleagues to understand the relationship between a specific area of the brain and its effect on complex behaviors. Luria formulated a theory of brain-behavior relationships which emphasized that complex behaviors could be broken down into their respective components and studied separately, to determine which aspects of a "functional system" had been compromised. His evaluation procedure heavily emphasized qualitative methods based upon observation of the types of errors made by the patient. His selection of tests, method of administration, and test interpretation were tailor-made for the individual patient, based upon his extensive clinical experience and on his model of brain-behavior relationships. Luria's work emphasized the use of expert clinicians' judgement in deciding whether brain dysfunction was present, and if so, what the nature of the dysfunction was.

Through collaboration with Anna-Lise Christensen, a Danish psychologist, Luria's tests and method of neuropsychological assessment was introduced into the United States in 1975, under the title, *Luria's Neuropsychological Investigation.* Her test battery emphasized the flexible individualized approach toward specific patients, which had been developed by Luria. Unfortunately, it was generally not well received in the United States, since it required the neuropsychologist to have extensive training and a strong background in behavioral neurology. In an attempt to rectify this,

Charles Golden, Thomas Hammeke, and Arnold Purisch administered the several hundred test items contained in *Luria's Neuropsychological Investigation* to normal controls and later to neurological patients. They utilized discriminant function statistical analysis techniques, to determine which test items were sensitive to the presence of brain damage. Their research (Golden, Hammeke, and Purisch, 1978) resulted in a battery of 269 items, which could then be administered to a patient in two or three hours. This test battery was eventually named the Luria-Nebraska Neuropsychological Battery and has been gradually gaining acceptance and becoming more frequently utilized, since it was first introduced in 1978.

Within the past several years, efforts have been made to utilize microcomputers to evaluate patients with specific cognitive impairments. For example, Robert Sbordone and Steven Hall, developed the Sbordone-Hall Memory Battery, which is a computerized neuropsychological test, which evaluates a variety of memory functions. These investigators and their colleagues have also developed other computerized tests to evaluate complex attention, speed of mental processing, and problem solving skills. In addition, other investigators have attempted to develop computer programs which duplicate many of the paper and pencil tests, that were developed in the past for neuropsychological assessment. Over the past several years, an increasing number of computer programs have been developed for neuropsychological assessment. Additionally, computer programs have been written by the developers of some of the neuropsychological tests, which provide comprehensive scoring and clinical formulation of test data. The reliability and validity of computer-administered tests are still under study, but the development of these procedures appears to promise greater precision in measurement and lower costs in test administration.

Chapter 2

The Neuropsychologist: Education and Training

The clinical neuropsychologist has attained a doctorate in Psychology (usually in the area of Clinical Psychology) from an accredited university. By virtue of having this training, the neuropsychologist has a broad background in the assessment and treatment of patients with various types of emotional and behavioral problems. The psychologist is also grounded in such basic knowledge areas as learning, cognitive functioning, psychopathology, physiological psychology, perception, memory, personality theory, statistics, and research design. Completion of the doctoral degree indicates that the individual has completed rigorous training at the graduate level, which usually takes between four and six years to complete on a full-time basis. This training includes course work, seminars, practicas, and supervision by faculty and/or neuropsychologists engaged in full-time practice.

While virtually all psychologists have taken course work which briefly covers topics such as neuroanatomy and the functional organization of the brain, these courses are generally insufficient to appreciate the brain-behavior relationships necessary for the practice of clinical neuropsychology. More recently, an increasing number of doctoral programs are offering their students courses and supervision in neuropsychological assessment. Unfortunately, many of these courses are taught by individuals whose experience and expertise is often limited in this area. As a consequence, many students will learn how to administer, score, and interpret a specific test battery, such as the Halstead-Reitan Neuropsychological Battery, without learning much in the way of behavioral neurology or how to take an adequate neuropsychological history. These individuals often supplement the course(s) they have received during their doctoral training with professional seminars that are frequently offered throughout the year. The content of these seminars, however, is typically geared toward learning how to administer, score, and interpret specific psychological test batteries. While the seminars usually offer some training and understanding of brain-behavior relationships, it is typically cursory and generally inadequate for what is needed to attain expertise in the field of neuropsychology. The situation is analogous to training someone who has never seen a schizophrenic patient to administer and score Rorschach inkblots in the hope that they will be able to diagnose schizophrenia someday on the basis of just the test scores.

The majority of clinical neuropsychologists obtain their specialty training in the field of neuropsychology at the post-doctoral level. Ideally, this should be performed at a medical school or hospital setting that provides them with access to individuals having expertise in neuroanatomy, neurology, neurosurgery, psychiatry, and medicine to acquaint them with the various medical aspects of brain-behavior relationships. During their post-doctoral training program, neuropsychologists will typically receive extensive training in the basic neurosciences. This frequently includes neuroanatomy (anatomy of the brain), neuropathology (diseases of the brain), and clinical or behavioral neurology (symptoms and neurobehavioral syndromes resulting from injury or diseases of the brain). In addition, neuropsychologists are taught to administer a wide variety of neuropsychological tests to patients with well-documented neurological and/or neuropsychiatric disorders. Neuropsychologists are then taught to write comprehensive reports under the supervision of a qualified neuropsychologist. The neuropsychologist trainee also takes a variety of courses in brain-behavior relationships that are taught both by neuropsychologists and neurologists. Such training typically lasts one or two years and would be the functional equivalent of a residency program in a medical specialty.

A variety of ongoing seminars, workshops, and teaching rounds, such as neurobehavioral rounds, neurology rounds, neuropsychology case conferences, etc., are available to neuropsychologists for purposes of continuing education. In addition, the International Neuropsychological Society and the National Academy of Neuropsychologists both offer three- and four-day seminars each year at their respective annual conferences. During these seminars experts in various areas of neuropsychology and neurology are invited to give workshops or lecture on specific topics to provide continuing education in the field of clinical neuropsychology. In addition, professional journals are published on a monthly or bimonthly basis to keep neuropsychologists abreast of the latest research and clinical findings in this growing field. Included within these journals are the reliability and validity of specific neuropsychological tests, relationships between specific test scores and neuropathological findings and specific neurological disorders. Current notions regarding cerebral localization are reviewed as are diagnosis, predictors of recovery, and the relationship between specific neuropsychological tests, neurodiagnostic tests, and neurological examinations.

Some of these journals are listed below:

Annals of Neurology
Archives of Clinical Neuropsychology
Biological Psychiatry
Brain and Cognition
Brain and Language
Brain Injury
Cortex
Journal of Clinical Psychology
Journal of Clinical and Experimental Neuropsychology
Journal of Head Trauma Rehabilitation
Journal of Nervous and Mental Diseases
Journal of Neurology, Neurosurgery and Psychiatry
Neurology
Neuroscience
Neuropsychologia
Perceptual and Motor Skills
Rehabilitation Psychology
The Clinical Neuropsychologist
The International Journal of Clinical Neuropsychology

Experience in Clinical Neuropsychology

It should be obvious to attorneys that many psychologists who offer neuropsychological testing may have, in fact, very limited experience evaluating and/or treating patients who have sustained either brain injuries or post-traumatic stress disorders. For many psychologists in private practice, limited experience evaluating patients with neurological injuries is the rule rather than the exception. Obviously, there are many reasons for this. For example, the psychologist offering such services may have recently completed a three-day workshop on the administration of particular neuropsychological tests and now wishes to offer such services to the consumer. Unfortunately, this individual may have never previously seen a patient with a brain injury or neurological disorder or, if they have, they may not have been aware that they have done so. He or she may be operating under the naive assumption, which is often inadvertently conveyed by the presenters of such workshops, that the results of the neuropsychological tests can stand alone and that a background in brain-behavior relationships, neuropathology, neurology, and the neurosciences is unnecessary. In other words, the assumption made is that the test results are sufficient to permit the psychologist to offer an opinion regarding damages and causation. (Author's note: One can easily recognize these reports since they are typically very brief—usually two pages long—and contain very little in the way of a chronological history of the patient's injury, including treatments and rehabilitation, and very little in the way of background information about the patient. The content of these reports typically contain the actual test scores and a set of descriptive statements describing the areas of the brain that are believed to be damaged and the degree of severity of the patient's problems. These reports typically lack any description of the patient's performance during testing and fail to discuss any possible extraneous factors, such as peripheral motor problems, medications, chronic pain and discomfort, orthopedic problems, visual difficulties, etc., which might confound test interpretation or mitigate the particular psychologist's conclusions. These psychologist's may receive one or two referrals each month from a medical colleague or attorney to rule out "organicity." The vast majority of these particular psychologists have probably seen less than 50 cases where there has been some type of neurological disorder present and have probably seen no more than 10 individuals who have sustained brain injuries. In addition, these psychologists are typically unaware of the various problems that exist in evaluating patients with brain injuries. Most of these individuals rely almost entirely on the results of their neuropsychological testing, which, as mentioned above, can be contaminated by a variety of extraneous factors.)

The majority of psychologists who offer neuropsychological testing have received little or no clinical supervision in neuropsychology. For example, while many psychologists have taken workshops in neuropsychological assessment (how to administer, score, and interpret a particular neuropsychological test battery), they rarely seek or receive supervision after they have completed the workshop. As a consequence, their errors in test scoring and/or interpretation may go unchecked. For example, several years ago this examiner was asked to review a neuropsychological test report that was written by a particular psychologist. The psychologist concluded in his report that the patient showed evidence of rather significant cognitive deficits, which he attributed to the patient's industrial injury. Careful review, however, of the psychologist's report revealed that the psychologist failed to use age appropriate norms (the patient was 63 years old), since the psychologist had compared him to test norms which had been designed for 25-year-old patients. The psychologist was unaware that test norms for 60-year-old patients were available, since after completing the workshop he had never sought or received any supervision and was unaware that it was improper to compare the performance of a 63-year-old patient to a 25-year-old patient. When the patient's test scores were compared to scores expected for persons his age, no evidence was found of impairment, since his scores placed him within the normal range for persons his age. When this author later telephoned the psychologist and discussed this issue, the psychologist admitted that he was unaware of these norms and had been using these norms to evaluate all the patients he had tested since completing the workshop.

The theoretical orientation of the psychologist can influence the way in which he or she views the particular complaints of a patient who has been referred to them with a history of neurological disorder or brain injury. For example, Sbordone and Rudd (1986) found that one-third of the psychologists practicing within the community failed to recognize rather salient underlying neurological disorders when they were asked to read a clinical vignette which contained a description of a patient who presented with psychological complaints. Careful analysis of the clinical training and theoretical orientation of the psychologists revealed that psychologists who had a psychodynamic or behavioral orientation were less likely to recognize the underlying neurological disorder. Thus, a psychologist with limited training and experience in evaluating patients with brain injuries may reach the spurious conclusion that a particular patient's problems reflect motivational or psychological factors rather than brain injury. For example, the author recently reviewed the report of a clinical psychologist who had been asked to perform psychological testing on a patient who had sustained a severe brain injury. Although the psychologist was aware that the patient had been rendered comatose for two days following her injury and had a residual left-sided hemiparesis (weakness and restricted movements of the entire left side of the body), and had been diagnosed as having a cerebral contusion based on the results of computerized tomography. The psychologist, who had had a strong psychoanalytic orientation, noted the patient's irritability, poor frustration tolerance, impulsivity, distractibility, and inappropriate behavior, and interpreted this as evidence of "passive-aggressive behavior," which he attributed to a faulty relationship she had had with her mother between the ages of four and five years old. Unfortunately, the psychologist failed to recognize that the patient's behavior was consistent with damage to the orbital surfaces of her frontal lobes, which typically occurs following cerebral contusions and results in the patient's inability to regulate their emotions or behavior. Thus, because of this psychologist's particular theoretical orientation and lack of knowledge of neurobehavioral syndromes, he overlooked the fact that this patient had sustained a severe brain injury, which was clearly documented in her medical records.

The type of setting in which patients are seen may contribute to the biases held by the particular psychologist. For example, Sbordone and Rudd (1986) found that psychologists who completed their clinical training in counseling centers were unlikely to recognize the presence of an underlying neurological disorder when they were asked to carefully read several clinical vignettes and determine which type of treatment or referral would be most appropriate for these patients. A high percentage of these psychologists felt that such patients had psychological problems that could be treated appropriately through such modalities as individual or group psychotherapy. Similarly, psychologists working in the departments of neurology and neurosurgery are likely to view the behavioral problems of patients seen in these settings as secondary to their underlying neurological disorders. Thus, they may err in the direction of ignoring motivational, environmental, or psychological factors in their assessment of the causation of the patient's behavior.

Most psychologists have had little, if any, experience in the rehabilitation of patients who have sustained brain injuries. Consequently, their conclusions regarding the relative permanency of the severity of the patient's problems and their prognosis for the future regarding the patient's ability to return to competitive employment, school, or their household responsibilities, may be limited. Consistent with this is the fact that most psychologists are unfamiliar with the field of cognitive rehabilitation and have had little or no experience in teaching patients the use of compensatory techniques to minimize their behavioral and cognitive deficits following brain injury. Thus, their conclusions may be overly pessimistic since through the use of rehabilitation techniques, many of these patients are often able to perform a variety of activities and tasks that increase their ability to function in the everyday world. Rehabilitation psychologists may, conversely, be overly optimistic because this is what they "sell."

Many psychologists may lack real world experience with patients who have sustained neurologic injuries or trauma, and may base their conclusions and opinions entirely on their neuropsychological test findings. This can lead to a number of erroneous conclusions about the patient since many of the neuropsychological tests that are typically utilized to assess patients with brain injuries have a number of serious shortcomings. For example, the test items themselves may lack sufficient "ecological validity" in the sense that they may be insensitive to cognitive or behavioral impairments that may only occur in real-world situations. The tests may fail to assess the patient's ability to generalize their newly acquired skills from one setting to another. Because of the psychologist's inexperience with specific neurological disorders, such as frontal lobe syndromes, the psychologist may only report the test data and neglect information obtained from significant others or behavioral observations of the patient during an independent test administration (Sbordone, 1990). As a consequence, the conclusions reached by the neuropsychologist, based largely on his or her inexperience in evaluating or treating patients with such disorders, particularly in rehabilitation settings, will most likely result in spurious conclusions about the patient's ability to return to work, school, or perform household activities. For example, a patient who had sustained a closed head injury was referred to a psychologist for neuropsychological testing. The psychologist reported that the patient denied having any problems or difficulties, but the psychologist failed to interview the patient's family or significant others. He reported that the patient tested with an IQ of 122, which led him to conclude that the patient could return to college. When the patient's family learned of the psychologist's findings, they phoned the psychologist and informed him that the patient's personality had changed dramatically since the accident in that he had become extremely irritable, easily frustrated, used foul language, appeared crude, had become egocentric, and was insensitive to the needs and welfare of others. The psychologist informed them that he had actually observed several of these behaviors during the patient examination, but felt that since the patient did so well on IQ testing, that he would have little difficulty completing school or working in the field of business. (Author's note: The patient returned to school and began experiencing significant academic and conduct difficulties. The patient eventually failed all his classes, even though he had a 3.2 GPA prior to his accident.)

Many psychologists, particularly those with minimal training and experience in neuropsychology, may also have limited forensic experience. As a consequence, we now have a psychologist who lacks competence in the area in which he or she has been designated as an expert and lacks experience on the complicated medicolegal issues involved in the case. It has been the experience of this author that this combination of incompetence and inexperience is potentially deadly. For example, Dr. J. was asked by an attorney to evaluate a plaintiff who had sustained a traumatic brain injury. Later, when the psychologist was deposed, he admitted that the patient was severely depressed when he conducted his examination and may have been mildly intoxicated. The psychologist was unable to adequately explain why he had tested this patient in the first place. When the patient was asked if he had ever had a problem with alcohol, he admitted that he had had a drinking problem for a number of years. The case settled two days later for an amount which was substantially lower than the plaintiff's attorney's demand prior to the deposition.

The attorney who utilizes a clinical psychologist rather than a neuropsychologist to evaluate a client, particularly one who is improperly trained or who lacks expertise in assessing brain damage, runs the risk of weakening the damages part of the case if the defense hires a neuropsychologist who points out that the plaintiff's expert lacked the proper training, experience, and expertise to support his or her opinions. If the plaintiff's attorney either loses the case or receives a paltry judgement because of this, the attorney may be sued by his client for malpractice for failing to utilize the services of an appropriate expert. Thus, in the "battle of experts," the testimony of a clinical neuropsychologist would most likely be superior to that of a clinical psychologist, particularly if the discrepancy between the training, background, and experience is substantial.

Competence

In medicine, Specialty Boards have existed for a number of years to ensure that a particular medical specialist was competent in the area of his specialty. To qualify for Board Certification, the medical specialist would have had to complete residency training in that particular area and successfully complete a series of written, practice, and oral examinations. For many years, such certification did not exist in the field of clinical neuropsychology, which often resulted in considerable embarrassment to the profession by so-called "instant neuropsychologists" who began sending out business cards notifying legal, medical, and other psychological professionals, that they had expertise in clinical neuropsychology as a result of completing a three-day workshop in the administration of a particular neuropsychological test battery. Within the past six years, Board Certification in Clinical Neuropsychology has become available. The American Board of Professional Neuropsychology (ABPN) was formed in late 1983. It served as an independent certification board that designated two levels of competency in clinical neuropsychology. Psychologists who had a minimum of two years and less than five years of experience in the field were eligible for "Certified" status, provided they could meet other criteria of experience and training. Psychologists with five or more years of experience could qualify for eligibility for "Diplomate" status. Because the Board did not provide rigorous testing procedures, psychologists with recognized experience in clinical neuropsychology were granted either Certified or Diplomate status. As a consequence, certification status by this Board does not guarantee that the individual is competent, but only that they have had at least two years of experience and completed the minimal standards of training in this field. Unfortunately, many psychologists who have managed to gain "Certified" status have stated under their name and degree, "Certified, American Board of Professional Neuropsychology," which often creates the erroneous impression that they have achieved the same certification that is familiar to the medical community, even though their clinical competence had not been formally evaluated through a rigorous examination process. More recently, there has been a growing movement within the American Board of Professional Neuropsychology to offer a rigorous clinical examination to psychologists who have already been granted Diplomates. Such individuals, upon passing the clinical examination, would then be able to place an asterisk next to their Diplomate, which would specify that they had passed a rigorous clinical examination and were found to be competent in their specialty area of neuropsychology.

The American Board of Clinical Neuropsychology (ABCN) was formed in 1984 and is affiliated with the American Board of Professional Psychology. The Board has developed a number of stringent criteria for certification of psychologists as clinical neuropsychologists. In addition to meeting the basic requirements for the American Board of Professional Psychology, the applicants for the American Board of Clinical Neuropsychology need to have a minimum of five years of relevant experience and training. Applicants are asked to indicate the training they received during their pre-doctoral and post-doctoral training in areas such as the basic neurosciences, neuroanatomy, neuropathology, clinical neurology, psychological assessment, clinical neuropsychological assessment, psychopathology, and psychological intervention. If the applicant has received sufficient training in these areas, the applicant is then asked to submit two samples of their neuropsychological test reports. These sample reports are then carefully scrutinized by two or more members of the Board, who are typically neuropsychologists whose knowledge and competence is well-recognized. If the work samples are found to be acceptable, then the applicant is invited to take a 200-item, written examination that evaluates the applicant's background and knowledge of the neurosciences, neurology, psychiatry, psychopharmacology, and clinical neuropsychology. The failure rate for the work samples is reported to be more than 50%. In addition, the applicant is given three individual examinations to evaluate their clinical competence within a hypothetical clinical situation, their professional judgement, ethics, and knowledge and contributions within the field of neuropsychology. The failure rate for the oral examinations has also been reported to be 40%. Upon successful completion of the above written and oral examinations, the applicant is awarded a Diplomate from the American Board of Clinical Neuropsychology that specifies the applicant has achieved the highest standards possible and is regarded as highly competent in the field of neuropsychology. At the time of this writing, approximately 150 psychologists have been awarded a Diplomate from the American Board of Clinical Neuropsychology. It should also be pointed out that many competent neuropsychologists have not yet taken or completed their Boards.

TABLE 1
AMERICAN BOARD OF CLINICAL NEUROPSYCHOLOGY, INC. ELIGIBILITY CRITERIA

A. Doctoral degree in psychology from a regionally accredited university

B. Licensed or certified at the level of independent practice in some state or province

C. Areas of training and experience:
1. Basic neurosciences
2. Neuroanatomy
3. Neuropathology
4. Clinical neurology
5. Psychological assessment
6. Clinical neuropsychological assessment
7. Psychopathology
8. Psychological intervention

D. Five years of post-doctoral professional experience in psychology which may include:
1. Clinical service
2. Research
3. Teaching
4. Administration

E. Three or more years of clinical neuropsychological experience defined as follows:
1. Equivalent of at least one year of full-time supervised clinical neuropsychology experience at the post-doctoral level (6 months may be credited for documented pre-doctoral specialty internship in neuropsychology)

   and
2. Equivalent of at least one year of additional experience as a clinical neuropsychologist

   or
3. In the absence of any supervised clinical experience, the equivalent of three years of unsupervised post-doctoral experience as a clinical neuropsychologist

Chapter 3

Clinical Neuropsychology: Comparison to Other Specialties

Comparison of Clinical Neuropsychologists with Clinical Psychologists

While both clinical psychologists and clinical neuropsychologists hold a Doctorate (Ph.D.) in the field of Psychology, the clinical neuropsychologist has typically received advanced training (usually at the post-doctoral level). Such training typically consists of courses and seminars in neuroanatomy, neuropathology, neurology, neuropharmacology, and clinical neuropsychology.

CLINICAL PSYCHOLOGISTS

The clinical psychologist specializes in the assessment and treatment of patients with "psychological" problems such as anxiety, depression, marital difficulties, work or occupational conflicts, sexual difficulties, child custody, poor self-esteem, paranoia, and stress-related disorders. These problems are typically caused by losses, divorces, work pressures, unrealistic expectations, and the demands of everyday living. In many cases, however, the cause of these problems may relate to impaired mother-child relationships, unhappy childhoods, emotional neglect, or psychological trauma (e.g., rape, sexual molestation, death of a child or parent, job termination, or rejection). The clinical psychologist often utilizes psychological tests such as the Wechsler Adult Intelligence Scale, the Minnesota Multiphasic Personality Inventory, and the Rorschach to evaluate a patient's intellectual functioning, personality style, and/or current emotional problems, and determine the proper course of treatment. This course typically consists of one or more of the following treatment modalities: individual, marital, family or group psychotherapy, relaxation therapy, desensitization, or biofeedback. While there are many different schools of thought regarding the treatment of patients with emotional or psychological problems, most psychologists ascribe to the assumption that most emotional or psychological problems are the result of maladaptive learning or are the result of intrapsychic conflicts stemming from the interaction of one's childhood experiences and current emotional or environmental stressors. However, many of these problems may actually represent psychologic manifestations of a medical illness or endocrine, metabolic, or neurological disorder (Jefferson and Marshall, 1981).

Clinical psychologists typically receive little or no training in such areas as neuroanatomy, neurology, or neuropathology. While they may at times be asked to "rule out organicity," this is usually done by the administration, scoring, and interpretation of tests such as the Wechsler Adult Intelligence Scale and/or Bender-Gestalt tests. As mentioned previously, however, some clinical psychologists who have taken courses in the administration, scoring, and interpretation of either the Halstead-Reitan or Luria-Nebraska Neuropsychological Batteries may utilize these batteries in addition to the Wechsler Adult Intelligence Scale and Bender-Gestalt tests to determine whether a particular patient is brain-damaged or "organic."

The major limitations of clinical psychologists are their relative lack of training or expertise in the neurosciences, neuroanatomy, neuropathology, or neurology, as well as their relative unfamiliarity and lack of experience in assessing patients with neurological disorders. As a consequence, they may overlook factors in the patient's history (e.g., hypothyroidism, medical problems, prior injuries, medications, or motivational or emotional factors), which may confound clinical interpretation of the test results. Consequently, the conclusions of the clinical psychologist may be erroneous regarding causation (Purisch and Sbordone, 1987).

CLINICAL NEUROPSYCHOLOGISTS

The clinical neuropsychologist primarily works with patients having neurological disorders or insults and is trained to recognize the cognitive, emotional, or behavioral manifestations of brain injury or disease. The clinical neuropsychologist uses tests or procedures which have been specifically designed to assess cognitive or behavioral impairments secondary to brain dysfunction or damage. The neuropsychologist is also typically aware of the relative sensitivity or insensitivity of these tests to detect cognitive or behavioral impairments secondary to focal or diffuse brain damage. Because of the neuropsychologist's background and understanding of the relationship between neurological and psychiatric disorders, the neuropsychologist has a greater appreciation and understanding of the influence of extraneous factors such as fatigue, medications, peripheral neuropathies, depression, medical diseases, and medications on test performance. The neuropsychologist typically gathers a comprehensive background and clinical history of the patient which chronicles the onset of the patient's symptoms in relationship to the injury, various neurodiagnostic or neurological examinations, and changes in functioning secondary to rehabilitation and various forms of treatment. A standardized history-taking technique has been produced by Siegal et al. (1980).

The neuropsychologist may also utilize a wider variety of neuropsychological tests than the clinical psychologist, which may have more sensitivity to the patient's cognitive impairments following traumatic brain damage than standardized test batteries (e.g., the Wechsler Adult Intelligence Scale or the Halstead-Reitan Neuropsychological Battery). The neuropsychologist's conclusions regarding the presence or absence of brain impairment or damage is typically based on an understanding of the patient's neurological disease or injury, interviews with significant others, review of the various medical or neurological records, comprehensive history obtained from the patient and/or significant others, behavioral observations of the patient, and interpretation of test scores and performances. Table 2 presents a comparison between clinical psychologists and clinical neuropsychologists.

While the clinical psychologist and clinical neuropsychologist typically are both trained to provide psychotherapy, the primary function of the clinical neuropsychologist is to provide neuropsychological consultation to referring physicians, attorneys, and other professionals. Thus, the clinical neuropsychologist may spend the overwhelming majority of his or her time performing neuropsychological assessments, reviewing records, and writing reports. Thus, a clinical neuropsychologist typically treats fewer patients than the clinical psychologist, since the practice of the clinical neuropsychologist is concerned primarily with assessment and consultation to other professionals. Part of this, however, also reflects the fact that many patients with neurological impairments or brain injuries are relatively poor candidates for psychotherapy because of the severity of their cognitive or behavioral problems, particularly during the first one to two years post-injury. For example, such patients are highly distractible, are relatively unaware of their problems, and may be unable to retain what transpired during therapy sessions. They may also have difficulty transferring what they have "learned" verbally in their therapy sessions into the "real world."

TABLE 2
COMPARISON OF CLINICAL PSYCHOLOGY AND CLINICAL NEUROPSYCHOLOGY

Clinical Psychology	Clinical Neuropsychology
Training in Clinical Psychology (Ph.D)	Same, plus post-doctoral training in Clinical Neuropsychology and/or specialty degree in Clinical Neuropsychology
State licensure in Psychology	State licensure in Psychology
Board certification with the American Board of Professional Psychology (A.B.P.P.) in Clinical Psychology	Board certification with the American Board of Professional Neuropsychology (A.B.P.N.) or the American Board of Clinical Neuropsychology (A.B.C.N.)
Work with patients with psychiatric or emotional problems	Work with patients with either psychiatric or neurologic problems
Abnormal behavior, emotion, and cognition are diagnosed and treated from a psychosocial perspective with little emphasis to underlying neural substrate	The interactions of psychosocial and underlying neurological factors are emphasized in the diagnosis and treatment of patients
Abilities assessed utilizing psychometric tests, patient history, behavioral observations, and interviews	Abilities assessed utilizing psychometric tests, specialized neuropsychological tests, behavioral observations, medical records, neurodiagnostic test findings, background history and clinical interviews
Personality assessed utilizing objective and projective personality tests and interviews with patient's family	Same
Clinical interview, history, behavioral observations and mental status exam focus upon psychosocial and psychiatric variables, i.e., symptoms and character traits	Same, plus additional emphasis upon medical history and manifestations of neurological disorder and its effect on patient's behavior
Neurological inferences limited to the identification presence or absence of brain dysfunction and superficial description of functional impairments	Same, plus additional inferences are made about localization of brain dysfunction, prognosis, treatment, etiology of patient's neuropsychological disorder
Treatment with psychotherapy and family intervention	Psychotherapy, cognitive rehabilitation, family interventions, and monitoring of medical and neurosurgical interventions

Adapted from *Trauma*, and reprinted with permission from Matthew Bender & Co., Inc.

CASE STUDY

A clinical psychologist was referred a 35-year-old woman by her attorney in a case alleging toxic exposure to industrial chemicals during the course of her employment. The patient claimed that she had developed memory and concentration difficulties, dizziness, hair loss, numbness and tingling in her fingers. A weight gain of approximately 40 pounds was evident. The psychologist, who was unfamiliar with the neuropsychological sequelae resulting from chemical exposure, administered the Wechsler Adult Intelligence Scale, which revealed a 15 point difference between her verbal and performance IQ scores, with her performance IQ being lower. He administered the Halstead-Reitan Neuropsychological Battery and reported that the patient performed poorly on most of the tests obtained within this battery. He also noted that the patient complained of severe memory difficulties, an inability to use her hands, and a variety of somatic and cognitive difficulties. He concluded that the results of neuropsychological testing demonstrated that the plaintiff had sustained brain damage as a result of exposure to industrial solvents during the course of her employment.

The patient was sent to a clinical neuropsychologist by the attorney representing the defendant. The neuropsychologist obtained a careful background history from the patient, which revealed that the patient had a long-standing history of stress-related emotional and physical problems stemming back to her adolescence. He also found that the plaintiff had a history of hypothyroidism and had been involved in a motor vehicle accident two years ago, wherein she sustained a probable concussion. He also noted that the plaintiff had been involved in a highly distressing relationship with her boyfriend, who lived with her. To cope with these problems, the plaintiff consumed large amounts of alcohol and street drugs. The neuropsychologist also pointed out that the plaintiff's performance on the Wechsler Adult Intelligence Scale was atypical for the patients that he had personally examined in the past with histories of solvent exposure. He also felt that the applicant's performance on the Halstead-Reitan Neuropsychological Battery was more consistent with patients having a history of traumatic brain injury or hypothyroidism. He administered a number of neuropsychological tests which corroborated this and led him to conclude that the applicant's complaints were most likely due to non-industrial factors.

Comparison of Clinical Neuropsychologists and Psychiatrists

PSYCHIATRISTS

Unlike the clinical neuropsychologist, the psychiatrist has a medical degree and has completed medical school and a residency in psychiatry. The psychiatrist is concerned with the diagnosis and treatment of emotional disorders. Psychiatrists generally treat patients with disorders such as schizophrenia, major depression, bipolar depressive disorders (manic depressive illness), severe neuroses, acting out adolescents, paranoia, as well as patients with organic brain syndromes. Psychiatrists have typically received training in neurology (usually consisting of both course work and a rotation on neurology).

Psychiatrists typically do not administer psychological tests to patients, since they are not qualified to score and interpret such tests. However, psychiatrists frequently utilize the results of psychological and/or neuropsychological tests (which have been administered, scored, and interpreted by a clinical psychologist or neuropsychologist) in arriving at their conclusions. Psychiatrists typically conduct a clinical interview, history, and mental status examination, which is typically qualitative, nonstandardized, and subjective. It is usually based on the psychiatrist's training, theoretical orientation, and experience. The vast majority of psychiatrists have had little experience evaluating and/or treating patients who have sustained traumatic brain injuries. Their treatment of patients typically consists of either psychotherapy and/or psychopharmacological treatment (prescribing medications which are specifically designed to alleviate a patient's mental confusion, emotional problems, or mood). Since there has been increasing evidence that many of the classic psychiatric disorders, such as schizophrenia and depression, appear to be caused by a combination of genetic, organic, and environmental factors, psychiatrists have become increasingly aware of the relationship between specific psychiatric symptomatology and nervous system dysfunction.

TABLE 3
COMPARISON OF PSYCHIATRY AND CLINICAL NEUROPSYCHOLOGY

Psychiatry	Clinical Neuropsychology
Medical training and Psychiatry residency (M.D.)	Clinical Psychology and Neuropsychology (Ph.D. or Psy.D.) degree plus post-doctoral training in clinical neuropsychology
Work typically with psychiatrically impaired populations	Work with psychiatrically and neurologically impaired populations
Abnormal behavior, emotional, and cognitive disorders are diagnosed and treated from a psychosocial and/or medical/biological perspective	Psychosocial factors and underlying neural mechanisms are both emphasized in diagnosis and treatment of cognitive, psychiatric, and behavioral disorders
Clinical assessment of emotional and organic status accomplished by a clinical interview, history, and mental status examination (a qualitative, nonstandard, and subjective procedure)	Same, plus additional extensive (6-8 hours) assessment utilizing qualitative, standardized, and objective neuropsychological and personality tests
Medical procedures, such as biological tests for depression, may be prescribed	Medical procedures cannot be prescribed, but are reviewed in patient's medical history
Treatment usually consists of psychotherapy, medication, and other somatic approaches (e.g., electroconvulsive shock therapy)	Treatment consists of psychotherapy, cognitive rehabilitation, biofeedback, and environmental and behavioral modification

Adapted from *Trauma*, and reprinted with permission from Matthew Bender & Co., Inc.

CLINICAL NEUROPSYCHOLOGISTS

Clinical neuropsychologists, by comparison, typically spend considerably more time evaluating patients than do psychiatrists. For example, most psychiatric evaluations last from one to two hours, while a neuropsychological examination (obtaining a history, interviewing the significant others, and the administration of neuropsychological tests) typically takes between six to eight hours. While the histories obtained from psychiatrists and clinical neuropsychologists are often similar, their mental status examinations are dramatically different. For example, the clinical neuropsychologist may administer as many as 25 different neuropsychological tests to evaluate a patient's intellectual, cognitive, behavioral, and emotional functioning, while the psychiatrist either administers no tests or relies on the test interpretations of a clinical psychologist (who may work in the psychiatrist's office) or computerized psychological test interpretations (e.g., MMPI). Table 3 presents a comparison between psychiatrists and clinical neuropsychologists.

Since the neuropsychologist typically has had more experience with patients with neurological impairment, the neuropsychologist's examination is usually more sensitive to the underlying neurological aspects of the patient's complaints and symptoms. For example, the psychiatric examination is typically insensitive to frontal lobe disorders, in that such patients typically fail to show evidence of language, psychiatric, or cognitive problems when interviewed. On the other hand, these patients will usually demonstrate significant impairments on neuropsychological testing consistent with frontal lobe pathology.

CASE STUDY

Neuropsychological testing was requested by a psychiatrist of a 29-year-old male patient who had recently been admitted to the psychiatric unit of a large hospital. The psychiatrist initially diagnosed the patient as schizophrenic because the patient appeared delusional and exhibited a flat affect. A review of this patient's medical records revealed that the patient had taken a probable overdose of barbiturates which had resulted in a cardiac arrest. The patient was discovered by his mother. He was not breathing and appeared blue. The paramedics were summoned and arrived a few minutes later. They started emergency resuscitation procedures which were eventually successful. The patient, however, spent the next three days in a coma, after which he was noted to be extremely lethargic, confused, disoriented, and extremely forgetful. The patient denied having any cognitive problems (which served as the basis of his treating psychiatrist, that the patient was delusional).

Neuropsychological testing revealed a variety of severe profound cognitive impairments consistent with hypoxic encephalopathy and diffuse brain damage secondary to a lack of oxygen to the brain. The neuropsychologist recommended that the psychiatrist reconsider the use of Haloperidol (an antipsychotic medication which is used for treating patients with schizophrenia). The neuropsychologist also recommended that the patient be referred to an acute brain injury rehabilitation unit which was highly structured (unlike the psychiatric unit) and had considerable experience treating such patients. The psychiatrist concurred with the neuropsychologist's recommendations and admitted that he had had no previous experience with such patients.

Comparison Between Clinical Neuropsychologists and Neurologists

NEUROLOGISTS

A neurologist is a medical school graduate who has completed a three-year residency in the field of Neurology. Neurologists are concerned with the diagnosis and treatment of disorders of the nervous system. They work almost exclusively with patients who have some form of neurological disease or dysfunction. This would include patients who have sustained cerebral concussions, mild or severe head trauma, hypoxic encephalopathy, Alzheimer's disease, Parkinson's disease, intracranial neoplasia (brain tumors), cerebrovascular disorders (strokes), obstructive hydrocephalus, infectious diseases of the brain or nervous system, spinal cord injuries, and a variety of other neurological diseases and disorders including peripheral neuropathy and neurological symptoms secondary to a variety of medical illnesses.

NEUROLOGICAL EXAMINATION

The neurological examination consists of elicitation of the chief complaints and history of the present illness, past medical history, family and social history, examination of the scalp and skull, peripheral nerves, cranial nerves, motor function, reflexes, sensation, and autonomic functions. Mental function, including language and motor speech, are assessed in a mental status exam. The neurological examination generally takes between 45 minutes and one hour. It can also be accompanied by neuroradiological and diagnostic tests, such as x-rays, computerized tomography, electroencephalography, MRI, and topographical brain mapping. In addition, the neurologist may perform electromyography (EMG) and electric stimulation studies of peripheral nerves and muscle tissue. The neurologist can also perform examinations of the cerebrospinal fluid and order a number of different medical tests to rule out a variety of medical disorders. Typically, however, the neurologist will frequently order an EEG study and CT or MRI scan when a patient is referred with a suspected brain injury of traumatic etiology. Unfortunately, in many cases these tests may be negative, even though the medical evidence may be overwhelming that the patient has sustained a significant traumatic brain injury (e.g., the patient has a Glasgow Coma Scale score of 4 or was comatose for several weeks post-injury). Thus, while these tests may be "objective" in the sense that they cannot be directly manipulated by the patient, they may be insensitive to various kinds of brain trauma. This is particularly true in cases involving mild brain injury, where the frequency of negative CT scans and EEG studies has been reported to be in excess of 90% (Rimel, Giordani, Barth, Boll, and Jane, 1981).

CLINICAL NEUROPSYCHOLOGISTS

While neurologists have considerable expertise in evaluating the structural integrity of the nervous system, they may lack an appreciation of the neurobehavioral sequelae of such injuries. This would include an examination of what has been referred to as the patient's "higher cortical" or "executive functions." Included within this would be the patient's problem solving skills, judgement, reasoning, higher order motor skills, memory (particularly under conditions of interference), insight, higher level perceptual functioning, cognitive flexibility, and higher level attentional and concentration skills. While the neurologist has expertise in the diagnosis of specific disorders of the central nervous system (brain and spinal cord), the neuropsychologist is typically able to determine the effects of this disorder on the patient's intellectual functioning, including attention, concentration, and memory skills, perception, and language. Higher order motor skills, problem solving, reasoning, judgement, and abstract thinking, are also assessed as is behavior in structured and unstructured settings, emotional functioning, and social interpersonal relationships. As a result of their respective areas of expertise, neurologists frequently refer patients who have sustained various forms of brain insults to neuropsychologists for assessment since the clinical neuropsychologist spends considerably more time evaluating the patient's mental status through a combination of interview techniques and neuropsycholgical testing. Table 4 presents a comparison between neurologists and clinical neuropsychologists.

TABLE 4
COMPARISON OF NEUROLOGY AND CLINICAL NEUROPSYCHOLOGY

Neurology	Clinical Neuropsychology
Medical training and Neurology Residency (M.D.)	Clinical Psychology and Neuropsychology training (Ph.D.)
Diagnosis of brain damage and neurological disorders	Identification of emotional and behavioral deficits associated with brain damage and neurological disorders
Work with neurologically impaired populations	Work with neurologically and psychiatrically impaired populations
Neurological exam: qualitative nonstandardized subjectively interpreted relatively brief (less than one hour)	Neuropsychological testing: quantified standardized objective lengthy (6-8 hours)
Emphasis typically focuses on assessing basic motor and sensory abilities. Mental status exam is typically very brief and focuses on orientation to surroundings, attention, recent memory, language, and constructional skills.	Much greater emphasis upon assessing patient's higher cognitive functions: attention, perception, language, memory, executive functions, judgement, motor skills, reasoning abstract thinking, problem solving, intellectual abilities, and personality/ emotional functioning
Little emphasis on psychosocial and psychiatric factors	Considerable emphasis on psychosocial and psychiatric factors
Can prescribe medical diagnostic procedures (e.g., CT scan, MRI, EEG)	Cannot prescribe medical diagnostic procedures, but can review findings of such tests
Treatment with medication	Treatment with psychotherapy and cognitive rehabilitation, biofeedback, and environmental and behavioral modification

Chapter 4

Neuroanatomy

It is necessary for the attorney involved in cases involving brain trauma to understand a few fundamental facts about neuroanatomy, although this is one of the most difficult courses offered in medical school. Hence, the attorney will be provided with a simplified overview of the brain, particularly vis-à-vis the functional significance of certain areas of the brain and their behavioral and psychological implications.

The Brain

The brain weighs approximately three pounds. It is surrounded by a bony chamber or vault known as the skull. Between the skull and the cerebral hemispheres lie three coverings, or membranes, which are termed the meninges. The outermost membrane is known as the dura mater. It is comprised of thick elastic material which adheres to the inner surface of the skull. Below the dura mater is the arachnoid membrane. The third membrane is known as the pia mater. The outermost covering of the brain, the dura mater, forms what is known as the falx cerebri, which divides the two cerebral hemispheres. The dura mater also performs a protective covering (tentorium cerebelli) which divides the most posterior part of the cerebral hemispheres from the cerebellum. In addition, the dura mater separates the two cerebellar hemispheres and forms the falx cerebelli. Located between the dura mater and the underlying subarachnoid membrane is cerebrospinal fluid which surrounds the brain and serves as a sort of shock absorber whenever the skull makes contact with an immovable object or is rapidly accelerated or decelerated.

The cerebral hemispheres are roughly symmetrical (e.g., left vs. right). The importance of the cerebral hemispheres within neuropsychology cannot be overemphasized, since they are concerned with such functions as intelligence, language, perception, judgement, memory, problem solving, knowing, thinking, social behavior, personality, and emotions. The surface of the cerebral hemispheres is made up of convolutions causing it to appear to be made of various hills and valleys. The hills are called gyri, while the valleys are known as sulci. The brain's convolutions permit the surface of the brain to be folded into a much smaller area so that it can be fitted into the skull, since 80% of the brain's surface remains hidden from view in its sulci. In this respect, it should be noted that the number of convolutions within the brain increases as one goes up the phylogenetic scale. For example, animals such as rats have considerably fewer convolutions than cats or dogs, while humans have considerably more convolutions than the latter.

THE CEREBRAL LOBES OF THE BRAIN

The cerebral hemispheres can be further divided into four lobes on the basis of four large sulci which form the lobe's boundaries (see Fig. 1). For example, the frontal lobe, the largest lobe of the

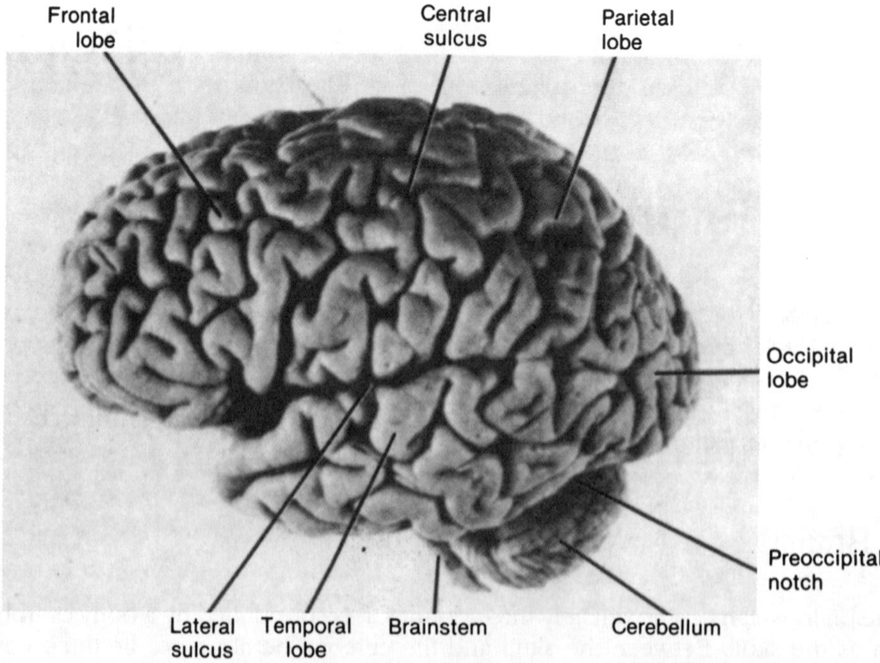

Fig. 1. Major Regions of the Adult Brain as Seen in a Lateral View

Reproduced by permission from: Nolte, John: *The human brain*, ed. 2, St. Louis, 1988, The C.V. Mosby Co.

brain, comprises approximately 44% of the total mass of the cerebral hemispheres, and lies anterior (toward the front of the head) to the central sulcus. This sulcus divides the frontal from the parietal lobes. Thus, the parietal lobe is located posterior to (behind) the central sulcus. Located directly below the frontal and parietal lobes, and separated by a very large sulcus, which is known as the lateral fissure, is the temporal lobe. Thus, the temporal lobe is inferior to (below) the frontal and parietal lobes. The occipital lobe lies at the most posterior aspect (toward the back) of the cerebral hemispheres. The cerebral hemispheres house a bundle of fibers (corpus callosum) deep within the brain. These deep, subcortical structures connect the two cerebral hemispheres and allow information to be transmitted from one side of the brain to the other. Research studies (Sperry, 1968) have demonstrated that severing the corpus callosum produces an individual with two brains that are unable to communicate with each other. For example, a blindfolded person following this type of surgical procedure (which is known as a split brain preparation to treat certain types of seizure disorders) would be unable to identify an object such as an orange if it was placed in his left hand but could later identify it on the basis of its weight, size, and texture from other objects such as an apple or a peach. The reason for this is that sensory information coming from the left hand is transmitted to the right side of the brain, which in the overwhelming majority of individuals, lacks the capacity for anything but the most rudimentary language production. The right side of the brain is better able to analyze this object and determine that it is an orange. However, it cannot send this information to the left side of the brain so that the person cannot verbally name it as "an orange." This same individual has little difficulty recognizing the orange by touch and feel alone when he is allowed to touch and feel other objects, since the knowledge of this object is known by the right hemisphere. Thus, the corpus callosum allows different parts of the brain to process information regarding a specific event relatively independently in an integrated fashion synthesizing many of the brain's functions.

The occipital, parietal, and temporal lobes can each be broken down into three cortical zones according to Luria (1965) to understand how the brain receives, analyzes, and stores sensory information arriving from various parts of the body through the senses. (see Fig. 2).

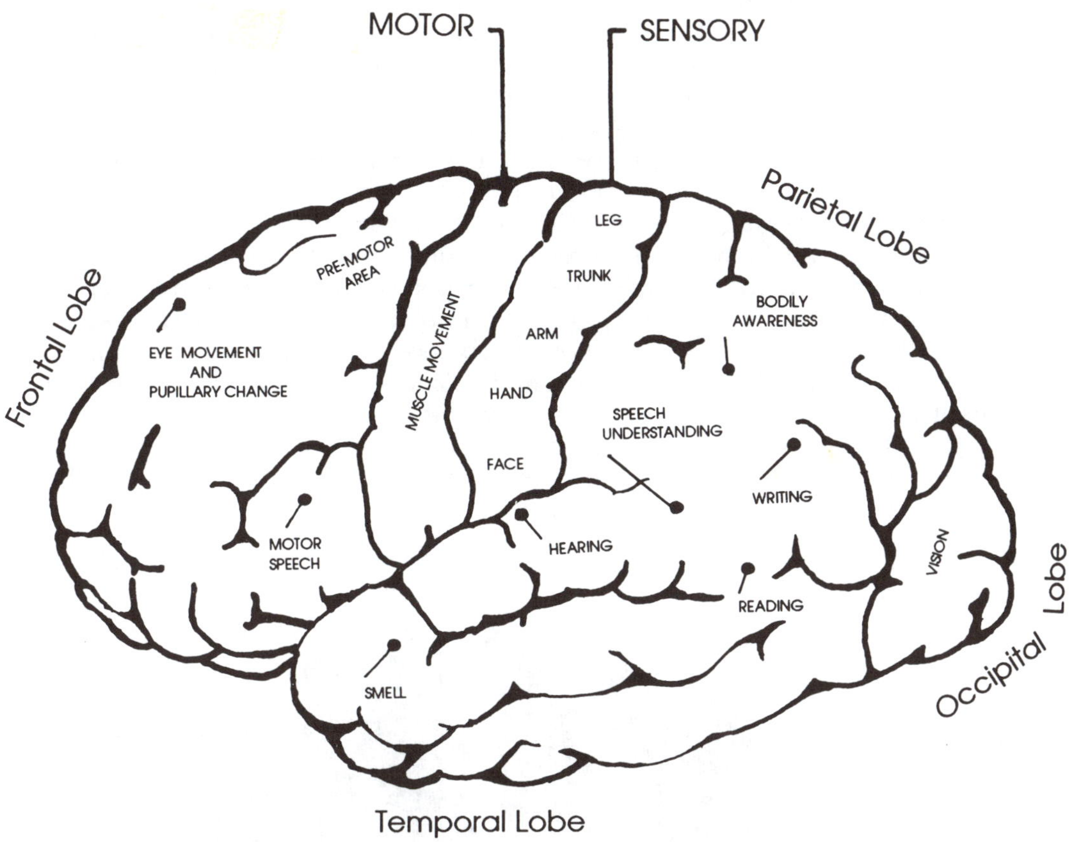

Fig. 2. Functional "Road Map" of the Brain

Schematic drawing shows how functions are defined in terms of geographical relationship to the lobes in which they are situated.

Adapted from *Trauma* and reprinted with permission from Matthew Bender & Co., Inc.

PRIMARY AND SECONDARY CORTICAL LOBES

According to Luria's (1966) model of brain-behavior relationships, each of these lobes contains neurons (nerve cells) which only respond to a specific sensory modality. For example, the primary cortical zones located in the occipital lobe respond only to visual information, while the primary cortical zones in the parietal lobe respond to only tactile (touch) and kinesthetic (movement feedback) information. The primary zone in the temporal zone responds to only auditory information. Thus, damage to any of these primary zones would result in the inability of the brain to process a specific type of information. The areas surrounding the primary cortical zones within each respective lobe are known as secondary cortical zones, since information arriving at the primary cortical zones is transferred to the secondary zones so that the brain can formulate a perception or elaborated image of the raw sensory information which it receives. For example, when the primary cortical zone in the occipital lobes is damaged, the patient will develop what has been described as "cortical blindness." If the primary cortical zone in the occipital lobes is preserved and damage occurs to the secondary areas (which frequently occurs in patients who sustain hypoxic encephalopathy), these individuals will develop "visual agnosia" and be unable to recognize the object which they can, however, see. For example, such patients may be unable to visually recognize such objects as a watch or pen by sight alone, but will have little or no difficulty recognizing such objects by touch. Within the occipital lobe, the primary sensory cortex is located in the most posterior area of the occipital lobe, while the area which surrounds it anteriorly comprises the secondary cortical zone, according to Luria.

The primary cortical zone within the parietal lobe is situated directly behind (posterior) the central sulcus and is located in the most anterior part of the parietal lobe. When damage occurs to specific parts of this zone, a person will experience a corresponding numbness in an area of the body which corresponds to this region (see Fig. 3). When the secondary zones which are located posteriorly to the primary zones are damaged (in the absence of primary lobe damage), the individual might not be able to distinguish a quarter from a dime which he is holding in the hand directly contralateral (opposite) to the site of brain injury. This condition is known as "astereognosis," which is a form of tactile agnosia. It should be noted that patients who sustain strokes will frequently exhibit this condition on the side of their body which is contralateral (opposite) to the site of their stroke.

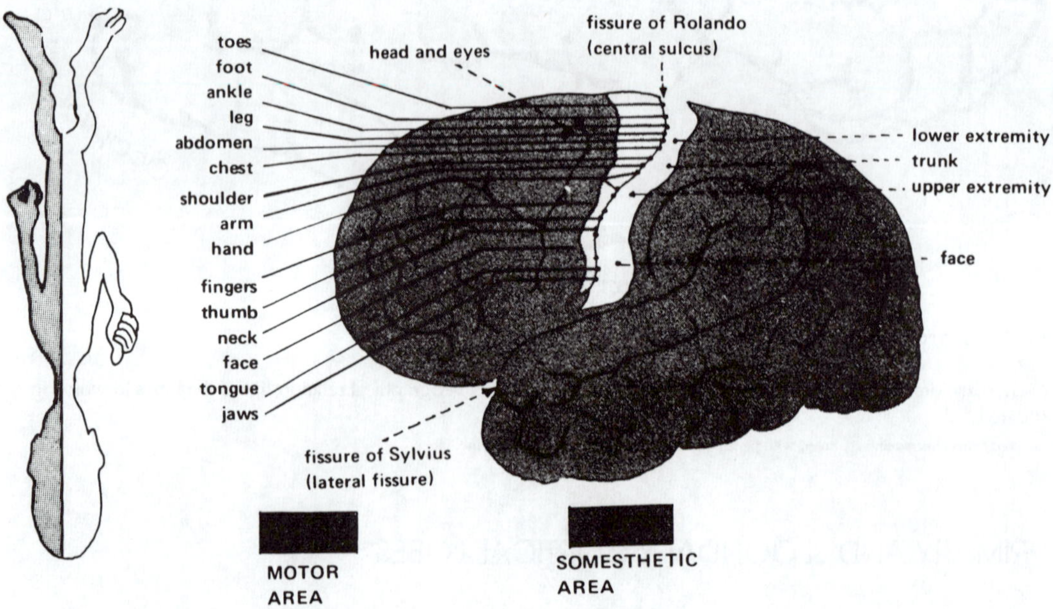

Fig. 3. Schematic Drawing of Motor and Somesthetic Areas

In front of the Rolandic Fissure is the precentral gyrus on which lies the motor strip. This is the motor projection area which bears a point-to-point relationship (projection) to all the muscles under voluntary control. Damage to the motor strip results in paralysis of the associated muscles.

On the postcentral gyrus, just behind the Rolandic Fissure, lies the sensory or somesthetic (body-feeling) area which has a point-to-point representation with specific body regions for sensation. Mild damage to any part of the somesthetic strip results in numbness in the corresponding body region; and destruction in the somesthetic strip causes the total loss of feeling in the corresponding part.

The primary cortical zone of the temporal lobe is responsible for the reception of auditory information. When damage occurs to this region, the patient will exhibit what has been termed "cortical deafness." The primary cortical zone in the temporal lobe is found in the superior temporal gyrus. The secondary cortical zone is located just below (inferior to) the primary cortical zone and is located within the middle and inferior gyri of the temporal lobe. When this specific area of the brain is damaged in the left hemisphere, the patient's ability to decipher speech sounds or phonemes will be severely compromised. Difficulty comprehending word meanings ensues after damage to the surrounding secondary zone. As a consequence, the patient typically will be unable to follow simple commands such as, "Raise your right hand over your head and touch your stomach with your left hand." When this area is damaged in the right hemisphere, the patient's ability to follow whole body commands such as, "Turn around twice and walk to the door," will be compromised, but will not be affected if the damage is restricted to the left hemisphere. In addition, the patient's ability to comprehend or recognize environmental sounds, such as the singing of birds, music, or the sound of a waterfall, will be compromised. It should also be noted that when right-handed patients sustain an injury to the secondary cortical zone in the left hemisphere, they are likely to exhibit frequent word substitution (paraphasic) errors. For example, the patient may use the word "spoon" when attempting to say the word "fork." The patient may also use the word "chuck" when attempting to say the word "chair." The patient may also be able to speak in a fluent manner without making any sense whatsoever. This condition is known as "fluent aphasia" or Wernicke's aphasia.

TERTIARY CORTICAL LOBES

The tertiary cortical zones of the brain integrate information contained within the various secondary cortical zones and their respective sensory modalities. The tertiary cortical zones are frequently referred to as "association" cortices and are found at the borders of the parietal (somatosensory), temporal (auditory), and occipital (visual) secondary cortical zones. They convert concrete perceptions into abstract thoughts. According to Luria, an injury to the tertiary sensory zone, which integrates the parietal and occipital secondary cortical zones, would result in a patient having considerable difficulty solving the following problem: A father is 45. He is 19 years older than his son. How old are the two of them together? Patients with tertiary zone lesions in the left cerebral hemisphere are unable to solve this problem as a result of impaired simultaneous spatial synthesis.

FRONTAL LOBES

The frontal lobes of the brain are primarily responsible for the initiation, organization, planning, execution, and regulation of complex motor movements and actions. The primary cortical zone for movement is found in the posterior frontal lobe just anterior to the central sulcus (Rolandic fissure). Voluntary movements of the body are initiated in this region. Injuries to this region are likely to produce an inability to perform voluntary movements on the contralateral side of the body. Within this region lies the corticospinal tract, which travels downward (posteriorly) through the internal capsule (passageway), midbrain (cerebral peduncles) and continues through the brain stem to the medulla oblongata, where it decussates (crosses over to the opposite side of the brain) before it travels down the lateral corticospinal tract, where it eventually exits the spinal cord through the peripheral nervous system (outside of the brain and spinal cord) directly to the body's muscles which are innervated by nerve fibers.

The primary motor region, the precentral gyrus, contains the sites for the initiation of specific movements of various parts of the body. This region (see Fig. 3) is distributed like an upside-down homunculus (man). The motor areas for the initiation of movements of the face and hands are located in the inferior aspects (close to the temporal lobe), while the regions for the back and lower extremities are located more anteriorly and dorsally (highest area of the cerebral hemispheres) and medially (near the longitudinal fissure). The secondary cortical zones of the frontal lobe have been termed the "premotor region" and are located in the adjacent anterior regions of the frontal lobe (see Fig. 2). The secondary cortical zones for motor functioning play a prominent role in the organization of movements and specific motor skills. Thus, complex motor skills are controlled by secondary motor zones of the motor cortex. The secondary cortical zones, which control the movements of the feet and legs, are located in the uppermost part of the frontal lobe. A strong relationship exits between the size of the secondary motor zones and the degree of control over the muscles of the hand and other body parts. Areas of the body which contain numerous muscles, such as the face and hands, and are involved in complex motor movements, tend to have a disproportionately large number of nerve fibers located in the secondary motor cortical zones. When these regions are injured, often the patient can no longer produce organized or complex motor movements.

The tertiary zones of the motor cortex are located in the most anterior regions of the frontal lobe. This zone is referred to as the orbital frontal cortex. These zones play a prominent role in carrying out executive functions which involve the planning, organization, initiation, execution, and regulation of complex motor skills and actions. Injuries to the tertiary zone will result in impulsive behavior, poor judgement, an inability to recognize errors or regulate behavior, and repeated mistakes in spite of being told that they are incorrect. These patients also show deficits in the initiation of spontaneous behavior and motivation. They exhibit severe impairments on problem solving and higher order intellectual tasks. These patients are typically easily distracted and have considerable difficulty shifting from one task to another. As a consequence, they are likely to exhibit perseverations (repeating the same action) and frequently show evidence of confabulation (their recall of recent events is either colored by their imagination or by certain aspects of the material). For example, the patient is asked to perform a task in which he must add three to each new number, beginning with the number one. The patient begins correctly by stating, "1, 4, 7," but then continues with, "8, 9, 10." Thus, the patient has lost the "motor program" for performing the particular task. The patient's behavior is then replaced by a well-learned or stereotyped activity such as counting. The patient, however, shows no awareness that he has made an error, and when asked what he was asked to do, he replies, "Count by threes." Thus, the patient recalls the task but quickly loses it, and shows no awareness of having made this error, even when he is later asked what he has been instructed to do.

The Limbic System

Within the temporal lobes lies the limbic system, which is a set of anatomically linked structures which extend anteriorly into the frontal lobe and posteriorly into the midbrain (the areas surrounding and including the upper part of the brain stem). Included within the limbic system are the thalamus, mammillary bodies, and fornix. These structures play a prominent role in the learning and retention of new information and in the generation and regulation of emotional behavior. When these structures are damaged, the patient has difficulty learning new information. For

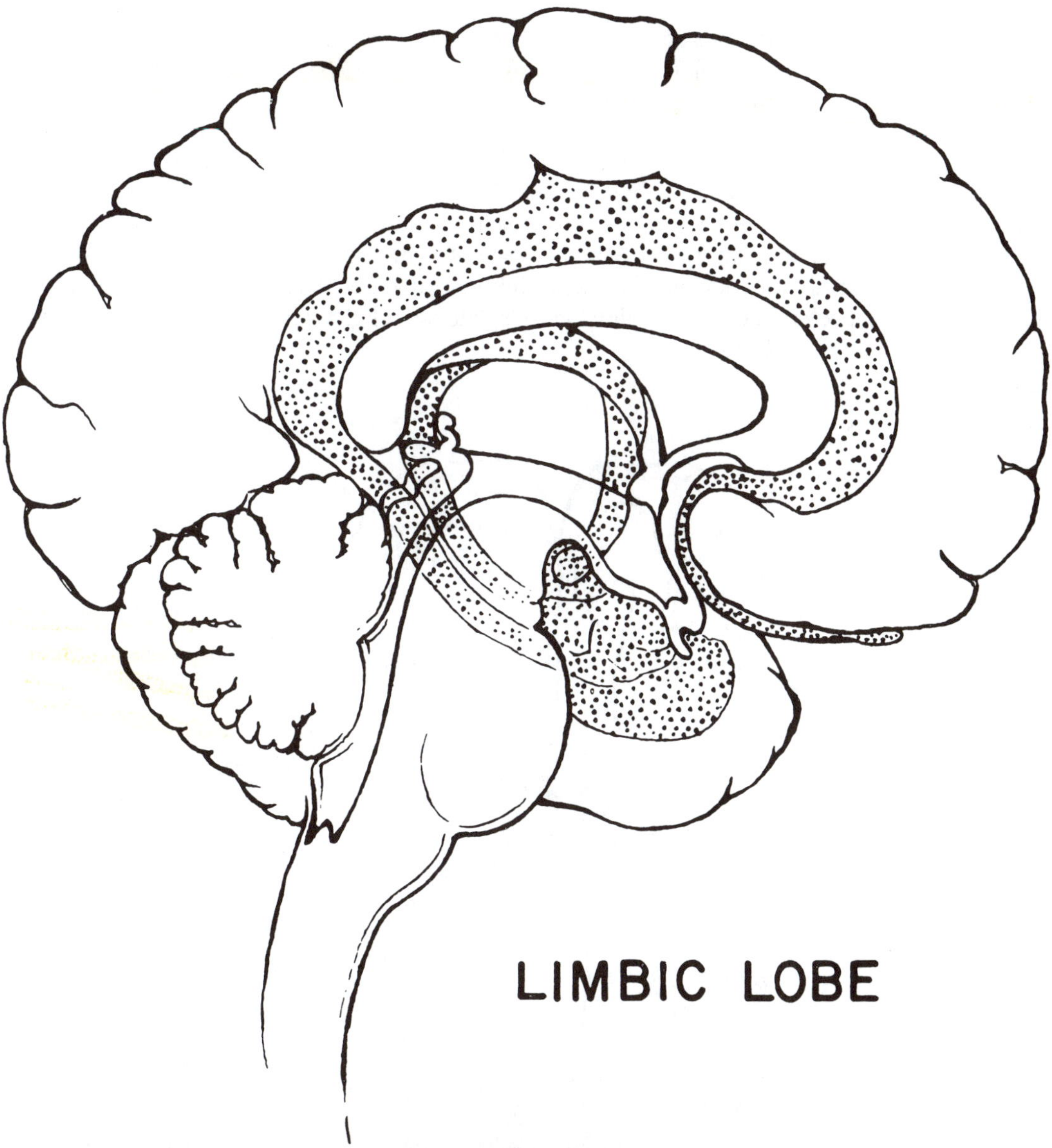

Fig. 4. Schematic Drawing of Medial Aspect of Hemisphere of Brain

This drawing shows the extent of the limbic lobe (shaded area). It includes the cingulate gyrus above and the complex structures of the old "olfactory" brain and portions of the frontal lobe (occipital gyri) and temporal lobe, which are related to memory and emotionality.

example, the patient may be given a story to recall in which a woman who lives in South Boston and works as a cleaning lady is robbed of $15 on her way home one evening. She has four children who have not eaten for two days. She informs the police, who feel sorry for her plight and take up a collection in order to help her feed her children. The patient is then asked to repeat this story. The patient states, "It is about a woman who is robbed," but he cannot recall any of the details of this story. One hour later, the patient is again asked to recall this story but has no recollection that he had ever been given a story to recall. The memory impairment in these patients is most severe when bilateral damage occurs to these structures. In such cases, the patient will exhibit evidence of profound memory impairment for recent events. These patients are typically unable to recall what they did only a few moments ago or have no recollection of ever having been examined by a particular physician, even though the physician may have spent over 30 minutes with the patient.

Damage to the limbic system can frequently result in a variety of emotional, perceptual, sexual, or psychiatric disorders and epilepsy. For example, patients who sustain limbic system damage will frequently display rapid mood swings, frequent outbursts of anger, irritability, marked alteration in sexual drive and preference, visual hallucinations, intense religious feelings, bizarre thinking, and severe psychiatric problems.

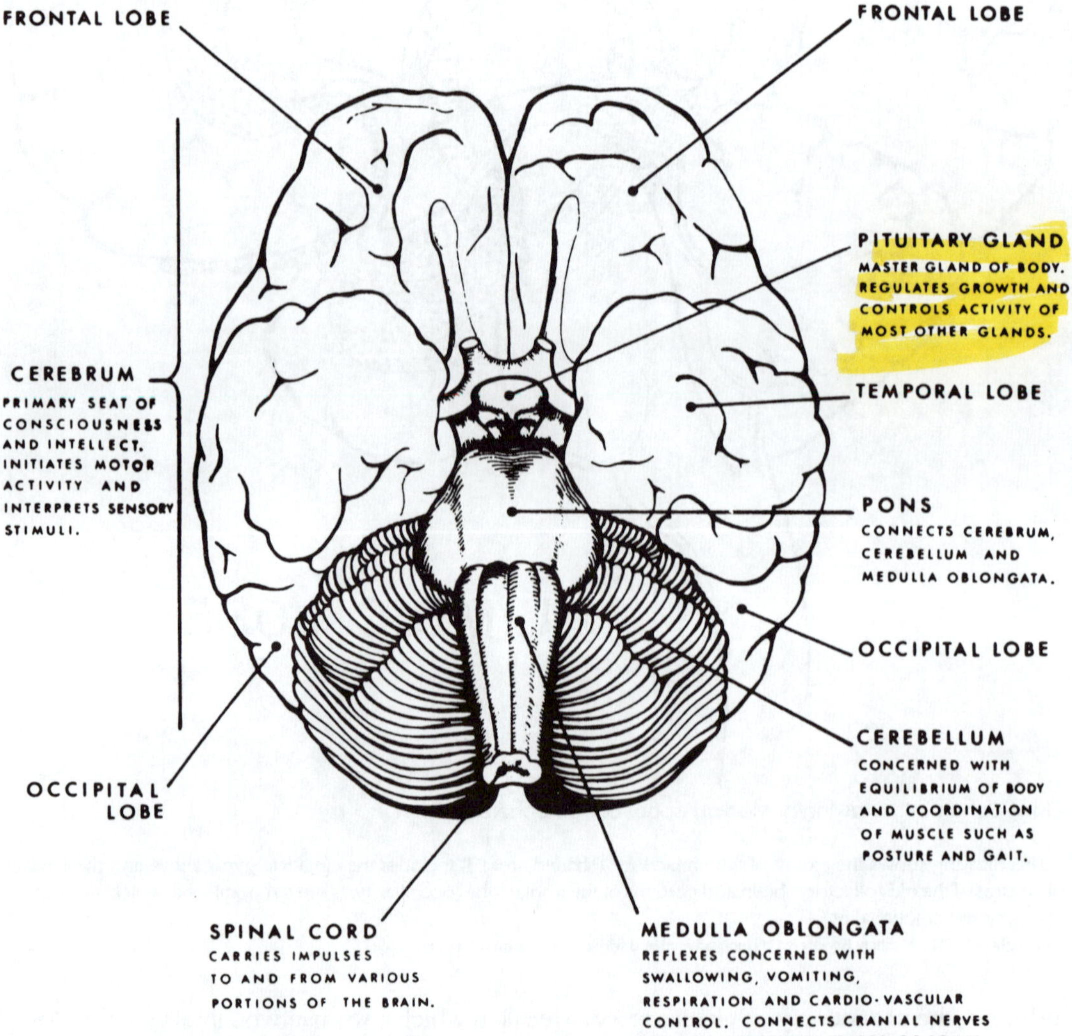

Fig. 5. Structures Located on "Underneath" Surfaces of Brain

This schematic, functional view is as though the brain had been removed from the skull and you are looking "up" at it.

THE BRAIN STEM

The brain stem provides a direct link from the spinal cord to the cerebral hemispheres (see Fig. 5). Contained within the brain stem are the medulla oblongata, pons, midbrain, and diencephalon. The brain stem serves several functions, the first of which provides a pathway for information coming directly from the brain to the spinal cord (the cerebrospinal tract) and provides a pathway for information traveling from the spinal cord to the thalamus (spinothalamic tract), where it is then relayed to other parts of the brain. The brain stem contains the 12 cranial nerves, which play a major role in all of our special senses (smell, sight, hearing, touch, balance, and taste).

The brain stem houses the neural centers for cardiovascular activity, consciousness, and respiration. It plays a major role in complex motor patterns. Lying within the core of the brain stem is the reticular formation, which serves to activate the brain and improve its efficiency. The brain stem also plays a major role in attention and sleep. Damage to the reticular system results in drowsiness, stupor, or even coma. Damage to the lower brain stem, particularly when it is severe, can result in death, since the nerve centers which maintain our life support systems are located within the medulla oblongata.

The pons (which in Latin means *bridge*) is located in the anterior portion midway up the brain stem. Visually, it resembles a large bulge or pouch and contains fibers which relay information between the motor cortex of the frontal lobes to the cerebellum for fine motor coordination and balance. The regulation of various stages of sleep is also controlled by areas within the pons.

Finally, the diencephalon, which is located at the most dorsal (highest) level of the brain stem, contains two very important structures (the thalamus and hypothalamus). The former receives information from the spinal cord (spinal thalamic tract) and relays this information to various brain structures. It also serves as a relay center within the brain and allows information to be sent from one part of the brain to another part. As a result of its primary function as a relay center for various forms of sensory and motor information, it plays a major role in such functions as attention, orientation, concentration, learning, memory, perception of the environment, language, and emotional functioning. The hypothalamus, although very small, is extremely complex and has been shown to play a major role in activities such as appetite, thirst, fatigue, sexual libido, the need for sleep, temperature regulation, weight control, and the generation of raw emotion which, as discussed earlier, is modulated by the limbic system in concert with the frontal lobes.

The cerebellum lies directly below the occipital and parietal lobes and directly behind (posterior) the brain stem and adjacent to the pons. The cerebellum plays a major role in coordinating and regulating fine motor control, as it receives information from the motor cortex via the pons. Damage to the cerebellum is likely to result in ataxia (poorly regulated and jerky movements which produce balance difficulties).

The Cerebrovascular System

The brain requires a constant and copious supply of blood to fulfill its needs for oxygen. For example, any blockage of the blood supply to the brain, even for only five seconds, will result in a loss of consciousness. When the brain is deprived of oxygen for three minutes or longer, the cells in specific areas of the brain will begin to die. Loss of oxygen for 8 to 10 minutes or longer will typically produce widespread brain damage (hypoxic encephalopathy). Thus, the brain must receive a constant and generous supply of oxygen to function properly. It relies exclusively on its cerebrovascular system for its supply of oxygen. The cerebrovascular system can be broken down into the internal carotid arterial system and the vertebral artery system.

INTERNAL CAROTID ARTERY SYSTEM

The internal carotid artery system is composed of arteries which enter the skull from the common carotid artery located in the neck. Shortly after it enters the skull, it divides into two anterior cerebral arteries which travel anteriorally along the longitudinal fissure, and then, posteriorly, towards the parietal occipital fissure. This system supplies blood and oxygen to the medial surface of the cerebral hemispheres. The second branch of the internal carotid artery forms the middle cerebral artery system and supplies blood and oxygen to the lateral areas of the frontal and parietal lobes, as well as the superior and middle temporal lobes. The middle cerebral artery contains smaller branches (striae), which furnish blood to the internal capsule, which contains bundles of descending motor fibers, which originate in the motor strip located in the posterior frontal lobes.

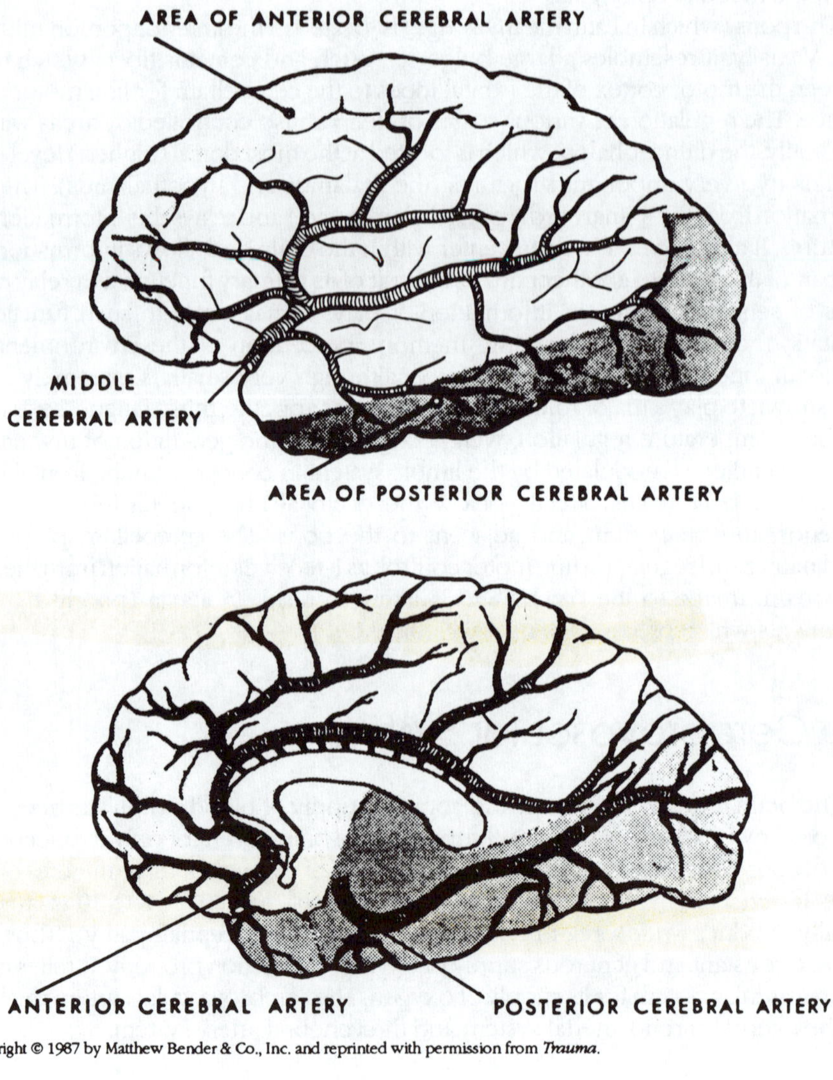

Fig. 6. Schematic Drawing of Vital Cerebral Arteries

VERTEBRAL ARTERY SYSTEM

The vertebral artery system is comprised of arteries which travel along the cervical vertebrae in the neck through the foramen magnum (a large opening at the base of the skull), where they travel across the posterior surface of the medulla oblongata. As they pass further up the brain stem, they merge just below the level of the pons to form the basilar artery. As the basilar artery travels past the pons, it branches into the posterior cerebral artery system and the posterior communicating artery system. The vertebral basilar artery system supplies blood and oxygen to the brain stem, cerebellum, and to the inferior temporal lobes.

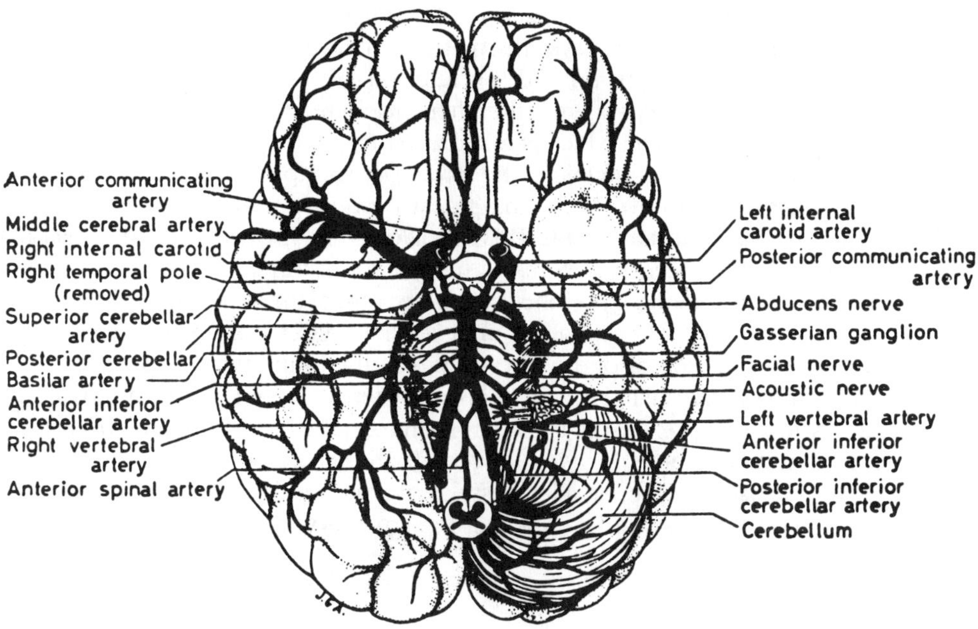

Fig. 7. Schematic Drawing of Arteries on Underside of Brain

The two vertebral arteries enter the cranial cavity from the neck and unite at the upper end of the medulla to form the basilar artery. The basilar artery terminates by dividing into the two posterior cerebral arteries and the two posterior communicating arteries. The internal carotid artery ends by dividing into the anterior cerebral and middle cerebral arteries.

The Circle of Willis is formed by the anastomosis of the posterior communicating arteries with the branches of the internal carotid artery behind and the anastomosis of the two anterior communicating branches in front.

All three artery systems (anterior, middle, and vertebral) connect together at the base of the brain and form what has been called the Circle of Willis. Through this connection, blood from one side of the brain can travel to the other side of the brain when one of the branches located on the opposite side becomes obstructed and is unable to provide an adequate amount of blood and oxygen.

Damage to the Cerebrovascular System

Any obstruction of a cerebral blood vessel (stroke) or a significant reduction in the amount of oxygen contained within the blood (hypoxia) can produce damage to specific parts of the brain or widespread brain damage (ischemia). For example, a lack of oxygen caused by cardiac arrest will most likely cause damage to the hippocampi located within the temporal lobes, which plays a major role in the learning of new information. If the patient is deprived of oxygen for more than several minutes, the brain cells located in the watershed zones (areas of the brain which lie between the areas of the brain perfused by the three arterial systems) are likely to be severely damaged. As a consequence, the patient is likely to develop visual agnosia, balance and coordination difficulties, and problems executing hand-eye coordination tasks. When a blockage or interruption of the blood supply occurs in one of the artery systems, that area of the brain, which is normally supplied blood and oxygen by this system, will die. This is referred to as a stroke. For example, a stroke involving the middle cerebral artery system in the left hemisphere will most likely produce a severe impairment in language functioning which is called aphasia.

In cases involving traumatic brain injury, the forces of the impact can cause a rupture of the veins within the membranes that cover the brain. This can produce a gradual accumulation of blood which can displace the brain and its contents. This condition is known as a subdural hematoma and is typically accompanied by such symptoms as mental confusion, lethargy, excessive fatigue, disorientation, and diminished cognitive functioning. Because of the slow buildup of blood in the brain, this condition may not be recognized until several weeks post-injury. Traumatic brain injuries can also cause a tearing of one of the arteries in the brain, which results in a massive hemorrhage within the skull, resulting in a rapid displacement of the brain, which can often result in death secondary to a compression of the brain stem (e.g., damage to the medulla oblongata which contains the neural centers for vital functions). In these cases, surgical intervention is necessary to save the patient's life. Smaller vessels can rupture following trauma resulting in microscopic lesions which can produce behavioral impairments without being visualized on CT or MRI brain scans.

The Cerebroventricular System

The cerebroventricular system is comprised of four ventricles (cavities) within the brain, which generate and circulate cerebral spinal fluid (CSF). CSF serves as a protective liquid cushion or shock absorber for the brain and spinal cord. Each lateral ventricle lies within a cerebral hemisphere. The anterior portion of the lateral ventricles reside in the frontal lobes, while the major portion of the ventricles lies within the frontal and parietal lobes. The ventricles extend posteriorly into the occipital lobe. The lateral ventricles also extend posteriorly into the temporal lobe. Within the lateral ventricles lie the choroid plexus, which manufactures the cerebral spinal fluid. CSF flows downward in the lateral ventricles through an opening (the Foramen of Monro) into the third ventricle, which lies within the diencephalon. The third ventricle contains choroid plexus and also produces cerebral spinal fluid. After the cerebral spinal fluid flows downward and out through the third ventricle, it passes through a long, narrow chamber which is known as the Aqueduct of Sylvius into the fourth ventricle, which is located within the brain stem. It also contains choroid plexus and is capable of producing cerebral spinal fluid. When cerebral spinal fluid exits the fourth ventricle, it circulates over the surface of the brain in the subarachnoid space located between the dura mater and the underlying subarachnoid membrane. The cerebral spinal fluid also travels down the spinal cord.

Brain Damage Caused by Hydrocephalus

When an obstruction occurs within the cerebral spinal fluid system or when its drainage system, located within the arachnoid villi, is blocked, the cerebral spinal fluid will accumulate, causing an expansion of the ventricular system which compresses the surrounding brain material. This condition, which is known as hydrocephalus, requires neurosurgical intervention consisting of the placement of a ventricular peritoneal shunt procedure which allows excessive cerebral spinal fluid to flow out of the brain and into the patient's stomach. Hydrocephalus is commonly seen following traumatic brain injuries, particularly if there has been some hemorrhaging within the brain. Patients who sustain this condition will typically exhibit the progressive development of such symptoms as lethargy, incontinence, balance difficulties, problems with recent memory, and mental confusion.

Chapter 5

Neuropathological Aspects of Neurobehavioral Disorders

It is essential that the attorney understand the neuropathological aspects of the various neuropatholgical disorders listed below which are frequently seen in Personal Injury or Workers' Compensation cases:

1. Minor head trauma
2. Cerebral concussion
3. Cerebral contusion
4. Severe traumatic brain damage (Diffuse axonal brain damage)
5. Secondary brain damage
6. Frontal lobe damage
7. Post-traumatic epilepsy
8. Post-traumatic psychiatric disorders
9. Post-traumatic hydrocephalus
10. Hypoxic encephalopathy
11. Memory disorders
12. Dementia
13. Toxic exposure (Toxic-metabolic encephalopathy)
14. Post-traumatic stress disorder

Minor Head Trauma

Approximately 8.8 million Americans sustain some form of head trauma each year. The overwhelming majority of these injuries are considered "minor" based upon several independent criteria which have been established by medical experts. The Glasgow Coma Scale (GCS), developed by two well-known neurosurgeons, Drs. Teasdale and Jennett (1981), consists of determining the patient's best motor, verbal, and eye opening responses following head trauma. Scores on this test can range from a low of 3 to as high as 15. The patient's score can be quickly determined by a physician or paramedic. Scores of 7 or less indicate that the patient is in coma. Some physicians have suggested that scores of 13 to 15 are indicative of mild brain injury, while scores ranging from 8 to 12 are indicative of moderate head injury. Scores of 7 or less are generally felt to be indicative of severe head trauma. This method of determining the severity of head trauma is not without its problems, since the vast majority of patients who sustain cerebral contusions (bruises on the surface of their brain) will have relatively high Glasgow Coma Scale scores (e.g., 13 or 14), but in actuality may be more impaired at one or two years post-injury than individuals with much lower Glasgow Coma Scale scores.

The duration of post-traumatic amnesia has been frequently utilized to determine the severity of head trauma. This is defined as the length of time after injury it takes for the patient's memory of ongoing events to become continuous. Thus, when the patient first begins to recall events following the injury in a chronological order, the period of post-traumatic amnesia has ended. According to this scale, patients who have post-traumatic amnesia of less than one hour are defined as having sustained a mild brain injury. However, research has shown that this scale tends to be unreliable in cases where the duration of post-traumatic amnesia is brief. For example, many patients who have sustained cerebral contusions may report a period of amnesia lasting for only a few seconds or minutes, but will exhibit rather dramatic changes in their personality, cognitive functioning, and behavior which would not be expected based on their relatively short duration of post-traumatic amnesia (PTA). Considerable skill is required in the interviewing of these patients to differentiate between isolated "islands" of memory versus truly continuous intact memory processing since the unskilled examiner will underestimate the duration of PTA. Collateral interviews with family members are helpful in establishing PTA.

The author has developed another criteria (Sbordone, in press) based upon the magnitude of the discrepancy between the number of complaints provided by the head-injured patient and those provided by significant others (family members or close friends) who have observed this patient since the head injury. The author has found that patients with minor head injuries will typically report several physical and cognitive difficulties stemming from their head trauma, which are typically relatively mild in severity; however, when the significant others are interviewed, they will report observing most of the same problems described by the patient and report several which have not been mentioned by the patient (e.g., irritability, temper tantrums, personality change, and changes in sexuality).

Cerebral Concussion

The most common form of mild head injury is a cerebral concussion. It may involve a brief loss of consciousness often following a rapid acceleration/deceleration injury (which simply means that the head is typically jerked back and forth in response to rapid mechanical acceleration/deceleration forces). Such injuries are commonly observed in motor vehicle accidents. Physical impact to the head is not necessary for a concussion to occur.

Research studies (e.g., Gennarelli, 1986) have shown that nerve fibers in the upper part of the brain stem tend to be stretched and damaged. This results in microhemorrhaging in this region. Research studies (Barth et al., 1986; Sekino et al., 1981) have shown that physical evidence of these injuries, based on neurodiagnostic tests and procedures such as CT scans, MRI scans, and EEG studies, is difficult to detect since these tests are typically normal because of their insensitivity to such types of injury.

Individuals who sustain cerebral concussions will typically be unable to recall the event (e.g., accident or fall) or physical impact (e.g., striking of their head on the dashboard or steering wheel). While patients with this disorder need not lose consciousness, they typically have amnesia lasting at least from a few seconds to several minutes. They may also appear confused and bewildered and begin exhibiting changes in their personality and cognitive and behavioral functioning shortly after such injuries. Most commonly, they are observed to be irritable, to fatigue easily, exhibit an increased need for sleep, and have diminished frustration tolerance. Attention-concentration difficulties are often present. These patients will often report being bothered by bright lights or loud noises. Such behaviors are most commonly observed by their spouses and family, as well as by their coworkers or employers.

POST-CONCUSSIVE SYNDROME

Cerebral concussions are very common, since it has been estimated that one out of every five college students has experienced at least one concussion by the time they reach college. In higher risk groups, such as individuals who ride motorcycles or who have histories of antisocial behavior, it is not uncommon to find that more than 50% of the individuals in this group have sustained at least one concussion. The symptoms of a cerebral concussion have frequently been reported to constitute a "post-concussive syndrome." Unfortunately, the symptoms of a post-concussive syndrome are quite varied and reflect a variety of factors. Research has also shown that approximately one-third of patients who sustain cerebral concussions are likely to complain of persistent cognitive difficulties at one year post-injury and that by three years post-injury, 15% are still complaining of such difficulties. The statistics, however, do not take into account a significant number of individuals who fail to complain of cognitive or behavioral difficulties but who are observed by significant others to exhibit significant cognitive or psychological impairments following their head trauma (Binder, 1986).

Patients who sustain cerebral concussions will rarely, if ever, develop frequent nightmares, intrusive recollections of the traumatic event, or experience considerable difficulty talking about their accident. They also typically do not become upset when exposed to events which remind them of their accident or resulted in their head trauma. They rarely develop a fear of driving or avoid stimuli or events which remind them of their accident or trauma. Patients with such problems are unlikely to have sustained a cerebral concussion, since their excellent recollection of the accident suggests that they were never rendered unconscious or developed post-traumatic amnesia. This suggests that their brain was most likely not injured and that their complaints and symptoms (which typically include complaints of forgetfulness and concentration difficulties) constitute a psychological reaction to a stressful event, rather than to a brain injury, per se. Such individuals have developed a post-traumatic stress disorder which is frequently misdiagnosed by their examining or treating physicians as a cerebral concussion or brain injury.

Cerebral Contusions

A cerebral contusion is a bruise on the surface of the brain. Patients who sustain such injuries typically strike their head on the ground or against a hard surface. While cerebral contusions may not necessarily result in a loss of consciousness, they typically result in significant and often relatively permanent alterations in personality, cognitive functioning, and behavior. Postmortem and CT studies of cerebral contusions (Alexander, 1984) indicate that the orbital frontal and inferior temporal areas of the brain are most likely to be damaged as a result of skull anomalies.

ORBITAL FRONTAL LOBE DAMAGE

Patients who sustain damage to the orbital frontal lobes will typically exhibit a pattern of disinhibition, characterized by inappropriate social comments, inappropriate or antisocial behavior, marked personality change, poor judgement and insight, and poor emotional control (Cummings, 1985).

TEMPORAL LOBE DAMAGE

Damage to the temporal lobes is likely to result in a pattern of brief, sudden outbursts of temper following relatively minor provocations or stresses, which are often followed by emotional distress or remorse (Bach-Y-Rita et al., 1971). In addition, patients who sustain temporal lobe damage are likely to exhibit memory disorders for recent events, as well as psychiatric difficulties, particularly depression, violence, rapid mood swings, pressured speech, and hallucinations. Patients who sustain prominent right frontal temporal lobe contusions are likely to exhibit a pattern of manic and depressive mood swings lasting one or two days each, which may not be seen until the patient is at least several months post-injury and which can persist for years (Sbordone, 1985). Patients with predominant left frontal temporal lobe injuries frequently become severely depressed and may seriously contemplate or attempt suicide (Lishman, 1968).

"OBJECTIVE" VERIFICATION OF DAMAGE

Verification of orbital frontal or temporal lobe damage by "objective" tests, such as the EEG, CT, or MRI scans, is often disappointing. While these tests may sometimes be sensitive to the presence of such injuries within the first few days following trauma, their ability to provide "objective" evidence of such injuries declines rapidly as a function of time. Thus, while evidence of abnormal findings may be seen during the first two or three days post-injury, an EEG or CT scan done one week or more following the patient's injury will often be normal. However, in some individuals, the CT or MRI scans may show brain atrophy at six to 12 months post-injury, which reflects the patient's earlier brain trauma (Sbordone et al., in press).

Diffuse Axonal Brain Damage

Diffuse axonal (white matter containing nerve fibers) brain damage typically occurs when the head is exposed to rapid acceleration/deceleration forces. These forces cause a shearing of the white matter of the brain and produce wide-spread damage to predominantly midbrain and subcortical brain areas. Such patients will typically become comatose at the scene of the accident and remain in this condition for many hours, days, weeks, and even months. The coma typically results from extensive midbrain damage, since this particular area plays a prominent role in wakefulness. Patients with diffuse axonal brain damage typically exhibit a variety of severe cognitive, motor, and behavioral difficulties which are typically recognizable even by the untrained observer, particularly when there is prominent brain stem damage. These individuals often exhibit marked to severe impairments on tasks involving speed of cognitive processing, problem solving, memory, attention and concentration, language, and perception. They also typically exhibit a substantial reduction in their intellectual functioning, which often severely compromises their ability to continue with their academic studies, work, or to perform household tasks and activities. Such patients frequently exhibit subtle (or obvious) impairment of their physical abilities, such as motor speed, coordination, and balance. A surprising number of patients who sustain diffuse axonal injuries will exhibit "normal" CT scans, even though there is unequivocal evidence of severe brain injury in that they have spent several weeks or months in coma (Astrup, 1989).

It is important to recognize that many individuals who sustain traumatic brain injury may have a combination of these three types of brain damage. For example, a patient can have a cerebral concussion and cerebral contusion. Similarly, a patient who is involved in a high speed motor vehicle accident may sustain a cerebral contusion and diffuse axonal brain injury. In such cases, it is important to recognize that such patients are typically more impaired, since their cognitive, emotional, and behavioral impairments will reflect a combination of such injuries.

Secondary Brain Damage

INTRACRANIAL HEMATOMA

The more severe the brain injury, the greater the likelihood of secondary brain damage. Secondary brain damage refers to additional insults to the damaged brain, which may begin several minutes, hours, days, and even weeks post-injury. Regardless of the severity of the head injury, the likelihood of intracranial hemorrhage is considerable. The classic clinical picture of an intracranial hematoma is that of a short period of unconsciousness, followed by the patient regaining consciousness, and then a secondary loss of consciousness due to pressure on the brain by the expanding hematoma within the space enclosed by the skull. If the hematoma remains undetected and untreated by neurosurgical intervention or medical treatment, the patient will show a progressive deterioration of neurological functioning, followed by decreased respiratory and cardiovascular functioning, followed by death. Occasionally, the expanding hematoma may not be diagnosed by the emergency room physician, resulting in the patient being sent home without special precautions for head trauma. These precautions include monitoring the patient's behavior on an hourly basis, checking for vomiting or changes in the patient's neurological functioning. The patient should also be awakened every hour to ensure that the patient's neurological status has not changed. If the patient cannot be aroused, this suggests the patient's neurological status has changed as a result of secondary brain damage most likely due to compression of the brain and brain stem, which can often result in death. For example, the patient may have sustained a cerebral contusion during a motor vehicle accident or fall which is likely to have produced focal brain damage to the orbital frontal and inferior temporal lobes. However, with an expanding intracranial hematoma (massive clot of blood), the contents of the brain are pushed from one side of the brain to the other, as well as pushed downward into the brain stem resulting in a compromise in the vital functions due to compression of the lower brain stem (medulla oblongata).

BRAIN SWELLING

Brain swelling, known as cerebral edema, is a common phenomenon and frequently occurs following severe head trauma. There is some controversy as to the precise mechanism of brain swelling. In cases involving cerebral contusions or brain lacerations, brain swelling appears to be due to the accumulation of water in the intracellular and/or interstitial space, while brain swelling in diffuse axonal injuries is most likely caused by the swelling and congestion of the blood vessels within the brain (Miller, 1983).

ELEVATED INTRACRANIAL PRESSURE

As a result of intracranial hemorrhaging and/or brain swelling within the skull, the patient's intracranial pressure is typically elevated. Many neurosurgeons will surgically insert an intracranial pressure monitor into the skull of the comatose, brain-injured patient to monitor intracranial pressure, since significant elevations in the patient's intracranial pressure will significantly reduce cerebral blood flow which frequently results in hypoxic insults and/or death. In a normal adult, the intracranial pressure should remain between 0 to 10 mmHg while the patient is lying flat on his or her back. When the pressure exceeds 20 mmHg, it falls into the abnormal range. When the intracranial pressure reaches 40 mmHg, then the patient's neurological functioning has been seriously compromised and is likely to result in the patient's death (Miller, 1975, 1977, 1983). Acute medical treatment, including the use of medications, may also be used to reduce swelling. Acute care records should be reviewed for symptoms of increased intracranial pressure.

INTRACRANIAL HEMATOMA

As mentioned before, the presence of intracranial hematoma causes displacement and distortion of the brain away from the expanding hematoma. This results in neurologic dysfunction which is typically seen in the contralateral motor and sensory functions. As this process continues, herniation of the brain's outer coverings can occur. For example, in many cases, an intracranial hematoma in the medial portion of the temporal lobe will produce a herniation of the tentorium cerebelli, which leads to a compression of the cerebral peduncle, resulting in progressive motor dysfunction. When the brain stem becomes compressed, the upper part of the brain stem which contains the reticular activating system (which keeps us alert and awake) becomes dysfunctional, resulting in a loss of consciousness. As the process of herniation continues, the oculomotor nerve becomes compressed, resulting in a third nerve palsy (the pupil on the same side of the lesion becomes fixed and dilated and is unresponsive to light). With further herniation, there is greater compression on the lower part of the brain stem, which results in changes in the patient's respiration and blood pressure, which frequently results in death. In many cases when death is averted through neurosurgical intervention, the patient will often be left with a severe amnestic (memory) disorder as a result of compression of the basilar vertebral artery by the cerebellum (Long, 1989; Miller, 1983).

HYPOXIC BRAIN DAMAGE

The vast majority of patients who sustain severe traumatic brain injuries are likely to experience hypoxic brain damage as a result of cerebral ischemia (a marked reduction in the amount of blood perfusing the brain). This frequently occurs as a result of brain swelling and raised intracranial pressure. It is exceedingly common, since it was found to occur in 91% of 151 patients who had died from severe head injuries, and was found on postmortem examination to be widespread (Graham, Adams, and Doyle, 1970). Other causes of ischemia include arterial hypotension and hypoxemia (a reduction in the oxygen carrying capacity of the blood following injury), cerebral vasospasm, and disruption of cerebral vascular autoregulation. While ischemic damage is widespread, it occurs most commonly in the hippocampis, basal ganglia, and in the watershed zones between the major cerebral arteries (Miller, 1983).

HYDROCEPHALUS

Hydrocephalus (an abnormal dilation of the cerebral ventricles) frequently occurs following intracranial hemorrhages which tend to clog up the arachnoid villi and thus prevent the excessive amount of cerebral spinal fluid from exiting the brain. When this occurs, the brain continues producing cerebral spinal fluid, which causes the cerebral ventricles to dilate and compress the brain. This frequently results in a characteristic pattern of neurologic dysfunction characterized by lethargy, mental confusion, problems with recent memory, balance difficulties, frequent falling, and incontinence. However, in many cases, the ventricles of the brain, particularly 6 to 12 months post-injury, will often become dilated as a result of a traumatic loss of brain tissue (usually white matter) following a traumatic brain injury. Thus, the presence of dilated ventricles post-injury can provide strong evidence that the patient had sustained a severe brain injury. This dilation usually will be even more evident after a year has passed.

INTRACRANIAL INFECTIONS

Intracranial infections are not uncommon and frequently arise following skull fractures, particularly when the dural membrane (the outer covering of the brain) has been torn or injured. This frequently results in a leakage of cerebrospinal fluid through the nasal septum (rhinorrhea) or ear canal (otorrhea). If this condition is not recognized and treated, the patient is likely to develop an intracranial infection which is likely to result in meningitis, encephalitis, or brain abscess. This can result in further damage to the brain and morbidity.

ARTERIAL HYPOEXEMIA

Arterial hypoxemia is the most common system insult seen in the severely head-injured patients upon their arrival in the emergency room. Whenever the level of arterial PO_2 falls below 600 mmHg, the amount of oxygen which can be carried in the blood falls dramatically. While the brain attempts to compensate for this by cerebral vasodilation, this mechanism is frequently impaired as a result of the traumatic brain injury. This results in a marked reduction in oxygen to the most severely damaged parts of the brain, resulting in hypoxic insults and necrosis (tissue death) of these areas (Miller, 1983).

REDUCTION OF CEREBRAL BLOOD FLOW

Patients who sustain severe traumatic brain injuries are extremely vulnerable to a reduction of blood pressure, since this typically results in a reduction of cerebral blood flow. This condition is referred to as arterial hypotension. This condition, however, is rarely produced by the brain injury but is more frequently seen when the patient sustains multiple trauma, including injuries to the abdomen, ribs, and fractures.

POST-TRAUMATIC EPILEPSY

Post-traumatic epilepsy can occur at any time following a head injury. While the overall incidence of post-traumatic epilepsy has been reported to be 5%, patients who sustain skull fractures, prominent parietal and/or temporal lobe damage, intracranial hematoma, intracranial infections, or penetrating injuries to the brain tend to have a much higher incidence of post-traumatic epilepsy (e.g., over 40%) (Long, 1989).

Post-traumatic epilepsy can present in a variety of different forms. Approximately half of the patients develop classic Grand Mal or generalized seizures, which are potentially hazardous, particularly if the patient is engaged in driving a motor vehicle or working at heights. These highly salient events will typically be noticed by others, who frequently call for medical assistance. Approximately 20% of patients with post-traumatic epilepsy may exhibit subtle behavioral changes which may not be recognizable to an external observer. For example, such individuals may stare off into space or develop a sudden fear or feel detached from one's surroundings. Other patients may develop deja vu experiences (a feeling that an experience happened before) or olfactory hallucinations (to experience the smell of rotten eggs or a specific odor). Other patients may exhibit complex automatisms, such as saluting, crossing a room, or repeating certain phrases. Generally these behaviors may only last a few seconds and are typically not recognized as being manifestations of a seizure disorder. For other patients, they may execute a series of complex activities, such as ending up in a restaurant they never intended to go to, without any recollection of how they got there. Many of these individuals may be seen as neurotic and, in some cases, even psychotic because of the relative bizarreness of the behavioral manifestations of their seizure disorder (Jennett, 1983).

The prediction of patients who are likely to develop late-onset post-traumatic epilepsy can be calculated based on three major factors: whether or not the patient had sustained an acute intracranial hematoma, had epilepsy during the first week post-injury, and whether or not the patient had sustained a depressed skull fracture. For patients who had sustained an intracranial hematoma within two weeks following their accident, the risk of post-traumatic epilepsy has been found to be approximately 35% over the next four years. Approximately 25% of the patients who sustained seizures during the first week are likely to develop seizures in the future. Depending on these factors, the risk of post-traumatic epilepsy can range from less than 3% to greater than 60% (Jennett, 1975).

Frontal Lobe Damage

The frontal lobes are frequently damaged during motor vehicle accidents, falls, or following blunt head trauma. The frontal lobes play a prominent role in the planning, organization, initiation, regulation, and monitoring of our behavior. Any injury to the frontal lobes, regardless of how small, is likely to result in an alteration in personality, behavior, cognitive functioning, or in interactions with others. The frontal lobes are not a homogenous entity and can be divided into three functionally specialized subregions, based on their location. Each of the three major areas of the frontal lobes, when damaged, tend to produce a predictable group of symptoms (i.e., syndrome).

ORBITAL FRONTAL LOBE DAMAGE

Patients who sustain orbital frontal lobe damage, which most frequently occurs when the patient sustains a cerebral contusion, is likely to produce a pattern of emotional and behavioral disinhibition. This disinhibition is characterized by a dramatic change in the patient's personality, diminished frustration tolerance, irritability, and impulsive behavior. Egocentricity, loss of affection toward significant others, lack of concern for the welfare of others, and frequent rapid mood swings accompany inappropriate social behavior or comments. Antisocial acts, crude or coarse language, and loss of social tact may be present. Euphoria and alterations in sexual activity or drive is common. Typically, these patients have little or no awareness of these changes and usually deny having any problems. In many cases, these patients may appear hyperactive and tell inappropriate jokes. However, when these patients are seen in highly structured settings, such as in a doctor's or attorney's office, these behaviors may not be observed. When these patients are administered standardized neuropsychological test batteries, they frequently show no evidence of abnormalities (Damasio, 1985). However, neuropsychologists who have had considerable experience with this type of patient frequently utilize qualitative or specialized tests, as well as interviews with significant others, to detect these patients' behavioral and emotional impairments (Sbordone, in press).

PRIMARY ROLE OF ORBITAL FRONTAL LOBE

The primary role of the orbital frontal cortex appears to be that of inhibiting the limbic system (emotional center within the brain). Thus, damage to this region results in the patient's inability to regulate his or her emotions or behavior. The principal cognitive deficits seen in this syndrome involve the impairment of judgement and planning skills and the ability to remain "on-track" in complex situations. Unfortunately, many clinical psychologists are unaware of the specific role that the orbital frontal lobes play in the regulation of behavior. They test these patients in a highly structured setting and administer a standardized neuropsychological test battery which contains very clear instructions. As a consequence, the quantitative test performances of these patients are typically "normal." This finding usually results in the psychologist erroneously concluding that the patient has not sustained a traumatic brain injury, even though the patient's significant others and family consistently report a dramatic change in the patient's behavior since the injury. Psychologists with expertise in clinical neuropsychology, and who have worked with this population in the past, are likely to use more qualitative and specialized tests that are more sensitive to the types of deficits exhibited by these patients. The neuropsychologist is also likely to interview the patient's family and significant others, paying careful attention to the patient's behavior (e.g., frank denial of any problems or difficulties, euphoric mood, etc.). The large discrepancy between the patient's complaints and those of significant others are a hallmark of frontal lobe injuries. Patients who sustain orbital frontal lobe damage will frequently return to school, but often show diminished motivation and incentive. They may exhibit a number of inappropriate and even bizarre behaviors in the classroom, which is likely to result in suspension and/or referral to a psychiatrist or counselor who may fail to understand the relationship between the patient's frontal lobe injury and inappropriate behavior.

DORSAL LATERAL DAMAGE

Patients who sustain more severe brain injuries are likely to sustain damage to the frontal convexity or dorsal lateral surfaces of the frontal lobes. Patients who sustain damage to this region typically appear apathetic, depressed (pseudodepression), and have emotionally "blunted" affect. They will also exhibit a number of significant cognitive impairments during neuropsychological testing. These patients typically demonstrate an inability to plan, organize, initiate, regulate, or monitor their behavior. These patients are usually distractable and have difficulty following through on tasks because of their inability to maintain an ongoing task. Frequently, they exhibit a marked discrepancy between what they say and what they do. For example, a patient may indicate that he is going to go to the store and buy some groceries, but in actuality, spends the rest of the day sitting at home and watching TV. These patients also show marked deficits in their abstract thinking, conceptual, and problem solving skills. They are unable to inhibit competing stimuli or events in their environment, and as a consequence, are easily distractable and find it impossible to do two things at once. They also perseverate or confabulate when they are asked to recall events of the recent or remote past (Stuss and Benson, 1986).

PATIENTS WITH FRONTAL LOBE DAMAGE APPEAR "NORMAL"

Oddly enough, these patients typically appear normal in that they exhibit little evidence of gross language impairments, motor problems, nor do they appear to have any significant psychiatric problems. They do, however, appear somewhat strange and may exhibit poor grooming and personal hygiene. For example, the author vividly recalls seeing a board-certified dermatologist in his office several years ago, who had graduated and completed his residency at a very well-respected Eastern medical center. Even though the doctor was wearing a suit, his shirt was hanging out of his pants and his trousers were unzipped. He also had a large coffee stain on his tie and each of his socks were a different color. He had apparently eaten breakfast prior to coming in to the author's office, since there were residues of the food he had eaten on his face and clothes. He also had not shaved or bathed for several days, and there was a noticeable body odor. In spite of these obvious problems, he denied that anything was wrong with him. When some of these above problems were pointed out to him, he failed to rectify them and did not seem the least bit embarrassed or troubled. Neuropsychological testing corroborated this patient's cognitive and behavioral deficits secondary to the frontal lobe injury he sustained in a motor vehicle accident one year earlier.

DAMAGE TO THE MEDIAL FRONTAL LOBES

Damage to the medial frontal lobes (the area between two cerebral hemispheres) typically produces a mute state characterized by lack of spontaneous movement, sparse verbalizations, and a lack of responsiveness to the environment (Cummings, 1985). Many of these patients are inappropriately diagnosed as being "catatonic" or "depressed" and may be mistakenly placed on antidepressant medications. This area of the brain appears to have strong connections with the limbic system and the upper brain stem, which contains the ascending reticular activating system. This system prepares the brain for emergencies and plays a central role in arousal and alerting the cerebral cortex of the arrival of important information about the environment.

CAUSES OF FRONTAL LOBE DAMAGE

The most common cause of bilateral, orbital frontal lobe damage is blunt head trauma. Damage to the orbital frontal lobes can occur following cerebral neoplasia (tumors), particularly those arising from the pituitary fossa, olfactory groove, or sphenoid ridge. In addition, aneurysms in the anterior communicating artery can function as mass lesions and may rupture into this region. The most common cause of frontal convexity damage is brain trauma. However, this problem can also be caused by compressive neoplasia (meningiomas) and intrinsic tumors (gliomas) and degenerative diseases (e.g., Alzheimer's disease), as well as demyelinating disorders (Cummings, 1985). The most common cause of medial frontal lobe damage is usually vascular lesions, hydrocephalus, or neoplasms. It should be noted, however, that chronic alcohol abuse, particularly over a period of 20 to 30 years, is likely to damage the frontal lobes and produce cognitive behavioral changes similar to patients who have sustained traumatic brain injuries. These problems would include impaired memory, poor abstraction skills, impaired problem solving skills, impaired conceptualization, visual-spatial impairments, verbal fluency difficulties, and impulsivity (Parsons and Farr, 1981). A competent neuropsychologist, however, should have little difficulty differentiating between cognitive difficulties caused by chronic alcoholism and frontal lobe dysfunction caused by an injury.

Post-traumatic Epilepsy

DEFINITION

Epilepsy refers to a group of disorders within the brain which result in recurrent seizures resulting from disturbed electrical activity within the brain. The seizures can take a variety of different forms, including episodes of disturbed movement, sensation, perception, and behavior and are frequently accompanied by alterations of consciousness. It has been estimated that at least 2% of the population suffers from some form of epilepsy. The onset of epilepsy, regardless of its particular etiology, tends to occur relatively early in life (Trimble and Thompson, 1986).

MAJOR CATEGORIES

Epilepsy can be divided into two major categories: idiopathic and symptomatic. In idiopathic epilepsy, some form of inherited mechanism is thought to produce a propensity for low seizure thresholds in the brain. In the latter category, the etiology of the patient's seizures is likely due to some type of injury or disease that occurs after birth. This would include head trauma, brain tumors, intracranial infections, vascular lesions, and cerebral hypoxia. It should also be recognized that some individuals may have a genetic predisposition to develop seizures following brain insult. Seizures can be broken down into two major categories: partial or generalized.

PARTIAL SEIZURES

Partial seizures can be further broken down into seizures where there is no impairment of consciousness (partial seizures with elementary symptomatology) and seizures that are accompanied by alterations of consciousness (partial seizures with complex symptomatology). Patients with partial complex seizures typically present with a variety of experiences, including hallucinations, affective disturbances (rapid mood swings), thought disturbances, and are typically complex in their manifestations. It should be noted that while patients generally do not lose consciousness during partial seizures, they are typically unable to respond to their environment in a fully purposeful and meaningful fashion. For example, during a seizure, the patient may be unable to respond if their name is called or to a red light or to a pedestrian crossing the street if they are operating a motor vehicle.

GENERALIZED SEIZURES

Generalized seizures are accompanied by a loss of consciousness or a transient lapse of consciousness. Included are such types as myoclonic seizures (sudden jerks of the body), clonic seizures, tonic attacks and tonic/clonic seizures (often referred to as Grand Mal epilepsy), atonic seizures, and akinetic attacks. Included with this category are Petit Mal seizures which may be unnoticed by observers and consist of brief absences.

ETIOLOGY AND DIAGNOSIS OF SEIZURES

It should be recognized that all epileptic seizures, regardless of their particular type, originate in the brain. The diagnosis of a seizure disorder is typically made by a medical neurologist and is usually based by actually observing a seizure episode or making the diagnosis of a seizure based upon the description of the patient's behavior from family members, if they are considered reliable informants. An impairment of consciousness, or seizure-like activity, can be produced by a variety of causes that lie outside of the brain, such as vasovagal syncopal episodes, cardiac arrhythmias, transient ischemic episodes, migraine headaches, hypoglycemia, and dissociative psychological or emotional states (pseudoseizures). To rule out seizures of noncerebral origin, it is essential that the patient undergo a careful neurological examination, including an electroencephalogram (EEG). This is important for patients who have had only one seizure episode, since this episode could be in response to such factors as sleep deprivation, fasting, and drug or alcohol withdrawal. If there is no evidence of neurological disease, and these latter factors are found to be present, and if the EEG reveals no evidence of epileptiform activity, then the diagnosis of epilepsy is likely to have been made in error (Ehle and Holman, 1980). Response to antiepileptic drug treatment can be helpful in establishing the diagnosis of epilepsy (Schmidt and Wilder, 1968), although this could be due to "placebo" or the mild antidepressant effects of the medication (i.e., Tegretol) in patients with psuedo-seizures of functional eitology.

DIFFICULTY OBTAINING "OBJECTIVE VERIFICATION"

The difficulty in evaluating patients who are suspected of having epilepsy is that the electroencephalogram is a relatively crude neurophysiological instrument, since it must record the electrical activity of the brain through the relatively thick insulating tissues of the head (hair, scalp, bones, blood vessels, etc.) (Kligman and Goldberg, 1975). It is also handicapped by being unable to detect electrical potentials more than a few millimeters from the most superficial layers of the brain. An additional problem is that the EEG recordings are usually made for 30 minutes or less. Thus, the EEG only samples a relatively small portion of the electrical activity of a 24-hour day (Dodrill, 1981).

PSYCHOLOGICAL MANIFESTATIONS OF TEMPORAL LOBE SEIZURES

Patients who develop temporal lobe seizures (partial complex seizures which originate in one of the temporal lobes) are likely to exhibit a wide range of psychiatric and psychological problems. Research studies (Bear et al., 1982) have shown that patients with temporal lobe epilepsy, in comparison to patients with functional psychiatric disorders, tend to exhibit a significantly greater frequency of behaviors such as excessive interpersonal clinging (viscosity), repetitive preoccupation with peripheral details (circumstantiality), religious and philosophical preoccupations, humorless sobriety, a tendency toward paranoid over-interpretation, and excessive moralistic concerns. Patients with temporal lobe epilepsy have a predilection for aggressive behavior and for acts of violence, although unlike patients with character disorders, they are more likely to accept responsibility for their violent outbursts and are likely to exhibit severe remorse and guilt following them. Patients with temporal lobe epilepsy often exhibit a propensity to write excessively (hypergraphia), have decreased sexual interest and drive (hyposexuality), frequently have difficulty getting to the point when they are asked to explain a particular event (circumstantiality). Similarly, they often show a deepened affect toward the world around them. Additionally, patients with temporal lobe epilepsy may exhibit frequent mood changes, emotional lability (crying easily), and may become hyper-religious. Finally, it should be recognized that these symptoms may not appear until several months or years following the first onset of temporal lobe epilepsy which may have been caused by an earlier traumatic brain injury.

Post-traumatic Psychiatric Disorders

Post-traumatic psychiatric disorders refer to the development of psychiatric symptoms following a traumatic injury. When the traumatic injury is psychological—in the sense that it does not involve brain damage—the patient will develop either an adjustment disorder or a post-traumatic stress disorder.

ADJUSTMENT DISORDER

An adjustment disorder is characterized by symptoms such as anxiety, depressed mood, conduct disturbances, physical complaints, or social withdrawal. These symptoms are likely to effect the patient's occupational, academic, or social relationships. An adjustment disorder, which can last up to six months, typically resolves gradually with or without psychological or psychiatric treatment.

POST-TRAUMATIC STRESS DISORDER

A post-traumatic stress disorder is characterized by frequent nightmares of the disturbing event, recurrent and intrusive recollections of the event, intense psychological distress while discussing the event or exposed to stimuli which remind the patient of the event, sleep difficulties, flashbacks, startle responses, memory and concentration difficulties, irritability, social withdrawal, emotional detachment, and deliberate efforts to avoid thoughts or feelings associated with the traumatic event.

TYPE OF DISORDER IS RELATED TO STRESSOR

Typically, when patients are exposed to stressors, such as job termination, divorce, debilitating physical injuries, death of a loved one, and financial or business difficulties, they are likely to develop an adjustment disorder or reaction. However, when the stressors are extremely severe or catastrophic and fall out of range of usual human experiences and would be extremely distressing to almost anyone (e.g., serious threat to one's life or family, sudden destruction of one's home or community, or witnessing someone being killed or seriously injured as the result of an accident or physical violence) the patient is likely to develop a post-traumatic stress disorder.

PSYCHIATRIC SYMPTOMS CAUSED BY BRAIN DAMAGE

Psychiatric symptoms which arise as a consequence of brain damage are likely to be varied and may not manifest themselves for several months to as long as several years post-injury. The symptoms of such disorders are likely to include depression, emotional lability, rapid mood swings, paranoia, aggressive or violent behavior, excessive guilt, changes in affect, manic episodes (characterized by shopping sprees, hyperactivity, grandiose thinking, euphoria, rapid speech, and a decreased need for sleep), suicidal behavior, visual hallucinations, impulsive and/or antisocial behavior, and changes in sexual functioning.

THE RELATIONSHIP BETWEEN SYMPTOMS AND SITE OF BRAIN DAMAGE

The particular constellation of psychiatric symptoms typically reflects the site of brain damage, the premorbid personality and coping style of the patient, and the duration of time since injury. For example, patients who sustain prominent frontal lobe damage are likely to exhibit symptoms such as emotional lability, changes in affect, insensitivity to the needs and welfare of others, and impulsive and/or antisocial behavior. Damage to the right frontal temporal lobe is likely to produce a rapid cycling manic-depressive disorder, characterized by grandiosity, denial, hyperactivity (which may last for one to two days), followed by depression, suicidal thoughts, physical complaints, and increased need for sleep (which may last one to two days). These symptoms generally do not appear until at least six months post-injury and may not appear until several years post-injury (Sbordone, 1988, 1990). Patients who exhibit the former symptoms are frequently diagnosed as having an organic personality disorder or syndrome, while patients with the latter disorder are likely to be diagnosed as having an organic mood disorder or syndrome. The diagnosis of an organic mood or personality disorder secondary to brain injury should be corroborated by the results of neuropsychological testing, the patient's medical records, interviews with significant others, and behavioral observations of the patient.

Post-traumatic Hydrocephalus

Hydrocephalus refers to the swelling or enlargement of the cerebral ventricles within the brain. This disorder can be caused by a number of conditions, the most common of which is some form of obstruction which prevents excessive cerebrospinal fluid from being absorbed via the arachnoid villi into the body. Hydrocephalus is commonly seen in patients who sustain traumatic brain injuries but may not be detected until several weeks or months post-injury. It is commonly seen in elderly patients who slip or fall in their home and strike their head. Patients who develop hydrocephalus often appear lethargic, drowsy, and may exhibit gait or balance difficulties, suffer from incontinence, and a variety of cognitive impairments, particularly with recent memory. Any delay in referring this patient to an appropriate medical specialist, such as a neurologist or neurosurgeon, or in obtaining treatment, which typically consists of surgical placement of a ventroperitoneal shunt, is likely to produce secondary brain damage. This secondary brain damage then serves to aggravate the patient's primary brain injury secondary to their blunt head trauma. It has been estimated that the majority of patients who are referred for neurosurgical intervention to alleviate this condition will show a marked improvement in their symptoms and behavior following treatment. Thus, it is crucial that this condition be quickly recognized by the patient's treating doctors to spare the damaged brain from any further damage.

Hypoxic Encephalopathy

Hypoxic encephalopathy refers to a loss of neurons and brain tissue as the result of an insufficient amount of oxygen to the brain. This disorder is frequently seen in patients who have overdosed on drugs, drowned, or who have been exposed to oxygen replacing gasses such as carbon monoxide for a sufficient length of time. It is also seen in patients who have sustained cardiac arrests or whose brains did not get sufficient oxygenation as a result of multiple trauma sustained during a severe motor vehicle accident. Patients with hypoxic encephalopathies may exhibit severe, if not profound, problems with recent memory, and display mental confusion, psychomotor retardation, gait and balance difficulties, ataxic (jerky) movements, and a depressed appearance. These patients will also display poor judgement, as well as a limited ability to process new information and may become confused when they are required to process more than one event at a time. The clinical course of these patients frequently depends upon the duration of coma following their cerebral insult. Research studies have shown that when patients are in comas for 48 hours or longer, they, most likely, will be left with permanent cognitive and behavioral impairments for the remainder of their lives. Thus, the prognosis for patients who have sustained severe hypoxic encephalopathies is typically poor.

Memory Disorders

AMNESIA

Amnesia refers to a condition in which the patient's ability to learn new information is impaired despite relatively normal attention and concentration skills. The ability to recall remote information (e.g., the name of the high school the patient attended or names of childhood friends and teachers) may be spared in many amnesias (Benson, 1978). The vast majority of patients who have been exposed to some form of severe trauma will complain of problems with their recent memory. One must, however, distinguish between complaints of memory difficulties and true impairments of recent memory. For example, patients who have severe amnesia rarely complain of memory difficulties. When asked to describe their memory, they will typically say, "It's fine," even though they cannot recall what they did several minutes ago, what they ate for breakfast that morning, or what they did the night before the examination. Patients who complain, however, of severe memory problems most likely either have very mild amnesia or are extremely nervous, depressed, or histrionic. Similarly, patients who complain of numerous problems and difficulties typically have an intact memory for recent events. Patients with severe amnesia rarely, if ever, complain of any problems or difficulties unless they are currently experiencing muscular pain or discomfort in some part of their body. Thus, their complaints are typically confined to their current somatic problems. Patients who complain of problems with their remote memory usually are depressed, since such memories are typically preserved following brain trauma.

CAUSES OF AMNESIA

Amnesia is often seen in patients who have sustained head trauma, cerebral anoxia, brain tumors, cerebral vascular accidents (strokes), or have a history of acute cardiopulmonary arrest. Electroconvulsive therapy, insulin overdose, and surgical removal of the temporal lobes may also produce amnesia. Patients who have a history of excessive drinking, which may result in Wernicke-Korsakoff's syndrome, will typically exhibit severe amnesia. Amnesia is most commonly seen in patients who have Alzheimer's disease. Any insult to the hippocampus, which is located in the temporal lobes, as a result of hypoxia or trauma, is likely to produce a profound impairment in recent memory. Patients who sustain significant frontal lobe injuries are likely to exhibit memory impairments for recent events, which frequently take the form of confabulation, distortions, and intrusion errors. For example, these patients quickly lose their mental set while recalling a list of words and begin recalling a different list of words or simply repeat the instructions provided by the examiner.

The primary site for disturbances of recent memory appears to be within the limbic system and originates in the hippocampi and mammillary bodies located within the temporal lobes and brain stem. The hippocampi receive information from the parahippocampal temporal lobe, which receives information from different regions of the brain, particularly from the parietal and frontal lobes. After being processed in the hippocampi, this information is sent to the fornix, which sends the information to the septum, mammillary bodies, and thalamus for further processing. Any injury to this limbic system or any part of it is likely to produce amnesia when this circuit is broken (Cummings, 1985).

Neuropsychological assessment is invaluable in assessing patients who are suspected of having amnesia or to rule out amnesia in patients who present with symptoms such as, "My biggest problem is my memory. I can't remember anything. My memory is simply terrible. For example, yesterday my wife told me about my brother-in-law and an hour later I completely forgot what she had said." Neuropsychological testing can also determine whether the patient's memory problems are due to faulty encoding (organization) of new information or impaired storage. Memory impairments are frequently seen in patients who have impaired concentration or attentional skills, which may be due to the patient's inability to encode this information at the time it was presented. Encoding difficulties may also be due to high levels of anxiety.

Dementia

Dementia refers to a pathological state in which the patient's cognitive and behavioral functioning is significantly impaired. Demented patients may show impairments of memory, language, visual-spatial skills, abstract thinking, conceptualization, impaired mental arithmetic, and impoverished judgement and problem solving skills. Typically, the term dementia was reserved for cognitive disorders of the elderly and is rarely used to characterize the psychological functioning of young adults. Dementia can be simply broken down into treatable and untreatable etiologies. Untreatable etiologies include such disorders as Alzheimer's and Pick's disease. Treatable dementias include medical disorders which significantly alter the metabolic activity of the brain and frequently produce significant impairments in concentration-attention, problem solving skills, judgement, and in recent memory. Correct identification of the etiology of the patient's dementia and subsequent treatment will often result in a marked alleviation of the patient's cognitive impairments. Dementia can also be caused by a series of small cerebral vascular accidents (strokes) within the brain. This condition is likely to create a variety of significant cognitive impairments along with areas of preserved mental functioning. This is known as multi-infarct dementia. Patients with this disorder often have a history of hypertension and/or cardiac difficulties.

Dementia can also be produced by a variety of medications which lower levels of acetylcholine and dopamine within the brain, which result in impairments in problem solving, recent memory and mental confusion. It should also be noted that patients who are placed on anti-convulsant medications, such as Dilantin and especially Phenobarbital, typically show a significant reduction in their cognitive functioning which is alleviated when the patients are taken off these medications. Exposure to a variety of metals (lead, mercury, manganese, arsenic, thallium) and a variety of organic solvents (trichloroethylene tolune, carbon tetrachloride, and carbon disulfide), carbon monoxide, and insecticides is likely to produce dementia (Cummings, 1985). In many cases, elimination of exposure to these substances results in a gradual improvement in the patient's condition.

PSEUDODEMENTIA

Patients who present with numerous complaints of severe amnesia and cognitive problems, which upon careful neuropsychological testing are found to be groundless, are often diagnosed as having pseudodementia, particularly if their complaints appear to be caused by psychiatric problems (e.g., depression) or if they are expressed in a histrionic fashion and accompanied by displays of anger and tears. These patients tend to have little insight into their emotional problems and continue to complain of severe memory problems, even though they are able to provide their treating or examining doctor with a detailed chronological history of their illness and the development of their symptoms.

Patients with a history of endocrine disorders (e.g., hypothyroidism, hypoglycemia, etc.) will frequently exhibit forgetfulness and mild cognitive difficulties until their disorder can be treated by an appropriate medical specialist (usually with medications). Patients with a history of bipolar depression (manic depressive illness) can appear demented during the depressed phase of their illness. Thus, it is essential to take a careful history, which includes interviews with significant others and a review of the patient's past medical records to rule out this possibility. Patients with hysterical conversion disorders will often present with the superficial appearance of a dementia. These patients are typically able to provide a rather detailed chronological history of their illness or symptoms (which contradicts their complaint of memory difficulties) and even though they often describe the severity of their memory problems as "extremely severe," it is usually stated in either a bland or dramatic manner.

CASE STUDY

The author was asked to consult on a case in which a 42-year-old woman reported that she sustained a head injury when a small piece of insulation material fell from the ceiling and struck her on the head as she was working. She denied a loss of consciousness and was able to easily recall the events which occurred immediately prior to, during, and following her injury. The patient was able to provide 30 complaints, each of which was very detailed and elaborate. She described her problems with her recent memory as "profound" but was able to provide this examiner with numerous examples of her "poor memory," which were quite detailed and, thus, contradicted her complaints of memory difficulties. When the patient was asked to describe her childhood, she stated, "It was fine." When asked questions about her childhood, however, particularly her relationship with her parents, she claimed that she could not recall anything about her childhood. When she was asked where she spent the first 10 years of her life, she stated, "Somewhere in Europe." However, when she was asked to be more specific, she stated, "I can't remember." When she was asked to indicate if there had been any problems in her life since her marriage, she vehemently denied any problems and stated that her marriage was "perfect." Her husband, however, when interviewed, reported a history of alcoholism, extra-marital affairs, and drug abuse. The patient indicated that she had been married three times previously and that each of her husbands had been unfaithful to her and had physically abused her. When she was asked how she handled this in the past, she stated, "It really didn't bother me. I took it well." The patient was also asked about her 15-year-old daughter who had recently run away from home and become pregnant. The patient replied, "My daughter is fine. She's doing well." It was also learned during the interview that her 17-year-old son had recently been arrested for selling drugs. Once again, the patient denied that this incident had created any psychological problems or difficulties for her. In spite of these admissions, she denied that there were any external problems in her life which were contributing to her memory difficulties.

Neuropsychological testing revealed a pattern of atypical responses on memory testing consistent with patients who are repressing long-standing and current emotional problems, particularly strong feelings of anger and rage, consistent with pseudodementia.

Testing further indicated that the patient was likely to convert her emotional problems into a variety of somatic complaints to draw attention to herself, since she apparently had not felt any caring or attention from other a family members. Later it was learned that this patient had spent the first 10 years of her life in a concentration camp where both of her parents were killed.

Toxic-metabolic Encephalopathy

Toxic-metabolic encephalopathy refers to a pattern of psychological, cognitive, behavioral, and emotional disturbances following exposure to industrial or toxic substances which are known to have neurotoxic effects on the brain. Such disorders are likely to produce a picture of apathy, clouded consciousness, inattentiveness, lethargy, fatigue, and impaired recent memory functions. Psychomotor retardation, anxiety, poor judgement and insight, and a depressed-looking appearance are often characteristic of toxic encephalopathy. Such behaviors may reflect acute or chronic exposure to a variety of chemicals or industrial solvents which have been described in the previous section. Neuropsychological assessment can be invaluable in either documenting or refuting the plaintiff's complaints of such difficulties.

Post-traumatic Stress Disorder

Post-traumatic stress disorder (PTSD) refers to the psychological reaction of individuals who have been exposed to an event which falls outside of the usual range of human experience (e.g., a serious threat to one's life or physical integrity; serious harm to one's children, spouse, or other close relatives and friends; sudden destruction of one's home or community; seeing another person seriously injured or killed as a result of physical violence or accident; or learning that one's child has been kidnapped, tortured, or killed). Automobile accidents can produce PTSD if the event falls outside of the range of human experience (e.g., caused the individual to fear serious physical injuries, losing his or her life, or witness serious injury or the death of a child, spouse, or close friend). Individuals who develop PTSD typically begin experiencing a variety of symptoms which can include recurrent and intrusive recollections of the traumatic event, distressing dreams of the event, flashbacks, insomnia, concentration and memory difficulties, irritability, social withdrawal, diminished interest in previously enjoyed activities, avoidance of events which resemble the distressing event, a driving phobia (particularly if the traumatic event involved a motor vehicle accident), and becoming very upset when asked to discuss the distressing event or when exposed to stimuli (e.g., movies, TV shows, the screeching of brakes, or accidents) which remind them of the traumatic event.

Patients who develop a post-traumatic stress disorder often become depressed and anxious and frequently complain that they are "going crazy" or "losing their minds." However, they are very reluctant to talk about the traumatic incident and typically become extremely nervous and frequently begin sobbing when they are forced to describe it.

CASE STUDY

A 35-year-old woman was traveling in her automobile accompanied by her six-year-old son. While she was wearing her seat belt, her son had managed to remove his seat belt so that he could have a better view of the road ahead. A few minutes later, an oncoming truck made a sudden, illegal U-turn directly in front of the patient's vehicle. The patient recalled seeing her car heading toward the truck and vividly recalled watching her son's face smash into the windshield and his body drop limp to the floor of the car. She thought her son had been killed and noticed blood all over his face and clothing. She could not release her seat belt and was trapped in the seat of her car unable to reach or touch her son. She began screaming for help, however, the paramedics did not arrive until approximately 20 minutes later; during this time she assumed that her son had been killed and blamed herself for his death. Even though her son had sustained a concussion and had been rendered unconscious, he had not sustained any serious injuries following this incident. The patient experienced as many as 100 flashbacks per day of watching her son smash his face into the windshield of her car and of the events leading up to and following the accident. She was unable to sleep at night because of repetitious thoughts and flashbacks of the accident. When she was finally able to fall asleep, she began experiencing severe nightmares. She became irritable and began complaining of memory and concentration difficulties because she had struck the left side of her head on the door jam during the accident and had sustained a scalp hematoma. Her treating doctor diagnosed her as having a traumatic brain injury. Over the next four years, the patient continued to complain of memory and concentration difficulties and appeared to be unable to work or to get on with her life. When she underwent neuropsychological assessment, she exhibited virtually all of the symptoms of a post-traumatic stress disorder, but relatively intact attentional, concentration, and memory functioning. When she was asked to recall the accident, she began shaking all over and hyperventilating as if she were re-experiencing it. She also began sobbing and indicated that she did not want to discuss the accident because it was so emotionally painful for her to talk about it. She admitted that she had not informed any of her treating doctors of the incident involving her son during her motor vehicle accident because it caused her so much grief even to think about it. The diagnosis of post-traumatic stress disorder was made based upon the history obtained from the patient, a review of the patient's medical records, behavioral observations of the patient, and the results of neuropsychological testing, with the latter having produced negative results with respect to the question of brain injury.

CRITERIA TO DETECT INDIVIDUALS WHO DISPLAY FICTITIOUS SYMPTOMS OF PTSD

Many individuals, however, who file claims for post-traumatic stress disorders do not meet the criteria for PTSD, as set forth in the Diagnostic and Statistical Manual of Mental Disorders (DSM III-R). For example, while some individuals may complain of symptoms generally consistent with PTSD, they display some of the following behaviors, which suggests that their symptoms are fictitious:

1. They appear eager to discuss the accident and their symptoms.

2. They strongly emphasize how their lives have been completely devastated by the accident.

3. They express a desire for revenge or to "get back" at the driver of the other vehicle or others.

4. They emphasize how much money they need to be happy again.

5. They appear "slick" or devious.

6. They have a history of similar motor vehicle accidents in the past.

7. They have a history of criminal activity and/or drug or alcohol abuse.

8. They carry their accident and medical records with them when they are seen for independent medical or neuropsychological evaluations.

9. They had a poor employment history prior to their accident.

10. They have a pre-existing history of emotional problems or characterological difficulties (e.g., had been arrested or fired for lying, forgery, or participating in some form of criminal activity).

PTSD VS. BRAIN DAMAGE

Patients who sustain post-traumatic stress disorders are unlikely to have sustained a traumatic brain injury, particularly when they are able to vividly recall the events immediately preceding, during, and following the accident. This indicates that their brain was operating at full efficiency during the time the accident occurred. The presence of nightmares, flashbacks, or intrusive recollections of the distressing event indicates that they most likely did not sustain post-traumatic amnesia, bewilderment, or confusion. The presence of nightmares, flashbacks, intrusive recollections of the event and their emotional reactions to events which resemble the distressing event are idiosyncratic to PTSD and are generally not seen in patients who have sustained brain injuries. An exception to this is when the patient who sustains a traumatic brain injury awakens in their vehicle after being unconscious for an unspecified period of time and is out of the period of post-traumatic amnesia. Exposure to any distressing events following this, such as news that a particular person has been killed or injured during the accident, or to a traumatic event (e.g., such as fearing being killed or seriously injured) can elicit a post-traumatic stress disorder at that time.

Chapter 6

Neuropsychological Assessment

Neuropsychological assessment refers to the complex process that the neuropsychologist goes through to reach his or her conclusions regarding the effect of a specific injury on the patient's cognitive and emotional functioning, and its effect on the patient's quality of life, ability to work, attend school, and perform activities of daily living, including shopping, cooking, cleaning, handling finances, paying bills, and dealing with one's family. This assessment process typically includes identifying specific areas of the brain which have been damaged and demonstrating the relative severity of the patient's cognitive and emotional impairments. Psychologists unfamiliar with medicolegal reports may often exclude any relationship between a specific injury and a patient's neuropsychological impairments. Part of the reason for this is that neuropsychologists are typically asked by physicians or other psychologists to identify the patient's impairments and how they impact upon the patient's life. For example, referral questions typically address such issues as, "Can this specific patient return to school or work? If he or she returns to work or school, what kinds of problems can we expect to arise?" Thus, neuropsychologists without medicolegal experience may be relatively insensitive to causation issues, unless their importance is carefully emphasized by the referring attorney. Since this issue is so important to attorneys, and should be so to neuropsychologists involved in medicolegal cases, it is essential that a variety of confounding or extraneous factors be ruled out so that the relationship between a specific event (e.g., accident or fall) and the patient's neuropsychological impairments be made as unequivocally clear as possible. This is best done by performing a careful and systematic neuropsychological assessment, which includes a variety of data bases such as:

1. A detailed, chronological history of the patient's injury should always be obtained. This includes information acquired directly from the patient, significant others, and from available medical records.

2. An extensive background history is obtained from the patient. This should include the patient's developmental, linguistic, educational, family, military, occupational, legal, cultural, religious, marital, sexual, medical, and psychiatric history.

3. Observations are made of the patient's behavior during the interview, breaks, and testing during both structured and unstructured settings. This should also include interviews with significant others and family members in order to determine their observations of the patient's behavior in familiar settings.

4. A careful review of the patient's academic, vocational, medical, psychiatric/psychological, legal, and military records should be performed in order to supplement patient and family interview data.

5. The administration of a wide variety of specialized tests, which have been designed to evaluate the patient's cognitive, emotional, and behavioral functioning.

6. Careful analysis of the test results, using both quantitative and qualitative scoring methods based upon the neuropsychologist's experience, expertise, and training in neuropsychology.

7. Conclusions regarding the patient's impairments, or lack of, based upon an integration of all of the above data bases. This involves ruling out other probable causes of the patient's impairments and/or determining the relative contributions of these factors on the patient's present condition.

8. Determination of the patient's prognosis and long-term cognitive, behavioral, and emotional difficulties.

9. Determination of the types of treatments that are needed, such as rehabilitation, psychiatric treatment, cognitive rehabilitation, etc., to improve the patient's quality of life and to alleviate or minimize the effects the patient's neuropsychological impairments have upon his or her daily functioning.

10. Determination of the effect that the patient's impairments have upon the family and/or significant others.

11. Description of any potential problems, such as epilepsy, depression, psychiatric conditions, etc., which may arise in the future that are likely to result in the need for medical, psychological, or other services.

The next section of this book will cover each of these areas in greater detail.

Clinical Interview with Patient and Significant Others

It is essential that the patient be carefully interviewed by a qualified neuropsychologist prior to the administration of neuropsychological tests. The reasons for this should seem obvious to defense attorneys, but may not be obvious to attorneys representing the plaintiff. For example, if the patient has sustained an alleged head injury, it is essential to determine if the patient can provide a chronological history of the events immediately preceding, during, and following the motor vehicle accident. If the patient is able to provide a clear, continuous recollection of these events and suffered no loss of consciousness, head trauma, confusion, bewilderment, or deterioration of neurological functioning (e.g., epidural hematoma), then it is highly unlikely that the patient sustained a brain injury during this motor vehicle accident.

CASE STUDY

The neuropsychologist was referred a 27-year-old woman for neuropsychological testing after she had been suspected of having a traumatic brain injury as the result of a motor vehicle accident. The neuropsychologist asked the patient, "What was going on in your head at the time that this event was occurring?" The patient replied, "I was just frightened out of my mind and thought I was going to be killed. I remember looking at the ceiling and saying to myself, I guess this is going to be it. I guess I will never live long enough to fulfill all the dreams I've had." Upon further questioning, the neuropsychologist discovered that the patient became extremely frightened when she noticed blood on her forehead, arising from a superficial cut, just above her eye. The patient started sobbing and stated, "I began smelling smoke and thought the car was going to explode. I thought I was going to be killed." The patient then recalled that she tried unsuccessfully to get out of the car, but that the doors had jammed. She thought she was going to be trapped in the car and engulfed in flames. She admitted that over the next several weeks she developed numerous flashbacks of the accident, had nightmares, and became extremely anxious whenever she was exposed to stimuli or events that reminded her of the accident. She also admitted that she had never told her examining doctors this story, because none of them had ever asked her what had been going on in her head at the time the accident occurred. Her doctors had seemed particularly interested in the fact that she had sustained the head injury, which was in actuality, a small scalp hematoma and laceration above her right eye, and that she was experiencing concentration and attentional difficulties following the accident. She also recalled that she had been diagnosed as having sustained a cerebral concussion, and probable brain injury, because of her complaints of attention and concentration difficulties, both of which are frequently reported in patients who sustain post-traumatic stress disorders. In other words, she sustained a psychological injury, rather than a brain injury. Thus, the clinical interview of the patient helped considerably in ruling out the presence of a brain injury. It should also be noted that the patient's performance on neuropsychological testing revealed a pattern of test performances which were inconsistent with brain damage.

PATIENT'S DESCRIPTION OF ACCIDENT

Patients who have sustained traumatic brain injuries are unable to recall the accident and exhibit evidence of post-traumatic amnesia lasting several minutes, hours, days, or even weeks. In direct contrast to the patient who has sustained a post-traumatic stress disorder, the brain-injured patient typically provides a poor or spotty recollection of the accident and of the events which occurred subsequently thereafter. For example, when patients are asked to describe the accident, they will often respond, "I don't remember." Yet, if they are asked to describe the events which occurred immediately after the accident, they will typically say, "I don't remember," and virtually never become upset or begin sobbing. When asked to describe the first event they recall after the accident, they are likely to say, "I remember being on a table in the emergency room and talking to a doctor." When the patient is asked, "What do you recall the doctor saying to you, or you saying to him, the patient typically responds, "I remember him saying something about my head. That's all I can remember." When asked, "What's the next thing you remember?" the patient typically responds, "I remember my aunt visiting me while I was in the hospital." When asked, "What do you remember about the visit?", the patient is likely to say, "She asked me how I was doing and I told her fine." Thus, one can easily see that the chronology of events provided by the brain-injured patient is vastly different from that provided by an individual who sustained a post-traumatic stress disorder.

COMPLAINTS OF PATIENT DURING INTERVIEW

The particular complaints of the patient obtained during the clinical interview are of considerable importance. For example, typically there is an inverse relationship between the number of complaints given by the patient and the severity of their brain injury in cases where the patient was actually rendered unconscious. During the first six months post-injury, patients with significant brain damage are likely to deny or minimize their cognitive or behavioral problems.

CASE STUDY

A 17-year-old female was rendered unconscious for approximately three days following a motor vehicle accident and had amnesia for two weeks. She was seen at five months post-injury and complained of only mild shoulder and back pain. She never complained of any cognitive, emotional, or social difficulties. Her attorney even asked her if she had developed any memory difficulties or other cognitive difficulties as a result of the accident. She replied, "No." He had also referred his client to a neurologist who was neither a specialist nor an expert in the field of traumatic brain injuries or behavioral neurology. He reported that her neurological examination, including an EEG and CT scan, was normal. Based on this information, the attorney considered settling the case for $10,000, even though the policy limits of the defendant's insurance were $100,000. A colleague, however, suggested that before he settled the case, he should refer his client for neuropsychological assessment. The attorney asked how much this was going to cost and when informed that it would be approximately $1,500, he balked at this figure and decided he would save his client this expense and settle the case. However, his curiosity about the possibility of a brain injury resulted in his telephoning the neuropsychologist who had been recommended to him. The neuropsychologist informed him that patients, during this stage of recovery following brain injury, typically exhibit a great deal of denial. This suggested that his client had, in fact, sustained a significant brain injury. The attorney reluctantly referred his client to the neuropsychologist for examination. The neuropsychologist called the attorney after the examination and informed him that his client had sustained significant damage to her frontal lobes and had exhibited a variety of neuropsychological impairments of moderate to marked severity. The neuropsychologist also advised the attorney not to settle the case, until it could be determined, based upon follow-up evaluations, what his client's residual and/or or future neuropsychological problems were likely to be. The neuropsychologist also informed the attorney that in his experience, patients with similar injuries and neuropsychological test profiles were at considerable risk to develop a number of serious psychiatric problems and that she should be carefully watched for these. One month later, his client began exhibiting bizarre behavior and was placed in a psychiatric unit, where she spent the next three months, at a cost of approximately $1,000 per day. Her treating doctors felt that she had sustained an organic mood disorder secondary to her brain injury and indicated that this condition would most likely require ongoing psychiatric treatment for the remainder of her life.

IMPORTANCE OF OBTAINING A BACKGROUND HISTORY FROM PATIENT

Some plaintiffs with alleged head injuries may provide as many as 20 to 30 complaints. The most frequent of these complaints tends to be problems with recent memory. These complaints are typically expressed as follows: "My biggest problem is my recent memory. I can't remember anything. If someone tells me anything, five minutes later I can't even remember it. For example, yesterday my wife told me to buy some groceries at the store. Do you know, that when I went to the store I completely forgot what she had told me to buy. After I got home, I remembered that she told me to buy some whipped cream and crackers. I felt so bad. You see, Doctor, doesn't that show you what a terrible memory I have? Why can't I remember anything?" This type of individual will typically complain of numerous physical problems, specifically pain in their neck, upper, and lower back. When these individuals are asked to quantify the severity of their pain, they will typically say, "My pain is horrible. My neck hurts constantly. On a scale of one to 10, my neck pain is nine and a half right now, and sometimes it goes up to 10." This is often stated with a bland affect and with no physical evidence of pain or discomfort.

An overwhelming number of these individuals have a history of traumatic childhoods, marriages, or life events. However, in many cases, these individuals typically deny having had any problems or difficulties prior to their accident or injury. When asked to describe their childhoods, they frequently describe them in idealistic terms, as if they were looking through "rose-colored glasses."

CASE STUDY

A 48-year-old female was referred for numerous complaints of cognitive and somatic difficulties following a relatively minor motor vehicle accident. During the interview she claimed that her childhood was "great," and denied ever arguing with either of her parents or siblings throughout her childhood or adolescence. She also denied having had any of the usual childhood diseases and claimed that she had "never been sick a day in her life" up until her accident a few years ago. When asked to describe the unhappiest memory of her childhood, she stated, "I never had any, my childhood was perfect." She also denied that she had ever missed a day of school or had ever seen a doctor, prior to her accident. However, during a five-hour clinical interview, this woman revealed that she had been abandoned by her biological mother when she was four, and had been raised by an aunt, whose husband sexually molested her between the ages of five and 12. She admitted that she was frequently physically abused by her aunt, as well. She also stated that whenever she became upset or angry she would be severely punished by being sent to her room, physically beaten, and then forced to go for two days without food or water. As is the case with many abuse victims, she began repressing her emotional pain and tried to keep "a smile on my face at all times and pretend that I was happy." She indicated that she got married at 17, to get away from home. However, her husband physically abused her and drank heavily. He also had numerous extramarital affairs which he attributed to her sexual frigidity. She had married two additional times, each time hoping to find someone to take care of her and treat her well. Unfortunately, she married men who were irresponsible, selfish, had drinking problems, and psychologically and physically abused her. She had, however, never previously confided this to anyone and tried to deny and repress these problems. It should be noted that in this author's experience, this type of history is not uncommon and can be seen in as many as one out of every three women who provide numerous, exaggerated complaints of cognitive and somatic problems.

USE OF CLINICAL HISTORY TO DETECT MALINGERING

The clinical history can be useful in ferreting out malingerers since the more sophisticated malingerers will provide the interviewer with textbook-like presentations of their symptoms.

CASE STUDY

A 38-year-old male arrived for his scheduled appointment approximately one hour late, but provided no excuse or apology. He appeared arrogant and suspicious. When he was asked questions regarding his injury, he stated, "Well haven't you read the records? Why don't you read the records, so that you can find out what happened to me. I don't think I need to tell you that." After it was impressed upon him that it was essential that he provide the examiner with his subjective recollections of the event, he stated, "I sustained a contrecoup brain injury to my frontal and occipital lobes. I had post-traumatic amnesia for 15 minutes. I have a severe brain injury and I can't work." Later when he was asked questions about the injury, he acted suspicious and stated, "You guys are all alike. All you do is work for the insurance companies. You really don't care what happens to us, all you're interested in is making money." He then stated, "I don't see why you are asking me all these questions, you've already made up your mind anyway, it is a waste of my time coming here. You are asking me these questions so you can prove that I didn't have a brain injury." When the patient was asked what had happened to him after the accident, he stated several times, "I don't know. It's in my records." When he was asked if he had ever had any of these problems before, he said, "What difference does that make whether I had them or not? It doesn't make any difference. The fact is I have a brain injury and I can't work." When the patient was asked to describe his employment history, he stated, "I can't remember that because of my brain injury." When he was asked if he had ever been fired from any job he had in the past, he stated, "What do you want to know that for? That's not important, what's really important is that I can't work and I have a brain injury."

TYPICAL BACKGROUND HISTORY OF MALINGERERS

In the experience of this author, many malingerers have poor employment histories, have been arrested in the past, and frequently have a history of drug or alcohol abuse. As children, they had either been placed on probation or had been arrested for antisocial behaviors, such as burglary, theft, driving under the influence, or excessive speeding tickets. They often have a history of being fired from their jobs because of arguments and fights with supervisors. Their childhood histories generally include an absence of love and affection. Their fathers or mothers typically had alcohol or drug problems. These patients often dropped out of school in the 10th or 11th grade, claiming that, "School was too boring." While in high school, they had frequent problems getting along with authority figures and were suspended or expelled from school on at least one occasion. As adults, there is often a history of being arrested for driving under the influence or for felonies such as buying stolen merchandise, writing bad checks, sale and distribution of narcotics, assault and battery, or carrying deadly weapons. They typically use rationalization and externalization to explain their shortcomings. For example, "I was fired because my supervisor was jealous of me. He knew that I was a good worker and that everyone respected me. He was afraid that I would eventually get his job."

DIFFERENT SCHOOLS OF THOUGHT ABOUT THE IMPORTANCE OF CLINICAL HISTORY

Thus, one can see that the clinical interview frequently reveals a great deal of information about the plaintiff, the type of injury sustained, and the severity of the injury. The history can also provide considerable insight into the plaintiff's motives, or lack thereof, in filing a claim. Unfortunately, some neuropsychologists do not feel that such information is essential in reaching a diagnosis, or in determining the patient's neuropsychological impairments. For example, one school of thought, which is typically associated with adherents of the Halstead-Reitan Neuropsychological Battery, has strongly argued that all that is necessary to interpret the psychometric test data is to know the patient's age, sex, handedness, highest grade completed, and occupation. Adherents of this particular school of thought strongly argue that taking a clinical history only serves to confuse test interpretation and that the diagnosis of brain dysfunction should be made on the test data alone. While the author strongly disagrees with this school of thought, there are a significant number of psychologists and neuropsychologists who adhere to this philosophy. Another school of thought argues that obtaining a careful and detailed clinical background history will allow the clinician to formulate specific hypotheses about the patient's impairments, and that this information is vital in making an assessment of brain dysfunction. Thus, testing serves to corroborate or refute such hypotheses. While both schools of thought have their respective merits, the attorney should be aware of the particular philosophy held by the neuropsychologist with respect to the relative importance of the clinical interview and history in the assessment process.

NECESSITY TO INTERVIEW SIGNIFICANT OTHERS

During the interview, the neuropsychologist should attempt to obtain a chronological history of the patient's injury, including all treatments received and the relative effectiveness of such treatments in alleviating the patient's condition and/or complaints. However, patients who sustain significant traumatic brain injuries are typically poor historians, particularly for events which have occurred since their injury. Consequently, the examiner must rely on information obtained from the patient's family and/or from significant others, such as friends, coworkers, and employers. These interviews frequently reveal the kinds of problems and difficulties the patient has exhibited since their accident. In the vast majority of cases, the family will disclose a variety of cognitive and behavioral problems, including a dramatic change in the patient's personality. Memory problems for recent events, mental confusion, irritability, temper outbursts, and rapid changes in mood are likely to be reported. The family may also report poor judgement, impulsive behavior, impaired problem solving skills, diminished frustration tolerance, impaired interpersonal skills, strained relationships with others, diminished motivation and initiative, and a loss of sensitivity to the needs and welfare of others.

Family members and significant others typically have the benefit of having known the patient well prior to the injury and are, therefore, usually able to detect relatively subtle changes in the patient's behavior that may not be detected by psychologically or medically trained professionals. In addition, the family environment is usually fairly unstructured which permits the brain-injured patient to exhibit many of their cognitive, behavioral, and emotional problems at home, which are less likely to be exhibited in the structured environment of the doctors' office. The two problems, however, that are faced when utilizing this information are its potential accuracy and that the emotional problems of the informants may color their observations and reports. For example, the patient's family may exaggerate the patient's problems or complaints for purposes of financial gain, or they may minimize the patient's problems because of denial arising out of their own emotional problems in denying grief, in coping with the patient's injury, with frequent visits to the hospital, or the patient's behavior at home. They often fantasize that the patient has not really been injured or will suddenly "snap out" of his or her problems. The author has found that careful attention to the specific types of complaints provided by family members and significant others can be extremely helpful in understanding the nature of the patient's cognitive and behavioral problems.

For example, the brain-injured patient typically complains of one or two problems, while the patient's family and/or significant others will provide a list of a dozen or more problems that appear to be consistent with the type of brain injury that the patient has sustained. However, the patient and family may provide the examiner with a list of 20 or 30 complaints which appear to be exaggerated. For example, if both the patient and family complain that the patient's memory is bad, or that he or she can't remember anything, then collusion must be suspected.

Families who utilize denial as a way of coping with their loved one's brain injury typically appear emotional, distraught, and tired, but are generally pleasant. They will often say, "Our son's doing real great. We haven't noticed any problems in him, since he got out of the hospital. He's been home now for nearly a week and he appears to be doing great. We plan on sending him back to school next week." The examiner, however, asks the patient's mother, "Wasn't your son in a coma following his automobile accident?" She says, "I don't remember if he was or not." The examiner carefully reviews the patient's medical records and finds that the patient spent three weeks in a coma, had been placed on a ventilator for 10 days, and the CT scan showed evidence of diffuse brain injury with prominent frontal lobe damage. These records also revealed that the patient had been hospitalized for four months and was noted to have severe cognitive impairments throughout his entire hospitalization. It should be recognized by the attorney that many family members cope with catastrophic events, such as a severe traumatic brain injury, by trying to deny that their son or daughter had actually been injured. Even though virtually all of these family members have been told numerous times by the patient's treating doctors that their son or daughter has had a severe brain injury, they somehow manage to repress this information and will often say, "I don't think anyone has ever told us that our son had a brain injury." Unfortunately, such denial and repression will frequently sap and drain away the family's emotional resources, which often results in a psychiatric crisis and hospitalization of one or more family members.

USE OF SIMPLE INDEX TO ESTIMATE THE SEVERITY OF BRAIN INJURY

The discrepancy between the number of complaints given by the patient and those provided by the patient's family or significant others (if we assume they are honest and reliable informants) is perhaps the best single indicator of the severity of a traumatic brain injury (Sbordone, in press). This information is fairly easy to obtain and should be obtained by the plaintiff's attorney, particularly when the patient is suspected of having sustained a traumatic brain injury. When the ratio of the family's and significant others' complaints is several times greater than the patient's, then there is a strong indication that the patient has sustained a severe traumatic brain injury. When the number of the family's complaints (barring denial and other psychological mechanisms) is only two times greater than that of the patient, then the patient most likely has sustained only a mild brain injury. Research in progress by the author and his colleagues will, hopefully, further define this relationship in terms of the time elapsed since the patient's injury and the number of complaints voiced. Clinically, however, the discrepancy between the patient's complaints and those of the family and significant others, remains in the author's mind, as an extremely valuable and relatively simple method for determining the severity of a patient's brain injury. The plaintiff's attorney can easily perform this task in his or her office by interviewing the patient and family members separately. It should be noted, in this regard, that the inverse is also true. For example, when the patient's complaints are far in excess of those of significant others, then it is then more likely that the patient has not sustained a traumatic brain injury and more likely has a functional (psychological) disorder, which may or may not be related to a specific accident or injury.

THE IMPORTANCE OF OBTAINING A CAREFUL AND COMPREHENSIVE BACKGROUND HISTORY

The importance of a careful and comprehensive background history cannot be overstressed. Unfortunately, the greatest single limitation in the history-taking process is the ability of the patient to provide a reliable and complete history. In many cases, where the patient is cognitively impaired, secondary to brain damage or pre-existing intellectual impairment, the patient's ability to provide this information is likely to be compromised. In such cases, it is essential that the patient be accompanied by a family member or a significant other, who can rectify the patient's faulty recollections of past events, furnish details of the patient's childhood, such as birth weight, childhood illnesses, or prior history of neurological disorders (e.g., a history of hyperactivity). Significant traumatic events, which the patient may deny or repress, may be reported by another informant. The informant may clarify specific information furnished by the patient, such as why the patient repeated the second grade or was taken to a psychiatrist during his or her childhood.

Obtaining a careful background history will frequently uncover a history of pre-existing neurological disease or psychological problems, such as head trauma, drowning episode, seizures, hyperactivity, dyslexia, left-handedness, stuttering, history of sexual molestation or rape, or drug abuse. This information should assist the neuropsychologist in interpreting the results of the neuropsychological test data, especially with respect to determining whether the test data reflect a pre-existing insult or problem or a recent injury. The following example illustrates the importance of obtaining background history and of assessing the contribution of previous neurological insults to the plaintiff's claim of brain damage allegedly sustained during an industrial accident.

CASE STUDY

A 52-year-old electrician was referred for neuropsychological testing by an attorney representing the defendant. The patient had fallen approximately 20 feet from a telephone pole while installing new equipment. The patient fractured both legs and, allegedly, sustained a traumatic brain injury. He was seen by a neuropsychologist, whose test data demonstrated strong evidence of diffuse brain damage. The plaintiff was later examined by another neuropsychologist who obtained a careful history which revealed that he was struck by an automobile when he was 10 and was comatose for one week. When he was 17, he became a professional boxer and fought in 25 bouts and had been knocked out 10 times. Six months prior to his industrial accident, he had noticed that he had been dropping objects and experienced balance and coordination difficulties. He described them as "drop attacks." He was seen by a neurologist who diagnosed his condition as vertebral basilar artery insufficiency syndrome. In this syndrome the blood supply to his brain stem, inferior temporal lobes, and cerebellum are significantly reduced, resulting in intermittent dysfunction, which, in this case, manifested itself as sudden falls, a tendency to drop objects, and balance and coordination difficulties. The patient was prescribed Persantine, a vasodilator, to alleviate this condition, which he did not take because it interfered with his consumption of 12 to 18 beers each day. He also admitted that he had consumed 12 beers at lunch prior to his fall. He also indicated that approximately three days after he was hospitalized, he began seeing "little green men under his bed," which was diagnosed as delirium tremens, a toxic delirium which follows alcohol withdrawal. When the neuropsychological test data of the plaintiff's neuropsychologist were examined in light of these past findings, the data were consistent with the patient's 30-year history of brain insults and chronic alcoholism. When the plaintiff's attorney learned of this information, he immediately dropped his client's claim of brain damage and focused exclusively upon his client's orthopedic injuries.

Table 5 presents the areas of information that should be obtained during a neuropsychological examination. Each of these areas will be carefully reviewed.

TABLE 5
PATIENT HISTORY

DEVELOPMENTAL
- Problems or drugs during pregnancy
- Place of birth
- Birth order
- Birth weight
- Problems during delivery
- Developmental milestones
- Childhood diseases
- Emotional problems during childhood and adolescence
- History of learning difficulties
- History of health problems
- History of hyperactivity
- History of physical or emotional trauma, head trauma, seizures, or neurological diseases

DOMINANCE
- Initial preference
- Changes in preference
- Familial history of sinistrality (left-handedness)
- Tasks performed with dominant and nondominant hands

LANGUAGE
- First language spoken
- Other languages spoken
- Preferred language
- History of speaking or language difficulties and treatment

EDUCATION
- Highest grade completed
- Grades obtained
- Best/preferred courses
- Worst/least preferred courses
- Extracurricular activities
- Awards and achievements
- Courses or grades completed
- History of remedial training
- History of conduct disturbances or expulsions
- Reasons for leaving school
- Additional schooling or nonacademic training

MILITARY SERVICE
- Branch and dates of service
- Jobs held with service
- Training received in service
- Combat history
- Rank at discharge
- Type of discharge

OCCUPATIONAL
- Present occupation
- Job duties
- Salary
- Last job held
- Previous occupations
- Longest job held
- History of job terminations/promotions
- Job aspirations

LEGAL
- Arrest history
- Types of offenses
- Time served in jail
- Current legal problems
- Law suits and litigation
- Prior court cases, disability claims

CULTURAL BACKGROUND
Country of birth
Ethnic background of patient and family
History of discrimination

RELIGIOUS
Religious background
Recent changes is religious beliefs, etc.
Church attendance
History of religious discrimination
Religious customs observed, beliefs, etc.

MARITAL HISTORY
Marital status
Number of years married
History of previous marriages
Education and occupation of spouse
Expectations placed on patient
Previous and current marital difficulties
Marital stability
Number and ages of children
Effect of children on patient

SEXUAL
Sexual preference
Changes in sexual preference
History of previous sexual problems
Changes in libido
Extramarital affairs

MEDICAL
History of major hospitalizations
Previous health problems
Previous surgery
Possible history of the following problems:
- Head trauma
- Cerebrovascular disorder
- Coronary dysfunction
- Hypoglycemia
- Anoxia or hypoxia
- Toxic or heavy metal exposure
- Substance abuse
- Alcoholism
- Cancer
- Hypertension
- Motor problems
- Diabetes
- Gastrointestinal disorder
- Respiratory problems
- Genital-urinary problems
- Headaches
- Vertigo
- Seizures
- Syncope

PSYCHIATRIC
History of previous emotional or psychiatric difficulties
History of suicidal behavior
Psychiatric treatment history
Psychiatric hospitalization history
History of use of psychiatric medications
Family history of psychiatric difficulties or treatment

CURRENT STRESSORS
Death or loss of spouse or family member
Divorce or marital separation
Marital difficulties
Job difficulties or termination
Financial difficulties
Sexual difficulties
Loss of friends
Conflicts with others
Academic difficulties
Business difficulties
Recent accidents, injuries, or illnesses
Recent relocation of self or family
Recent travel

FAMILY

Parents:
- Age and education
- Occupation
- Personality
- Marital status and history
- Alcohol and substance abuse history
- Psychiatric history
- Criminal history
- Health history
- Relationship with patient
- Neurological disorders
- Stability
- Divorce and/or separation history

Siblings:
- Number and ages of siblings
- Education and occupation
- Personality
- Marital status and history
- Alcohol and substance abuse history
- Psychiatric history
- Criminal history
- Health history
- Neurological disorder
- Relationship with patient
- Divorce and/or separation history

CLINICAL HISTORY
Complaints of patient and significant others
History of injury or illness
Loss of consciousness and/or duration of coma
Duration of post-traumatic amnesia
Neurological findings
Hospitalization history
Rehabilitation history
Current residual problems
Progress within past year
Effect of injury on patient and significant others
Expectations of patient and significant others
History of alcohol and/or drug use post-injury
Psychiatric or emotional problems since injury
History of head trauma or whiplash injury

Developmental

The presence of a low birth weight or prematurity suggests that the patient's mother may have smoked, drank, or was ill during pregnancy. Such individuals frequently have a childhood history of attention problems, hyperactivity, learning difficulties, temper tantrums, poor self-esteem, and behavioral difficulties. In some cases, forceps were used to remove the child from the birth canal, which may also produce brain injury. A surprising number of patients who sustain traumatic brain injuries, or develop neurological insults to their brain, have a childhood history of head trauma, hyperactivity, attentional difficulties, learning difficulties, emotional problems, and chronic health problems, such as asthma. Epilepsy is especially frequent in these children later in life.

As mentioned earlier, this author estimates that approximately one out of every three women who sustain traumatic brain injury, had been sexually molested or raped during their childhood. Many patients have a childhood history of terrifying nightmares, bed-wetting, or severe psychological abuse. Many came from broken homes or families where they were physically abused or even tortured. The following example illustrates the importance of obtaining a careful developmental history:

CASE STUDY

A 24-year-old, white male, was referred for neuropsychological assessment by his treating psychiatrist. His psychiatrist indicated that the patient had been involved in a motorcycle accident three years prior and had sustained a mild cerebral concussion, after which he began experiencing homicidal urges. The patient became frightened as a result of these urges and sought psychiatric treatment. The patient had been placed on Mellaril, an antipsychotic medication, and had been diagnosed as "paranoid schizophrenic." The psychiatrist had heard a neuropsychologist lecture on traumatic brain injuries and thought that it would be helpful for his patient to undergo neuropsychological assessment. While taking the developmental history, the neuropsychologist noted that the patient had a history of severe abdominal cramps during his childhood, for which he had been hospitalized. When the patient was asked what this condition had been diagnosed as, he stated, "I can't remember, but I think it starts with the letter P." The psychologist said, "Do you mean porphyria?" The patient said, "Yes." The patient also indicated that he never drank, smoked, or used drugs throughout his adolescence, since he wanted to be a professional football player, and was a physical fitness fanatic. At the time of his injury, he had been scheduled to try out for a professional football team. During his accident, he fractured his right arm and dislocated his shoulder. These injuries, unfortunately, ended his chances of playing professional football and also caused him severe pain and discomfort. He was prescribed a narcotic pain medication, which eased his pain, but caused him to develop homicidal impulses which terrified him and prompted him to seek psychiatric care. He also became depressed at the prospect of never being able to play professional football because of his orthopedic injuries and psychiatric problems. Football teams had become quickly disinterested in him when they learned of his psychiatric problems. As a way of coping with his depression and his loss of a life-long goal of playing professional football, he began drinking. This partially alleviated his emotional pain, but also aggravated his homicidal impulses. Porphyria is an inborn genetic disorder of metabolism, which produces a homicidal psychosis when patients ingest barbiturates and alcohol. Thus, the patient's homicidal impulses and psychosis were not directly caused by his head injury, but by the pain medications and alcohol he took following his head injury, because of his porphyria which had not been recognized by his treating physician. When his psychiatrist was informed that his patient had porphyria, he became extremely embarrassed and cursed himself for not taking a more careful history of his patient's past illnesses. The patient was advised to avoid using barbiturates and alcohol, which resulted in a dramatic improvement of his psychiatric problems.

Dominance

The preferred use of a particular hand, foot, or eye when performing tasks, is known as lateral dominance. Approximately 85% of people are right-handed. Virtually all of these individuals have their centers for language located in their left hemisphere. Approximately two-thirds of individuals who are left-handed also have their language centers located in the left hemisphere. Even though there are more right-handed women than men, the brains of women are less lateralized with respect to language than are men's. What this means is that patients who are left-handed, or who have a family history of sinistrality (one of their parents is left-handed), generally make a better recovery of their language skills following an injury to the left hemisphere of their brain than right-handed individuals.

Any changes in one's hand use during childhood (e.g., from left to right) could reflect compensatory use of the non-dominant hand following an ipsilateral (same hemisphere as the impaired hand or leg) injury. It could also reflect considerable pressure by family members, including harsh discipline to force the patient during childhood to use the right hand. In other words, knowledge of lateral dominance and its history, can help the neuropsychologist better appreciate the patient's neuropsychological test data and may improve the neuropsychologist's ability to prognosticate on recovery of language functions.

Language

The importance of gathering information about the history of languages spoken, or preferred languages, allows us to weigh the possible contribution of linguistic and/or cultural factors, when interpreting neuropsychological test data. Unfortunately, this factor is often ignored by some psychologists or neuropsychologists. Patients who have been raised in a different culture or speak a different language typically perform poorly on the Wechsler Adult Intelligence Scale, which is the most frequently used psychological test to assess intelligence. Such patients will often be given this test and typically found to have relatively low IQ scores. The IQ score is then compared to the patient's occupation (e.g., carpenter, electrician) which requires higher capabilities than would be expected on the basis of the patient's spuriously low IQ score and is then used to buttress the argument that there has been a substantial intellectual deterioration as the result of an alleged head injury.

CASE STUDY

A Samoan-born, 28-year-old male was seen for neuropsychological testing to evaluate his intellectual and cognitive functioning following a relatively mild head injury. The patient had lived in Samoa until he was 12 and then migrated to the United States. While his command of the English language seemed acceptable, his IQ on the Wechsler Adult Intelligence Scale was only 78, even though he had graduated from an American high school and had completed one year of junior college and had worked as a carpenter. The patient indicated that he had received above average grades in high school and had a 3.1 GPA in junior college. The psychologist argued that the brain injury had reduced his intellectual functioning approximately 30 points, based on his academic and occupational achievements. Three weeks later, the patient was administered the Raven Progressive Matrices Test, which is a relatively culture-free test of intellectual functioning, which places little, if any, emphasis on the patient's pre-existing linguistic or cultural background. The patient obtained an IQ of 115 on this test, which suggested that the psychologist's choice to administer the Weschler Adult Intelligence Scale to this patient most likely reflected his failure to consider the patient's prior linguistic and cultural background.

Education

A careful history of the patient's educational achievements, grades, failures, courses repeated, remedial training, expulsions, or reasons for leaving school, is important. Many patients who have a history of traumatic brain injuries or neurological insults have a pre-existing history of significant academic problems, such as poor grades, history of remedial or special education classes, problems in arithmetic and/or reading, conduct disturbances or expulsions, and dropping out of school prior to graduation. Poor grades in school can reflect a variety of factors, such as poor motivation or limited intelligence, pre-existing neurological disorders, hyperactivity, or dyslexia, as well as antisocial or rebellious behavior. Family problems, divorce, economic difficulties, and illnesses, may be gleaned from the history or records. Many patients, however, do not provide accurate information about their grades or academic achievements. As a consequence, one cannot assume, based on the history furnished by the patient, that such information is accurate. In many cases, patients will report that they graduated from high school with A's and B's, when, in fact, they dropped out of the ninth grade with failing grades. School records and interviews with teachers and peers may be helpful in this regard.

Academic performances indirectly give us valuable insights into the patient's pre-existing level of intellectual functioning, as well as identify specific problem areas.

CASE STUDY

A 19-year-old patient was referred for neuropsychological assessment after he was struck on the left side of his head by a policeman's night stick, during a physical altercation. While he was not rendered unconscious, he claimed that this injury had significantly affected his ability to learn new information that was essential in his job as a parts supplier. His position required him to review catalogs containing specifications for new parts and their characteristics. He claimed that he could no longer read following this injury and, as a consequence, was unable to work. Neuropsychological testing indicated that he performed poorly on the reading tasks, tests of vocabulary, verbal fluency, and verbal memory. A review of his academic transcripts indicated that the patient had a history of dyslexia which was identified during the second grade, and had been in remedial classes for poor readers. The patient's grades in school were poor (D's and F's). The patient dropped out of school in the ninth grade, after repeating the fourth and fifth grades. While it is possible that the patient may have sustained some form of brain injury during his altercation with the police officer, his prior academic records clearly revealed a history of pre-existing problems in each of the areas which neuropsychological testing had indicated. It should also be noted that this particular patient informed the psychologist who initially examined him that he had graduated from high school with honors and had never had a prior history of reading or academic difficulties before his injury. When these discrepancies were later pointed out to this psychologist, during a deposition, the psychologist admitted that he had not reviewed the patient's academic records and felt that his test data was consistent with the patient's academic records and did not indicate that the patient had sustained a brain injury. Neuropsychological testing can also be used to assess current levels of functioning in comparison with those provided by school records in establishing the nature, severity, and extent of deficits and their impact upon current functioning.

Military Service

The majority of males have served in the military. In many cases, these individuals served or witnessed combat in Vietnam. Many refuse to discuss these experiences, suggesting that they may have sustained a post-traumatic stress disorder as a result of witnessing the tragedies of war. This is particularly important if the patient is claiming a post-traumatic stress disorder (e.g., nightmares, severe levels of anxiety, difficulty sleeping, etc.) following job termination or a motor vehicle accident.

A surprising number of individuals fail to complete their military obligations and are given undesirable or medical discharges. In such cases, it is important to establish the factual basis for these problems, which may have considerable bearing on the patient's present complaints or alleged damages.

CASE STUDY

A patient was referred by his treating physician for a neuropsychological assessment after he had been involved in a motor vehicle accident. While the patient did not lose consciousness or develop post-traumatic amnesia, he began to complain of anxiety, nightmares, concentration and memory difficulties, and a variety of other somatic problems. He had been informed by his neurologist that he most likely sustained a traumatic brain injury.

A lengthy interview with this patient, however, revealed that he had been discharged from the service four years ago, after he began experiencing anxiety reactions, consisting of nightmares, hyperventilation, sleep difficulties, headaches, and gastrointestinal problems when his relationship with a woman, whom he had known for three months, abruptly ended. He had been placed on a psychiatric unit at an Army hospital, where he was diagnosed as having a generalized anxiety reaction and adjustment disorder and was placed on Valium. After three months, he returned to work duties, but could not tolerate the stresses and demands of his job as a cook. Once again, he developed psychiatric problems. The Army decided that this patient was unfit for military duty, for psychiatric reasons, and gave him a medical discharge under honorable conditions. His treating neurologist was unaware of this information and later changed his diagnosis when he became aware of this information. He then referred the patient to a psychiatrist, who placed the patient on tranquilizers. During psychotherapy, the patient admitted that he had wrecked his girlfriend's car during his accident. When his girlfriend found out that he had wrecked her "beloved" car, she became infuriated and abruptly terminated their relationship. Thus, replicating the earlier trauma and reviving the patient's earlier PTSD symptoms.

LEGAL PROBLEMS DURING MILITARY SERVICE

The patient's rank at discharge is often helpful in determining whether they had received any punitive actions such as court-martials or demotions. This information can provide the neuropsychologist with valuable insights into the patient's character and may shed light on the patient's motivation for pursuing litigation.

CASE STUDY

A 35-year-old male had been involved in a motor vehicle accident while he was sitting at a stop sign, in which his car was rear-ended by another car that was traveling approximately 15 miles an hour. The patient complained of severe low back pain and problems with recent memory. He claimed that he could no longer work because of the severity of these problems. He indicated that he had served in the Army and had attained the rank of captain. When he was asked about his military career, he indicated that he had served in the Army for eight years and resigned his commission. When he was asked why he resigned his commission, he stated that he wanted to get out of the Army. His story, however, contained some elements of implausibility. The psychologist persisted in asking the same questions again, until the patient admitted that he had been given the choice of resigning his commission or being court-martialled for engaging in illegal activities, while serving as an Army officer. He later admitted that he had been involved in illegal gambling activities and had been engaged in the sale of stolen merchandise and had been part of a ring of Army personnel who had been suspected of illegally selling military weapons to third world countries. When he was later asked if he had ever been arrested after being discharged from the Army, he indicated that he had been arrested three times for embezzlement, but had managed to enlist the services of a "smart attorney," who was able to beat all three charges. An interview with his wife revealed that her husband was still involved in a number of illegal activities, including drug smuggling. Neuropsychological test data revealed a pattern of performances consistent with malingering and psychopathic personality traits. The patient's attorney was contacted by the neuropsychologist and informed that there were strong indications that his client was malingering. The attorney indicated that he had suspected this because of several inconsistencies in the patient's story. He also indicated that he was unaware of his client's past criminal background and present criminal activities. He indicated that he would recommend to his client to settle his case as quickly as possible or seek the services of a new attorney.

Occupational

The patient's occupational history, including job duties, salary, previous occupations, longest job held, and history of job termination, allows us to determine the patient's level of cognitive functioning, as well as areas of strength and weakness, prior to a specific injury. A careful description of the patient's job duties allows the neuropsychologist to evaluate the patient's ability to return to a specific job or occupation, given an understanding of the particular cognitive, physical, or social demands of that position. For example, patients with traumatic brain injuries typically have a great deal of difficulty processing two or more events at the same time. They become frustrated easily and frequently have difficulty recalling recent information.

CASE STUDY

A 24-year-old female stockbroker sustained a mild head trauma in an automobile accident. She was briefly rendered unconscious and was amnesic for approximately 20 minutes post-injury. When she returned to work, she found herself unable to handle all of the stock quotations coming in and perform her duties as a stockbroker. Her clients began to sense that her ability to provide them with insights into the market's activity had become flawed. As a consequence, she began losing clients and became depressed, feeling that life was no longer worth living. She attempted suicide and was placed on a psychiatric unit for two weeks. After her discharge, she continued receiving outpatient psychiatric treatment. After three months, she tried to return to her job, but once again could not handle the cognitive demands of her job. She continued to feel like a failure and remained depressed with frequent suicidal ideation.

She was referred for neuropsychological assessment by her psychiatrist. Testing revealed that while this patient was extremely bright (IQ = 148), she had considerable difficulty on tasks involving higher level attention, recent memory, speed of cognitive processing, and problem solving. The patient was encouraged to return to work at a less demanding job, to which she reluctantly agreed. The new position consisted of managing a beauty salon. The cognitive demands of this position were far less complex than those of a stockbroker. Even though the patient continued to demonstrate impairments on follow-up neuropsychological testing, she was able to handle the cognitive demands of her new job which improved both her mood and outlook on life. As a consequence, she no longer required psychiatric treatment nor felt suicidal.

PATIENTS WITH POOR PRIOR WORK HISTORIES

Many patients who sustain traumatic brain injuries have had poor prior work histories. Many of these patients were unable to hold down jobs because of a combination of personality, intellectual, or motivational deficits. However, when these patients sustain brain injury, their ability to hold down a job may become virtually non-existent because of the combination of pre-existing factors and their brain injury.

The type of work a particular patient has done prior to their brain injury, irrespective of the number of years of education they have received or their grades, will often serve as a crude index of their pre-existing cognitive skills and abilities.

DETERMINING PRE-EXISTING COGNITIVE SKILLS AND ABILITIES

CASE STUDY

A 27-year-old male was referred for neuropsychological assessment by his physician after he had been involved in a motorcycle accident during which he sustained a cerebral concussion. He had been employed as an auto mechanic and specialized in working on exotic foreign cars, even though he had only completed the ninth grade and had done poorly in school because of a history of dyslexia. His visual-spatial and motor skills, however, had been superb. He had been an outstanding athlete who excelled in skiing, surfing, tennis, and baseball. He had always been able to take anything apart and quickly put it back together again, and began working on cars when he was 14. By the time he was 19, he was regarded as one of the top foreign car mechanics in the city. Following his accident, he returned to work but found himself making a number of unacceptable mistakes which resulted in a number of reprimands from his employer and his eventual termination. He was able to find work in his field, because of his excellent reputation as a mechanic, but found himself continually making mistakes. It required twice as long to perform auto repairs than it did prior to his accident. He had been seen by a clinical psychologist who found him to have a Full Scale IQ of 103 on the Wechsler Adult Intelligence Scale. Testing revealed that the patient's performance IQ was 14 points higher than his verbal IQ. This indicated that his visual spatial and motor skills were better than his verbal abilities. The psychologist informed the patient that there was "nothing wrong with his visual perceptual abilities" and that his problems were most likely due to "psychological factors" such as, depression or anxiety. The patient was later seen by a neuropsychologist who found that while the patient's perceptual abilities tested within the normal range, his abilities had been exceptional prior to his accident. For example, the neuropsychologist interviewed the patient's employers and coworkers, who each attested to the patient's exceptional visual-spatial and motor skills prior to his accident and indicated that he was no longer the same mechanic he had been prior to his accident, or possessed the exceptional visual-spatial skills he once had.

Legal

The prior litigation history or criminal activities of a patient who alleges amnesia, numerous cognitive difficulties, or severe and disabling pain and discomfort, can be of considerable importance in determining whether the plaintiff is honestly reporting the details and circumstances of a particular accident. A surprising number of individuals who alleged head injuries have been arrested in the past for nonvehicular offenses. Many of these people have been arrested for felonies including burglary, embezzlement, grand theft, attempted murder, drug usage and sales, or assault and battery. While some of these men and women have never been convicted, they often provide histories of what has been termed "antisocial behavior" consisting of incorrigibility, fighting, lying, criminal activities, and irresponsible behavior during childhood. The author has found that the past history of malingerers is often consistent with these behaviors, since such individuals are typically manipulative, have poorly developed consciences, and have little regard for honesty or the welfare of others. When one considers that malingering involves deceit and dishonesty designed to secure financial gains through fraudulent means, the past history of the individual's arrests and litigation history becomes important. Such individuals rarely profit from experience and rarely, if ever, change their "spots."

CASE STUDY

The 35-year-old wife of an auto mechanic was involved in a single car accident which she claimed had occurred as a result of defective brakes that had recently been replaced by an auto dealer. Her husband claimed that he inspected her vehicle following the accident and determined, based upon his expertise as an auto mechanic specializing in brake repair, that her brakes were defective and that they had been improperly installed by the auto dealer. His wife sustained a cerebral concussion in the accident and subsequently developed significant cognitive and behavioral problems. Neuropsychological assessment was requested by the defendants to assess the severity of the patient's neuropsychological damages. The neuropsychologist insisted on interviewing the patient and her husband to gather a careful background history. While interviewing the plaintiff's husband, it was discovered that he had been arrested on numerous occasions in the past for a variety of felonies including embezzlement, drug smuggling, attempted murder, writing bad checks, and grand theft auto. Thus, the claims of the patient and her spouse were viewed with considerable skepticism.

It is also important to determine whether the patient has ever been previously involved in a personal injury action or has ever filed a Workers' Compensation claim. Additionally, it is also helpful to know whether any members of their immediate family have ever been arrested or involved in litigation.

CASE STUDY

A 17-year-old male was referred for neuropsychological assessment by his neurologist. He had been involved in a car accident while riding a motorcycle and had sustained a very slight head injury. He did not lose consciousness, and failed to exhibit post-traumatic amnesia. Approximately three months following his accident, he was kicked out of school for poor grades and antisocial behavior. One of his treating doctors attributed these problems to his traumatic head injury. His neurologist was unclear as to whether or not there was any relationship between his traumatic head injury and subsequent antisocial behavior and academic difficulties. Neuropsychological testing revealed no evidence of brain injury or cognitive dysfunction, but strong indication of an antisocial personality, as well as a prior history of drug abuse, criminal activity, pathological lying, and excessive truancies. The patient's family members were also interviewed. During this interview, the family admitted that the patient's 19-year-old brother had been expelled from school two years earlier and had recently been incarcerated for selling drugs, carrying a deadly weapon, and attempted murder. The parents indicated that they had divorced five years ago and had not remarried. As a consequence of their busy schedules, they had not been able to provide their sons with adequate supervision or discipline. The neuropsychologist phoned the patient's neurologist and indicated that the patient's academic difficulties and antisocial behavior most likely reflected the patient's dysfunctional family and the natural progression of pre-existing characterological traits which had no bearing to the accident since the patient's 19-year-old brother had manifested a pattern of similar behavior when he was 17 years old and had never been involved in a motor vehicle accident. (Author's note: It should be noted that exacerbations of previously existing personality traits can occur secondary to traumatic brain injury, and that neuropsychological testing may fail to reflect the effects of traumatic brain injury.)

Cultural Background

The cultural background of the patient will frequently color the manner in which the patient describes his or her symptoms as well as the manner in which the family is likely to cope with the patient's neurological or psychological problems. Consequently, the patient and/or family may not divulge specific details or complain of specific problems for fear of violating the norms of their culture. Recognition of this factor can alert the neuropsychologist to these issues.

CASE STUDY

A 17-year-old East Indian female was referred by her attorney for neuropsychological assessment. When the patient was seen at seven months post-injury, with her family, both the patient and family denied any cognitive, emotional, or behavioral problems since the patient's injury. The neuropsychologist was puzzled since the patient had sustained a severe head trauma and had been in a coma for nearly five days. The neuropsychologist decided to investigate this issue further and discovered that the admission of problems to strangers was considered taboo. The neuropsychologist enlisted the support of an East Indian psychiatrist who interviewed the patient and her family in their native language. The psychiatrist had been raised in a nearby province. The psychiatrist reported that the family had, in fact, noticed a dramatic change in the patient's behavior which included violent outbursts toward other family members. The patient, who had previously been a very demure and quiet individual, had physically assaulted both of her parents and had tried to kill her older brother during a verbal altercation. They had also observed that her memory for recent events was extremely poor and that she had become extremely impulsive and showed little regard or concern for the welfare of other family members. Neuropsychological assessment found strong evidence of frontal lobe dysfunction and test findings consistent with temporal lobe epilepsy. These findings were also consistent with the problems which had been observed by her family. However, because of the family's cultural background, they did not feel that it was proper to admit to such difficulties to strangers or persons outside of their culture. Thus, this plaintiff's difficulties were under-reported.

PRIOR HISTORY OF DISCRIMINATION

Many individuals who grew up in particular cultural backgrounds may be exposed to discrimination which may create interpersonal difficulties for them when they become adults and are engaged in competitive employment. Changes in the patient's perceptions of others and emotional coping skills following brain damage can cause these individuals to develop a paranoid psychosis which can significantly jeopardize their ability to work or deal with others.

CASE STUDY

A 47-year-old male was referred for neuropsychological testing after he was exposed to industrial solvents during his work at a chemical factory. As a Black, growing up in the South, he had been exposed to a great deal of prejudice. He had learned, however, to live with these feelings and was generally able to work with white coworkers and superiors with relatively little difficulty. His job involved daily exposure to a variety of industrial solvents. After three years, he became increasingly paranoid and felt that his white coworkers and superiors were plotting to kill him. As a consequence, he would not eat with them for fear that they might poison his food. He also feared that they were going to inject him with some type of poison upon any type of physical contact he had with them. He was referred to a physician who suspected that his paranoid psychosis may have been related to exposure to the various industrial solvents during his employment. Neuropsychological testing revealed mild memory and concentration deficits and organizational, perceptual, and problem solving deficits consistent with toxic encephalopathy. Tests of personality and emotional functioning corroborated the patient's paranoid psychosis and its relationship to his brain injury. The neuropsychologist phoned the patient's referring physician and informed him that he felt that the patient's toxic encephalopathy had markedly aggravated the patient's pre-existing paranoia and had seriously reduced the patient's coping skills resulting in a paranoid psychosis.

Religious

While a patient's particular religious views may not seem important, they may help the neuropsychologist understand how a particular individual may cope with emotional stresses and/or cognitive deficits secondary to brain injury. Patients who are raised in strict or Fundamentalist religions are at a higher risk to develop psychiatric problems following brain damage or psychological trauma.

CASE STUDY

A 36-year-old female was referred for neuropsychological testing by her treating neurologist after she became depressed and paranoid after sustaining a cerebral concussion in a motor vehicle accident three months earlier. Her religious upbringing had stressed the importance of keeping one's feelings under rigid control and that failure to control one's feelings, anger in particular, was sinful. After she sustained a cerebral concussion, she found herself irritable and experiencing frequent temper outbursts in which she swore at her family. Her family made her feel guilty and told her that she was not following the word of God and that she needed to pray harder for the strength to resist these sinful temptations. Unfortunately, her prayers were not enough and she continued to lose her temper over the slightest reasons. Her family continued to blame her and called her "a sinner." They contributed to her fear that the Devil was controlling her mind and that she was going straight to Hell. She became both severely paranoid and depressed. Neuropsychological assessment identified the patient's cognitive impairments and relative inability to regulate her emotions and behavior. The neuropsychologist gently informed the patient that her problems were not the work of the Devil and were the result of her concussion. He also assured her that they should improve gradually over time. The patient felt relieved and asked the neuropsychologist to meet with her family to explain his findings. While the patient's family was initially reluctant to meet with the neuropsychologist, the meeting went well in the sense that the family received some understanding of the patient's symptoms and became more accepting of her behavior.

Marital Status and History

The marital status and history of a patient who has sustained a brain injury or who complains of a variety of cognitive or somatic problems secondary to an alleged brain injury is important since marital stressors can create severe psychological and emotional stressors. In addition, brain injuries, because of their cognitive, emotional, and behavioral sequelae, will aggravate pre-existing marital conflicts. When these stressors are added to a brain injury, they can significantly exacerbate the patient's cognitive, emotional, or behavioral problems. A variety of potential marital stressors should be reviewed during the history, including extramarital affairs, incest, alcoholism, drug abuse, financial difficulties, and problems with children or in-laws.

CASE STUDY

A 30-year-old female had been employed at a film studio, where she was occasionally exposed to industrial solvents. For the past year, she had been complaining of concentration difficulties and severe memory problems. She also claimed that she could no longer work because of these difficulties and had filed a Workers' Compensation claim of brain damage secondary to exposure to toxic solvents. Her attorney had sent her to a clinical psychologist, rather than to a neuropsychologist, who administered the Halstead-Reitan Neuropsychological Battery which found evidence of "brain damage." The psychologist claimed that the patient was no longer capable of working and was totally disabled. The patient was then referred to a qualified neuropsychologist who took a careful and lengthy history from the patient. During the interview, the patient indicated that she was now on her third marriage and had suspected that her third husband had been sexually molesting her two daughters. She also indicated that she first suspected this approximately one and a half years ago, one month prior to the onset of her symptoms. She admitted that she could not believe that her husband would do that and had been terrified to confront him on this issue for fear that he would leave her. She also admitted that when her two previous husbands left her, she became extremely depressed and anxious each time. She saw herself as unattractive and feared that if her present husband left her, she would never find another man. She admitted that she had difficulty sleeping at night and found herself very tense and "uptight." Additionally, her relationship with her two daughters had become strained. They also began developing academic and emotional problems which caused her to feel guilty.

Neuropsychological testing revealed mild cognitive problems that appeared to be secondary to her depressed mood, internal psychological conflicts, and high levels of anxiety. Because of her fear of recognizing or accepting the emotionally painful situation at home regarding her children and her husband, she attributed her cognitive and emotional problems to the chemicals she was occasionally exposed to at work after she had been read an article that indicated chronic exposure to such chemicals could cause brain damage.

Sexual

Sexual difficulties are extremely common following brain damage. Patients who sustain traumatic brain injuries, hypoxic encephalopathy, strokes, or a progressive neurological disorder, such as Alzheimer's or Pick's Disease, typically show a marked alteration of sexual desire—usually severe reduction. However, patients who sustain post-traumatic stress disorders, or become severely depressed or psychotic, will also exhibit loss of sexual desire and functioning. To complicate matters even further, many of the medications that these patients are prescribed for mental confusion, depression, or bizarre thinking, may also create sexual problems. In addition, patients who develop temporal lobe epilepsy secondary to traumatic brain injury will also, in time, demonstrate diminished sexual drive. However, approximately half of these individuals will show an alteration in their sexual conduct, such as, having sex with someone of the same or different gender or become sexually aroused by inanimate objects. Patients who sustain frontal lobe pathology may demonstrate hypersexuality characterized by excessive sexual activity including extramarital affairs and frequent masturbation. Thus, one can see that alterations in sexual functioning are typically the rule, rather than the exception, following significant brain or psychological trauma. On the other hand, when patients deny any changes in sexual functioning or interest, and also allege they have sustained a brain injury, one must carefully check with the patient's spouse or significant others to corroborate this. Normal sexual functioning in these cases is rare, in the author's experience, and suggests that the patient may not have sustained a brain injury. The author has also found that the more severe the patient's brain or psychological trauma, the longer the period of decrease or loss in sexual libido. In cases where there has been severe brain injury, one frequently finds that the patient has completely lost all sexual drive and, in males particularly, the ability to develop or maintain an erection. Since sexual dysfunction can frequently result from rather severe marital conflicts and emotional turbulence within the family, patients who exhibit emotional and behavioral sequelae secondary to psychological trauma will also report diminished sexual libido. Thus, sexual dysfunction is generally the rule, whether it be directly caused by the primary injury or trauma, or secondarily by the various emotional problems or conflicts it creates with spouses and/or significant others.

CASE STUDY

A 35-year-old female was referred for neuropsychological testing by an attorney representing the defendants in a Workers' Compensation case. The applicant maintained that she had been struck on the head while working when part of the ceiling directly above her collapsed during a rainstorm and had struck her on the side of the head as she was working at her desk. She was unclear as to whether or not she lost consciousness, but was able to provide the neuropsychologist with an excellent history of the events that occurred prior to, during, and following the accident. While she reported no complaints or difficulties for the first week following her accident, she claimed that one week following her accident, she began experiencing severe problems with her recent memory, as well as rather significant attentional difficulties. She also claimed to have developed constant, severe headaches which she said had been present 24 hours a day since they first began one week post-injury. She also complained of a number of cognitive, emotional, and social difficulties, as well as being severely depressed. However, when she was asked if there had been any change or decrease in her sexual functioning, she denied this and claimed that she and her husband had always enjoyed a satisfying sexual relationship throughout their entire marriage and that the accident had not altered this in any way. Her husband was interviewed. He also denied any changes in his wife's sexual behavior or functioning since her accident.

Neuropsychological testing revealed an atypical test profile suggestive of both motivational difficulties and of a hysterical conversion disorder. This patient had also been given numerous neurodiagnostic tests, including several CT scans, EEG's, EMG's, and topographical brain mapping studies, all of which had been negative. It should also be noted that when the patient appeared in the author's office, she exhibited no physical evidence of pain or discomfort and appeared quite healthy looking with no evidence of sleep problems or difficulties, despite her claim that she "had not slept for the past three months." The neuropsychologist also noted that the patient's affect was bland during the interview and that she also exhibited a "la belle indifference" while describing her numerous symptoms and their severity. This is consistent with classical signs of a conversion neurosis. This was later corroborated by neuropsychological testing and by physical observation of the patient's behavior (e.g., The patient dressed seductively and appeared to flirt with the examining doctors.).

Medical

Since a number of medical disorders can affect cerebral functioning and produce cognitive, emotional, and social sequelae following brain damage or neurological insults, it is essential that the patient's medical history be carefully reviewed. This would include the childhood and adult medical problems of the patient, their treatment, and any residual recurrent medical problems. Unfortunately, many patients may provide an inaccurate or incomplete medical history. As previously mentioned, a surprising number of patients who sustain traumatic brain injury, or report a variety of cognitive or emotional problems following an accident, have a prior history of head trauma, substance abuse, alcoholism, or childhood neurological disorders. Of particular note is that problems such as cerebrovascular disorders, coronary dysfunction, hypoglycemia, anoxia/hypoxia, drownings, toxic or heavy metal exposure, substance abuse, alcoholism, hypertension, diabetes, gastrointestinal disorders, respiratory problems, neoplasia, migraine, endocrine disorders, and other medical disorders, frequently produce a number of significant cognitive problems which can be detected upon careful neuropsychological testing. The presence of two or more of these disorders in the same patient often makes it difficult to differentiate between the symptoms of a relatively recent brain injury and cognitive difficulties secondary to the patient's medical problems.

It is also important to determine how the patient has coped with his or her medical problems in the past. For example, patients who are prone to conversion disorders tend to have a history of lingering complaints or medical problems. Such patients frequently have a lengthy medical history, even though they may deny seeing doctors on a regular basis prior to their accident. In one such case, the author recalls that a patient with a conversion disorder claimed she could not recall seeing a physician during the 10 years prior to her accident. She even denied routine physicals, Pap smears, or any type of medical visits. The author requested that this patient's prior medical records be subpoenaed. A review of these records revealed that the patient had seen a total of 225 different physicians during the 10 years prior to her accident. In fact, there was overwhelming evidence that she had had each one of the problems she had alleged to have had as a result of her alleged head injury prior to her accident.

SOME PSYCHOLOGISTS MAY FAIL TO APPRECIATE THE CONTRIBUTION OF THE PATIENT'S PRIOR MEDICAL HISTORY

Some psychologists, partially because of their lack of medical training, fail to inquire into the patient's prior medical history and may not understand the symptoms of a particular medical or neurological disorder.

CASE STUDY

A 28-year-old, obese woman was referred for neuropsychological assessment by her husband, a clinical psychologist in private practice. He complained that his wife had become depressed, gained weight, and was irritable, anxious, and had complained of concentration and memory difficulties during the past year. He wondered whether these symptoms were related to a fall she had sustained while working around her home. The patient arrived weighing approximately 280 pounds and complained of fatigue, sleep difficulties, hypersomnia (excessive sleeping), nervousness, excessive sweating, tachycardia, and a weight gain of over 80 pounds during the last six months. She was asked whether or not she had ever had a history of endocrine disorders and stated that she had been diagnosed as having hypothyroidism approximately five years ago and had been placed on Synthroid, which she voluntarily stopped taking approximately six months ago because of her health and religious convictions. She felt that this medication was not a natural substance and, therefore, should not be taken since it violated her body. She indicated that she had been seeing a clinical psychologist, to whom her husband had referred her approximately three months ago, for psychotherapy. While she enjoyed psychotherapy, she felt that her emotional and cognitive problems had increased as well as a weight gain of 40 pounds since she had entered treatment. She admitted that her self-esteem had become extremely poor and that she had contemplated suicide. Neuropsychological assessment revealed a pattern of cognitive impairments which were generally consistent with metabolic disorders, such as hypothyroidism. The neuropsychologist phoned her husband and advised him to take his wife to her internist to have her undergo a careful physical and medical examination. The medical examination and laboratory tests were positive for an underactive thyroid. She was placed on Synthroid again. After three weeks, her mood improved considerably and she was no longer complaining of cognitive difficulties, anxiety, and a depressed mood. She also began exercising and had lost 15 pounds. Her energy level improved considerably, which was accompanied by a marked improvement in her self-esteem.

Psychiatric

Some patients who present with a variety of cognitive and/or emotional complaints will have a pre-existing history of psychiatric difficulties, which may include suicide attempts, psychiatric hospitalizations, or being prescribed tranquilizers, antidepressants, or other psychotropic medications. Since there is growing evidence that many psychiatric disorders, particularly depression, manic-depressive illness, and schizophrenia are to a large extent genetically determined, it is essential that the neuropsychologist obtain a careful personal and family history of psychiatric illness from the patient. The help and cooperation of other family members is invaluable. Unfortunately, many patients or family members are often reluctant to admit to a history of psychiatric illness because of the shame or stigma involved with such an admission. The author has found that families frequently say, "No," when they are asked the question, "Is there a family history of mental illness?" On the other hand, if they are asked, "Has anyone in the family ever had a history of being depressed for more than one month? Has anyone ever gone on frequent shopping sprees or has anyone ever been given Valium or any other medications for their nerves? Has anyone ever heard voices?" it will often produce an affirmative response, since many people typically do not know what constitutes a "mental disorder" or a "psychiatric illness." This is particularly true for foreign-born and poorly educated patients.

CASE STUDY

The author consented to serve as the Agreed Medical Examiner in a Workers' Compensation case in which the applicant, a 53-year-old Hispanic female, had complained of memory difficulties and attentional problems. She reported sleeplessness, nervousness, headaches, and a variety of aches and pains throughout her body. These complaints allegedly appeared after she was involved in an industrial accident while riding as a passenger in a company vehicle. Her car was rear-ended by another car that was traveling approximately 10 miles per hour. The patient was wearing her seat belt and did not sustain any visible physical injuries, any loss of consciousness, or amnesia for the event. She claimed that her problems had increased over the past two years since her injury and had become disabling. The patient had only completed three years of formal education and spoke relatively little English, even though she had lived in the United States for nearly 20 years. She lived in a barrio and admitted that she rarely watched the news and read very little. Although she had been seen by numerous psychiatrists and physicians who disagreed about the cause of her symptoms, a careful review of their records indicated that the patient was often asked questions like, "Have you ever had a history of depression?" or, "Is there a family history of psychiatric illness?" When the patient was asked if she knew what these terms meant, she replied, "No." However, when she was asked if she had ever been given any medicines for her nerves, she replied, "Yes," and pulled out an old bottle of tranquilizers from her purse. When asked if she ever felt sad for a long period of time or had ever lost weight or gained weight because of sadness, she replied, "Yes." When she was asked to elaborate on that, she indicated that she had "felt terrible" five years earlier after her 22-year-old son had been killed following a motor vehicle accident. She admitted that she could not function for nearly two years following this. She also admitted that 10 years earlier, she had felt the same way after her husband had abandoned her and their children.

Neuropsychological assessment revealed that the applicant had an IQ of 75, using a relatively culture-free test of intellectual functioning which required very little verbalization or language. This score was felt to be consistent with her occupational achievements as a nurse's aide in a nursing home. When her performance on neuropsychological tests was corrected for her age, low intelligence, and her limited educational achievements, it fell within the normal range. She admitted that during the past three years, she felt abandoned by her children who had moved out and rarely visited or phoned her. She also admitted that she lived in a dangerous neighborhood, in which drive-by shootings and muggings were common. She then indicated that her next-door neighbor had been beaten and robbed at gunpoint two years ago. This had frightened her. She admitted that she frequently woke up in the middle of the night whenever she heard a noise in the house and would immediately begin breathing rapidly and feared that she was going to be killed by some unknown assailant. To make matters worse, she also admitted that her oldest son had been arrested and convicted of murdering his girlfriend approximately two years ago. As a consequence, her grandchildren were being raised by his brother's ex-wife, who worked as a prostitute to support her cocaine addiction.

Current Stressors

A number of patients who are referred for neuropsychological testing to evaluate their cognitive, behavioral, or emotional functioning secondary to a specific accident may be currently undergoing stresses in their life which are unrelated to the accident. Such stressors may be of sufficient magnitude to create a number of disabling psychological symptoms and, hence, cloud the assessment of any problems created by a specific accident or injury. Current stressors, such as the death or loss of a family member, divorce or marital separation, marital difficulties, job difficulties or termination, financial difficulties, loss of friends, academic or business difficulties, or sexual difficulties can create serious psychological problems which may even mimic a brain injury or post-traumatic stress disorder.

CASE STUDY

A 36-year-old male was referred by his physician for neuropsychological assessment to evaluate the patient's cognitive functioning after he had slipped and fallen at work, which caused him to strike his head on the ground. He denied a loss of consciousness but reported that he had a severe headache and experienced some mild confusion since his fall. He arrived for his scheduled appointment at 9 a.m. but appeared extremely fatigued and nervous. When the examiner inquired why he appeared fatigued, he indicated that he had not slept much during the past week as a result of the untimely death of his mother. He also indicated that he had been having considerable financial difficulties and was over $30,000 in debt. Finally, he admitted that his wife had recently asked for a divorce and that his two sons had been arrested for possession and sale of drug paraphernalia. He appeared so tired that he began dozing off during the clinical interview. There were dark circles under his eyes. He also appeared disheveled and preoccupied with the stressors that had been occurring in his life. Neuropsychological testing was put off for three months, at which time the patient phoned and indicated that his wife had agreed to remain with him and that his sons had been placed on probation. He admitted that he felt much more relaxed and had been sleeping better. When he was seen for neuropsychological assessment, he appeared much more relaxed and did not appear fatigued. He even admitted that had he been tested three months earlier when he was first seen, he would have performed extremely poorly on each of the tests he was administered because he had been so preoccupied with the loss of his mother, financial difficulties, his wife's demand for a divorce, and the arrest of his two sons.

Unfortunately, many patients who sustain either brain trauma, psychological trauma, or both, experience a variety of severe stressors following their injury. These stressors only serve to exacerbate their cognitive, emotional, and behavioral difficulties, and may also produce a secondary depression which serves to add a "psychological insult" to the patient's "neurological injury." This is likely to produce an exacerbation of the patient's neurological symptoms and problems. This combination may create the impression that the patient is actually becoming worse. Unfortunately, many health professionals, including psychologists, may either ignore or fail to recognize the stressors and inform the patient that his or her neurological injury was worse than originally believed and that they will most likely have these problems for the rest of his or her life. This negative prognosis only serves to take away any hope that the patient might have had for recovery and, thus, adds additional stress to the patient's problems. This typically results in a marked deterioration of the patient's functioning, which only serves to reinforce the patient's and the doctor's belief that things will only get worse and not better. Thus, the patient will often develop "iatrogenic" problems due to the failure of one or more of his treating doctors to recognize the various stresses that the injury has placed on the patient and the consequent aggravation they have had on the patient's initial problems.

Family

A history of the patient's family can often provide considerable insight into the patient's complaints and current psychological or even medical problems. A family history should include the ages of both parents, step-parents, their years of education, occupations, personalities, health status, and a description of how they interacted with the patient during the patient's formative years, adolescence, and adulthood. It should also include the marriages, marital status, and the manner in which the patient's parents, step-parents, siblings, and step-siblings were perceived, as well as their interactions with the patient. This history should also include the questions about the substance abuse history of the parents and other family members, as well as the family's psychiatric history, including treatments, hospitalizations, and current whereabouts. Many patients who present with a variety of cognitive, somatic, and behavioral problems frequently come from dysfunctional families characterized by parental neglect, physical abuse, sexual molestation, abandonment, divorce, poor relations with parents, alcoholism, substance abuse, significant health problems, and psychiatric illness.

Gathering this information is also important in evaluating the brain-injured patient, since many of these individuals will often be forced to reside with their families. This may be very upsetting to these patients and their families and create considerable stress which will most likely exacerbate the patient's problems. This information can also be extremely helpful in planning treatments and rehabilitation for such patients, since the pathology of the family may be so severe that the patient's needs may be best served by placing the patient in a long-term care facility if the family's active cooperation cannot be enlisted.

The following example serves to illustrate the importance of gathering a careful family history.

CASE STUDY

A 36-year-old male had been referred for neuropsychological assessment after he had fallen at work and struck his head on the leg of a chair. He admitted that he had not lost consciousness but had felt "dizzy" after the accident. He denied any vomiting or nausea. He also denied amnesia for events immediately prior to, during, or following the injury. He complained, however, of severe headaches, upper and lower back pain (which he described as extremely severe), excessive memory difficulties ("My memory is terrible. I can't remember anything."), sleep difficulties, and episodes of hyperventilation. During a lengthy interview, he admitted that his father had abandoned his family prior to his birth. Approximately six months after his birth, his mother deserted him, so he was raised by his maternal grandparents. He described his grandfather as "ornery and mean" and vividly recalled being beaten with a thick belt as a child on numerous occasions whenever he broke one of his grandparents' rules. Both of his grandparents drank heavily. Throughout his childhood, he never felt loved nor experienced any degree of caring. He described his childhood as "miserable" because his grandparents forced him to submit to their extremely moralistic and cynical views of the world. He was never permitted to cry in front of them. Whenever he did this, his grandfather would call him a "sissy" and "beat him to a pulp." His grandmother hated him because he reminded her of her father, whom she despised. He was not permitted to have any of his friends visit their home, nor was he allowed to participate in any sports activities. He was forced to read the Bible for two hours every evening, even though it prevented him from doing his homework. This resulted in barely passing grades in school. His grandparents forced him to leave school prematurely and to give up his ambition of becoming an artist. Instead, he was forced to work at his grandfather's garage as a mechanic—which he did not enjoy—and had to accept a meager salary, which was far below the standards of the industry.

While at work, his grandfather constantly criticized him and frequently called him a "bastard." He left home when he was 21. His grandparents never forgave him for this and blamed him for all of their problems. This caused him to feel extremely guilty. To cope with his poor self-esteem and general unhappiness, he began drinking heavily. He constantly wondered about the whereabouts of both of his biological parents. One day he found out where his biological father lived and decided to pay him a surprise visit. His father denied that he had ever fathered the patient and told him that he never wanted to see him again. The patient also tried to visit his mother, whom he discovered had been living in a town located only 25 miles away. When he visited his mother, he discovered that she was a heroin addict and worked as a prostitute. Rather than appearing happy and pleased to see her son again, she blamed him for her drug addiction problems and told him, "I wish I had gotten an abortion."

Neuropsychological assessment revealed that the patient had been chronically depressed since his childhood and that he showed strong tendencies to somaticize his pent-up emotional problems. Testing of his cognitive functioning revealed no convincing evidence of neuropsychological impairment, but found the patient to be a very socially withdrawn, unhappy individual who repressed strong feelings of rage toward his family for the unhappiness they had caused him throughout his entire life. He also admitted that his principal reminded him of his stepfather, had made numerous unreasonable demands on him, and had never been understanding or accepting of him. Personality testing also revealed that the patient enjoyed the attention he received from his treating medical doctors, whom he felt generally cared about him. He also admitted that his symptoms and complaints had not changed to any significant degree over the past three years since his injury. He also admitted that he had been seeing a total of eight different doctors each week for his numerous complaints. He found them to be accepting, understanding, and compassionate people with whom he enjoyed talking. The neuropsychologist phoned the patient's referring physician and indicated that the patient's pre-existing emotional needs as a result of having been deprived of understanding, acceptance, and dignity as a child, had been met by his treating doctors, which had only served to reinforce his complaints and provide him with considerable secondary gains. The neuropsychologist also recommended psychotherapy in place of the medical treatments the patient had been receiving.

Siblings

The patient's siblings can also serve as a rough index of the patient's neuropsychological functioning, provided that the patient and his or her siblings were roughly comparable in terms of their educational level, size, age, attitudes, personality, and abilities prior to an injury.

CASE STUDY

A 25-year-old male patient had sustained a depressed skull fracture and brain injury when he was hit by a wrench that had fallen 50 feet after it had been accidentally dropped by a coworker while the patient was working below on an oil rig. The patient was immediately rendered unconscious and developed an epidural hematoma which was surgically evacuated. The patient spent three days in a coma. The patient was referred for neuropsychological testing by his treating neurologist, who found the patient to be only minimally impaired during his neurological examination. The patient arrived for his scheduled examination accompanied by his identical twin brother. When the neuropsychologist learned that the patient had an identical twin brother, he asked the brother's permission to undergo neuropsychological testing to compare the patient's performances and to determine the extent and severity of the patient's brain injury in comparison to his twin's abilities. Neuropsychological testing revealed only slight to mild impairments in comparison to normative data. However, when the patient's test results were compared to those of his identical twin brother, evidence of rather significant differences were found, which suggested that the patient had sustained moderately severe impairments in his problem solving skills, recent memory, perceptual organization, and intellectual functioning. Later, the academic performances and IQ scores of the patient and his identical twin were compared. They revealed that both the patient and his brother had virtually identical IQ's—123 versus 124—and had obtained virtually identical grades in both high school and college. They were virtually identical in height and weight and were not easily distinguishable on a physical basis. Their personalities were similar, in that they both shared the same likes and dislikes and had dated two women who shared many of the same physical and personality characteristics.

The author has also found that the siblings of individuals who are diagnosed as having a conversion disorder or malingering are likely to have siblings with histories of antisocial behavior, drug abuse, alcoholism, or many of the same complaints which are elicited by the patient. In this particular case, this suggests that the patient's problems and complaints may be due to a combination of genetic, developmental, and learning factors which preceded the patient's accident or injury, since these behaviors have been exhibited by other family members with no history of brain or psychological trauma.

Behavioral Observations

Behavioral observations refer to direct observation of the patient's behavior from the time the patient enters the doctor's office, during the interview and testing, and in relatively structured and unstructured settings. Many patients who complain of severe problems with their memory will informally demonstrate what a superb memory they have outside of the formal testing situation. For example, they will frequently provide the examiner with an excellent chronological history of the events which have occurred to them, including the dates of their examinations by treating doctors, conversations with these doctors, and their work experiences. They will often describe numerous incidents that have occurred since their injury that are used to "document" their complaints of severe memory difficulties. These patients often arrive for their scheduled appointments precisely on time or even a few minutes early. When these patients are asked if they had any problems getting to the appointment on time, they will often state, "No, actually traffic on the way here was pretty good, although I had to take the exit on Harbor Boulevard to avoid a traffic accident up ahead." When asked if they had witnessed the accident on the side of the road, they might state, "Yes, I saw two fire trucks on the freeway and there were three ambulances and two people lying on the ground receiving cardiopulmonary resuscitation." These patients remember where they parked their car during the lunch break and are able to remember precisely how to return to the doctor's office after they had gone to lunch. They also recall what they had informed the doctor during the morning and often correct the doctor's errors of memory, such as, "I don't believe you asked me about my uncle when we were talking this morning. You only asked me about my father." Many of these patients indicate that they had taken a particular test before and can even recall many of the questions and how they answered when they were administered the test seven months ago. They can also describe the doctors' offices in which they were examined, as well as several unique characteristics of the doctor that distinguish him or her from other doctors they have seen in the past. They also recall, without any prompting, other appointments that they had during the day or later that evening. They also remember to call their wife at precisely 3:30. They are able to describe the family events that have gone on earlier in the day in fairly precise detail. However, when these same individuals are given a formal test of memory, they often perform quite poorly, and will frequently complain during testing, "I can't remember anything. My mind is a blank."

The question which arises, however, is, "What should the neuropsychologist focus on?" If the neuropsychologist focuses his or her attention on the patient's performance on formal tests of memory, then the patient is seen as having a severe, if not profound, memory disorder. However, if the neuropsychologist examines the behavior of the patient outside of the formal testing situation, as well as the patient's qualitative behavior during testing, such as the histrionic complaints of the patient observed during testing, then the neuropsychologist recognizes the patient's excellent memory. The author feels strongly that the neuropsychologist should use what can best be described as a "vector" approach, in which each observation, formal or informal, of the patient's behavior constitutes a vector. Upon gathering all sources of data or vectors, such as each of these vectors should be consistent with each other. The presence of inconsistent vectors, such as the discrepancy between the patient's behavior during informal settings and formal testing, should cause the neuropsychologist to carefully evaluate the patient's motivation or behavior during both settings. For example, when both vectors are consistent, the patient's behavior during informal and formal settings is basically the same. The patients will typically deny that they have a problem with their memory, yet will be unable to provide a chronological history of the events that occurred following a specific event or accident. They will often appear confused and request that the instructions be repeated several times. They typically have no recollection of ever seeing other doctors in the past and forget that their family has been sitting in the waiting room for several hours. They will not know the reason why they are being examined and will frequently forget the examiner's instructions. They will often get lost when they go to the restroom and frequently can be found wandering up and down the hallway, confused and not knowing why they are there for their scheduled appointment. They are typically taken by their spouses or significant others to their appointments, since they cannot be trusted to keep them on their own because of their severe problems with recent memory. These patients rarely complain of memory difficulties and appear to be trying to perform to the best of their ability on each of the tests they are administered. When they are asked to recall events or information they had witnessed or experienced 20 to 30 minutes earlier, they typically are unable to recall this information and do not appear perturbed for having this problem. They generally appear pleasant and virtually never direct the examiner's attention to their memory difficulties.

The behavioral observations of the examiner (see Table 6) would include the patient's appearance — grooming, dress, physical characteristics, personal hygiene, and disabilities. The patient's attitude toward assessment, which includes his or her cooperation and motivation to perform to the best of his or her abilities should also be observed. The patient's mental status, including his or her level of arousal, attention to the environment, and orientation to person, place, time, and purpose should be noted. Speech patterns and comprehension of language or the examiner's questions and instructions are noted and described. Memory for recent and remote events, overall cognitive and intellectual functioning, and ability to regulate one's behavior and recognize and/or correct one's errors should also be recorded.

The patient's affect and mood should be noted, to determine whether the patient was anxious, depressed, or exhibited hostility, euphoria, frequent mood swings, emotional lability, or suicidal or homicidal ideation. The patient's personality traits should also be carefully observed, as well as his or her coping mechanisms, particularly the awareness of their illness and their reactions to the examiner's questions and formal neuropsychological testing. Personality traits, such as grandiosity, hallucinations, flight of ideas, pathological lying, manipulativeness, or bizarre thinking, should be reported by the examiner. The examiner should also describe the patient's gait, balance, coordination, and ability to initiate, as well as terminate, their behaviors. Finally, the neuropsychologist should provide an overall impression of the patient's behavior during the assessment process which discusses the validity of the patient's performance during testing, as well as possible limitations or conditions which may confound interpretation of the patient's test results or overall neuropsychological functioning.

Review of Records

The patient's academic, vocational, medical, military, and psychiatric/psychological records should be carefully reviewed. These records frequently contain important information that helps the neuropsychologist interpret his or her neuropsychological test data.

TABLE 6
BEHAVIORAL OBSERVATIONS

APPEARANCE

Grooming
Dress
Physical characteristics
Disabilities

ATTITUDE TOWARDS ASSESSMENT

Cooperation
Motivation

MENTAL STATUS

Arousal
Attention
Orientation to surroundings
Speech
Comprehension
Memory
Cognition
Self regulation
Ability to recognize and self-correct errors
Judgement
Problem solving skills

AFFECT AND MOOD

Affect
Anxiety
Depression
Hostility
Euphoria
Suicidal or homicidal ideation
Emotional lability
Irritability
Poor frustration tolerance
Paranoia/suspiciousness
Depression

PERSONALITY TRAITS

Eccentric
Dramatic
Labile
Erratic
Demanding
Manipulative
Anxious
Compulsive
Suspicious
Intellectual
Oppositional
Dependent
Controlling
Detached/withdrawn

INSIGHT AND COPING MECHANISMS

Awareness/denial of problems/illness
Reactions to errors/mistakes

PSYCHIATRIC DISORDER

Hallucinations
Delusions
Paranoia
Bizarre thinking
Schizophrenia
Manic-depressive illness
Depression
Loose association
Tangential thinking

OVERALL IMPRESSIONS

Validity or limitation of test results
Motivation of patient during testing
Integration of behavioral observations with test results
Integration of test results with observations of significant others
Ecological validity of test findings

ACADEMIC

Academic records frequently contain the patient's grades, IQ, scholastic rating, and scores on specific achievement and aptitude tests. Grades reflect a combination of intelligence, diligence, motivation, peer competition, and the grading system used by a particular teacher or school. Good grades typically indicate that the individual had been an intelligent and well-motivated individual. Poor grades, on the other hand, can reflect either low intelligence, poor motivation, emotional problems, a history of drug or alcohol abuse, or over-involvement in extracurricular activities. Working while attending school, pregnancy, emotional trauma, divorce, and/or a dysfunctional family system may also produce poor grades. It is difficult to determine which of these factors are responsible for a patient's poor academic performance. This can only be determined by interviewing the patient, reviewing other academic records, including the progress notes of the patient's teachers, IQ and test scores of the patient, and querying the patient's family and/or significant others. For example, an individual with an IQ of 82 would not be expected to perform well academically, nor would an individual who had a history of dyslexia (impaired reading skills), or hyperactivity, who has an IQ of 105. Bright individuals, with IQ's of 125 or higher, may not do well in school because they often find their teachers and/or assignments boring, particularly if they are not placed in classes for brighter or gifted students. Individuals with character disorders, such as an antisocial personality, generally do poorly in school because of excessive absences and negative attitudes toward school and their teachers. These individuals may also be under the influence of alcohol and/or drugs during class and typically are too irresponsible to complete homework assignments or prepare for tests. Individuals whose parents are going through severe marital conflicts or divorce may be so preoccupied with the emotional turmoil in their family that they may be unable to study or concentrate on their homework. Women who become pregnant out of wedlock or who are sexually molested are prone to develop serious emotional problems, which are likely to significantly compromise their academic performance. Thus, it is much easier to draw conclusions about good grades than about the causes of average or poor grades.

VOCATIONAL

Vocational records can assist the neuropsychologist in understanding the various cognitive, social, and behavioral demands that the job environment placed on the patient prior to his or her injury. Such information is also valuable in helping the neuropsychologist decide if the patient is ready to return to work following brain injury or requires vocational rehabilitation. Vocational records can also help identify patients with pre-existing characterological difficulties such as paranoia, rebelliousness, hostility, irresponsibility, manipulativeness, and undependability. It should be noted that many individuals who sustain traumatic brain injuries often have a pre-existing history of vocational problems as a result of characterological difficulties. This information can help the neuropsychologist determine the degree to which the injury has aggravated the patient's pre-existing vocational problems.

MEDICAL

A patient's medical records, particularly those which pre-existed the patient's injury, will frequently contain illnesses, problems, and treatments that the patient can either not recall or denies at the time of his or her examination. In certain cases, the sheer volume of the patient's medical records which pre-existed a specific accident or injury are often sufficient to allow the psychologist to raise hypotheses regarding the patient's psychiatric condition.

CASE STUDY

A patient was referred for neuropsychological assessment for toxic exposure to cleaning solvents while working as a pulmonary therapist in a large hospital. The patient arrived for her scheduled appointment nearly two hours late, and stated to the doctor's secretary, "I don't want him giving me any of those psychological tests. There is nothing wrong with me psychologically." Within a minute or two, the patient began hyperventilating and fell to the floor. While gasping for air, she demanded that the paramedics be called to take her to the hospital. The paramedics were summoned. The patient was taken to a nearby hospital where she was released several hours later with instructions to return to the psychologist's office. When the patient returned, she did not wish to be interviewed and wanted to go home, claiming that, "I could have another attack at any time." The psychologist asked her if she had ever had a prior history of breathing difficulties. The patient adamantly denied that she had ever had a prior history and became angry at the doctor for even asking her this question. The patient then indicated that she had been hospitalized 31 times during the past two years for respiratory problems after she claimed that she had accidentally inhaled a cleaning solution while working. The patient refused to take any psychological tests and stated that she had to get home because she feared she would have another attack.

The psychologist phoned the referring source, an attorney representing the insurance carrier, and recommended that every effort be made to obtain this patient's past medical records. The attorney indicated that he was not aware that this patient had ever seen a physician prior to her industrial accident and did not believe there were any records available. The psychologist indicated that from his experience, he felt that the patient showed symptoms and behavioral characteristics consistent with Munchausen's syndrome, a factitious disorder which is deliberately maintained by the patient to avoid work and other responsibilities. The attorney hired an investigator to check hospitals within a 50 mile geographic area of the patient's home. The attorney was amazed when he discovered that for the 10 years prior to the applicant's industrial injury, the patient had spent an average of 32 weeks per year hospitalized over the 10-year period. These hospital records indicated that whenever her treating doctors suggested that there might be a psychological or psychiatric basis for her problems, the patient became extremely angry and left the hospital against medical advice. These records also indicated that this patient had been hospitalized and received treatment at over 40 different hospitals and indicated that none of the hospitals knew that she had ever been treated at another hospital. The applicant denied she ever had these problems before or had ever been hospitalized. The records corroborated the psychologist's impression that the patient had Munchausen's syndrome.

MILITARY

The patient's military records, if applicable, can provide valuable insights into how the patient had handled stress, discipline, authority, and interacted with others. These records may also contain information about the patient's medical problems while serving in the military, as well as any disciplinary or punitive actions he or she may have received. Contained within these records are the Armed Forces qualifying test scores, which can often be utilized to provide an estimate of the patient's prior intellectual functioning. These records may also contain information about the types of duties and responsibilities the patient performed while serving in the military and the type of discharge received.

PSYCHIATRIC/PSYCHOLOGICAL

The patient's psychiatric and psychological records prior to and following their injury or accident can alert the psychologist to any pre-existing emotional problems and/or treatments. This information will frequently discuss the patient's background history, as well as identify any external stressors which are unrelated to a specific injury or accident. These records frequently contain psychological and occasionally neuropsychological test data, including narrative computerized reports of tests such as the MMPI.

Chapter 7

Neuropsychological Testing

The neuropsychological assessment process includes the administration of a battery of specific tests which have been designed to evaluate the patient's abilities in the following areas: attention, concentration, perception, learning, memory, language, visual-spatial skills, motor skills, higher order motor skills, planning, organizational skills, behavioral regulation skills, cognitive flexibility, abstract and conceptual skills, problem solving, and judgement. In addition, the neuropsychological examination frequently includes tests to evaluate the patient's personality and emotional functioning.

The specific tests which are utilized to evaluate these functions depends largely upon the training, experience, and expertise of the clinical psychologist or neuropsychologist. While some neuropsychologists routinely administer standardized neuropsychological batteries, such as the Halstead-Reitan or the Luria-Nebraska Neuropsychological Batteries, the majority of neuropsychologists administer what has been termed "flexible" batteries (Sweet and Moberg, 1990), which are a composite of different tests that have been selected for any of the following reasons: the cultural and linguistic background of the patient, the specific type of problems created by the patient's injury, the complaints of the patient and/or significant others, time since injury, specific referral questions or issues (e.g., rule out organicity, determine if this patient is capable of returning to school on a full-time basis, etc.), specific tests the patient has been administered in the past, the duration of time since previous testing, specific medicolegal issues (e.g., Is this patient malingering?), the patient's perceptual and motor skills (e.g., The patient may be visually impaired, deaf, or may be unable to use his or her right arm), current emotional or psychiatric problems (e.g., The patient may be severely depressed or psychotic), the amount of time allotted for assessment, the patient's endurance and tendency to fatigue, and the particular patient/examiner interaction (e.g., The examiner may notice a particular cognitive impairment during the administration of one test which may result in the administration of another test to explore this impairment).

Test Validity

Neuropsychological tests can be conceptually viewed as a series of instruments which attempt to measure a patient's cognitive or behavioral functioning in a particular area. Because numerous tests have been developed to evaluate specific functions, the neuropsychologist's choice of one particular test or battery over others may reflect the particular test's validity or reliability. Validity can be defined as the likelihood by which a particular test is able to measure what it purports to measure. There are several different types of validity. In cases involving brain injury, criterion validity, or the degree to which a particular neuropsychological test is able to predict or correlate with specific external criteria, is the most widely preferred criteria used by neuropsychologists. This typically involves identifying a group of patients who have sustained a particular type of injury (e.g., brain damage or frontal lobe injury) and measuring the ability of a specific neuropsychological test to predict the percentage of individuals who fall into a specific category (e.g., brain damage). For example, a neuropsychologist is interested in studying the criterion validity of two particular neuropsychological tests to detect brain damage. He administers Tests A & B to a group of 100 individuals who have all sustained brain damage by some external criteria (e.g., duration of coma, CT scan findings, abnormal EEG findings, neurological examination, etc.). He also administers both tests to a group of 100 psychiatric patients with no history of brain damage. The neuropsychologist finds that Test A identifies 80% of the patients in the brain-damaged group as brain-damaged but incorrectly identifies 20% of the psychiatric patients as brain-damaged. Test B, on the other hand, identifies only 60% of the brain-damaged patients as brain-damaged and identifies 40% of the psychiatric group as brain-damaged. In terms of criterion validity, the criterion validity of Test A is .80, whereas the criterion validity of Test B is only .60. Thus, criterion validity refers to the relative sensitivity of a particular test in terms of its ability to detect individuals belonging to a particular group of patients (brain injury versus psychiatric).

"Hit Rates"

The manuals of many neuropsychological tests or batteries report what have been described as "hit rates," which refers to the percentage of correct classifications made strictly on the basis of a particular test score. For example, most of the widely used neuropsychological tests report hit rates ranging from 70 to 90%, which means that the prediction or categorization of a particular individual as falling into a group of brain-damaged patients based on his or her test score will be correct between 70 and 90% of the time. This also means that the chances of incorrectly classifying this particular individual ranges between 10 and 30%. This is generally accepted as having sufficient validity for purposes of discriminating between brain-damaged patients and normal controls. The problem, however, is that when one attempts to differentiate between brain-damaged patients and psychiatric patients, the hit rates tend to become much lower. Part of the reason for this is that patients with psychiatric disorders may have an underlying neurologic substrate (e.g., Alzheimer's Disease), may be taking psychotropic medications which effect their cognitive functioning, or may be so depressed, psychotic, or so emotionally disturbed at the time of testing that they perform as poorly as patients with brain damage. Another problem arises, however, when one attempts to use a particular neuropsychological test or battery to differentiate between patients who are brain-damaged and individuals involved in personal injury litigation. For example, the litigation group may include individuals who may be motivated to perform poorly for purposes of secondary gain. Thus, the patient's poor score on a particular test may cause him or her to be incorrectly identified as "brain-damaged" rather than as a malingerer.

The attorney should also be cautioned that a hit rate of 95% on one particular test or battery does not necessarily mean that it is a better test than another test which reports a hit rate of only 75%. For example, the first test may have utilized controls consisting largely of college freshman, while the controls utilized by the lower hit rate test may have consisted of hospitalized patients. Thus, a test with a higher hit rate should not be interpreted as more sensitive to brain damage unless the control groups utilized in both studies are roughly equivalent.

Studies with the most widely used standardized neuropsychological batteries, the Halstead-Reitan and Luria-Nebraska, have reported hit rates in excess of 90% in discriminating the neuropsychological test performance of brain-damaged and nonbrain-damaged patient groups (Golden, Hammeke, and Purisch, 1978; Wheeler and Reitan, 1974). Despite these apparent impressive results, one must evaluate what is meant by the term "brain-damaged." It may refer to diverse patients with different neurological etiologies such as Alzheimer's Disease, cerebral vascular disorders, brain tumors, hydrocephalus, hypoxic encephalopathies, penetrating missile wounds to the brain, intracranial abscesses or infections, or encephalitis. It could also refer to patients whose brain damage was produced by surgery (e.g., frontal lobotomy), viral infections (e.g., encephalitis), bullet wounds (e.g., penetrating missile wounds), crush injuries, cardiac arrest (e.g., hypoxic encephalopathy), ruptured aneurysm or stroke, heavy metal or toxic exposure, chronic alcoholism, blunt trauma, or acceleration/deceleration forces (e.g., diffuse axonal damage). Thus, the attorney should attempt to determine the particular reference group of "brain-damaged" patients the study utilized, and if such a comparison group is valid for the particular patient being tested. For example, if a patient with a subtle brain injury is compared to a normative group of patients with severe and profound brain damage, the test may not identify this patient as "brain-damaged."

Reliability

The reliability of a particular neuropsychological test or battery refers to the consistency to which a particular test or battery achieves the same score or scores when used on two or more occasions. For example, if two psychological tests (A & B) are given to a group of patients suspected of having "brain damage" one week apart, and if 90% of these individuals obtain the same score one week later, then the reliability of Test A will be .90; however, if only half of the individuals given Test B obtain similar scores one week later, then the reliability of Test B will be .50. Test-retest reliability can be affected by a variety of factors, such as changes in the patient's condition, the patient's environment, starting or discontinuing a particular medication which is known to alter cognitive functioning, the attitude of the individual tested from one week to the next (e.g., the patient may say, "Oh shucks, I've taken this test before. I really don't want to take it again."), placing the patient in a particular treatment program to improve his or her cognitive functioning, and a variety of other factors (e.g., depression, anxiety, illness, fatigue, etc.). Obviously, when the time between test administration increases, the reliability of the test used is likely to decrease, particularly if it is a test which is sensitive to acute conditions (e.g., depression, mental confusion, fatigue, etc.). On the other hand, tests which rely heavily on well-learned information acquired over the person's lifetime are likely to be extremely reliable over a fairly long time. For example, the Wechsler Adult Intelligence Scale (WAIS-R) appears to be heavily dependent on what has been termed "crystallized intelligence" (well-learned intellectual abilities), such that patients who sustain traumatic brain injuries frequently show little change in their IQ scores pre- and post-head injury. Thus, the reliability of IQ scores may be quite high, but its validity (in terms of identifying patients with brain damage) may be quite low.

Inter-rater Reliability

The reliability between two or more observers (e.g., psychologists, etc.) can also be determined. This is known as inter-rater reliability. It essentially refers to the consistency between the measurements or ratings of two or more observers when they are asked to evaluate a specific problem or patient. High scores in inter-rater reliability refer to a high degree of concordance between two or more psychologists or examiners using a particular test instrument. For example, Dr. Jones administers an IQ test (WAIS-R) to a plaintiff and reports that the plaintiff achieves an IQ of 100. One week later, Dr. Smith, the defense expert, administers the same test and reports that the plaintiff has an IQ of 145. Because of the marked discrepancy between the plaintiff's IQ scores, the patient is referred to Dr. Hood, who reports that the patient's IQ is 65. The plaintiff's attorney becomes very concerned and hires Dr. Tracy to investigate this matter. Dr. Tracy finds that Dr. Smith had never received training in administration of this test and had added the patient's scores incorrectly. He goes over Dr. Jones' results and finds that Dr. Jones has had extensive experience administering this test and had administered and scored this test properly. He meets with Dr. Hood, whom he discovers is nearly deaf and wears a hearing aide. Dr. Hood also wears thick bifocal lenses but admits that on that particular day, the battery in his hearing aide had worn out and he had misplaced his glasses. Dr. Tracy concludes that these factors were most likely responsible for the plaintiff's low score when he was tested by Dr. Hood.

With this humorous example in mind, it is not an uncommon experience for attorneys to discover that two psychologists, who have examined the same individual in a medicolegal case, report different test scores. This most likely reflects a combination of the following factors: differences in the examiner's experience, background, and training, the particular test norms utilized, the number of tests given by the examiner, the type of feedback provided by the examiner, whether or not the patient was given frequent breaks or went to lunch, the time of day the testing occurred, the amount of time allotted for testing, the particular expectations of the examiner, the biases and prejudices of the examiner, scoring and interpretation errors, and a variety of extraneous factors (e.g., the temperature of the room during testing, distractions during testing, etc.).

CASE STUDY

A 24-year-old Hispanic male was referred for neuropsychological assessment after he fell and sustained a cerebral concussion during an industrial accident. The applicant was referred by his attorney to a psychologist who administered the Halstead-Reitan Neuropsychological Battery which required eight hours to administer. The psychologist reported that the patient obtained an impairment index of 1.0, indicative of severe brain impairment. Two weeks later, the patient was referred to a qualified neuropsychologist specializing in traumatic brain injuries. The neuropsychologist noted that when the patient arrived for his scheduled appointment, he was extremely anxious and upset. The neuropsychologist asked the patient why he felt so nervous and upset. The patient indicated that one month ago he discovered that his wife had been cheating on him, which caused him to become very upset. As a consequence, he had not been able to sleep at night and had been having numerous fights with his wife since that time. The neuropsychologist then asked if this had affected him when he underwent neuropsychological testing two weeks earlier. The patient indicated that he had not slept at all the night before he had undergone the previous neuropsychological testing. He also indicated that the psychologist had spent very little time with him, it seemed, and appeared uninterested in his marital problems. This made him angry and depressed. He also indicated that the psychologist had informed him during one of the tests, "It looks like you have sustained a severe brain injury." When he asked the psychologist what this meant, the psychologist indicated, "Your brain has been pulverized. The score on this test means that your brain got wiped out and that more than likely you will never be able to work or function normally again." The patient admitted that he felt devastated upon hearing this. After this, he became so anxious and upset that he could not even perform a simple task without making an error.

The neuropsychologist learned that the patient had sustained a relatively slight concussion and essentially had made a fairly good recovery, which was complicated by his marital difficulties, high levels of anxiety, and acute depression. The neuropsychologist spent nearly an hour with the patient discussing some of the things he could do to improve his marriage and cope with his wife's problems. The patient felt relieved and enjoyed the opportunity to discuss these issues. He was then administered a variety of neuropsychological tests. The patient's performance on these tests revealed that the overwhelming majority of his problems appeared to be due to emotional factors and that he was showing some very slight residual cognitive problems secondary to his head injury. The patient felt relieved that his brain had not been "pulverized" and expressed his utmost gratitude to the neuropsychologist for his willingness to help him with his problems and for making him feel better.

Use of Psychological Assistants

Many neuropsychologists employ psychological assistants, or technicians, who administer psychological and neuropsychological tests to their patients. In some cases, the neuropsychologist may spend little or no time with the patient and, therefore, must rely entirely on the test results and observations of the patient's behavior, through the eyes of their assistant or technician. On one hand, this approach can be considered fairly objective, in the sense that the psychological assistant or technician may know virtually nothing about the patient's legal case, or not know whether the patient was referred by their attorney, insurance company, or the defendant's attorney. The psychologist and neuropsychologist, upon receiving the test results, then generate a written report, which is usually dictated and typed by the psychologist's secretary or typing service. Typically, such reports are primarily based on the patient's test scores. On the other hand, this approach assumes that each patient is motivated to perform to the best of his or her ability during testing and that the test data adequately reflects the patient's true level of neuropsychological functioning.

Ecological Validity

Many of the neuropsychological tests administered to patients suspected of having a brain injury may lack "ecological validity" in the sense that the particular scores derived from such tests may have little bearing on the patient's ability to function in their environment or society (Sbordone, 1988). For example, some psychologists prefer to devote the entire day to a particular patient, during which time they administer all of the tests that the patient is scheduled to receive. Other psychologists may spread the tests out over several days or weeks, during which time they may spend an hour or two administering tests to the patient during each visit. The primary advantage of the latter approach, is that the patient tends to be more rested and is less likely to exhibit the effects of fatigue. However, if one of the reasons why this person is being tested is to determine this particular patient's ability to work, or return to his job, then such testing may not be ecologically valid, since it may not provide us with sufficient information as to whether or not this patient can tolerate eight hours of cognitive activities, or what will happen when the patient becomes fatigued at work after several hours.

CASE STUDY

A 25-year-old electrician, was referred by his treating physician for a neuropsychological assessment. His medical records indicated that he had sustained a head injury at work, when he fell approximately 10 feet while installing an electrical circuit. This patient was seen approximately five months post-injury. He arrived for his scheduled appointment at 9:00 a.m. and appeared cognitively intact and quite normal. His responses to the questions during the interview appeared logical and coherent. He was given some neuropsychological tests at approximately 10 a.m. His performances on these tests were generally intact and revealed no evidence of cognitive impairment. However, during the afternoon, the patient's cognitive functioning began to deteriorate. By 4:00 p.m., the patient could not recall four digits forward, or three digits backward, although that morning he had no difficulty recalling seven digits forward and five digits backward. He also appeared bewildered and confused, made numerous errors, and exhibited evidence of impulsivity and poor judgement. Thus, under conditions of fatigue, the behavioral manifestations of his brain injury became readily apparent and were essentially disabling. Because his job involved working on power lines, which contained 10,000 volts of electricity, any errors of judgement made on his job, were likely to be fatal. The neuropsychologist phoned his referring doctor and said that in his opinion, he did not feel that the patient was ready to return to work at this time. The neuropsychologist recommended that the patient be re-evaluated in three months. When the patient returned, after three months, he indicated that approximately one week after his last appointment, he had tried to repair a broken electrical circuit in his home one evening, after he had spent the day with some friends. He admitted that he had nearly electrocuted himself. He said that normally, he would have not had any problem performing this task, but as a result of becoming fatigued, he became confused and grabbed the wrong wire. Follow-up neuropsychological testing, however, revealed that the patient had improved considerably in the sense that he failed to exhibit any significant deterioration in his cognitive functioning after several hours of neuropsychological testing. The psychologist then phoned the patient's physician and indicated that he felt that the patient had sufficiently recovered from a neuropsychological perspective and was now capable of returning to his job. The patient was seen again after three months and reported no significant problems or difficulties and indicated that he was doing fine. This was corroborated by telephone conversations with his supervisor and employer. If a neuropsychologist had tested this patient for only one or two hours per session, the patient's cognitive functioning under conditions of fatigue would not have been detected. Thus, the neuropsychologist, most likely, would have erroneously concluded that the patient was capable of returning to work when he was first seen.

Conditions During Testing May Actually Mask Brain Damage

The actual length of time required for neuropsychological testing varies, according to the number and type of tests administered, as well as the particular training and expertise of the neuropsychologist. In most instances, neuropsychological testing generally takes between four and eight hours. Patients who are younger, brighter, and relatively cognitively intact, may require only four hours, while patients who either require the services of a translator, are depressed, or have sustained significant brain damage, may require eight hours, or longer. When testing such patients, the neuropsychologist must be sure that the patient adequately understands the examiner's questions and/or test instructions. In many cases, the test instructions will have to be repeated several times, for the patient to respond appropriately. In addition, patients may be provided with examples, cues, and prompts to permit them to initiate and complete the particular test that they are being administered. This often creates difficulties interpreting their test scores, from a quantitative perspective, since such techniques often serve to minimize, or mask a patient's cognitive impairments, particularly when there is significant frontal lobe damage. Under such conditions, many patients with significant brain damage, are able to initiate and complete neuropsychological tests and may even perform within the normal range. However, in the absence of such prompts, cues, repeated instructions, and examples, the patient would normally be unable to initiate or complete such tests. Unfortunately, many psychologists and neuropsychologists fail to adequately discuss their particular interactions with the patient and the various cues and prompts they utilized during neuropsychological testing. Without this information, it may be erroneously assumed that the patient's performance on this test was an adequate reflection of his or her present level of cognitive functioning. In other words, a brain-damaged patient's ability to perform adequately on a particular neuropsychological test may be dependent on the presence of external cues, prompts, examples, and repeated instructions provided by the examining neuropsychologist, who has effectively compensated for the patient's cognitive impairments caused by brain injury. Thus, the neuropsychologist may erroneously conclude that the patient is cognitively intact and is able to return to work without realizing that his or her actions during testing may have essentially eliminated or minimized the patient's neuropsychological impairments. This issue will be discussed in greater detail when qualitative methods of neuropsychological assessment are presented.

Neuropsychological Tests

In this section, we will examine many of the widely used psychological and neuropsychological tests. Each of these tests will be described in terms of its purpose, administration, validity, reliability, and strengths and limitations, keeping in mind also that, "no test is any better than the person who administers it." We shall begin by examining the most widely used psychological tests to evaluate patients who have been referred to clinical psychologists with a history of neurological and/or psychological trauma.

WECHSLER ADULT INTELLIGENCE SCALE

The Wechsler Adult Intelligence Scale-Revised (WAIS-R) has been specifically designed to evaluate a patient's intellectual functioning and is the most widely used psychological test today. It consists of six verbal subtests (Information, Comprehension, Arithmetic, Digit Span, Similarity, and Vocabulary) and five performance subtests (Picture Completion, Picture Arrangement, Block Design, Object Assembly, and Digit Symbol). Each of these tests is individually administered by the examiner. The test is appropriate for individuals ranging in age from 16 to 74 (Wechsler, 1981). The norms utilized on this test were derived from representative groups of the adult population in the United States, based on the 1970 U.S. Census Report. The test authors carefully considered such variables as age, sex, race (e.g., white vs. nonwhite), occupation, geographic location, education, and urban-rural residence, to ensure that the groups selected adequately represented the U.S. adult population (Spruill, 1984).

The WAIS-R verbal subtests evaluate the patient's ability to answer questions regarding academic topics (e.g., Whose name is generally associated with the theory of relativity?), historical (e.g., Name five presidents of the United States since 1950.), and cultural (Who was Martin Luther King?) Such questions would be found in the Information subtests. Within the Comprehension subtest would be questions regarding the meanings of common sayings, or what types of actions or behavior would be expected in particular cultural or social situations. The Arithmetic subtest provides the patient with specific mental arithmetic tasks. The Digit Span subtest consists of having the patient repeat strings of numbers forward and backward. The Similarity subtest presents the patient with two common objects and asks how these objects are related (e.g., How are a table and chair related?) The Vocabulary subtest asks the patient to provide a definition of specific orally presented words (e.g., What does the word "winter" mean?).

The WAIS-R performance subtests evaluate the patient's visual-spatial and constructional skills. In the Picture Completion subtest, the patient is shown drawings of objects which contain a missing part. The Picture Arrangement subtest contains a series of pictures, which when properly arranged by the patient, will present a pictorial sequence of logical events. The Block Design subtest requires the patient to manipulate small blocks which contain different colored sides, to reproduce specific printed designs. The Object Assembly subtest involves putting together pieces to form a complete object (e.g., a hand), similar to that of a jigsaw puzzle. The Digit Symbol subtest is a coding task, in which the patient must substitute one symbol for another, based on a specific code, as quickly as possible.

Each of these subtests are administered in a particular order. For scoring purposes, it is essential that the patient's literal responses be recorded on the test booklet. According to the manual for administration and scoring, the examiner may at times query the patient on specific verbal subtests or when the patient fails to comprehend the test instructions. Within each of the 11 subtests, the easiest items are presented first, to allow the patient to "learn how to take the test." Five of the 11 subtests are timed, which means that the patient receives a higher score if a particular test item is solved quickly.

The WAIS-R (Wechsler, 1981) manual describes how the test should be administered and the types of responses and/or prompts permitted by the examiner. The manual defines how a specific test item will be scored. Occasionally, however, patients will provide responses which are not contained in the manual, hence the examiner must extrapolate a particular score, based on its proximity to samples contained in the manual. The scoring procedure results in numeric scores for each of the 11 subtests, which are converted into standard scores based on their statistical variability from the norm. The patient's standard score on each of the 11 subtests can also be corrected for age. Thus, the same numeric score for a 20-year-old on the Digit Symbol subtest, is likely to produce a higher standard score if the same numeric score had been obtained by a 60-year-old patient. This is because some of the subtests (particularly the Performance subtest), are sensitive to the effects of age and tend to become lower with increasing age. Part of this, however, may reflect the fact that older patients may have had fewer years of formal schooling than younger patients.

The patient's scores on the verbal and performance subtests determine the patient's verbal (VIQ) and performance (PIQ) intelligence quotients. The patient's full scale intelligence quotient (FSIQ) represents a composite of the patient's verbal and performance intellectual quotient. Full scale IQ scores, ranging from 90 to 109, comprise 50% of the adult population and are considered to fall within the average range. When the patient's IQ exceeds 109, but is less than 120, then the patient is regarded as having above average intelligence. When the patient's IQ exceeds 120, then the patient is seen as having superior intellectual functioning. IQ's of 130, or higher, are considered to represent very superior intellectual functioning. IQ's less than 90, but greater than 80, are considered to fall into the range of low-average intellectual functioning. When the patient's score falls between 70 and 79, they are considered to have borderline intellectual functioning. Scores of 69 or less fall into the mentally retarded range. Approximately 95% of the population falls between IQ scores of 70 and 130. The administration of the entire test battery typically requires between 60 and 90 minutes. Some psychologists prefer to use abbreviated forms of the test, in which they will administer fewer than 11 of the subtests (often only five or six subtests) to save time (Lezak, 1983).

Validity

Based on research studies, IQ coefficients have been found to correlate well with the patient's grade point average, at all levels of education. Thus, the WAIS-R has been frequently used by psychologists and other health professionals to predict academic achievements or success (Spruill, 1984). For example, if a patient expresses an interest in going on to college to study engineering and obtains an IQ of only 92, more than likely he may be dissuaded by the school psychologist from applying to a four-year college in the field of engineering and may be persuaded into either going to a junior college, or attending a trade school. On the other hand, if a particular student is found to have a very high IQ (e.g., 142), he may be encouraged to enter college, rather than becoming a plumber or carpenter. However, it should be pointed out that vocational success and a particular person's IQ score, have a much lower correlation. This is partly based on the semantic difficulty created by the term "vocational success" as well as the numerous factors that may contribute to one becoming successful in a particular vocation.

Reliability

Research studies have shown that while the overall reliability of the WAIS-R is high, the reliability of the individual subtests ranges considerably (from 0.96 on the Vocabulary subtest, to 0.52 for the Object Assembly subtest). The WAIS-R has generally demonstrated very high reliability in assessing normal controls and psychiatric patients (except for their performance on the Arithmetic subtests, as a result of the use of psychotropic medications). The reliability for psychiatric and brain-injured patients is likely to be somewhat different, depending on the severity of the patient's psychiatric disorder, the type of medications the patient is taking, the type of brain injury involved, the time since injury, and the length of time between test administrations (Spruill, 1984).

Strengths and Limitations

The WAIS-R is a relatively easy test to administer and score. The manual is well-written, easy to read, and generally provides clear directions for scoring. It is effective in determining IQ scores which range from 45 to 150. It is widely used in a variety of settings and has been based on a representative sample of normative population groups within the United States. IQ scores obtained through this test have been shown to correlate highly with the patient's grade point average throughout school (Lezak, 1983).

The chief limitation of the WAIS-R is that it was never designed to evaluate patients who sustained brain damage. Many of the WAIS-R subtests appear relatively insensitive to brain injury and frequently result in surprisingly high scores, which most likely do not reflect a brain-injured patient's cognitive functioning in "real world" or unstructured situations. It is also inappropriate for patients who have significant visual or motor impairments (e.g., diplopia, hemiparesis, visual agnosia, or aphasia). The author has found that a brain-injured patient's IQ scores can be adversely affected by emotional factors (e.g., depression) and may create the spurious impression that the patient's cognitive functioning is deteriorating, even though the patient's performance on more sensitive neuropsychological tests may have significantly improved (Sbordone, 1987).

Much of the popular folklore about the brain can be attributed to the use of the Wechsler Adult Intelligence Scale, in assessing patients who have undergone neurosurgical intervention. For example, the IQ's of patients who have undergone prefrontal lobotomies have been reported to increase an average of two points following surgery. In addition, many investigators have reported little or no change in the patient's IQ score, following removal of damaged brain tissue. As a consequence of the use of the WAIS-R to evaluate brain-damaged individuals in the past rather than using appropriate neuropsychological tests, the myth that we only use a very small (2%) part of our brain developed. The author sadly recalls the parents of a patient who had sustained a severe brain injury, which involved resection of the right temporal lobe, saying, "Our son should be all right, since they only took out 10% of his brain and we only use 2% of our brain anyway." Patients who are raised in a different culture and/or whose command of English is limited may receive spuriously low IQ scores. The WAIS-R is also not particularly suited for patients who have aphasic difficulties, or who are motorically, visually, or auditorally impaired. Finally, patients who are placed on anticonvulsant medications (e.g., Dilantin) or antipsychotic medications (e.g., Thorazine, Mellaril, Haldol, etc.) are likely to obtain lower IQ scores.

BENDER-GESTALT TEST

The Bender-Gestalt test is most widely used by psychologists to evaluate "organicity." The use of this term by a psychologist usually indicates that the psychologist has had little, if any, training in behavioral neurology and lacks an adequate understanding of neurological disorders. This test consists of nine geometric designs which are presented individually on a 4 x 6 inch card to the patient, who must draw them as accurately as possible on a blank sheet of 8-1/2 x 11 inch paper. When the patient completes the first drawing, the second card is placed on top of the first until all nine cards have been reproduced. This test is designed to evaluate the patient's perceptual tendencies to organize visual stimuli into configural "Gestalts." It is appropriate for patients who are three years and older (including geriatric patients) because it is a simple test and can be administered in a relatively short time. It has achieved considerable popularity among clinical psychologists in the United States. However, it has been regarded by some as extremely over-rated. Like any test, its effectiveness depends on the skill, training, and experience of the examiner (Whitworth, 1984).

A number of different scoring systems exist based upon the accuracy and organization of the patient's drawings, which consider factors such as the relative size of the drawings (compared to the test stimuli) and their relative placement on the sheet of paper, the particular distortions of the reproductions, which may include inversions or rotations of the figures, as well as evidence of perceptual and/or fine motor problems. The results of the Bender-Gestalt can either be interpreted in terms of emotional disturbance, maturational development, or "organic" brain function.

Validity

Investigators, such as Koppitz (1964; 1975), have conducted numerous validity and reliability studies involving this test with young children. Koppitz reported correlation coefficients (Author's note: This is a mathematical relationship between two variables and should not be construed as a percentage. For example, correlations of 1.0 represent a perfect correlation or relationship between two variables. Correlations of .0 indicate that no correlation exists between two variables.) ranging from approximately .50 to as high as .80 between this test and intelligence test scores. Studies by Lezak (1976) indicated that this test has been effective in discriminating between psychiatric and brain-injured patients as well as normal controls. Koppitz obtained correct diagnoses ranging from 74 to 91%. Studies by Heaton, Boade, and Johnson (1978) reported that this test could correctly discriminate between psychiatric and organic groups with an 84% accuracy.

Reliability

Research which examined the test-retest reliability of this test taken two weeks apart with kindergarten children reported reliability coefficients of .90. When the same group of kindergarten children were given the test eight months apart, the test-retest reliability coefficient dropped to approximately 0.5 (Whitworth, 1984). It should be pointed out that as children become older, their test-retest scores on this test become higher. Children, in the absence of brain injury or significant emotional disturbances, tend to improve in their scores on this test as they become older. For example, children who are 10 or older typically make perfect scores on this test.

Strengths and Limitations

One of the major strengths of this test is its ease in administration and how relatively quickly it can be administered. It has been in use for over 50 years. As a consequence, there have been well over a thousand studies done on its clinical effectiveness, validity, and reliability. While it has often been employed as a screening test for brain damage, along with other neuropsychological tests, it has often been misused when the clinician relies solely on this instrument and neglects to administer other neuropsychological tests or take a careful clinical and background history of the patient. Because of the numerous scoring systems which exist, there is no one accepted scoring system for the diagnosis of organicity. Because of its ease in test administration, it is too frequently misused or abused by untrained, inexperienced, and even unethical examiners (Whitworth, 1984).

Standardized Neuropsychological Test Batteries

Many neuropsychologists utilize a standardized neuropsychological battery to evaluate patients suspected of having brain dysfunction or damage. There are several advantages (and disadvantages) in utilizing a standardized neuropsychological battery. The first advantage is that the battery usually contains norms to compare a patient's scores to brain-damaged patients and normal controls, a manual which describes the administration and scoring of the various tests contained within the battery, specific tests to be administered to the patient, and research studies which demonstrate its validity and reliability. The second major advantage is that the neuropsychological test batteries typically do not require that the examiner be well-versed in neuroanatomy or behavioral neurology, since the battery frequently attempts to serve as a "stand alone" instrument to detect brain damage. The third major advantage is that most neuropsychological batteries are relatively easy to administer and score. The fourth major advantage is that they can usually be administered by technicians or psychological assistants (individuals who generally have a college degree and are frequently working toward an advanced degree in the field of psychology). Typically, an individual can be trained to administer and score a neuropsychological test battery in several days.

The vast majority of psychologists and neuropsychologists who utilize standardized neuropsychological test batteries have taken a workshop to learn how to administer, score, and even interpret the results of a particular standardized neuropsychological test battery. The workshops generally last between two and five days. These workshops usually include a cursory overview of the neuroanatomy of the brain and its pathology, brain-behavior relationships, a description of each test, and how to properly administer and score the tests contained within the battery. Following this, specific profiles of test scores are examined to illustrate how neuropsychological interpretations should be made. Unfortunately, the author does not know of any workshops which offer the student the opportunity to actually test a patient under supervision. While the workshops typically provide the trainee with the test scores of patients who have previously been examined by one of the instructors, the major problem is that relatively few of the psychologists who complete these workshops seek or receive supervision from qualified and experienced neuropsychologists after they have completed the workshop. Unfortunately, many psychologists, particularly those with little or no background in behavioral neurology, neuroanatomy, or brain-behavior relationships often feel that they are now "competent" to offer "neuropsychological testing" services. The author vividly recalls speaking to a psychologist several years ago who had never heard of neuropsychology and knew virtually nothing about brain-behavior relationships because she had completed her Ph.D. in counseling in the Department of Education rather than in the Department of Psychology. (Author's note: Many state licensing boards allow such individuals to apply for licensure as a psychologist, although, in the last several years, there has been a growing trend to restrict licensure to individuals who have completed a Ph.D. in the field of psychology.) After she was given a brief description of the field of neuropsychology, she indicated that she had recently received a brochure in the mail which advertised a three-day seminar on how to administer and score a particular standardized neuropsychological battery. After the conversation, she decided to enroll in the course. One week after she completed the course, the author received an announcement, which had also been sent to other psychologists, physicians, and attorneys in the area, that indicated that she was now accepting referrals for neuropsychological testing. (Author's note: While it should be noted that this psychologist's behavior is generally frowned upon by other members of the psychological profession and violates the Code of Ethics of the American Psychological Association, it only serves to demonstrate how little training some psychologists have received in the administration, scoring, and interpretation of neuropsychological test batteries.)

The two most widely used standardized neuropsychological test batteries will now be presented to provide the reader with an understanding of their administration, scoring, and methods of interpretation. In addition, studies relating to the validity and reliability of these batteries will also be presented, as well as the various strengths and weaknesses of the batteries, particularly in medicolegal cases.

HALSTEAD-REITAN NEUROPSYCHOLOGICAL BATTERY

The Halstead-Reitan Neuropsychological Test Battery and allied procedures are perhaps the best known and one of the most widely used neuropsychological test batteries. It was developed over 40 years ago to measure a broad range of cognitive abilities which were thought to be dependent on the integrity of the brain. Therefore, impairments in specific cognitive functions could identify brain damage or dysfunction (Reitan, 1955). The Halstead-Reitan Battery consists of adult, intermediate children (9-14 years), and young children (5-8 years) versions. Each battery is designed to include a minimum of 14 neuropsychological tests capable of measuring up to 26 different brain-behavior relationships. The Halstead-Reitan Battery also includes the Wechsler Adult Intelligence Scale, the Minnesota Multiphasic Personality Inventory, and an academic achievement measure, such as the Wide Range Achievement Test (Whitworth, 1984).

The complete Halstead-Reitan Battery consists of the following tests: The Halstead Category Test, the Tactual Performance Test, the Seashore Rhythm Test, the Speech Sounds Perception Test, the Finger Oscillation (Tapping) Test, the Trail Making Test, the Grip Strength Test, the Sensory Perceptual Examination, the Tactual Perceptual Examination (Tactile Finger Localization and Fingertip Number Writing Perception Tests and Tactile Form Recognition Test), the Modified Halstead-Wepman Aphasia Screening Test, the Wechsler Adult Intelligence Scale, and the Minnesota Multiphasic Personality Inventory. Each of these tests are described below:

HALSTEAD CATEGORY TEST

The Halstead Category test is a nonverbal test which measures a person's ability to formulate abstract principles based on feedback after each specific test item. The test consists of 208 stimuli which are shown on slides. Each test item suggests a number ranging from one to four. The patient is instructed to determine or guess a particular number based on their conceptualization of the abstract principle represented by the slide. After the patient decides on a particular response, they must depress one of four levers obtained on the instrument, which are numbered from one to four. When the subject has depressed the correct number, a door chime will ring, indicating that they have made the correct response. If, on the other hand, they depress one of the incorrect numbers, they will hear the sound of a buzzer. Based on this feedback, correct or incorrect, they must determine the underlying principle in each of seven different subtests. Traditionally the items for the Category test have been presented on a relatively small viewing screen located on a box. More recently, some psychologists have begun using the booklet version of this test, which is much easier to use, in that it is portable. The major difference, however, is that the examiner must indicate whether the patient's responses are "correct" or "incorrect" (Lezak, 1983).

The Category test requires anywhere from 45 minutes to as long as two hours to complete, depending on the characteristics of the person being administered the test. For example, nonbrain-injured individuals of average or above average intelligence generally take one hour to complete this test. Patients who are elderly, or who have sustained severe diffuse brain damage, may require two hours or longer. It is important that the patient be told at the beginning of each of the seven subtests that there is an underlying principle which they must deduce that may be the same or different from the principles found in the other subtests. The only exception to this is that when the patients are given the seventh subtest, they are told to answer the items the same as they had previously done during the six prior subtests (Whitworth, 1984).

The scoring for this test consists of the total number of errors made by the patient. Reitan (1955) recommended a cut-off score of 51 or more errors that he has, based on his empirical research, found to statistically discriminate between brain-damaged and neurologically intact groups of relatively young adult patients. More recently, however, Fromm-Auch and Yeudall (1983) reported an extremely wide range of normative scores (means) for normal subjects taking this test, ranging from a low of 22.8 to as high as 59.4 errors. This review suggests that using the cut-off score of 51 errors can incorrectly categorize a normal patient as "brain-damaged" as often as 60% of the time. The use of this cut-off score when testing visually impaired or normal elderly patients can result in an even higher percentage of "false positive" errors (e.g., erroneously categorized as brain-damaged).

TACTUAL PERFORMANCE TEST

This test consists of placing a blindfold on a patient and having the patient place 10 blocks of different shapes into a specially designed form board. The patient's task is to place each of the blocks into their respective shaped holes as quickly as possible. The patient begins with his or her preferred hand and uses only that hand until all of the blocks are completed. The patient begins the second trial with their nonpreferred hand until all the blocks are correctly placed. Typically, the patient's score improves between 30 and 40% on the second trial because of learning effects. On the third trial, the patient is instructed to use both hands. After the patient completes all three trials, the blindfold is removed, and the patient is instructed to draw a diagram which illustrates the placement of the various blocks as best as they can recall. Their drawing is then scored for memory (the number of blocks of various shapes they can recall) and localization (the exact number of blocks placed in their correct relative position). Scoring is further achieved by computing the total amount of time the patient requires to complete all three trials (Lezak, 1983).

Reitan (1955) recommended a cut-off of 15.7 minutes (942 seconds) to discriminate between the performance of brain-injured and normal patients. The patient's score on the localization scale is considered a highly sensitive indicator of brain injury, since it measures a variety of cognitive functions such as speed of cognitive processing, the patient's tactile and kinesthetic abilities, nonverbal learning, and incidental memory (the ability to recall information or events which the patient was not specifically instructed to learn or recall) (Boll, 1982). Studies have shown (Wheeler, Burke, and Reitan, 1963) that using the localization cut-off score of five, 85% of the brain-injured group could be differentiated from normal controls while psychiatric patients could be differentiated from brain-injured patients with 64% accuracy. Other investigators (Golden, 1978) have reported similar findings. Golden (1978; 1979) also found that by using a cut-off score of four or five correct on the memory scale, he was able to achieve similar findings. In addition to quantitative measurements, qualitative evaluation of the patient's performances between his preferred and nonpreferred hand, or with both hands, is helpful in determining whether the injury is predominantly in the left or right hemisphere or is present throughout the entire brain (diffuse brain damage). Poor performance on this test can also reflect anterior brain injuries (e.g., frontal lobes) based on comparison to other tests contained within the battery.

Poor performances on this test can be due to a variety of factors, such as anxiety (e.g., patients who are insecure or paranoid frequently become very upset and anxious when a blindfold is placed on them in a relatively small room in the presence of a virtual stranger with the door closed), peripheral motor problems (e.g., injury to one of the patient's hands, motor weakness secondary to cervical radiculopathy, loss of a finger or injury to the arm or wrist), peripheral neuropathy (e.g., injury or disease of the nerves within the arm or shoulder), sweaty hands (e.g., causing the patient to drop the blocks on the floor), physical pain or discomfort caused by bending or stretching or by remaining seated for 15 to 20 minutes, auditory or perceptual difficulties (e.g., the patient is unable to hear or understand the test instructions), or the presence of a severe headache.

SEASHORE RHYTHM TEST

The Seashore Rhythm Test requires the patient to determine if two pairs of musical rhythms are the same or different. The patient is presented with a tape recording and after a brief practice session is provided with three sets of 10 test items. After each pair of rhythms is presented, the patient must decide if they were the same or different by writing down S (same) or D (different) on a sheet of paper. After the patient is given all three sets which total 30 test items, the patient's score can be determined by comparing the patient's actual scores to the test manual (Lezak, 1983).

A score of six or more errors has been used as the "cut-off point" to discriminate between brain-injured and nonbrain-injured patients. Poor performance on this test has frequently been found in patients who sustain damage to the right temporal lobe, since the task itself places heavy emphasis on nonlinguistic auditory perception and concentration. Poor performance on this test can also reflect damage to other parts of the brain, such as subcortical or diffuse brain damage or injuries to the frontal lobes, but can also be seen in neurologically intact patients who are nervous, psychotic, or markedly depressed.

SPEECH SOUNDS PERCEPTION TEST

The Speech Sounds Perception Test consists of presenting a total of 60 nonsense words which are variants of the "ee" sound via a tape recorder. The subject is instructed to listen to each word and then underline one of four words (one of which is the correct word). The patient receives no feedback from the examiner after they have completed the first test item. The patient is given six sets of 10 words, which are numbered by the speaker on the tape. For example, the tape states, "The fifth word is freep." After the test instructions are presented to the patient and the patient is administered three sample test items, the test is started. Once the test has begun, the examiner cannot stop the tape or interrupt the patient until the entire 60 test items are completed (Whitworth, 1984).

Scoring consists of matching the patient's responses to the manual to determine the number of errors the patient made. Reitan (1955) recommended a cut-off point of eight or more errors be used to differentiate between brain-damaged patients and normal controls. This test tends to be sensitive to both diffuse brain damage and left hemisphere lesions. It is also sensitive to severe frontal lobe pathology, since the task requires a fairly high level of concentration and attention to a task which is actually quite boring. Poor performance on this test, however, can often be found in patients whose native language is not English or who have a pre-existing history of dyslexia or a developmental auditory perceptual disorder, impaired visual acuity (e.g., the patient has difficulty seeing the written words), psychosis (e.g., the patient attributes a bizarre connotation or meaning to the word which alters his or her response choice), or patients who are severely depressed or fatigued (e.g., they may begin to drift off during the test and may not attend to the test stimuli, since the task itself is boring and monotonous).

FINGER OSCILLATION (TAPPING) TEST

The Finger Tapping Test measures the patient's ability to depress a lever which is attached to a counter with his or her index finger. The patient initially uses his preferred hand and then the nonpreferred hand. The patient is given five consecutive trials of 10 seconds each for both hands. Scoring consists of the average number of taps for each hand. The average young adult typically is able to provide 55 taps with his or her preferred hand and approximately 50 with his or her nonpreferred hand. The nonpreferred hand is usually 5 to 10% slower than the preferred hand. Reitan (1955) recommends that a cut-off score of 50 or less be used for the preferred hand to discriminate between brain-damaged patients and normal controls. A patient's performance on this test can be used to determine the laterality (side of the brain) of brain damage. For example, if the patient's performance with his or her nonpreferred (left) hand is 25% less than his or her preferred (right) hand, and in the absence of any peripheral, psychological, or orthopedic problems, there is good reason to believe that the patient may have sustained a right hemispheric injury.

While poor performance on this test can reflect subcortical or diffuse brain damage (when a patient's performance in both hands is very slow), or unilateral (confined to one side of the brain) brain damage, patients who have been placed on high dosages of anticonvulsant medications (Dilantin or Phenobarbital) are likely to perform slowly. Patients who have a history of injuries to either hand or arm or who have developed radiculopathies involving C5 and C6 will often have difficulty on this task. In addition, patients who are extremely nervous or markedly depressed will often perform relatively poorly. Since this particular test is directly under the patient's voluntary motor control, it is prone to conscious manipulation, since a patient can control his or her rate of speed by visual observation of the response counter.

TRAIL MAKING TEST

The Trail Making Test consists of two parts, A and B. On Part A, the patient is instructed to connect 25 circles which are distributed on a sheet of white paper and are numbered from 1 through 25 in ascending order. On Part B, the patient's task is to connect circles containing either numbers or letters in alternate sequence, such as beginning with 1 and going to A, going to 2, then going to B, etc. On both tasks, the patient is instructed to work as quickly as possible and is provided with practice items prior to beginning the test. The scoring is based on the amount of time the patient takes to complete each task. Some neuropsychologists, however, also employ qualitative measures in evaluating a patient's performance on this test. For example, the number of errors the patient makes (after the patient has made an error, the instructor is required to gently provide the patient with a cue, such as "Which letter follows D?" or "You went from number 5 to number 6. You should have gone to a letter instead," the number of times the patient lifts the pencil off of the paper (the patient can be instructed to keep the pencil on the paper at all times), or the number of cues provided by the examiner for the patient to complete the task. This test involves visual scanning, cognitive flexibility, and visual-motor tracking (Lezak, 1983). A poor performance on Part A often reflects subcortical and occasionally right hemisphere brain injury. Poor performance on Part B typically reflects left hemisphere brain damage. Poor performance on both Parts A and B frequently reflects diffuse brain damage (Golden, 1979).

The use of "cut-off scores" for this particular test has been difficult, since it has resulted in an extremely high percentage of false positive errors in the classification of brain-damaged patients. For example, using cut-off scores of more than 50 seconds for Part A and 129 seconds for Part B resulted in misclassification of 92% of 70-year-old normal controls as brain-damaged (Davies,

1968). A patient's performance on the Trail Making test has been found to increase significantly with age. For example, the average score for normal control subjects, ranging from 20 to 39 years old, is 69 seconds, while the average score for normal control subjects, ranging from 70 to 79 years old, is 196 seconds (Davies 1968).

Many neuropsychologists may utilize the ratio of the patient's performance on Parts A and B to determine the laterality of the patient's brain injury. For example, if the patient requires three times or more longer to complete Part B than Part A, then there is a good likelihood that the patient's left hemisphere has been damaged or that there is more damage in the left hemisphere than the right hemisphere. Poor performances, however, can also reflect visual difficulties (e.g., the patient failed to bring their glasses to the examiner's office), high levels of anxiety, marked depression, histrionic behavior (e.g., the patient begins crying during the middle of the test, stating, "I can't do this. I can't do this. Oh, God, please help me. Oh, God, please help me."), physical injury or peripheral neurological impairment of the patient's arm or hand (e.g., fractured wrist, C5-6 radiculopathy, crush injury to patient's arm, etc.), or the patient's inability to recite the alphabet (e.g., this is typically found in patients whose English is very limited, or who have been raised in a different culture), a severe headache, or physical pain or discomfort which is likely to affect the patient's ability to concentrate. Since this test is under the patient's voluntary control, it is possible for the patient to manipulate their performance. For example, the patient can deliberately slow down their performance on this test to simulate the performance of patients with brain damage. While this can occur, it has been the author's experience that such individuals (malingerers) typically do not make loss of set errors, such as going from 1 to 2, rather than from 1 to A.

GRIP STRENGTH TEST

The Grip Strength test consists of measuring the grip strength of each hand with a dynamometer. The patient is typically given two or three trials with each hand. The average of all of the trials administered serves as the patient's score for each hand. It has been generally accepted that the strength of the patient's preferred hand (dominant hand) should generally be between 5% and 10% stronger than the patient's nonpreferred hand. Differences of greater than 10% are frequently interpreted as evidence of brain damage or dysfunction in the contralateral hemisphere of the significantly weaker hand (Whitworth, 1984). For example, if the patient's grip strength is 50 kilograms with their preferred hand, but only 35 kilograms with their nonpreferred hand, then there is a good likelihood that the patient has sustained an injury in the right hemisphere unless this can be explained by other factors, such as injury to the nonpreferred hand. While norms exist for both males and females on this test, the most preferred method of analysis appears to be the relative disproportion in performance between the dominant and nondominant hand.

Poor performances on this test can be due to a number of factors including an injury to one of the patient's arms, hands, or fingers, a radiculopathy involving either C5, C6, or C7, peripheral neuropathy (e.g., damage to the ulnar or radial nerve), pain or discomfort in one of the patient's shoulders, arms, hands, or fingers; or histrionic behavior (e.g., the patient loudly states, "I have no strength in this hand. Can't you see how weak it is?"), and marked depression (e.g., the patient fails to put forth the necessary effort because of the severity of their depression). This particular test easily lends itself to conscious manipulation. The author vividly recalls administering this test to an extremely muscular young man (whose biceps were nearly 19 inches) only to have him produce a grip strength of only 1 kilogram each hand. It should also be noted that the patient's face became quite distorted while taking this test, apparently to convince the examiner that he was putting forth his "best effort."

SENSORY-PERCEPTUAL EXAMINATION

The Sensory-Perceptual Examination contains a number of different tests to determine the patient's ability to perceive stimuli to each side of their body. In the tactile perception test, the patient's hands are placed on a table with the palms down. After the patient's eyes are closed, the examiner touches the back of each hand lightly in a random sequence. This same procedure is also done to both sides of the patient's face. The examiner must also adjust the amount of pressure placed on the back of the patient's face or hand, so that they are roughly similar. The examiner then touches either both hands or sides of the face simultaneously and asks the patient to indicate which side was touched. When a patient consistently reports that one side of the body has been touched when both sides of the body are touched, the patient has given evidence of a "suppression error" which suggests that the patient most likely has sustained a contralateral (the side of the brain directly opposite to the patient's hand) brain injury. Thus, the examiner can often localize the particular hemisphere which has been damaged, particularly when the injury involves one of the parietal lobes (Lezak, 1983).

A similar type of test has been developed to assess the patient's ability to perceive auditory stimuli. For example, the examiner stands directly behind the patient who has his or her eyes closed. The examiner makes a small noise by rubbing his fingers together approximately six inches away from the patient's left or right ear. Initially, this is done to determine whether the patient can perceive this auditory stimuli in each ear. Following this, the examiner simultaneously rubs the fingers of both hands together near both of the patient's ears. The patient is instructed to indicate which side the sound is coming from. If the patient consistently fails to identify the sound arriving at one of their ears (right or left), then it is likely that a suppression of the sound arriving in that ear has occurred as a result of an injury to the contralateral hemisphere. It should be noted, however, that this particular test requires considerable experience on the part of the examiner since it is necessary for the examiner to place his hands equally distant from the patient's ears and that the level of sound made by the examiner (by rubbing the fingers together) be approximately equal (Whitowrth, 1984).

The patient's visual fields are also examined. This consists of the examiner sitting approximately three feet in front of a sitting patient. The examiner then outstretches his or her arms while the patient's eyes are directly focused on the examiner's nose. The examiner then instructs the patient to indicate whether he or she notices anything moving at the periphery of their visual field while focusing their vision on the examiner's nose. The examiner tests the patient's upper, middle, and lower visual fields by making slight movements of his or her fingers and moving them closer to the patient until they are detected. This is done separately for both sides, which is then followed by simultaneous movements of the examiner's fingers of both hands in the patient's upper, middle, and lower visual fields. Scoring is determined by the number of "sensory suppressions" or "imperceptions" made by the patient during simultaneous stimulation. Some patients will show a reduction in their peripheral vision or be totally unable to recognize any movements in their left or right visual fields. This condition is known as homonymous hemianopsia. In other patients, there may be a partial loss in either the upper or lower visual field (upper or lower quadrantanopsia) (Golden, 1979).

Tactual Perceptual Examination

During these various tests described above, the patient should never be informed that they will receive bilateral rather than unilateral stimulation. It is also important that the examiner ensure that the patient cannot "cheat" in the sense that they do not fully close their eyes when their hands or face are touched. This problem can be prevented by placing a visual obstacle, such as a book or piece of cardboard, over the patient's hands so they cannot perceive which hands are being touched. Some examiners prefer, however, to use a device in which the patient's hand is inserted into a large open box which provides a greater visual obstacle.

TACTILE FINGER LOCALIZATION AND FINGERTIP NUMBER WRITING PERCEPTION TESTS

The patient is administered a test of finger agnosia which consists of touching the patient's fingers while their eyes are closed or a visual obstacle has been placed in front of them. The patient's fingers are touched in a random order four times each. The patient must report the name or number of each finger touched. Scoring consists of the number of errors out of a total of 20 trials. The examiner writes numbers (3, 4, 5, or 6) on the fingertips of the patient's hands with the patient's eyes closed or a visual obstacle present. The examiner then writes one of four numbers on one of the patient's fingertips in a random order so that each one of the patient's five fingers has been given each one of these numbers, making a total of 20. This is done for each hand. The patient must identify which number he perceives that the examiner has written. When a patient makes significantly more errors on one hand than the other, there is a good likelihood that the area of the brain contralateral to the hand in which the significantly greater number of errors occurred most likely has been damaged (Golden, 1979; Lezak, 1983).

TACTILE FORM RECOGNITION TEST

The patient's ability to discriminate between different coins (a penny, a nickel, and a dime) is then tested. Initially, the patient must identify by touch alone, while blindfolded or with their eyes closed, whether the coin placed in their left or right hand is a nickel, dime, or penny. Following this, the examiner places a coin of the same denomination, two nickels, two dimes or two pennies in both of the patient's hands, without indicating that both coins are the same. The examiner then asks the patient to identify what type of coin they are holding in each hand. Scoring is determined by the number of errors the patient makes with each hand. Immediately following this, the patient is administered the Tactile Form Recognition Test, which consists of a square, triangle, circle, and cross made out of plastic. The examiner places one of these shapes on the patient's hand after the patient has placed his or her hand through a large visual obstacle which prevents visual identification of the object. The patient's task is to identify the particular object by feeling the object and relying on kinesthetic information. The patient must then point with their free hand to the particular object which is located on the visual obstacle directly in front of them. This procedure is then repeated for the other hand and for both hands again. Scoring consists of the number of errors made with each hand and the amount of time required before the patient is able to provide the examiner with a response (Lezak, 1983).

Poor performance on these above tests can reflect a number of conditions including physical damage or injury, cervical radiculopathy, attention or concentration difficulties, high levels of anxiety or depression, paranoia (e.g., the patient becomes frightened when they are asked to close their eyes, or when an unfamiliar person is standing directly behind them in a small room with the door closed), chronic medical conditions (e.g., diabetes, poor circulation, etc.), hysteria (e.g., the patient begins sobbing during the examination and states, "I don't feel anything in my fingers or any part of my body. My body's completely numb."), or malingering (the patient reports feeling no sensation whatsoever on either side of their body in the absence of any type of neurological disease or injury). Since the scoring procedures depend heavily on the experience and expertise of the examiner, it is not uncommon for significant discrepancies to occur when a patient is given this examination by two different examiners (Whitworth, 1984).

APHASIA SCREENING TEST

The Aphasia Screening Test consists of a number of different tasks which serve as a brief screening device to evaluate whether the patient has any impairments in their language or nonlanguage skills. For example, the patient is asked to name specific objects (e.g., cross, triangle, square), read letters, numbers, and words ("the number 7," "seven"), perform arithmetic tasks (e.g., "85 - 27 =____," or "17 x 3 =____"), read and write sentences, pronounce words (e.g., "Massachusetts"), identify specific body parts (e.g., ear, elbow, hand), and determine left from right. Scoring is determined by the number of errors made by the patient and by assigning specific weights to the test items which the patient failed (Russell, Neuringer, and Goldstein, 1970).

Poor performances on this test can be due to a number of factors including high levels of anxiety, a prior history of dyslexia, limited education (e.g., the patient may have only completed the second or third grade), poor command of the English language, environmental deprivation (e.g., the patient may not know what a triangle is), borderline or retarded intellectual functioning, poor arithmetic skills, marked depression (e.g., the patient is so preoccupied with his wife leaving him or a particular problem that he cannot attend to the task), histrionic behavior (e.g., the patient dramatically states, "I can't draw any more. Ever since I had that accident, I can't use my right hand any more. I just can't use it. It just doesn't work any more."), psychotic thinking (e.g., when shown a cross and asked to identify it, the patient states, "It's a message from God telling me that I am Jesus Christ."), or malingering (e.g., "What is this test supposed to show anyway? I don't know what that is. Can't you see that I'm brain-injured? Why are you giving me these tests? They're just a waste of time. Can't you see from my records that I have a brain injury and can't do these things?").

WECHSLER ADULT INTELLIGENCE SCALE

The Wechsler-Bellevue Intelligence Scale was originally utilized when this battery was first developed. More recently, however, the Wechsler Adult Intelligence Scale (Revised) is typically used, although there may be a few psychologists who persist in using the older version of this test. The reader should refer to pages 109 - 112 for a detailed description of this test.

MINNESOTA MULTIPHASIC PERSONALITY INVENTORY

This test is described later in the section under Tests of Personality and Emotional Functioning. While this test is administered as being part of the Halstead-Reitan Neuropsychological Battery, it has been the author's experience that the profile obtained from this test typically plays only a minimal role in the interpretation of the patient's scores on other tests contained within this battery. This, of course, may vary considerably and depend on the clinical expertise and experience of the psychologist or neuropsychologist interpreting the profile.

Methods of Scoring and Interpretation

In addition to the scoring methods described above, Reitan and his associates have developed an "Impairment Index" consisting of the relative proportion of tests which fall above their respective cut-off points for brain damage. Index scores can range from zero (none of the patient's scores fell into the brain-damaged range) to 1.0 (all of the patient's scores fell into the brain-damaged range). Reitan (1955) recommended that a cut-off score of 0.5 for the Impairment Index be used to differentiate brain-damaged patients from normal controls. It should be noted, however, that in utilizing his particular cut-off score as the patient's Impairment Index, 10 to 30% of normal controls will be erroneously categorized as "brain-damaged" while 10 to 20% individuals with brain damage will be incorrectly classified as "normal."

Validity and Reliability

Reitan (1955) performed the first validation of Halstead's neuropsychological procedures. This study reported that the Halstead-Reitan Battery could discriminate between brain-damaged and nonbrain-damaged controls in a statistically reliable manner. A subsequent cross validation study indicated that the Halstead-Reitan Battery was capable of significantly distinguishing between brain-damaged patients and normal controls at a statistically reliable level but somewhat less than reported by Reitan (Vega and Parsons, 1967). More recent validation studies (e.g., Filskov and Goldstein, 1974) have further corroborated the validity of this test in being able to discriminate between brain-damaged patients and normal controls. Whitworth (1984) reported that while the Halstead-Reitan Battery contains methodological difficulties, his review of this test battery indicates that it possesses high validity and reliability which appears to be largely based on its use of quantitative behavioral measurements.

STRENGTHS AND LIMITATIONS

Strengths

Among the many strengths of the Halstead-Reitan Battery are its impressive validity and reliability in discriminating between brain-damaged and psychiatric patients and normal controls. The battery has been widely used in a variety of hospital, outpatient, neurological, and psychiatric settings. The time required to learn how to administer and score the battery is typically less than one week. The use of quantitative scores and measurements is ideal for research studies. The neuropsychological test data of a particular patient can be compared to other patients and can be evaluated by other psychologists. Finally, the battery has been effective in determining the extent or severity of brain damage, the lateralization and localization of brain injury, and has been used to determine the patient's prognosis for recovery and rehabilitation potential.

Limitations

The Halstead-Reitan Neuropsychological Battery has many short-comings. Despite the numerous studies and publications which have appeared over the past 40 years attesting to its clinical sensitivity, reliability, and validity, no "cookbook" has ever been developed to assist the clinician in making accurate interpretations of the test data (Whitworth, 1984). The validity and reliability of the battery in discriminating between brain-damaged patients and individuals who are attempting to simulate brain damage, has been found to be generally poor. For example, Heaton and his associates (Heaton, Smith, Lehman, and Vogt, 1978) sent test data from the Halstead-Reitan Neuropsychological Battery to 10 experienced neuropsychologists and asked them to distinguish whether the patient's scores were either produced by a malingerer or a brain-injured patient. They found that the diagnostic accuracy ranged from chance level (e.g., no better than simply guessing) to approximately 20% better than chance. Each of these neuropsychologists was reported as having expertise and considerable experience in the administration, scoring, and interpretation of this battery. Heaton and his associates, however, reported that when qualitative rather than quantitative methods were utilized to evaluate the patient's performance on the neuropsychological tests they were administered, the neuropsychologists had little difficulty discriminating the brain-damaged patients from malingerers.

This study presents some serious difficulties for psychologists who utilize the Halstead-Reitan Battery and have adopted Reitan's philosophy that test interpretations be based entirely on the neuropsychological test data and that the patient's clinical and background information not be reviewed prior to test interpretation (e.g., "blind analysis"). Since neuropsychological test performances can be significantly affected by a variety of factors including prior physical injury, such as loss of finger, surgery, fractures, etc., pain and discomfort, headaches, poor vision, impaired hearing, cultural and linguistic factors, medications, various medical diseases (such as hypothyroidism, diabetes, pernicious anemia, endocrine disorders, etc.), psychotic thinking, paranoia, fatigue, depression, anxiety, histrionic behavior, or motivational factors, such as malingering, it is essential that the possible influence of such factors be ruled out to formulate a probable relationship between the patient's cognitive impairments and brain injury, or lack thereof.

Many psychologists who have taken the workshops offered by Reitan and his associates receive little or no supervision after they have completed the week-long workshop. Thus, they are likely to continue making specific errors in the interpretation of neuropsychological test scores. In addition, many psychologists may administer the battery only once a month, which does not permit them the opportunity to develop sufficient experience or expertise.

It has been generally recognized that the Halstead-Reitan Battery cannot detect all possible neuropsychological impairments. As a consequence, many neuropsychologists have supplemented the battery with additional tests, particularly those which examine the patient's memory and problem solving skills. The primary disadvantage of adding additional tests is that it increases the time required for neuropsychological testing to as long as 10 hours. This can be exhausting for the patient when the testing must be completed in one day, particularly when the patient is in the early stages of recovery from a brain injury. The use of the battery for individuals who are more than 60 years old results in an unacceptable number of categorizations of "brain damage" when, in fact, no such brain damage may exist.

Recent studies (Fromm, Auch, and Yeudall, 1983) revealed a surprising variability in the scores obtained from normal controls on the various tests contained within this battery. As mentioned earlier, these investigators reported that their review of the validation studies that have been performed on this battery, revealed an extremely large variability in test norms. This suggests that many of the cut-off scores used in the past are likely to result in a very high proportion of normal controls being misclassified as brain-damaged. While it has generally been believed that the administration of the Halstead-Reitan Battery is standardized, the vast majority of neuropsychologists are likely to modify the battery by using some but not all of the tests and will supplement these tests with other neuropsychological tests that were never intended to be utilized in conjunction with the Halstead-Reitan Battery, which may create serious difficulties in test-retest reliability when a patient is tested by several different neuropsychologists.

The equipment necessary for the administration of the complete Halstead-Reitan Battery is fairly expensive and difficult to transport because of its size and bulkiness. As a consequence, the neuropsychologist may use only those specific tests which can be carried within a briefcase. This would involve excluding the Category, Tactual Performance, and some other perceptual tests. Thus, the neuropsychologist would then be forced to rely on only those tests which were able to be administered (Whitworth, 1984).

LURIA-NEBRASKA NEUROPSYCHOLOGICAL BATTERY

The Luria-Nebraska Neuropsychological Battery (LNNB) is a comprehensive neuropsychological test battery that integrates the neuropsychological assessment procedures of the late Professor Alexander Romanavich Luria and the American psychometric tradition through the work of its authors (Golden, Hammeke, and Purisch, 1980). This battery contains a total of 269 test items which comprise 11 clinical scales, which are as follows: motor functions, rhythm and pitch, tactile and kinesthetic functions, visual functions, receptive language, expressive language, reading, writing, arithmetic, memory, and intellectual processes. In addition to these scales, three scales have been developed (based on the 269 test items) which are sensitive to brain impairment and recovery following brain injury and are known as the pathognomonic, profile elevation, and impairment scales. The battery also contains two lateralization scales — left hemisphere scale and right hemisphere scale. In addition, eight scales have been developed to localize brain damage to the following regions of the brain: left frontal, left sensory-motor, left parietal-occipital, left temporal, right frontal, right sensory-motor, right parietal-occipital, and right temporal lobe.

The Luria-Nebraska Neuropsychological Battery attempts to integrate the qualitative tradition of Luria by listing 66 different qualitative indices which the test examiner is asked to score. Thus, the Luria-Nebraska combines quantitative and qualitative information about the patient's performance. Learning how to administer this battery generally requires anywhere from several days to two weeks. However, the biggest problem is its interpretation, since it is derived from the work of Luria, who was both a medical neurologist and psychologist. Unlike the Halstead-Reitan Neuropsychological Battery, interpretation of the Luria-Nebraska is very complex and requires considerable background and training in the neurosciences, behavioral neurology, and neuroanatomy, as well as considerable familiarity with Luria's model of brain-behavior relationships and higher cortical functions. The entire test battery can usually be administered in two and a half to three hours. The test material necessary to administer this battery consists of the test protocol sheet (which contains the test items and their scoring indices), a number of visual stimuli, a set of audiotaped rhythm and pitched stimuli, and items such as a rubber band, a key, a nickel, a protractor, a rubber eraser, and a large paper clip (Franzen, 1985). Unlike the Halstead-Reitan, the Luria-Nebraska is portable and can be administered at the patient's bedside. It contains two forms (I and II) and was designed to be administered to patients 14 years and older.

The test scores of a particular patient for each of the 11 clinical scales can be placed on a profile sheet by which the examiner can visually examine the elevations on each of the clinical scales in terms of normative data (mean and standard deviation). Based on the patient's age and educational achievements, the patient's critical level can be statistically determined such that scales which exceed this critical level are considered to be statistically significant. When three or more of the clinical scales exceed the critical level, there is a good likelihood that the patient has brain impairment. This is not the same as brain damage, since it indicates that while no structural damage to the brain may be present, the functioning of the brain is impaired.

Unlike the Halstead-Reitan Battery, interpretation of the Luria-Nebraska Neuropsychological Battery must include a careful clinical history and background history from the patient to rule out many of the extraneous factors which may cause a particular patient to fail one or more test items. When combined with a careful review of the patient's medical, neurological, educational, psychiatric, psychological, and vocational records, it can, in the hands of a competent and qualified clinical neuropsychologist, provide a wealth of useful clinical information about the patient's cognitive and behavioral impairments. However, many of the psychologists who utilize this battery have a less than adequate background in clinical neuropsychology, behavioral neurology, neuroanatomy, neuropathology, and in Luria's theoretical concepts of brain-behavior relationships (Purisch and Sbordone, 1986). Test interpretation involves determining which scores are above the critical level, the degree of scatter among the scale scores, the elevation of the localization scales in reference to the critical level, careful examination of the individual test items to determine if the patient's performance is consistent with a particular pattern of neuropsychological impairment and/or disorder, and careful review of the patient's observed qualitative behaviors during test administration (Franzen, 1985).

Validity

A variety of validity studies (Hammeke, Golden, and Purisch, 1978) have shown that the Luria-Nebraska Neuropsychological Battery could discriminate brain-damaged patients from normal controls with a very statistically reliable level of significance. Correlations between the Luria-Nebraska and the Halstead-Reitan Neuropsychological Batteries have ranged from 0.60 to 0.96 (Shelley and Goldstein, 1982). Golden, Hammeke, and Purisch (1980) reported that a discriminant function analysis of the Halstead-Reitan and Luria-Nebraska Neuropsychological Batteries indicated that both batteries had a hit rate of 85% accurate classification in discriminating between brain-injured patients and normal controls.

Reliability

The test-retest reliability of the Luria-Nebraska Neuropsychological Battery reported correlation coefficients ranging as low as 0.77 to as high as 0.96 in each of the clinical and auxiliary scales used in the battery. The inter-rater reliability of this battery is reported to be excellent in that an overall 95% agreement rate between examiners has been reported (Golden, Hammeke, and Purisch, 1980).

Strengths and Limitations

Among the many strengths of this battery is that it rests on Luria's theoretical basis for brain-behavior relationships based on his investigations of over 67,000 patients with various forms of brain disorders and damage. The battery is portable and can easily be transported to the patient's bedside, unlike the Halstead-Reitan Battery. It is relatively easy to administer and takes only two and a half to three hours to administer in comparison to six to eight hours for the Halstead-Reitan Battery. It is supported by numerous validity and reliability studies which attest to its effectiveness in discriminating between brain-damaged patients, psychiatric patients, and normal controls. It provides a basis for the examiner to localize brain impairment and determine its severity. It relies on both quantitative and qualitative information as well as a careful clinical and background history of the patient to rule out extraneous causes of poor performance (described earlier when discussing the Halstead-Reitan Neuropsychological Battery). It allows the clinician to visually examine the patient's performance on each of the clinical and auxiliary scales and compare a particular scale in relation to others. Finally, the administration and scoring of the Luria-Nebraska Battery can be learned in less than two weeks.

The major shortcoming of this test is that it requires that the psychologist who interprets this battery has had sufficient background and training in the neurosciences, neuroanatomy, clinical neuropsychology, behavioral neurology, and is thoroughly familiar with Luria's theory of brain organization and behavior. Test interpretation is typically difficult since it requires the integration of many test scores, qualitative information about the patient's behavior during testing, a comprehensive and detailed clinical history, review of the patient's medical records, and background information about the patient. Thus, if any of this information is missing, the psychologist will most likely be handicapped to some degree in his or her ability to interpret the collected neuropsychological test data. Like the Halstead-Reitan Battery, many neuropsychologists supplement this battery with a variety of other tests, such as the Wisconsin Card Sorting Test or the Wechsler Memory Scale, to carefully evaluate the integrity of specific functions. The battery becomes insensitive in terms of its ability to detect cognitive impairments as the level of intellectual functioning of the patient increases. For example, patients with IQ's in excess of 125 are likely to demonstrate few impairments on this battery since they may be able to utilize their high level of intellectual functioning to compensate or conceal their cognitive impairments in certain areas (Franzen, 1985; Purisch and Sbordone, 1986).

Flexible Neuropsychological Test Batteries

The majority of neuropsychologists use what has been described as "flexible" batteries to evaluate patients who have been referred for neuropsychological assessment. Sweet and Moberg (1990) recently examined the types of neuropsychological tests and batteries used by board certified (Diplomates of the American Board of Clinical Neuropsychology) and nonboard-certified neuropsychologists. They found that a flexible neuropsychological approach or battery was utilized approximately four times as often as standardized neuropsychological batteries, such as the Halstead-Reitan or Luria-Nebraska).

A flexible neuropsychological test battery refers to a collection of tests and procedures which are used by a neuropsychologist to assess a particular patient and/or type of neurological disorder. In other words, the tests and procedures utilized are chosen to fit a patient, situation, or type of neurological disorder or injury. For example, patients who sustain severe traumatic brain injuries within three months of their injury will typically demonstrate marked cognitive confusion and fatigue very quickly when they are exposed to cognitive activities, after which they may become extremely emotional and aggressive. If this patient is administered a standardized neuropsychological battery, such as the Halstead-Reitan, which generally takes between six and eight hours to administer, the patient's performance (unless the examiner breaks up the examination into a number of short segments which may take several weeks to complete) will most likely be extremely poor because of the confounding influence of such factors as emotional outbursts, fatigue, or poor motivation. In other words, the results of neuropsychological testing will only tell us that the patient has sustained a severe traumatic brain injury but will not give us much information about what kinds of changes or improvements the patient has made since the injury.

A neuropsychologist, using a flexible approach, accepts the fact that the patient is confused and will be expected to fatigue in 10 to 15 minutes after testing has begun. The neuropsychologist also recognizes that at this stage in the brain-injured patient's recovery, it is important to establish the patient's orientation to his or her surroundings, attention and concentration skills, and recent memory, since if these primary functions are impaired, then the patient's higher level conceptual, problem solving, and intellectual functions will also be impaired, since these latter functions typically are dependent on the relatively intactness of more primary cognitive functions. If the patient is in a residential head injury program, the neuropsychologist knows that much of the patient's time during the day is taken up by the various rehabilitation therapists (e.g., speech, physical, and occupational) who are working with the patient during the day. The neuropsychologist also realizes that during the evening the patient's family arrives and spends several hours with the patient. The neuropsychologist decides to evaluate the patient at 7:45 a.m., since he expects that the patient will have completed breakfast and be fairly alert and rested. He also knows that by 8 a.m., the patient will be taken to physical therapy. The neuropsychologist then travels to the patient room, carrying with him some tests that can be administered at the patient's bedside. The neuropsychologist arrives at the patient's bedside and after introducing himself and briefly explaining the purpose of his visit, begins to ask the patient his or her name, age, date of birth, day of the week, month, year, and what type of place he or she is in. He then asks the patient if he knows the name of his doctor or of any of his treating therapists. He asks the patient what he had for breakfast that morning and how long he has been in the hospital. Then he asks the patient to repeat some digits forward and backward and to count backwards from 20 to one and add by threes (e.g., 1, 4, 7, etc.) and perform serial seven subtraction from 100 (e.g., 100, 93, 86, 79, etc.). Then Parts A & B of the Trail Making test are administered. Following this, he reads a short story to the patient and immediately after the story has been presented asks the patient to recall as much information as possible. Following this, he asks the patient, "How are a chair and table alike?" and what the proverb, "Strike while the iron is hot" means. He then asks the patient to "raise his right hand over his head, close his eyes, and touch his nose with his right hand." Following this, he asks the patient if he can recall some of the questions that the examiner asked him and how much time he believes the examiner had spent with him. Finally, he asks the patient to indicate the kinds of problems he has been experiencing recently and what kinds of things he would most likely be involved in today. The neuropsychologist thanks the patient for his time and leaves at 8 a.m. just as the speech pathologist enters the room.

The neuropsychologist took approximately 15 minutes to examine the patient using a combination of formal and informal neuropsychological tests. These tests were designed to evaluate the patient's orientation to his or her surroundings, attention and concentration skills, cognitive flexibility, visual-motor tracking, recent memory, and abstract thinking. As the patient's condition improves over the next few months, the neuropsychologist increases the length of his test battery and begins using more formal tests of neuropsychological functioning and focuses on a wider variety of cognitive abilities (e.g., perception, problem solving, intellectual functioning, etc.).

The use of flexible batteries is particularly suitable for elderly patients, minorities, or patients with unique problems (e.g., visually impaired, deaf, unable to speak, motor paralysis) and for specific types of neurological disorders (e.g., dementia, stroke, hypoxic encephalopathy, traumatic brain injury, etc.). A flexible battery approach permits the neuropsychologist to select the most appropriate and/or sensitive neuropsychological tests to evaluate the patient's cognitive and behavioral functioning.

The major difficulty created by the use of flexible neuropsychological test batteries is that the number and type of tests may vary considerably across different neuropsychologists. For example, one neuropsychologist may employ six or seven different tests, while another neuropsychologist may administer as many as 25 different tests. While many neuropsychologists administer many of the same tests when re-evaluating the same patient, some of the tests that are administered may also be different. (Author's note: This may reflect changes in the patient's cognitive functioning, improved endurance, or a change in the patient's complaints.) While this can often create serious problems for attorneys, it is the conclusions that are drawn from different tests which are of crucial importance. In some cases, however, the neuropsychologist's choice of tests will be inadequate in the sense that they may fail to adequately assess a particular complaint or cognitive impairment. For example, if a neuropsychologist has been referred a 67-year-old man and is asked by the patient's physician to rule out the possibility Alzheimer's Disease and administers the Wechsler Adult Intelligence Scale, Bender-Gestalt test, and Minnesota Multiphasic Personality Inventory, his choice of tests are not adequate to rule out Alzheimer's disease, since none of these tests examine the patient's recent memory, which is one of the prominent symptoms of this disease. In most cases, however, it is not the specific tests given that are of crucial importance, but the competence, expertise, and experience of the neuropsychologist who evaluates the referred patient.

CASE EXAMPLE

An attorney referred his client, a 24-year-old male, to a clinical psychologist he had used in the past to evaluate some of his other clients. The psychologist had taken a workshop in the Halstead-Reitan Battery three years ago and had given this battery approximately 50 times since taking the course. He had never taken any courses or received any training in behavioral neurology, neuroanatomy, or had ever been supervised by a qualified neuropsychologist. Most of the patients he examined and treated in his practice had either marital problems, sexual problems, or adjustment difficulties related to their jobs. He had been involved in approximately 10 medicolegal cases involving pain and suffering following slip and fall accidents. Each of these referrals came from the plaintiff's attorney. He had only examined two patients who had been involved in motor vehicle accidents and had complained of recent memory, concentration, and sleep difficulties. The attorney asked the psychologist if he would be willing to see a client who had been involved in a motor vehicle accident one year ago in which he was briefly rendered unconscious. Since his accident the client had been having emotional difficulties and had been prescribed tranquilizers by his family physician. The psychologist agreed to examine the attorney's client.

The psychologist examined the plaintiff and took a brief history and concluded that the plaintiff had no significant history of psychiatric or emotional problems, learning difficulties, or health problems prior to his accident. He interviewed the plaintiff and found that the plaintiff only complained of neck pain and discomfort. He administered the Halstead-Reitan Neuropsychological Battery, Wechsler Adult Intelligence Scale, and the Minnesota Multiphasic Personality Inventory. He found that the plaintiff achieved a full-scale IQ of 120 and an impairment index of 0.3 on the Halstead-Reitan Battery (which placed the plaintiff within the normal range) and found that the plaintiff's profile on the

MMPI indicated that he was mildly depressed and anxious. The psychologist concluded that he felt that the plaintiff most likely did not sustain any serious brain injury and that whatever problems the plaintiff had following his injury had largely resolved.

The plaintiff's attorney reviewed the psychologist's report and informed his client's family that the psychologist's report indicated that, basically, his client's problems had largely resolved and recommended that his client accept an offer of $10,000 to settle the case. The patient's wife, however, indicated that she had noticed a dramatic change in her husband's personality since his injury. She felt that he was no longer the same person he had once been and was frequently impulsive and displayed poor judgement. She also mentioned that he no longer showed any interest in sex and did not seem to be aware of many of the problems and difficulties that he exhibited. She also stated that even though her husband had gone back to work several months ago, she had received numerous phone calls from his supervisor asking her, "What is wrong with Jim? He just doesn't seem like the same person he once was." She also mentioned that he no longer spent any time with his two children nor appeared to be interested in the activities he previously enjoyed, such as rebuilding cars, fishing, hunting, and skiing, prior to his accident. She also mentioned that her husband had become confused and had gotten lost while driving on several occasions when she was a passenger in the car. She noticed that he seemed unaware that he was lost and that his mood was inappropriately euphoric.

After hearing this, the attorney wondered if perhaps the psychologist had been wrong in his conclusions about his client. He phoned the psychologist, who assured him that his client was nothing more than mildly depressed and anxious and that the results of neuropsychological testing did not reveal any significant cognitive impairments. He also stated that his client had superior intellectual functioning and should have no difficulty returning to work. Approximately one week later, the attorney received a brochure in the mail which announced that a one-day symposium would be held on traumatic brain injuries and that the speakers would include a neurologist and neuropsychologist. The attorney decided to attend the seminar, and to his amazement learned that his client's symptoms fit the characteristics of a cerebral contusion and orbital frontal lobe injury. During a break, he asked the neurologist and neuropsychologist if they would be willing to see his client and possibly serve as an expert witness in this case. They both agreed. His client was seen by the neurologist, who performed a topographical brain mapping study, which revealed bilateral frontal lobe damage. The neuropsychologist interviewed the patient's family and administered a wide variety of neuropsychological tests which focused in on the patient's executive functions, problem solving skills, and ability to regulate his moods and emotions. These tests revealed evidence of moderately severe impairment consistent with a bilateral injury to the orbital frontal lobes, as well as right temporal lobe damage. The neuropsychologist also recommended that the applicant be referred to an outpatient rehabilitation program for approximately three months of cognitive rehabilitation. The cost of this outpatient program, however, was $17,000 per month. The attorney was able to get the brain-injury program to accept his client on a lien, since the other party had admitted liability. After three months, the plaintiff was re-evaluated by both the neurologist and neuropsychologist, who indicated that the plaintiff still had some mild cognitive and behavioral difficulties which would most likely resolve over the next two years. The case eventually settled for $850,000.

Specific Neuropsychological Tests

Neuropsychologists who administer flexible batteries typically select their neuropsychological tests from the tests which are available to them in specific areas of functioning. In most cases, the neuropsychologist is interested in administering neuropsychological tests which assess the following areas: attention-concentration, memory, motor skills, sensory-perceptual skills, abstract thinking-conceptual skills, problem solving, language, spatial-perceptual and constructional skills, intelligence, academic skills, and psychological adjustment/emotional functioning. The tests which are frequently administered by neuropsychologists to assess these areas will be presented below, and can be found on Table 7.

TABLE 7
NEUROPSYCHOLOGICAL TESTS OFTEN USED TO ASSESS THE BRAIN-INJURED PATIENT

NEUROPSYCHOLOGICAL FUNCTIONS TO BE EVALUATED	TESTS ADMINISTERED
	General
Multiple	Luria-Nebraska Neuropsychological Battery Halstead-Reitan Neuropsychological Battery
	Specific
Attention	Digit Span Test Paced Auditory Serial Learning Test Sbordone Attention Battery Symbol-Digit Modalities Test Trail Making (A & B) Test
Memory	Benton Visual Retention Test Rey Auditory Verbal Learning Test Rey-Osterrieth Complex Figure Test Selective Reminding Test Sbordone-Hall Memory Battery Wechsler Memory Scale
Motor	Finger Tapping Test Grip Strength Test Grooved Pegboard Test
Sensory-Perceptual	Benton Facial Recognition Test Benton Judgement of Line Orientation Test Hooper Visual Organization Test Reitan-Klove Sensory-Perceptual Exam Visual Form Discrimination Test

Continued next page

Abstract Thinking	Proverbs Test Similarities Test
Conceptual Thinking, Problem Solving	Category Test Raven Progressive Matrices Wisconsin Card Sorting Test
Language	Aphasia Screening Test Boston Diagnostic Aphasia Examination Controlled Oral Word Association Test Boston Naming Test Token Test
General Intellectual Level	Raven Progressive Matrices Wechsler Adult Intelligence Scale (Revised)
Spatial-Perceptual, Constructional Skills	Rey-Osterrieth Complex Figure Test Object Assembly Test Tactual Performance Test Block Design (WAIS)
Academic Skills	Wide Range Achievement Test

Adapted from *Trauma*, and reprinted with permission from Matthew Bender and Co., Inc.

Attention-Concentration Skills

DIGIT SPAN TEST

The Digit Span test consists of orally presenting random number sequences, such as 3-8-6-2-9, to the patient at a rate of approximately one per second. The patient must repeat the digits in the exact sequence in which they were presented. The examiner typically begins by having the subject repeat only two or three digits and will increase the number of digits in the sequence until the subject is unable to repeat the sequence correctly. Following this, the examiner instructs the patient to repeat the orally presented digits backwards, so that if the examiner states, "5-2-9," the patient should respond "9-2-5." The examiner continues to add a digit every time the patient correctly performs the task. Scoring consists of the total number of digits the patient could correctly recall in the exact order they were presented (forward digit span) and the total number of digits they could recall in reverse order (backward digit span). Typically, whenever the patient makes an error on a particular sequence, the examiner will provide the patient with a different sequence containing the same number of digits. If the patient then fails that sequence, the examiner will stop testing the patient or begin the digits backward task. Most patients are able to recall seven digits forward and five digits backward. A difference of three or more digits between the patient's forward and backward score is more commonly observed in brain-damaged patients than in neurologically intact individuals (Lezak, 1983).

Strengths and Limitations

Poor performance on this test in terms of only being able to recall a few digits backward and forward, such as five forward and three backward, can be due to a variety of factors such as anxiety, depression, being preoccupied with unrelated thoughts, or brain dysfunction. The Digit Span test is more sensitive to left hemisphere brain damage (Newcombe, 1969). It is fairly resistant to the aging process in that a patient's performance will show relatively little deterioration on this test prior to the age of 60 (Kramer and Jarvik, 1979).

The Digit Span test is primarily a test of attention and is not generally regarded as an accurate test of recent memory. For example, patients with Korsakoff's syndrome (a disorder characterized by profound impairments in recent memory) typically perform this test well but cannot recall what happened five minutes ago. It is one of the subtests of the Wechsler Adult Intelligence Scale and is frequently used by neurologists, psychiatrists, and psychologists to evaluate the patient's attention and immediate memory. It has been the author's experience that poor scores on this test are more frequently observed in patients who are anxious and/or depressed than in patients who have sustained brain damage. Thus, to determine whether a particular patient's score is indicative of emotional problems or a brain injury, the psychologist or neuropsychologist must carefully evaluate a number of factors, such as the patient's complaints, the patient's performances on a variety of neuropsychological tests, external stressors in the patient's environment, the patient's behavior during testing, and the patient's profile on tests of emotional functioning. For example, the author was recently asked to review a report written by a clinical psychologist who had evaluated a patient involved in a motor vehicle accident during which there was no loss of consciousness, amnesia, nor any type of head trauma sustained. The psychologist concluded that the patient had sustained a brain injury because she could only recall five digits forward and three digits backward on the Digit Span test. The author noted, however, that the psychologist indicated that the patient appeared quite anxious during testing and complained of being depressed, anxious, having sleep difficulties, and feeling irritable. The patient's profile on the Minnesota Multiphasic Personality Inventory revealed that she was severely depressed and markedly anxious and had been experiencing a number of distressing dreams, nightmares, and fears consistent with a post-traumatic stress disorder. Further review of the patient's performances on tests of cognitive functioning revealed that she performed generally poorly on cognitive tasks of attention and concentration but performed well on more complex cognitive tasks such as memory, abstract thinking, and problem solving. The author also reviewed the patient's deposition and noted that she began experiencing nightmares, flashbacks, and intrusive recollections of the accident and was able to provide a detailed, chronological history of the events that occurred immediately prior to, during, and following the accident. The author concluded that the patient most likely sustained a post-traumatic stress disorder which caused her to become anxious and depressed. Thus, there was little evidence to support the psychologist's contention that she had sustained a brain injury.

The Digit Span test has not been found to correlate highly with the 10 other subtests on the Wechsler Adult Intelligence Scale. Thus, it appears to measure a very specific skill or ability. It has been used for many years by a variety of health professionals to assess attention and brain damage. It has been shown to be sensitive to brain damage, particularly in the left hemisphere. The Digits Backward score appears more sensitive to brain injury and age than the Digits Forward score. One, however, should not conclude that a particular patient has brain damage because they have performed poorly on this test, since poor performance on this test can be due to a variety of factors other than brain damage (see the example above).

PACED AUDITORY SERIAL ADDITION TEST

This test assesses the patient's ability to add 60 pairs of numbers ranging from 1 to 9. Each number is added to the number immediately preceding it. For example, if the patient is read the numbers "3-5-7-2-6-5," the patient must add the first two numbers and then the second and third numbers and the third and fourth numbers, respectively. Thus, the patient should correctly say, "8-12-9-8-11." The pace at which the numbers are presented is also varied. They are presented at either 1.2, 1.6, 2.0, or 2.4 seconds apart by the use of a tape recorder. The slower rate (2.4 seconds) is presented first. The patient is then read 60 digits at this rate, which is then followed by a faster presentation of 2.0 seconds apart, whereupon the patient is presented with 60 digits at that rate of speed. On trials three and four, the speed increases to 1.6 seconds and 1.2 seconds, respectively. The test consists of a total of 240 responses made by the patient. Scoring consists of the percentage of correct responses for each presentation rate (Lezak, 1983). As one might expect, the rate of correct responses diminishes considerably as the rate of presentation increases. For example, Gronwall and Wrightson (1974) and Gronwall (1977) reported that the percentage of correct responses decreased from 82% at the slowest rate (2.4 seconds) to 51% at the fastest rate (1.2 seconds) in normal controls.

Strengths and Limitations

This test appears sensitive to relatively subtle attentional impairments in patients who have sustained cerebral concussions or mild head trauma. Gronwall and Wrightson (1981) studied the ability of this test to detect subtle deficits in information processing in patients who had sustained cerebral concussions. They reported that patients performed significantly below normal controls following their injury but noted that their scores on this test returned to normal within 30 to 60 days. Gronwall (1977) has advocated using this test to determine whether a patient is able to return to his pre-injury social and vocational activities following mild head trauma.

This test is not widely used despite its presumed sensitivity to subtle brain damage. Poor performance on this test can reflect mechanical difficulties (e.g., difficulties with the tape recorder or quality of sound), anxiety, depression, inattention due to recent stressors, (e.g., financial difficulties, divorce, extramarital affair of spouse), physical pain or discomfort, headache, medications, hysteria, or inadequate motivation. Poor performance should also be corroborated by significant others, behavioral observations, and other neuropsychological test data.

SBORDONE ATTENTION BATTERY

This test consists of nine subtests in which the patient is required to perform several serial arithmetic or alpha-numeric tasks. For example, the patient is asked to count backwards from 20 to 1, perform serial three addition (e.g., 1, 4, 7, 10, etc.), alternating serial three and five addition (e.g., 3, 8, 11, 16, 19, etc.), serial seven subtraction (e.g., 93, 86, 79, etc.), serial 13 subtraction (e.g., 87, 74, 61, etc.), alternating three and five subtraction (e.g., 97, 92, 89, 84, etc.), indicate which capital letters in the alphabet contain only straight lines (e.g., A, V, F, etc.), and which letters of the alphabet rhyme with the word "tree" (e.g., B, C, D, G, etc.). This battery contains tests which have been frequently used in the past to evaluate attention and concentration skills, such as counting backwards, serial three addition, serial seven subtraction, etc., and tests such as alternating three and five addition, serial 13 addition and alternating three and five subtraction which the author developed. This battery was designed to be administered to patients suspected of having subtle attentional problems secondary to brain damage. It appears quite sensitive to patients with frontal lobe damage and can often detect patients with right or left hemisphere injuries by the types of errors made during testing. For example, patients with frontal lobe injuries are likely to exhibit loss of set errors while performing alternating three and five addition (e.g., 3, 8, 11, 14, 17, etc.). Patients with left hemisphere injuries are likely to make more arithmetic errors, while patients with right hemispheric injuries generally do poorly when they are asked to indicate which letters in the alphabet contain only straight lines or indicate which letters of the alphabet rhyme with the word "tree," both of which the patient must visualize in their head. Patients with subcortical disorders secondary to exposure to industrial solvents or carbon monoxide typically take much longer than usual and make errors on the simplest tasks in the battery (e.g., counting backwards, reciting the alphabet, or performing serial three addition), yet perform better on more difficult tasks (e.g., alternating three and five addition and serial seven subtraction). Scoring consists of recording the actual responses made by the patient, the patient's behavior during testing (e.g., patient required frequent cues and prompts from the examiner to complete the task), and the amount of time required to complete each test.

Strengths and Limitations

While no formal norms exist for this test, it was primarily designed to provide a qualitative assessment of patients suspected of having brain injury since the examiner must carefully record the patient's responses and make careful observations of the patient's behavior during testing across all nine tests to determine whether any meaningful pattern emerges. The patient's performance on this test must then be carefully compared to the patient's performance on other neuropsychological tests and the patient's complaints, history, interviews with significant others, and academic and medical records. Poor performance on this test can reflect a number of factors such as anxiety, depression, medications, psychotic thinking, drugs, alcohol, motivation, a poor academic background, auditory processing difficulties, memory impairment, and frontal lobe pathology. Histrionic patients frequently perform poorly on this test. For example, when they are asked to perform serial three addition, they frequently state, "I can't add 1, 4, 7, 10. My mind's blank. I can't go on any further. I just lost it. You see, this happens all the time. My mind constantly goes blank after I'm doing something." Interpretation of this battery depends on the competence and experience of the particular psychologist or neuropsychologist administering the test.

SYMBOL-DIGIT MODALITIES TEST

The Symbol-Digit Modalities test consists of a modification of the Digit Symbol Subtest of the Wechsler Adult Intelligence Scale. The patient must code symbols according to a key that describes nine symbol-numeric relationships. The patient is given a pencil and is given 10 practice items which initially begin with a symbol. They are then told that in the box below the symbol and they must fill in the particular number which is associated with the symbol they have been shown. They are then asked to examine the key, whereupon they see the number "1" directly below the first symbol. They are instructed to place that number below the symbol so that it corresponds exactly to the key. After completing all 10 practice items, they are instructed to work as quickly as possible without skipping any items when the examiner says, "Start" and to immediately stop when the examiner says, "Stop." The test lasts for a total of 90 seconds. Scoring consists of the number of correct responses made within the allowed time. Unlike the Digit Symbol test, the patient's oral responses can also be substituted and scored in cases where the patient has sustained an injury to their dominant arm or hand.

Strengths and Limitations

Smith (1968; 1973) obtained norms for a total of 420 normal controls, ranging from ages 18 to 74. He also obtained norms for brain-damaged patients. He reported that by using a cut-off score of 1.5 standard deviations below the mean (average score) for a particular age group, he was able to identify 86% of the brain-damaged group and 92% of the normal controls. It should also be noted that the patient's level of educational achievement has been found to be highly correlated with both written and oral administrations of this test (Lezak, 1983). Thus, a well-educated individual, such as a teacher, attorney, engineer, or physician, may score within the normal range, even though these individuals may have sustained brain damage. This will be discussed further in the section on Scoring and Test Interpretation.

An individual's performance on this test decreases with advancing age. As a consequence, norms have been developed for different age groups (18-24, 25-34, 35-44, 45-54, 55-64, and 65-74). Since this test involves visual scanning, attention, and visual motor activities, it is sensitive to diffuse and subcortical brain damage. Poor performances on this test, however, can be due to a wide range of factors, including use of antipsychotic or anticonvulsant medications, anxiety, depression, pain and discomfort, severe headache, chronic medical problems (e.g., hypoglycemia), fatigue, psychotic thinking, or poor motivation. To rule out these factors, it is essential that the neuropsychologist obtain a careful clinical and background history, review the patient's medical and psychiatric records, compare the patient's score on this test to his or her performance on other neuropsychological tests, observe the patient during testing, and interview significant others.

TRAIL MAKING TEST

The Trail Making test consists of two parts and is one of the tests used in the Halstead-Reitan Battery. The reader should refer to this test, which is found on pages 118 - 119. This test is widely used and serves as a measure of attention, visual scanning, and visual-motor tracking. It contains two parts which have been previously described. Part B is more difficult than Part A, since it requires the patient to shift sets (e.g., go from a number to a letter), rather than only connecting numbers. Whenever a patient makes an error, the examiner typically points out the error and may provide the patient with a cue or prompt. Scoring of this test is typically in terms of the number of seconds required to complete both parts. It is important to note that if the patient makes an error and is corrected or is given a cue or prompt, the timing of the patient must not stop. This test has been shown to be sensitive to brain damage and cognitive deterioration associated with advancing age.

Memory

BENTON VISUAL RETENTION TEST

The Benton Visual Retention test is designed to assess the patient's visual memory. This test consists of presenting 10 cards containing up to three geometric figures. The subject's task is to draw the geometric figures on a separate sheet of paper after the card containing the geometric figures has been removed. There are four different methods of administering this test (A, B, C, D). During Administration A, each of the cards are presented to the patient for 10 seconds after the patient has been informed that he or she will be asked to draw the contents of the card from memory on a sheet of paper which is the exact size (5 x 8 inches) of the card after the card has been removed by the examiner. In Administration B, the patient is only permitted five seconds to memorize each card before trying to draw it from memory. Administration C requires the patient to copy the contents of the card on a sheet of paper. After the patient has completed his or her drawing, the card and the drawing are removed. In Administration D, the patient is shown each card for 10 seconds; however, the patient must wait 15 seconds before beginning the drawing after the card has been removed (Benton, 1974).

Scoring consists of either the total number of drawings which are correct (out of a total of 10), or calculating the number of errors based on a scoring system developed by Benton. The latter scoring system permits a more qualitative analysis of the patient's errors and can provide richer information about the type of injury and its location in the brain. According to Benton's scoring system, a patient can make omission, distortion, perseveration, rotational, misplacement, or size errors.

There are two forms of the Benton Visual Retention test (Forms A and B) which are roughly equivalent. The test manual provides norms for patients ranging in age from 15 to 64 years old. The manual also contains expected correct and error scores according to the patient's estimated premorbid intellectual functioning (IQ). Thus, the scores obtained by a particular patient can be compared to his or her expected score based on their age and premorbid IQ. The interpretation of the patient's performance on this test is fairly straightforward and consists of comparing the patient's expected score (based on their age and premorbid IQ) and their actual score. When the patient's score is three points below the expected correct score, Benton argued that this suggests the presence of impairment. When the difference is four or more points below the expected score, there is a strong indication of impairment.

Strengths and Limitations

This test has been highly reliable over repeated administrations (Lezak, 1983). It also discriminates between brain-injured patients and normal controls with 60 to 70% accuracy and correctly categorizes normal controls with 80 to 90% accuracy (Golden, 1979). Its ability to discriminate between brain-damaged and psychiatric patients is less impressive, and qualitative analysis of the patient's errors typically reveal a pattern of errors (e.g., bizarre responses) that are idiosyncratic to psychotic or schizophrenic patients, but are rarely exhibited by brain-damaged patients. Benton (1974), in a series of studies (e.g., Benton and Spreen, 1961), carefully compared the errors made by normal controls who were instructed to simulate brain damage with the errors of brain-damaged patients. The malingerers made a much greater percentage of distortion errors and very few errors of omission and perseveration. Thus, utilizing a qualitative analysis of the errors made by both groups, Benton was able to easily distinguish malingerers from brain-damaged patients. Research studies have also demonstrated that brain-damaged patients tend to omit a peripheral geometric figure and make a high percentage of rotational and size errors unlike normal controls or malingerers.

An intact performance on this test does not rule out the possibility of brain damage, since the research studies cited above indicate that this test failed to identify between 30 and 40% of the brain-damaged patients. Poor performances, on the other hand, can be caused by a variety of factors including anxiety, psychotic behavior, severe pain and discomfort, headaches, fatigue, visual difficulties, constructional difficulties (e.g., the patient has never been able to draw well), inadequate motivation, hysteria, and malingering. As a note of caution, the diagnosis of brain damage should not be made on the basis of poor performance on this test unless it is supported by the patient's clinical and medical history, other neuropsychological test findings, corroboration by significant others, and the behavioral observations of the examiner.

REY AUDITORY VERBAL LEARNING TEST

This test consists of a list of 15 words (e.g., drum, curtain, bell, etc.) which are orally presented to the patient. The patient is instructed to remember as many of these words as possible. The examiner then reads the list of words at a rate of one per second. After the entire list of words is presented, the patient must recall them in any order he or she can. The examiner must write down the words the patient recalls in the order the patient recalls them as well as note whether the patient's responses are incorrect or repeated (i.e., given more than once during each trial). After the patient cannot recall any more words, the list of words is presented again to the patient. Once again the patient is asked to recall as many words as possible even though the patient may have said some of these words on the previous trial. The list is presented a total of five times. After the patient has completed the fifth trial, the examiner presents the patient with a list of 15 new words. Once again the patient is instructed to remember as many words as possible. After the patient is able to recall as many new words as possible (e.g., the second list is presented only one), the examiner instructs the patient to recall as many words as possible from the original list. Some neuropsychologists will also ask the patient to recall as many words as possible after a delay of 30 minutes. In addition, the patient is either presented with a short story or a list of 45 words which contain the 15 words from the first list. The patient is instructed to identify these words as the story is being slowly read to them or as the list of 45 words is orally presented to them. This serves as a test of recognition memory to determine if the patient's memory impairment is due to faulty encoding (e.g., processing difficulties at the time the information was initially presented or retrieved from memory) or storage loss (e.g., information was lost due to faulty storage).

Scoring consists of the total number of words the patient is able to recall during each of the five learning trials, the number of words recalled on the first trial of the second list, and the number of words from the first list after the interference trial (e.g., presentation of the second list of words). The patient's scores can be compared to norms for manual laborers, professionals, students, elderly laborers, and elderly professionals as well as to brain-damaged patients (Lezak, 1983).

Strengths and Limitations

Qualitative analysis of the patient's learning curve over five consecutive trials, the type and number of errors made, the patient's performance on the first trial of both lists, the relative loss of words recalled after the interference trial, and a comparison of the patient's performance on the fifth trial of the first list with the number of words recalled during the recognition test can provide the neuropsychologist with a greater understanding of the patient's performance so as to determine if the patient has sustained a brain injury. For example, brain-damaged patients are likely to show a flat learning curve over the first five consecutive learning trials, and have difficulty recalling the first list of words after being presented with the second list (interference trial). Most normal controls are usually able to recall 13 to 14 words by the end of five consecutive learning trials, while brain-damaged patients may only learn six to seven words. Normal controls are usually able to recall 11 to 12 words after the interference trial, while brain-damaged patients may only be able to recall three to four words and demonstrate a loss of approximately 40 to 50% of the originally learned words, while normal controls will demonstrate a loss of only 10 to 20%.

Poor performance on this test can also reflect such factors as severe anxiety, marked depression, psychotic thinking, severe pain or headache, inattention due to excessive ruminative mental activity (e.g., patient is obsessing about his wife's extramarital affairs or his supervisor), medications (e.g., high doses of pain or antipsychotic medication), alcoholic intoxication (e.g., patient has returned from lunch with a distinct odor of alcohol on his breath and appears inebriated), hysteria (e.g., patient states, "Oh God! I can't remember these words. My memory is gone. I'll never be normal again. Why, doctor, do I have this problem with my memory?"), and malingering (e.g., "I just can't remember any of those words. What is this test supposed to show anyway?"). Poor performance on this test should be corroborated with the clinical history, the patient's medical records, interviews with significant others, other neuropsychological test data, and observations of the patient's behavior.

REY-OSTERRIETH COMPLEX FIGURE TEST

This test consists of instructing the patient to copy a complex geometric figure on a sheet of white paper. Although it has been recommended that the patient be given five or six colored pencils when copying this figure, there has been a growing trend to simply give the patient a pencil to copy the figure. The amount of time taken to initially copy the figure is recorded. The standard procedure is to have the patient draw the figure again from memory after a delay of three minutes and again at 30 minutes or one hour. Some neuropsychologists who have extensive experience with this test may eliminate the necessity of having the patient draw this figure from memory three minutes after the figure and the patient's drawing are removed, and may only have the patient draw the figure from memory following a 30-minute to one-hour delay.

A scoring system was developed by Taylor (1969), which was adapted from the original work of Osterrieth (1944). This system allows the examiner to score the patient's copy and drawing from memory of the figure using 18 separate criterion units contained within the figure which can be scored separately. In addition, the examiner can provide partial credit (1/2 to 2 points) for each of the 18 units, depending on whether the unit was copied or drawn correctly, distorted, or absent depending on its particular placement. Thus, it is possible to score the patient's copy and memory of this figure. A score of 36 would constitute a perfect score during copying, while a score of 32 would place the subject at the 50th percentile with respect to normal controls. A score of 22 on the memory trial would place the subject at the 50th percentile in comparison to normal controls.

Over the past 10 years, several neuropsychologists have attempted to develop a qualitative method of evaluating the patient's performance on this test. For example, Binder (1981) found that patients with left hemisphere damage tend to break up the design into smaller units, while patients with right hemisphere damage are likely to omit many of the elements contained within the design. Lezak (1983) reported that, overall, patients with left-sided brain damage tend to simplify their copies than do patients with right hemisphere brain damage. In addition, patients with right hemisphere damage tend to produce much less accurate copies than do patients with left hemisphere damage following a stroke.

Poor performance on this test can reflect other factors besides brain damage. For example, patients who dislike drawing tasks, are very depressed, anxious, psychotic, have motor difficulties secondary to orthopedic problems, physical pain, hysteria, or are insufficiently motivated are likely to do poorly on this test. One should not conclude that a patient has brain damage based on a poor performance on this test unless it is supported by other test data and is consistent with the patient's medical records, observations of significant others, and the behavioral observations of the examiner.

SELECTIVE REMINDING TEST

The Selective Reminding test consists of the examiner presenting the patient with a list of words. After the list has been presented, the patient is instructed to recall as many words as possible from the list. Words which are not recalled by the patient are repeated by the examiner on the next trial. The trial is continued until the patient is able to repeat the entire list. Normal controls are typically able to recall a list of 10 words, such as animals, by the third trial on this test (Buschke and Fuld, 1974).

Strengths and Limitations

This test has been used with patients who have sustained traumatic brain injuries and has been found to identify patients who have sustained significant brain injuries, since these patients were unable to improve their performance over 12 consecutive trials (Levin, Grossman, Rose, and Teasdale, 1979). Poor performance can also reflect attentional difficulties, hearing loss, anxiety, depression, physical pain and discomfort, anticonvulsive or antipsychotic medications, headaches, chronic medical conditions (e.g., endocrine or metabolic disorders), low premorbid intellectual functioning, alcohol use, hysteria, malingering, or poor motivation.

SBORDONE-HALL MEMORY BATTERY

The Sbordone-Hall Memory Battery is administered, scored, and analyzed by a computer program written by its developers. Testing consists of placing the patient in front of a TV monitor located directly above a computer keyboard. The patient is told to follow the instructions that are displayed on the TV monitor. They are also instructed that they can enter their responses on the computer keyboard below. The program initially asks the patient for his or her name, age, and sex. It then presents an overview of the test and proceeds to administer a variety of different tests to evaluate the patient's memory. Specifically, it examines the patient's ability to learn information over trials and determines the patient's ability to retain this information under conditions of interference and ranges from several seconds to 20 to 30 minutes. It also assesses the patient's recognition memory for visual and verbal memory, as well as the patient's incidental memory. This test usually requires 45 to 60 minutes for administration.

Strengths and Limitations

The specific test stimuli used in his battery are either generated by the computer program or are selected by the computer program at random from a pool of test stimuli. The test provides easy redundant instructions and personalized interaction with each patient. Positive reinforcement is given while the patient is taking the test to keep the patient's motivation at acceptable levels. The program also provides the patient with brief rest periods to counteract the effects of fatigue and also provides automatic response cuing. The program produces a short (2-page) print-out which includes statistical comparisons of the patient's scores with norms from normal controls, psychiatric, and brain-injured patients. A 12-page printout of the patient's performance on each test can also be obtained. In addition, the test battery includes an automatic discriminant function analysis which compares a total of 60 of the patient's scores with those of normal controls and psychiatric patients to determine the likelihood that the patient's overall performance is more consistent with neuropsychologically intact controls or patients who have sustained some form of brain insult or injury. The program also performs an analysis of covariance, that corrects the patient's score according to the patient's age. Research on the reliability and validity of this battery by the author and his associates has shown that the test battery possesses adequate test-retest reliability and is capable of categorizing patients as either organic (brain-damaged) or nonorganic (normal or psychiatric) with an accuracy of over 90%.

This test battery requires the use of an Apple II or IBM computer system in addition to the computer software. If there is another person in the room while this test is being administered, the patient's attention may wander and result in their failure to register the test stimuli on the TV screen. Because the test requires nearly one hour to administer, patients who had been unable to sleep the night prior to their appointment for neuropsychological assessment tend to drift off or fall asleep while the test is in progress. To rule out this possibility, the patient's scores on each subtest should be carefully inspected by a neuropsychologist who has sufficient experience and expertise with this test battery. In addition, the test scores should be generally consistent with the observations of significant others, medical records, and history of the injury.

WECHSLER MEMORY SCALE

This test assesses the patient's memory for verbal and nonverbal stimuli, meaningful and abstract material under conditions of both immediate and delayed recall. The original test, developed by Wechsler in 1945, produced an overall memory quotient score which was criticized since it failed to provide any differentiation of different memory functions. A revised version of this test was published in 1987 and contained the following subtests: Questions on information and orientation to one's surroundings, Mental Control (e.g., repeat the alphabet and count by fours), Configural Memory (e.g., identify designs which had previously been shown), Logical Memory I (e.g., recall an orally presented story immediately after it is presented and after a delay of 30 minutes), Visual Paired Associates I (e.g., learn the color associated with six abstract line drawings), Verbal Paired Associates I (e.g., learn eight pairs of words), Visual Reproduction I (e.g., recall from memory simple geometric designs which had been shown to the patient for 10 seconds and removed), Digit Span (e.g., repeat digits forward and backward), Visual Memory Span (e.g., touch a series of colored squares in a specific order), Logical Memory II (e.g., recall a story which had been read 30 minutes earlier), Verbal Paired Associates II (e.g., recall as many as eight paired associates after a delay of 20 to 30 minutes), and Visual Reproduction II (The delayed recall trial of Visual Reproduction I test).

Strengths and Limitations

This test has been designed to evaluate the memory functioning of patients ranging in age from 16 through 74. Scoring consists of obtaining the total raw scores for each subtest. Following this, the examiner must give weights to the raw scores so that their statistical significance can be evaluated. Poor scores on this test are frequently made by patients whose native language is not English or who have generally low premorbid levels of intellectual functioning. The test does not measure the patient's ability to learn specific skills, nor does it measure the patient's olfactory and tactile memory. Additionally, it does not evaluate the patient's remote memory. For this test to be used in a meaningful way, it should be interpreted along with other neuropsychological tests, as well as compared to the history and background information obtained from the patient and significant others, and the patient's academic and medical records. Poor performances on this test can also reflect such factors as anxiety, depression, psychotic thinking, pain and discomfort, severe headache, fatigue, medications, hysteria, and inadequate motivation.

Motor Tests

FINGER TAPPING TEST

The Finger Tapping test is frequently used to evaluate a patient's motor speed. It is one of the tests contained within the Halstead-Reitan Battery and has been previously described. The reader should refer to page 118 for a detailed description of this test.

GRIP STRENGTH TEST

The Grip Strength test is designed to assess the strength of the patient's grip in each hand. It is one of the tests contained within the Halstead-Reitan Battery. The reader should refer to page 119 for a detailed description of this test.

GROOVED PEGBOARD TEST

The Grooved Pegboard test permits an assessment of the patient's fine motor coordination and manual dexterity. It consists of a small board that contains a total of 25 slotted holes in a 5 x 5 configuration. The pegs are inserted into grooved slots located in an adjacent metal dish. The patient is instructed to place the pegs into each of the slotted holes as quickly as possible, using only one hand. The patient typically begins with the preferred hand. After the patient has completed the task of filling each of the holes, the pegs are removed and placed back into the metal dish. The patient is then instructed to use his or her nonpreferred hand to perform the task and to work as quickly as possible. Patients are usually permitted several practice trials with each hand to familiarize them with the task. Scoring is determined by the amount of time the patient requires to complete the task with each hand (Lezak, 1983).

Strengths and Limitations

Because of the manual dexterity required for the patient to fit the pegs into the slotted holes, patients who sustain damage to the brain stem, cerebellum, or the cortical spinal motor pathways are likely to have considerable difficulty on this test. Norms have been developed according to the patient's age and educational achievement (e.g., less than Grade 12 or Grade 12 and above) for the preferred and nonpreferred hands (Fromm-Auch and Yeudall, 1983). Poor performance on this test may reflect visual difficulties, orthopedic injury, peripheral neurological impairment (e.g., C6-7 radiculopathy), anxiety (e.g., patient's hands become sweaty causing them to drop the metal pegs), depression (e.g., patient appears preoccupied with negative thoughts about self or future), physical pain or discomfort, hysterical behavior, malingering, medications, fatigue, or inadequate motivation. Poor performance should not be interpreted as evidence of brain damage unless these factors can be ruled out, and the test data are generally supported by the patient's medical records, observations of the patient's behavior and significant others, and other neuropsychological test data.

Sensory-Perceptual

BENTON FACIAL RECOGNITION TEST

This test was designed to assess the individual's ability to compare photographs of faces. The patient is shown a picture of a photograph of a person's face. Directly below this photograph are six photographs, each of which contains a photograph of someone's face. In the first section of the test, the patient is asked to identify the photograph from the six photographs located directly below. During the second section of the task, the patient is shown a photograph which contains only three-quarters of a person's face. The patient is instructed to examine the six photographs below and pick out three photographs of this individual. In the third section of the test, the patient must match this person's identity to photographs which have been taken under darkened lighting conditions. This test appears sensitive to subtle perceptual visual discrimination impairments. Since the patient need only point to the photographs, this test is only minimally dependent on the patient's linguistic skills and can be given to patients whose knowledge of English is limited. This test also places little emphasis on the patient's visual memory since it does not require that the patient memorize or learn the patient's face, since a photograph of the patient's face is always available for matching purposes (Benton, Hamsher, Varney, and Spreen, 1983).

Strengths and Limitations

The test usually takes approximately 15 minutes to administer, depending on whether the patient is cognitively intact or severely brain-injured. The examiner can choose to give the patient the short form, which contains only 13 items, or the long form, which contains 22 items. Correlation studies between scores obtained on the short and long forms have ranged between .88 and .94, which suggests that the use of the short form may be desirable to save valuable time. Normative data is provided with the test packet to permit the examiner to compare the person's scores to normal controls and brain-damaged patients (Lezak, 1983).

This test tends to be particularly sensitive to patients who have sustained posterior right hemisphere damage, but is generally insensitive to left hemisphere and frontal lobe damage. Poor performance on this test can also be produced by poor vision, high levels of anxiety, marked depression, low intellectual functioning, physical pain and discomfort, headache, concentration difficulties, psychotic thinking, histrionic behavior, poor motivation, and deliberate attempts to perform poorly, such as malingering. To rule out the likelihood of these factors, it is essential that the patient's score on this test be compared to other neuropsychological tests and that the examiner takes a careful background and clinical history, interviews significant others (e.g., to see if the patient has had any prior difficulty recognizing faces), as well as review the patient's medical records. In addition, the patient's behavior during testing should be carefully observed to determine if the patient's behavior is consistent with brain injury.

BENTON JUDGEMENT OF LINE ORIENTATION TEST

This test requires the patient to match a pair of angled lines which are shown on a card to 11 numbered lines, below which form a semicircle. The patient is required to either point to or name the numbers associated with the 11 lines below. The test consists of four practice items and 30 test items. The test has two forms (H and V), which contain exactly the same test items arranged in a different order (Benton, Hamsher, Varney, and Spreen, 1983).

Strengths and Limitations

This test tends to be sensitive to posterior right hemisphere damage, particularly in the right parietal lobe (Lezak, 1983). Scoring is performed by adding the number of correct test items the patient makes out of a possible 30. The test manual contains normative data to allow the examiner to compare the patient's score to determine its severity and clinical significance. Poor performance on this test may reflect visual acuity difficulties, test anxiety, severe depression, physical pain or discomfort, attentional difficulties, headache, medications (e.g., blurred vision as a side effect of an antipsychotic medication), fatigue, hysteria, psychotic thinking, malingering, and inadequate motivation.

HOOPER VISUAL ORGANIZATION TEST

This test consists of showing patients 30 pictures of objects that have been cut up and placed in different positions. The subject's task is to visually examine each picture and decide what it could possibly be if it were assembled. The patient must write down the name of the particular object, such as fish, ball, key, etc. The test items are generally arranged in terms of increasing difficulty.

Strengths and Limitations

This test tends to be sensitive to posterior brain damage, however, patients with frontal lobe damage will often test as impaired on specific items. The author has found that patients who sustain severe hypoxic or anoxic encephalopathies tend to do poorest on this test, in that their total score will frequently be less than 10 out of a possible 30, indicating severe impairment. Patients with frontal lobe pathology, particularly when it is more prominent in the right frontal lobe, will frequently exhibit problems in visual organization because of their tendency to examine only one object, rather than visually organizing the different objects into a single concept. For example, such patients are likely to have difficulty on Item 28, which forms a key. Patients with frontal lobe damage will typically look at only one of the three pieces, which resembles an Exacto knife, and identify the entire object as a "knife."

Research studies have shown that repeated administrations of this test did not result in any appreciable change in the patient's scores (Lezak, 1983), which indicates that its test-retest reliability is high. Poor performance on this test can reflect a variety of factors such as poor visual acuity, low intellectual functioning, high levels of anxiety, severe depression, psychotic thinking, brain damage, histrionic behavior, and malingering. The author has found that a qualitative analysis of the patient's errors can be quite valuable in determining whether the patient's responses are those expected from a brain-damaged patient or reflect psychotic thinking, malingering, or histrionic behavior. In addition, the author strongly recommends that the patient's score on this test be compared to the patient's medical history, complaints, background history, interviews with significant others, behavioral observations of the examiner, neurodiagnostic testing (e.g., visual evoked response study), and other neuropsychological tests to determine its validity.

REITAN-KLOVE SENSORY-PERCEPTUAL EXAMINATION

This test assesses the patient's sensory and perceptual functioning across a variety of modalities. It is one of the tests contained within the Halstead-Reitan Neuropsychological Battery.

VISUAL FORM DISCRIMINATION TEST

The Visual Form Discrimination test consists of a series of three geometric figures which the patient must match to one of four sets of designs. One of the designs is an exact replica, while the others may vary either subtly (e.g., one of the peripheral figures is too high or low) or is grossly distorted (e.g., one of the major figures is rotated 180°). The patient's performance on each of the 16 test items can be easily scored, since the subject's choices are numbered 1 to 4 (Benton, Hamsher, Varney, and Spreen, 1983).

Strengths and Limitations

This test has been found to be sensitive to posterior brain damage, particularly in the left parietal lobe. The test can be administered to patients who are unable to speak English, since it only requires that they point to one of four sets of figures on an 8-1/2 x 11" sheet of cardboard. The test also places little emphasis on the patient's visual memory since the patient need not recall the three geometric figures. They are only required to match it with one of the four alternatives. Most patients typically complete this test in 15 to 20 minutes, although patients with severe diffuse brain damage may take as long as 30 minutes. The test manual contains normative data to permit comparison of the patient's score to normal controls and brain-damaged patients. Poor performance on this test may be due to any number of factors, including brain damage, visual acuity difficulties, high levels of anxiety, visual field defects (e.g., the patient may not recognize stimuli located in the left or right visual field due to brain damage in the right or left parietal-occipital cortex, respectively), severe depression, histrionic behavior, psychotic thinking, or malingering. Poor performance on this test, in the absence of corroborating evidence from other neuropsychological test data, the neurological examination, neurodiagnostic tests (e.g., CT scan, EEG, etc.), the patient's history, complaints, behavioral observations, and interviews with significant others, should not be interpreted as an indication of brain damage.

Abstract Thinking

PROVERBS TEST

Patients who sustain brain injury, particularly when it is either diffuse or predominantly in the frontal lobes, typically have difficulty interpreting proverbs. For example, when they are asked to indicate what the proverb, "Strike while the iron is hot," means, they will say, "When the iron is hot, you strike it." Thus, the patient has failed to grasp the abstract principle contained within the proverb and has provided a concrete interpretation based on the physical properties contained within the proverb. Most neuropsychologists will provide a patient suspected of having a brain injury with several proverbs to interpret. Some of these proverbs may be, "A rolling stone gathers no moss," or "Shallow brooks are noisy." Some psychologists, however, may administer the Proverbs test, which contains 12 proverbs of roughly equal difficulty. The patient is given a sheet of paper and required to write what the proverb means. A three-point scoring system is used (e.g., 0, 1, 2), depending upon the level of abstract thinking contained in their answer. There is also a multiple choice version of this test which requires the patient to pick one of four possible answers.

Strengths and Limitations

A patient's interpretation of proverbs is highly correlated with their level of intellectual functioning. On the other hand, intelligent and well-educated patients who were raised in a different culture or whose native language is not English will often have difficulty interpreting the proverbs. Patients who are psychotic may produce bizarre interpretations. For example, if a psychotic patient is asked to interpret the proverb, "Strike while the iron is hot," the patient may say, "When you get this strike, it just goes strike and it goes up to infinity. That shows you that it's in the seventh dimension and it doesn't have any wheels." On other occasions, the patient may not fully understand what a proverb is and may require some examples of proverbs to provide them a sufficient understanding of what a proverb entails. This is frequently seen in patients with low intellectual function or limited educational or culturally deprived backgrounds.

SIMILARITIES TEST

The Similarities test is one of the six verbal subtests of the Wechsler Adult Intelligence Scale (Revised). The patient is asked how two objects, such as a table and a chair, go together.

Strengths and Limitations

Patients with significant frontal lobe or diffuse brain damage frequently say, "They are both made out of wood," or "You can sit on both." The correct answer, however, is that they are both "furniture." The author has found that patients with relatively mild frontal lobe damage frequently get this item correct if the examiner provides them with the cue, "They are both ... ?" Upon hearing this, the patient will frequently say, "... pieces of furniture." Without this cue, however, they typically continue to respond in a concrete fashion. The Similarities test, which has been described on pages 109 - 112, is sensitive to problems in abstract thinking. Once again, however, it should be noted that patients who are schizophrenic or depressed often exhibit concrete thinking on this test in the absence of brain damage. Therefore, it is essential that the neuropsychologist carefully evaluate the content of the patient's responses, observe the patient's behavior during testing, and carefully review the patient's background records, complaints, other neuropsychological test data, and interview the significant others or family members to corroborate this problem.

Conceptual Thinking/Problem Solving

CATEGORY TEST

The Category test assesses the patient's conceptual skills, since the patient must determine the underlying principle in each of six sets of test items. The patient must depress a lever after being visually shown one of the test items. The patient is informed whether his or her choice was incorrect or correct based on whether they hear a pleasant door chime or buzzer, respectively. This test is one of the tests contained within the Halstead-Reitan Neuropsychological Test Battery. A lengthy description of this test can be found on pages 115 - 116.

RAVEN PROGRESSIVE MATRICES

The Raven Progressive Matrices is a test of conceptual thinking and problem solving. Patients are presented with a rectangle containing a set of designs with one part missing. The patient is instructed to examine either six or eight parts (each of which will fit into the rectangle) and determine which of these alternatives is the correct one. The patient must then enter the number located directly above the chosen alternative onto a test sheet furnished by the examiner. The test consists of 60 items which are broken down into five sets of increasing conceptual difficulty. This test produces an IQ score which correlates with the WAIS-R. The test is particularly suited for patients whose native language is not English or who were raised in a different culture, since it places minimal emphasis on the patient's command of English or cultural background. There is also a 36-item version of this test (Colored Progressive Matrices test) which can be used with children or adults with low intellectual functioning. There is also an advanced version of this test which is designed for individuals with very high intellectual functioning (Lezak, 1983).

Although the test has no time limit, it is usually completed in 30 to 40 minutes. Patients who are markedly depressed or have brain damage typically require one hour. The patient's score on this test is determined by the number of correct items. The patient's score can then be compared to norms according to the person's age, which allows the examiner to derive an IQ score which is roughly comparable to the full-scale IQ obtained by the Wechsler Adult Intelligence Scale-R.

Strengths and Limitations

Since this test tends to be a relatively culture-free test of intellectual functioning and places little demand on the patient's motor skills, it is well-suited to assess the intellectual functioning of brain-damaged patients. Studies have shown (Lezak, 1983) that this test possesses adequate test-retest reliability, even when testing occurs as long as six months or twelve months apart. Its ability to discriminate between brain-damaged patients and normal controls is limited. However, it serves, in the author's opinion, as a fairly good indicator of the patient's premorbid intellectual functioning, since it does not appear to be particularly sensitive to brain damage, per se. Thus, the patient's performance on this test can be used as a "gauge" to determine how to interpret the patient's performance on other neuropsychological tests that are sensitive to brain damage. For example, if a patient who has sustained a traumatic brain injury obtains an IQ of 130 on this test (which is corroborated by his pre-accident academic records and IQ test scores), and scores at the 50th percentile (normal range) in comparison to normal controls (e.g., whose average IQ is approximately 100) on tests involving attention, speed of cognitive processing, memory, and problem solving, then his performance on these tests may be significantly lower than expected, based on his performance on the Raven and premorbid academic and vocational achievements. Thus, his normal scores on these tests could represent a deterioration in his cognitive functioning as a result of his brain injury.

Poor performance on this test may reflect visual acuity difficulties, severe anxiety or depression, significant pain and discomfort, headache, hysterical behavior, inadequate motivation, or malingering. The neuropsychologist should carefully inspect the patient's scores over each of the five trials to determine if the scores reflect inadequate motivation or malingering. A poor performance on this test should be corroborated with the patient's premorbid IQ scores, academic and vocational achievements, observations of significant others, behavioral observations of the examiner, and other test data.

WISCONSIN CARD SORTING TEST

The Wisconsin Card Sorting test evaluates the patient's problem solving skills, cognitive flexibility, ability to maintain a particular conceptual set, and concept formation. The current version of this test consists of 128 cards which contain up to four symbols (triangle, star, cross, or circle) which are in one of four colors (red, green, yellow, or blue). The examiner places four cards in a horizontal array in front of the patient. The patient's task is to match the top card in a pack of 64 cards directly below one of the four cards above. The patient is given only minimal instructions on this test; however, the object of the test is to have the patient sort according to an underlying principle which can be deduced by the feedback provided by the examiner after each card is sorted. Thus, if the patient correctly places his card under the correct card (one of the four cards), the examiner indicates, "That is correct." If, on the other hand, the patient incorrectly places his card under one of the three incorrect cards, the patient is informed, "That is incorrect." After a patient has made 10 consecutive correct responses, the underlying category automatically changes. For example, if the patient was sorting correctly according to color, the underlying concept will change to form (Lezak, 1983). Patients with frontal lobe damage frequently continue sorting according to color even though they continue receiving negative feedback from the examiner. The patient, however, is never informed that the underlying category has changed and must deduce this based on the feedback he or she receives after making a response. The underlying categories are Color, Form, and Number (e.g., number of symbols on the card). The patient is given a maximum of 128 cards to complete six categories. A patient's score on this test can be based on several different factors. For example, it can be based on the number of categories the patient completes before the supply of cards runs out. It can also be based on the total number of errors made by the patient, percentage of correct responses, number of perseverations, number of perseverative errors, trials required to complete the first category, percentage of conceptual level responses, number of failure to maintain set errors, and their ability to reduce their errors over trials. These classifications permit the examiner the opportunity to qualitatively analyze the patient's performance to determine the nature of the patient's impairments, as well their clinical significance.

Strengths and Limitations

This test has been shown to be sensitive to dorsolateral lesions of the frontal lobes, but is relatively insensitive to orbital frontal lesions (Stuss and Benson, 1986). The manual that accompanies this test contains norms for normal controls, patients with frontal lobe pathology, patients with brain injuries that do not include the frontal lobes, and patients with diffuse brain damage. Validity studies using this test have demonstrated an overall hit rate of 72% in its ability to discriminate between brain-damaged patients and normal controls. As was suggested above, a relatively good performance on this test does not rule out brain damage, since patients who sustain prominent damage to the orbital frontal lobes typically perform well on this test, particularly if they have a relatively high level of intellectual functioning. Poor performance on this test can also reflect visual impairment, color blindness, visual-perceptual difficulties, impaired hearing, psychotic thinking, severe depression or anxiety, histrionic behavior, or malingering. To rule out these possibilities, it is essential that the examiner obtain a careful history from the patient which includes a review of this patient's medical records, interviews with significant others, behavioral observations of the patient during testing and the clinical interview, and then to compare the patient's performance on this test with other neuropsychological tests.

Spatial-Perceptual and Constructional Skills

BLOCK DESIGN TEST

The Block Design test consists of assembling one-inch blocks with different colored sides to reproduce a specific printed design which may require four or nine blocks. This test is one of the performance subtests of the Wechsler Adult Intelligence Scale. Each successive design is more difficult than the preceding design. It is also a timed test. Four block designs have one-minute time limits, while the nine-block design test has a two-minute time limit. Bonus points can be earned by patients on seven of the nine test items on the WAIS-R. The WAIS-R manual carefully describes the instructions and procedure to be followed to administer and score this test. When testing brain-damaged patients, however, some neuropsychologists may utilize a more qualitative rather than quantitative approach when using this test to localize the site of the patient's brain injury, such as left or right hemisphere (Lezak, 1983).

Brain-damaged patients may not fully comprehend the test instructions according to the manner in which they are presented in the test manual. In such cases, however, the examiner may be forced to elaborate and provide several examples to the patient for better comprehension of the test instructions. While this may be necessary in many cases, the examiner should carefully note the various instructions, cues, and examples he or she provided the patient prior to and during the test. When this is done, however, it actually violates the procedures developed for this test. One school of thought strongly argues that it would be unwise to utilize the norms which have been developed for this test to such individuals, since the procedures utilized were not the same as those described in the manual. The author essentially agrees with this, since, in actuality, the examiner's behavior served to minimize the patient's confusion and compensate for the patient's organizational deficits. Without these instructions however, the patient would most likely have never been able to complete this test. Thus, it makes little sense for neuropsychologists to then compare the patient's performance to test norms. When this occurs, the patient's scores frequently only minimally reflect brain injury and result in misleading or spurious conclusions about whether the patient sustained brain injury. The author also recommends that the plaintiff's attorney should carefully question the psychologist or neuropsychologist who examined the patient to determine what instructions, examples, or information were provided to the patient prior to and during testing that were not contained in the WAIS-R test manual.

Strengths and Limitations

This test has been shown to be sensitive to brain damage, particularly when the injury is located either in the frontal lobes or parietal lobes. This test is also sensitive to patients with Alzheimer's disease, strokes, and hypoxic encephalopathy. For example, patients with subcortical brain damage typically work very slowly and exceed the time limits. Patients with left posterior hemisphere brain damage usually maintain the overall 2 x 2 or 3 x 3 configuration of their blocks but make considerable errors with regard to the internal details of their designs. Patients with right posterior hemisphere damage typically exhibit a loss of the overall 2 x 2 or 3 x 3 block configuration and produce reproductions that are grossly distorted. Thus, a careful qualitative analysis of the types of errors made by the patient can provide a greater understanding of the site of brain injury and its clinical significance. Poor performance on this test may also reflect such factors as poor visual acuity, orthopedic injury to one or both arms or hands, test anxiety, severe depression, significant physical pain or discomfort, headache, hysteria, malingering, or inadequate motivation. It is not indicative of the diagnosis of brain damage unless it is supported by other test data, including the patient's medical history, the neurological examination, neurodiagnostic tests, observations of significant others, and behavioral observations of the examiner.

OBJECT ASSEMBLY TEST

This test requires that the patient assemble cardboard figures of familiar objects, such as a mannequin, a profile of a person's face, a hand, and an elephant. The patient is not told what the object is and must deduce the identity of the object as he or she begins assembling it. A two-minute time limit is given for each object, with bonus points given for rapid completion of the task.

Strengths and Limitations

This test is one of the performance subtest of the Wechsler Adult Intelligence Scale-Revised and permits the psychologist or neuropsychologist to evaluate the patient's spatial-perceptual and constructional skills. When the patient is unable to complete one of the objects within the allotted time, the patient's score depends on how many pieces of the object were put together correctly before the testing time elapsed. Like the Block Design test, the Object Assembly test is sensitive to posterior brain injury, particularly in the right hemisphere, as well as dorsolateral frontal lobe damage. Because this test, like the Block Design test, requires skilled motor movements to assemble the various pieces, the patient's performance is likely to be poor if the patient has sustained a significant physical injury to either hand, has diplopia (double vision), is extremely anxious, visually impaired, or has motor ataxia (jerky movements of the arms or hands).

Patients with posterior right hemisphere damage typically perform poorly on this test. Patients with frontal lobe injuries show poor organization and planning skills. Like the Block Design test, patients with significant brain injuries may not comprehend the test instructions, which may cause the examiner to provide examples and/or instructions that considerably exceed the test instructions to the subject as described by the manual. When this occurs, the psychologist or neuropsychologist should provide a record of this including the rationale utilized to violate the instructions as set forth in the test manual. Comparison to test norms, under these circumstances, should not be permitted if the examiner has grossly violated the test instructions or procedures as set forth in the manual. The author recommends, instead, that the psychologist or neuropsychologist provide a descriptive account of the patient's performance from a qualitative perspective, since this typically illustrates the patient's cognitive impairments and highlights their clinical significance in relation to brain injury.

If a patient performs poorly on the Block Design test, he or she most likely will also perform poorly on the Object Assembly test, since these tests measure very similar abilities and appear to be mediated by similar brain mechanisms; however, the Object Assembly subtest appears to be more sensitive to right parietal damage than the Block Design test. Thus, patients who do well on the Object Assembly subtest, but perform poorly on the Block Design test, are unlikely to have sustained an injury to the right parietal lobe and have either sustained an injury to the left parietal lobe or may have performed poorly on the Block Design test as a result of a variety of non-neurological factors.

REY-OSTERRIETH COMPLEX FIGURE TEST

The Rey-Osterrieth Complex Figure test requires the patient to copy a complex geometric figure onto a sheet of paper with one regular or six colored pencils. A scoring system has been developed to quantitatively assess the accuracy of the patient's drawing. A detailed description of this test can be found on pages 139 - 140.

TACTUAL PERFORMANCE TEST

The Tactual Performance test evaluates the patient's constructional skills while blindfolded with each hand separately and with both hands working together. This test is part of the Halstead-Reitan Battery and has been described in detail on pages 116 - 117.

Academic Skills

WIDE RANGE ACHIEVEMENT TEST

The Wide Range Achievement test has been developed to assess the patient's spelling, reading, and arithmetic levels of competence. Children from ages 5 to 11 can be evaluated at Level I, while patients ranging in age from 12 to over 45 can be assessed at Level II. Some differences exist in the manner the patient's spelling and reading skills are evaluated at the two different levels because of the ages of the subjects being evaluated with Level I. The spelling test evaluates the patient's ability to spell a list of words of increasing difficulty. The arithmetic subtest includes addition, subtraction, multiplication, and division, as well as arithmetic problems involving fractions, percentages, and arithmetic conversions. It also contains computation of squares, roots, and a variety of algebraic problems. The patient is given 10 minutes to complete the arithmetic section. The reading section involves having the patient read individual words of increasing length and difficulty (Lezak, 1983).

Strengths and Limitations

Scoring on this test is relatively straight-forward, in that the patient's score consists of the total number of correct items achieved for the spelling, arithmetic, and reading subtests. These scores are then compared to age norms and can be converted into standard scores or percentiles, as well as the patient's grade equivalent in school. While this test was not specifically designed to evaluate patients with brain damage, it frequently identifies patients who have had a previous history of spelling or reading difficulties.

Patients with brain damage typically do poorly on the arithmetic subtest because of its 10-minute time limit. A careful analysis, however, of the patient's responses and errors on this test can often determine if the patient's errors reflected pre-injury arithmetic difficulties or brain injury. Poor performance on this test can reflect a variety of extraneous factors such as anticonvulsant or psychotropic medications, anxiety, poor vision, depression, psychotic thinking, histrionic behavior, or poor motivation. For the neuropsychologist to determine if the patient's poor performance has been caused by brain damage or was the result of a prior history of academic difficulties, dyslexia, or spelling difficulties, the neuropsychologist must carefully review the patient's academic and medical records, interview significant others, as well as carefully observe the patient's behavior during testing.

Language

APHASIA SCREENING TEST

The Aphasia Screening test is part of the Halstead-Reitan Battery and contains 51 test items which permit the examiner to screen patients for aphasic disturbances in approximately 15 to 20 minutes. A description of this test can be found on page 122.

BOSTON DIAGNOSTIC APHASIA EXAMINATION

This test provides a comprehensive assessment of the patient's aphasic difficulties. It contains a total of 34 subtests and evaluates the patient's communication and communication-related skills.

Strengths and Limitations

Neurologically intact patients typically require one hour to complete this test, while patients with brain injury can require as long as four hours to complete this test. While this test has been used by neuropsychologists, it is primarily used to evaluate disturbances in communication and language functioning following strokes (cerebral vascular accidents) and extensive damage to the left frontal-parietal, frontal-temporal, and temporal-parietal areas secondary to depressed skull fractures. Neuropsychologists using this instrument must have a strong background in aphasiology (the study of language disturbances caused by neurological injury), since clinical interpretation depends heavily on the examiner's training, experience, and background with this specific patient population.

BOSTON NAMING TEST

This test consists of 60 drawings of objects that become increasingly less familiar and difficult to name. For example, the patient may be presented with a drawing of a harmonica and asked to name it. If the patient is unable to name this object, he is given a cue such as, "It's a musical instrument." If the patient is still unable to name it, he is provided with the first syllable of the word "harmonica" as a cue. It is essential that the examiner note the amount of time required before the patient is able to provide a correct response and whether or not the patient was correct or incorrect after being provided with a stimulus cue or phonemic cue, such as, "It begins with "har". A patient's score is based on the number of objects which were successfully named without having to provide the patient with a phonemic cue.

Strengths and Limitations

The test manual and booklet provide normative data based on the patient's educational achievements (12 years of education or less, or more than 12 years of education) and age (e.g., 20-29, 30-39, 40-49, and 50-59 years old). The normative data contains means and standard deviations that permit the examiner to determine the degree of the patient's severity. Careful analysis of the patient's responses on each of the test items, as well as their responses to stimulus and phonemic cues, can be of considerable assistance in precisely identifying the nature of the patient's impairment and their clinical significance.

Poor scores on this test can reflect a variety of factors, such as premorbid cultural or linguistic differences (e.g., the patient was raised in a different culture or speaks English as a second language), low premorbid intellectual functioning, limited formal education, anxiety, depression, psychotic thinking, or inadequate motivation to perform well. Very poor performances on this test (scores of 35 or less) in the absence of word finding difficulties observed during the clinical interview should be suspect, particularly when this finding is not supported by the patient's medical records, clinical history, observations of significant others and family members, and other psychological test data.

CONTROLLED ORAL WORD ASSOCIATION TEST

This test consists of instructing the patient to name as many words as possible beginning with specific letters of the alphabet. Typically, the patient is given an example of the task requirements. For example, he is told, "I want you to say as many words as you can that begin with the letter 'M' without giving me people's names." In other words, he might say, "Marble, music, marriage, or magic." After this example, the patient is given the letter "F" and is instructed to state as many words as possible beginning with this letter. The patient is given one minute, during which time he must state as many words as he can that begin with that letter. The examiner must rapidly write down the patient's responses on a sheet of paper as the patient is engaged in this task. Immediately following this, the patient is given the letter "A" and instructed to provide as many words as he can beginning with that letter. As soon as this is completed, the patient is given the letter "S" and is given the same previous instructions. The patient's score is the total number of words provided by the patient during the three (F, A, S) trials.

Norms have been developed for both males and females according to their educational achievements (less than nine years, nine to 11 years, 12 to 15 years, and 16 or more years of formal education), and age group (25-54, 55-59, and 60-64). Based on the patient's years of formal education and age, points may be added to the patient's score to adjust for educational and age differences in patients. For example, a 56-year-old woman who has completed nine years of formal education would have 10 points added to her score. On the other hand, a 25-year-old college graduate would not have any points added to his score. The patient's percentile can be determined on the basis of his or her adjusted score. Adjusted scores of 53 or higher would place the patient above the 96th percentile and would indicate superior performance on this task. On the other hand, if the patient's performance is between 23 and 24, they are considered to have borderline impairment. Patients whose scores are 16 or less are considered to have severely defective performance (Lezak, 1983).

Strengths and Limitations

This test has been found to be a sensitive indicator of brain damage, particularly when the site of injury involves the left frontal-temporal area. Patients who sustain bilateral frontal-temporal lobe injuries typically make the lowest scores on this test. Poor performance on this test may also reflect such factors as test anxiety, depression, fatigue, cultural deprivation, prior linguistic background (e.g., patient's primary language is not English), significant physical pain and discomfort, headache, hysteria, malingering, or inadequate motivation. Poor performance on this test should be corroborated by other test data, the patient's medical records, observations of significant others, and the patient's clinical history.

TOKEN TEST

This test assesses the patient's ability to perform orally presented commands and has been found to be sensitive to patients with subtle receptive language deficits secondary to brain injury. The examiner presents a set of tokens which are made out of cardboard and consist of either circles or squares. Tokens come in two sizes (large and small). Some or all of the tokens may be placed directly in front of the patient, depending on specific test procedures. The examiner's commands to the patient range from being very straightforward and simple, such as, "Touch the white square," to "Before touching the yellow circle, pick up the red square." The test is composed of five parts which comprise a total of 62 test items.

Strengths and Limitations

Norms have been developed to compare the scores of nonaphasic and aphasic brain-damaged patients to normal controls. Since this test is fairly simple, neurologically intact patients should obtain near-perfect scores. Patients with aphasic difficulties typically make a significant number of errors on this task, particularly on Part 5. This test tends to be very sensitive to left temporal-parietal lobe damage.

Poor performance on this test can be also due to hearing difficulties (e.g., the patient forgot to wear his or her hearing aid or the batteries ran out), distractibility (e.g., the patient failed to attend to the orally presented command of the examiner), depression, severe anxiety, psychotic thinking, severe pain and discomfort during testing (which interferes with the patient's ability to attend to the examiner's commands), English as a second language, different cultural background, or inadequate motivation. Patients who perform poorly on this test are likely to exhibit receptive language difficulties during the clinical interview and during the administration of other neuropsychological tests. For example, the examiner is likely to observe that the patient's responses at times appear inappropriate, or that the patient seems confused after being asked a lengthy or complex question. The patient's family and/or significant others should also provide corroboration of this problem.

Personality/Emotional Adjustment

MINNESOTA MULTIPHASIC PERSONALITY INVENTORY

The Minnesota Multiphasic Personality Inventory (MMPI) is the most widely used personality inventory to assess a patient's level of adjustment, personality dynamics, attitude toward self and the world, and current emotional problems. The MMPI was never designed to, nor should it ever be used to, diagnose brain damage. The MMPI consists of 566 items, of which 16 items are repeated for scoring purposes. The test provides questions or statements which must be answered within a true/false format. A newer version of the test (MMPI-II) contains a total of 567 items. The newer version of the test has reworded and/or modified some of the questions. Both the old and new version contain three validity scales, the "L" (lie), the "F" (faking), and the "K" (defensiveness) scales. The patient's profile on these scales can provide valuable insights as to whether or not the patient is either malingering or denying his or her psychological problems, their competency to take the test, and whether or not they are defensive or are seeking out help for their emotional problems.

The MMPI contains 10 clinical scales: Hypochondriasis (HS), Depression (D), Hysteria (HY), Psychopathic Deviate (PD), Masculinity/Femininity (MF), Paranoia (PA), Psychasthenia (PT), Schizophrenia (SC), Mania (MA), and Social Introversion (SI). Scoring can be done by placing special templates over the patient's answer sheet or by entering the patient's raw scores for each item into a computer for scoring. The patient's scores for the three validity and 10 clinical scales are entered onto a profile sheet after the patient's raw scores are adjusted in terms of the elevation of the "K" scale. The psychologist can then examine the relative elevations of each of these scales in relationship to each other and determine the clinical significance of the patient's profile.

Patients who experience a great deal of concern over their bodily functions and who are likely to complain of a wide variety of physical problems, including pain and discomfort, are likely to have elevated scores on the hypochondriasis scale. It should be noted, however, that significant elevations on this scale can be due to real or imagined physical problems. Patients who experience suicidal thoughts, depression, poor self-esteem, sleep difficulties, loss of appetite, feelings of helplessness, dejection, lack of positive feelings, and apathy tend to score high on the depression scale. Patients who are unable to tolerate hostility and stress but tend to be very friendly, sociable, egocentric, immature, have unhappy marriages, and little insight into their emotional problems or needs tend to score high on the hysteria scale. Patients who have a history of criminal behavior, drug abuse, a general disregard for the rules of society, problems with law enforcement authorities, exhibit impulsive behavior or poor judgement, and are markedly egocentric tend to score high on the psychopathic deviate scale. Males who score high on the masculinity/femininity scale are either homosexual or confused about their sexual identity. They also feel insecure when placed in masculine roles. It should be noted, however, that well-educated males who are artistic, creative, or highly intellectual may also score high on this scale. Males who score low on this test typically have deep-seated feelings of insecurity about their masculinity and may attempt to compensate for these feelings of insecurity by acting "macho." Females who score high on this scale tend to be highly competitive, unemotional, and aggressive. They often resent males and are actively engaged in competition with them. Women who score low on this scale tend to be submissive, passive, sensitive, emotionally constricted, and self-pitying. Such women frequently have doubts regarding their femininity and prefer to date "macho" males.

Individuals who are hostile, resentful, and tend to blame others for their own failures, appear guarded or display excessive moral rigidity are likely to score high on the paranoia scale. It should also be noted that extremely low scores on this scale may represent a covert form of paranoia, since the person may attempt to conceal or deny their paranoia. Patients who are excessively anxious, nervous, have phobias, have trouble concentrating, are perfectionistic, and have difficulty coping with their environment often score high on the psychasthenia scale. Individuals who experience hallucinations, bizarre thoughts, appear odd, have difficulty expressing or dealing with their feelings, and frequently act inappropriately are likely to score high on the schizophrenia scale. It should also be noted that many brain-injured patients may score high on this test during the early stages of their injury, since they are typically confused, have difficulty regulating their behavior and emotions and have difficulty organizing their thinking. Individuals who tend to be grandiose, jump from one topic to another, appear happy virtually all of the time, yet display poor judgement and an endless supply of energy are likely to score high on the mania scale. Patients with brain injuries are likely to show elevations on this scale, as they try to cope with their diminished cognitive functioning by excessive over-activity. Individuals who enjoy being alone, are hard to get to know, and are seen by others as very sensitive tend to score high on the social introversion scale. On the other hand, low scores on this scale are frequently associated with patients who are often opportunistic and manipulative and yet may appear highly intelligent and confident of their abilities.

Strengths and Limitations

Numerous research studies have demonstrated the validity and reliability of the MMPI to diagnose patients with personality or emotional disorders. Psychologists who utilize this test should have extensive clinical training and expertise in making such interpretations. These interpretations should be generally consistent with the patient's clinical and background history, the observations of significant others, the patient's profile on other psychological tests (e.g., MCMI), and the behavioral observations of the examiner. Finally, it should again be strongly emphasized that the MMPI was never designed to diagnose brain injury. Unfortunately, one finds some psychiatrists or even psychologists who rely on the patient's MMPI profile to diagnose brain damage or "organicity." Instead, the patient's profile on this test can often be utilized to determine the presence of significant emotional problems which may account, at least in part, for the patient's relatively poor performance on neuropsychological tests which are highly sensitive to emotional factors (e.g., WAIS-R).

MILLON CLINICAL MULTIAXIAL INVENTORY

Like the MMPI, the Millon is a personality inventory that requires the patient to respond in a true/false format. It contains 175 questions which resulted from a lengthy validation process. Unlike the MMPI, the questions and patient's responses are contained within the same booklet. This booklet was designed for optical scanning or for computer scoring and interpretation. The MCMI has been designed for patients who are 17 or older.

The major strength in the MCMI is that it directly attempts to assess pre-existing personality traits or disorders, whereas in the MMPI such traits or disorders must be inferred by the interpretation of the examiner. This has considerable value in medicolegal cases, since one of the questions frequently asked is, "What kind of person was the plaintiff before she had her accident?" so that the effect of the accident on this patient's emotional problems can be carefully assessed. Computer programs have been written which generate a profile report that contains each of the scale scores and can serve as a screening device to identify patients who require more extensive evaluations. The computer program also provides a clinical narrative interpretive report containing a detailed analysis of the patient's personality and current emotional problems and symptoms. Contained within this computer-generated report are the current stressors the patient is under and suggestions for the patient's therapeutic management.

Strengths and Limitations

The MCMI has been shown to be a valid test, partly through the cross-validation sample techniques developed by its authors. Since it is a relatively new test in comparison to the MMPI, research studies on its use and effectiveness are, therefore, limited (McCabe, 1984). Like the MMPI, this test was never designed to identify or diagnose brain injury. Its primary value lies in its ability to describe the various emotional and adjustment problems such patients are likely to have following a post-traumatic stress disorder or brain injury. The neuropsychologist should, however, exercise great caution in assuming that the Axis II profile produced by this test, which describes premorbid or long-standing personality traits, accurately reflects the patient's long-standing personality traits when a significant duration of time has elapsed since the time of the injury or accident and when the patient is actually tested. This is based on the fact the test relies on the patient's responses (true/false) to specific test items to determine the patient's current emotional problems (e.g., Axis II). For example, the item (#43) "My own 'bad temper' has been a big cause of my troubles." This item has been designed to identify long-standing antisocial and/or borderline personality traits. If a patient sustains a traumatic brain injury that results in poor frustration tolerance, irritability, and aggressive outbursts towards others, and if the patient recognizes this problem and responds, "Yes," the patient is likely to be diagnosed as having long-standing antisocial or borderline personality traits even though such traits never existed prior to the patient's brain injury. Therefore, the neuropsychologist should exercise considerable caution when determining whether the patient had similar personality traits before and after a traumatic injury or accident. Such a determination should not be based solely on the results of the patient's MCMI, or even MMPI test profile, but should be based on a thorough clinical investigation which includes a review of the patient's prior academic, legal, medical, military, and occupational records, interview of the patient, and interviews with significant others. If the test profile corroborates this information, then it should be regarded as valid. If it disagrees or contradicts this information, then the psychologist or neuropsychologist should interpret the test profile as reflecting the problems the patient has developed since, or as a result of, their injury.

Summary

A summary of the strengths and weaknesses of each of the tests presented in this chapter can be found in Table 8.

TABLE 8

STRENGTHS AND LIMITATIONS OF NEUROPSYCHOLOGICAL TESTS

TESTS OF INTELLIGENCE

WECHSLER ADULT INTELLIGENCE SCALE-REVISED (WAIS-R)

Description

The WAIS-R has been designed to evaluate a patient's intellectual functioning. It consists of six verbal subtests and five performance subtests. It produces a verbal, performance, and full scale IQ score. The test is individually administered and is appropriate for individuals ranging in age from 16 to 74.

Strengths

1. Most widely used IQ test.
2. IQ correlates well with academic grade point average.
3. Easy to administer and score.
4. Test manual is clear and easy to read.
5. Produces verbal, performance, and full scale IQ scores.

Limitations

1. Was never designed to evaluate brain damage.
2. Many of the subtests are insensitive to brain damage.
3. IQ scores can be affected by emotional and motivational factors.
4. Patients raised in a different culture or whose command of English is limited may receive spuriously low IQ scores.
5. Not particularly suited for patients with aphasic difficulties, or who are motorically, visually, or auditorially impaired.
6. IQ scores can be negatively affected by anticonvulsant or a variety of antidepressant and antipsychotic medications.

STANDARDIZED NEUROPSYCHOLOGICAL TEST BATTERIES

HALSTEAD-REITAN NEUROPSYCHOLOGICAL BATTERY (HRNB)

Description

The HRNB is one of the most widely used neuropsychological test batteries. It consists of 12 tests which are individually administered. The battery takes approximately six to eight hours to administer.

Strengths

1. Validity studies demonstrate its ability to discriminate between brain-damaged patients and normal controls.
2. Has been shown to reliably discriminate between brain-damaged patients and psychiatric patients.
3. Extensive research done on battery.
4. Has been used in a variety of settings.
5. Ideal for research.
6. Utilized in determining the extent or severity of brain damage, and the lateralization and localization of brain damage.
7. Can be administered by psychological assistants or technicians.
8. The administration and scoring of the battery can be learned in one week.

Limitations

1. Teaching workshops provide no actual supervision of test administration or scoring.
2. Relatively poor at detecting malingering.
3. Clinical interpretations are based almost entirely on test scores.
4. Test scores can be influenced by a wide variety of non-neurological factors.
5. Considerable variability in test scores of normative controls.
6. "Cut-off" scores for brain damage can result in 30 percent chance of being wrong in diagnosing brain damage based on test scores. This increases considerably in older patients.
7. Testing usually takes between six to eight hours, but can take as long as 10 hours in patients with severe diffuse brain damage.
8. Battery is not able to detect all possible neuropsychological impairments, particularly recent memory.
9. Relatively few psychologists utilize the entire battery. Most psychologists use portions of the battery and other tests which were never designed to be included in the battery.
10. Battery is generally insensitive to orbital frontal lobe brain damage.
11. Battery needs to be supplemented by other neuropsychological tests.
12. Test interpretation requires background in behavioral neurology and neuroanatomy.

LURIA - NEBRASKA NEUROPSYCHOLOGICAL BATTERY (LNNB)

Description

The LNNB is a comprehensive neuropsychological test battery based on the assessment procedures of the late Professor Luria and the American psychometric tradition. It contains a total of 269 test items which comprise 11 clinical scales. It can be administered in two-and-one-half to three hours.

Strengths

1. Based on the neuropsychological assessment methods developed by Luria.
2. Possesses adequate validity and reliability.
3. Can be administered in only two-and-a-half to three hours.
4. Permits localization of brain impairment.
5. Corrects for patient's age and educational achievements.
6. Administration and scoring of test can be learned in less than two weeks.

Limitations

1. Test interpretation requires background in behavioral neurology and neuroanatomy.
2. Test interpretation is difficult.
3. Needs to be supplemented with other neuropsychological tests.
4. Tends to be insensitive to mild cognitive dysfunction in patients with IQ's of 125 or higher.
5. Background and historical information are necessary to reach accurate test interpretations.

TESTS OF ATTENTION AND CONCENTRATION

DIGIT-SPAN TEST (DST)

Description

The DST consists of orally presenting random number sequences to the patient, (e.g., 3-8-6-2-9). The patient then repeats the digits in the exact sequence they were presented. The patient must initially give the digits forwards and then later backwards.

Strengths

1. Serves as a sensitive measure of attention.
2. Frequently used by both physicians and psychologists.
3. Sensitive to brain injury.

Limitations

1. It is not an accurate test of recent memory.
2. Poor performance frequently reflects emotional factors (eg., anxiety, depression, etc.).
3. Interpretation of test results depends on a careful evaluation of a variety of factors (e.g., patient's behavior during testing, recent stressors, etc.)

PACED AUDITORY SERIAL ADDITION TEST (PASAT)

Description

The PASAT assesses the patient's ability to add 60 pairs of numbers ranging from one to nine. Each number is added to the number immediately preceding it. The pace at which the numbers are presented ranges from 1.2 to 2.4 seconds apart. The numbers are presented to the patient by a tape recorder. A total of 60 pairs of numbers are presented at time intervals of 2.4, 2.0, 1.6, and 1.2 seconds.

Strengths

1. Sensitive to relatively subtle attentional impairments following mild brain trauma.
2. Has been used to determine if brain-injured patients are able to return to work or school following mild head trauma.

Limitations

1. Test is not widely used.
2. Poor performance can also reflect non-neurological factors (e.g., anxiety).
3. Test results must be corroborated by other neuropsychological test data.

SBORDONE ATTENTION BATTERY (SAB)

Description

The SAB consists of nine subtests which require the patient to perform five serial arithmetic and four serial alphabetic tasks. The patient's ability to perform these tasks provides a measure of sustained attention. This test places heavy emphasis on a qualitative assessment of the patient's errors and coping strategies while taking each subtest.

Strengths

1. Serves as a sensitive measure of sustained attention.
2. Sensitive to subtle cognitive impairments following a mild head injury.
3. Provides clinician with rich qualitative information about the nature of the patient's brain-behavior relationships.

Limitations

1. No formal test norms exist for this test.
2. Test interpretation is based largely on the experience and expertise of the examiner.
3. Needs to be correlated with other neuropsychological tests and behavioral observations of examiner and significant others.

TRIAL MAKING TEST (TMT)

Description

The TMT consists of two parts, Part A and Part B. The patient must connect circles containing numbers ranging from 1 to 25 in a serial order in Part A, and circles containing either letters or numbers in an alternating sequence in Part B. This test is part of the Halstead-Reitan Neuropsychological Battery and serves as a measure of visuomotor tracking, visual scanning, and mental flexibility.

Strengths

1. Serves as a sensitive measure of visuomotor tracking and visual scanning.
2. Is sensitive to subtle cognitive impairments secondary to brain damage.
3. Produces quantitative data which can be used by other psychologists.

Limitations

1. Can be influenced by emotional or motivational factors.
2. Poor performance can also reflect non-neurological factors.
3. Test interpretation needs to be corroborated with the patient's performance on other neuropsychological tests.

TESTS OF MEMORY

BENTON VISUAL RETENTION TEST (BVRT)

Description

The BVRT is designed to assess visual memory. The test consists of 10 cards which contain up to three geometric figures. The patient must draw the presented figures on a sheet of paper after the card is removed.

Strengths

1. Test has been shown to be highly reliable over repeated administrations.
2. Can discriminate between brain-damaged patients and controls.
3. Qualitative analysis of the patient's errors can differentiate brain-injured from schizophrenic patients.
4. Has been used to distinguish between malingers and brain-injured patients.

Limitations

1. Intact performance on test does not rule out brain damage.
2. Poor test performance can be caused by a variety of non-neurological factors.
3. Conclusions regarding brain damage should be corroborated by other neuropsychological tests.

REY AUDITORY VERBAL LEARNING TEST (RAVLT)

Description

RAVLT consists of a list of 15 words which are orally presented to a patient for five consecutive trials. After each trial the patient must recall as many words as possible. Then the patient is orally presented with a second list of words for only one trial. The patient is then asked to recall the first list of words again.

Strengths

1. Patient's ability to learn new information can be measured over trials.
2. Patient's performance can be compared to appropriate norms for each trial.
3. Test is sensitive to subtle memory impairments seen following brain injury.

Limitations

1. Poor performance can also reflect a variety of non-neurological factors (eg., anxiety, motivation, etc.).
2. Poor performance needs to be corroborated with clinical history, the patient's medical records, interviews with significant others, and other neuropsychological test data.

REY-OSTERRIETH COMPLEX VISUAL FIGURE TEST

Description

The patient must initially copy a complex geometric figure on a sheet of paper. After a delay of three minutes and 30 minutes after the figure has been removed, the patient is instructed to draw the figure from memory.

Strengths

1. Serves as a sensitive test of visual memory.
2. Normative data and scoring system permits the examiner to compare the patient's drawings to normal controls.
3. Qualitative methods of analysis permit cerebral localization of impairments.

Limitations

1. Poor performance can also reflect a wide variety of non-neurological factors.
2. Conclusions about brain damage need to be supported by patient's history, medical records, interviews with significant others, behavioral observations, and other neuropsychological test data.

SELECTIVE REMINDING TEST (SRT)

Description

The SRT consists of presenting the patient with a list of words. After the list is presented the patient must recall as many words as possible from the list. Words which are not recalled are repeated by the examiner on the next trial. Trials are continued until the patient is able to repeat the entire list.

Strengths

1. It has been used with brain-injured patients.
2. Brain-injured patients frequently show impaired learning over trials.

Limitations

1. Not widely used.
2. Poor performance can also reflect non-neurological factors.

SBORDONE-HALL MEMORY BATTERY (SHMB)

Description

The SHMB is a computer-administered and scored memory test which examines up to 23 different memory functions. The patient is presented with test stimuli on a TV monitor and interacts with the computer through a keyboard. The entire test requires 45 to 60 minutes to complete.

Strengths

1. Specific test stimuli are generated or are randomly selected by a computer.
2. Test is easy to take.
3. Test provides brief rest periods to counteract the effects of fatigue.
4. Automatic statistical comparisons are made with normal controls, psychiatric, and brain-damaged patients.
5. Test performs a discriminant function analysis which determines whether the patient's performance on the test is consistent with brain-damaged patients.

Limitations

1. Requires computer system to use test.
2. Requires nearly one hour to administer test.
3. Poor performance may reflect non-neurological factors.
4. Test interpretation of scores are largely based on experience and expertise of examiner.
5. Validity of test scores should be ecologically valid and corroborated by other neuropsychological tests, and observations of significant others.

WECHSLER MEMORY SCALE-REVISED (WMS-R)

Description

The WMS assesses the patient's memory for verbal and nonverbal stimuli, meaningful and abstract material under conditions of both immediate and delayed recall. It was designed to evaluate memory functioning in patients ranging in age from 16 to 74.

Strengths

1. The most widely used test of memory.
2. Testing, scoring, and administration is relatively straightforward.
3. Adequate normative data and reliability.

Limitations

1. Was not designed to evaluate brain-injured patients.
2. Poor scores are frequently made by patients whose native language is not English or have low premorbid IQ's.
3. Test does not evaluate remote or olfactory memory.
4. Poor performance can reflect factors such as anxiety, depression, psychotic thinking, pain, fatigue, medications, hysteria, or inadequate motivation.

MOTOR TESTS

FINGER TAPPING TEST

Description

This test is used to evaluate motor speed. It is one of the tests contained within the Halstead-Reitan Battery.

Strengths

1. Produces quantitative data which can be compared to normative data.
2. Easy to administer.
3. Sensitive to subtle motor impairment.
4. Used in Halstead-Reitan Battery.

Limitations

1. Poor performance can be due to conscious manipulation of task.
2. Poor performance can reflect orthopedic or peripheral neurological disorders.

GRIP STRENGTH TEST

Description

Designed to assess strength of patient's grip in each hand. It is one of the tests used within the Halstead-Reitan Battery.

Strengths

1. Produces quantitative data which can be compared to normative data.
2. Easy to administer.
3. Sensitive to subtle motor weakness.
4. Used in Halstead-Reitan Battery.

Limitations

1. Poor performance can be due to conscious manipulation of task.
2. Poor performance can be due to orthopedic or peripheral neurological disorders.

GROOVED PEGBOARD TEST

Description

This test assesses fine motor coordination and manual dexterity by having the patient place metal pegs into grooved slots as quickly as possible.

Strengths

1. Provides quantitative data which can be compared to appropriate norms.
2. Easy to administer.
3. Sensitive to subtle fine motor impairments.
4. Used in Halstead-Reitan Battery.

Limitations

1. Poor performance can be due to conscious manipulation of task.
2. Poor performance can be due to orthopedic, visual, or motivational problems, anxiety, or peripheral neurological disorders.

SENSORY - PERCEPTUAL TESTS

BENTON FACIAL RECOGNITION TEST

Description

This test assesses the patient's ability to compare pictures of faces.

Strengths

1. Sensitive to subtle visual perceptual impairments.
2. Can be administered to patients whose knowledge of English is limited.
3. Places little emphasis on patient's memory.
4. Normative data allows examiner to compare patient's score to normal controls.

Limitations

1. Tends to be insensitive to left hemisphere or frontal lobe damage.
2. Poor performance can be caused by visual acuity difficulties, high levels of anxiety, poor motivation, pain, or psychotic thinking.
3. Test scores should be corroborated by the patient's medical records and other neuropsychological test data.

REITAN-KLOVE SENSORY PERCEPTUAL EXAMINATION

Description

This test assesses sensory and perceptual functioning across a variety of modalities. It is one of the tests contained within the Halstead-Reitan Battery.

Strengths

1. Provides a quantitative method of assessing patient's sensory and perceptual impairments.
2. One of the tests used in the Halstead-Reitan Battery.

Limitations

1. Poor performance can reflect a wide number of conditions, including physical damage or injury, anxiety, paranoia, hysteria, or malingering.
2. Scoring is highly subjective.

VISUAL FORM DISCRIMINATION TEST

Description

The test is designed to assess visual discrimination skills. It evaluates the patient's ability to match three geometric figures to one of four sets of designs.

Strengths

1. Sensitive to posterior brain damage, particularly in the left parietal lobe.
2. Places little emphasis on the patient's visual memory.
3. Requires only 15 to 20 minutes to administer.
4. Normative data allows comparison with normal controls and brain-damaged patients.

Limitations

1. Poor performance may be due to a wide range of factors including visual difficulties, anxiety, psychotic thinking, or malingering.
2. Test score should be corroborated by neurological studies and other neuropsychological test data.

TESTS OF ABSTRACT THINKING

PROVERBS TEST

Description

This test requires the patient to interpret 12 proverbs such as "Shallow brooks are noisy."

Strengths

1. Provides an index of the patient's abstract thinking skills following brain injury.
2. Relatively easy to administer.

Limitations

1. Lacks normative data for brain-damaged or normal controls.
2. Patients raised in a different culture or whose native language is not English generally do poorly on this test.
3. Poor performance can also reflect limited education, low intellectual functioning, or culturally deprived backgrounds.

SIMILARITIES TEST

Description

Is one of the six verbal subtests of the WAIS-R. The patient is asked how two objects go together (e.g., a table and chair).

Strengths

1. Sensitive to concrete thinking which is commonly observed in brain-damaged patients.
2. Adequate normative data.
3. Patient's score can be compared to other WAIS-R subtests.

Limitations

1. Tends to be insensitive to mild anterior brain damage or extensive posterior brain damage.
2. Poor performance can also been seen in psychotic or severely depressed patients.
3. Patient's performance needs to be correlated with the patient's medical history, complaints, other neuropsychological test data, and observations of significant others.

TESTS OF CONCEPTUAL THINKING/PROBLEM SOLVING

CATEGORY TEST

Description

Assesses the patient's conceptual and problem solving skills. The patient is shown 208 stimulus cards and must decide on whether it represents the numbers 1, 2, 3, or 4. The patient is provided feedback as to whether their answer is correct or incorrect. Based on this feedback they must determine the underlying concept on each of seven subtests.

Strengths

1. Provides a quantitative score.
2. Sensitive to diffuse brain damage.
3. Test is part of Halstead-Reitan Neuropsychological Battery.

Limitations

1. Normative control data varies considerably which creates a high risk of making false positive errors.
2. Equipment is bulky and not easy to transport.
3. Visually impaired or elderly patients can be inaccurately diagnosed as "brain-damaged."
4. Poor performance can reflect a variety of non-neurological factors, including low IQ, anxiety, depression, etc.

RAVEN PROGRESSIVE MATRICES

Description

Is a test of conceptual thinking and problem solving. Patients are presented with a rectangle containing a set of designs with one part missing and must decide which one of six or eight parts correctly completes the missing part. The test consists of 60 items which are broken down into five sets of 12 items of increasing conceptual difficulty.

Strengths

1. Serves as a relatively culture-free test of intellectual functioning.
2. Produces an IQ score.
3. Easy to administer.
4. Can serve as an estimate of the patient's premorbid intellectual functioning.

Limitations

1. Does not appear sensitive to brain damage, per se.
2. Poor performance may be caused by severe anxiety, poor visual acuity, physical pain, motivational difficulties, or malingering.
3. The patient's score should be corroborated by pre-injury academic records, achievements, and interviews with significant others.

WISCONSIN CARD SORTING TEST

Description

Evaluates the patient's problem solving skills, cognitive flexibility, ability to maintain a particular conceptual set, and concept formation. The patient is presented with 128 cards which they must match to one of four cards according to one of three categories (color, form, or number). The patient is informed whether they are correct or incorrect after each sorting response. The patient must deduce the underlying principle based on this feedback.

Strengths

1. Is a sensitive test for brain damage.
2. Has adequate validity studies and normative data.
3. Highly sensitive to frontal lobe pathology.

Limitations

1. Tends to be insensitive to orbital frontal lobe damage.
2. Inappropriate for color-blind or visually impaired patients.
3. The patient's performance is highly correlated with their IQ. Thus, patients with low IQ scores are likely to do poorly.
4. The patient's performance should be correlated with medical records and observations of significant others.

TESTS OF SPATIAL-PERCEPTUAL/CONSTRUCTION SKILLS

BLOCK DESIGN TEST

Description

Consists of assembling four or nine one-inch blocks with different colored sides to reproduce a specific geometric design.

Strengths

1. Sensitive to brain damage, particularly in the frontal or parietal lobes.
2. Qualitative scoring methods can be used to localize the site of injury.
3. One of the subtests of the WAIS-R.

Limitations

1. Poor performance can be due to poor visual acuity, orthopedic injury, anxiety, depression, physical pain and discomfort, or inadequate motivation.
2. The patient's performance should be corroborated by medical history, other neuropsychological test data, and behavioral observations of significant others.

REY-OSTERRIETH COMPLEX FIGURE TEST

Description

Patients must copy a complex geometric figure onto a sheet of paper to assess their perceptual/constructional skills.

Strengths

1. Is sensitive to subtle perceptual and constructional impairments.
2. Relatively easy to administer.
3. Qualitative scoring methods permit localization of brain injury.

Limitations

1. Poor performance can reflect a wide variety of non-neurological factors, including anxiety, visual difficulties, orthopedic problems, etc.
2. Since the patient's performance is under their conscious control, malingering always remains a possibility.

TACTUAL PERFORMANCE TEST

Description

Evaluates the patient's constructional skills while blind-folded, with each hand separately and with both hands working together.

Strengths

1. Provides quantitative data to evaluate severity of the patient's impairment.
2. Part of the Halstead-Reitan Neuropsychological Battery.
3. Possesses an adequate normative database.

Limitations

1. Poor performance may reflect a variety of non-neurological factors.
2. Norms used by different examiners may vary considerably.
3. Poor performance is often associated with increasing age.

TESTS OF ACADEMIC SKILLS

WIDE RANGE ACHIEVEMENT TEST (WRAT)

Description

This test assesses the patient's spelling, reading, and arithmetic levels of competence. Level I evaluates children from ages five to 11, while Level II can be used from age 12 up.

Strengths

1. Scores can be compared to age norms and converted into percentiles to determine grade equivalency.
2. Can be used to evaluate patients with previous history of learning difficulties.

Limitations

1. Not specifically designed to evaluate brain damage.
2. Brain-damaged patients can perform poorly on the arithmetic test because it is timed.
3. Poor performance can reflect a variety of non-neurological factors such as medications, poor vision, depression, anxiety, or poor motivation.

TESTS OF LANGUAGE

APHASIA SCREENING TEST

Description

Is a 51-item screening test to evaluate impairments in language and nonlanguage skills.

Strengths

1. Relatively simple to administer.
2. Used as a part of the Halstead-Reitan Neuropsychological Battery.

Limitations

1. The test has been criticized for its relative insensitivity to subtle aphasic disturbances.
2. Poor performance can be due to non-neurological factors such as anxiety, prior history of dyslexia, limited educational background, poor command of the English language, psychotic thinking, etc.

BOSTON DIAGNOSTIC APHASIA EXAMINATION

Description

Contains a total of 34 subtests to provide a comprehensive assessment of a patient's communication skills and aphasic impairments.

Strengths

1. Provides a comprehensive assessment of aphasic disturbances.
2. Extremely sensitive to subtle communication and aphasic disturbances.

Limitations

1. Testing may require up to four hours.
2. Examiner must have a strong background in aphasiology (i.e., study of language disturbances).

BOSTON NAMING TEST

Description

Consists of naming 60 drawings which become increasingly difficulty to name.

Strengths

1. Test manual provides normative data based on patient's educational achievements and age.
2. Sensitive to subtle confrontational naming deficits.

Limitations

1. Poor scores can reflect a variety of non-neurological factors.
2. The patient's performance on the test should be corroborated by observations of the patient's verbal behavior during the interview.

CONTROLLED ORAL WORD ASSOCIATION TEST

Description

Consists of having the patient orally generate as many words as possible over three one-minute trials beginning with specific letters.

Strengths

1. Normative data for both males and females is based on the patient's age and educational achievements.
2. Sensitive to subtle verbal fluency deficits following left frontotemporal damage.

Limitations

1. Poor performance can reflect such factors as test anxiety, depression, fatigue, the patient's prior linguistic background, physical pain and discomfort, and motivational difficulties.
2. Poor performance should be corroborated by other test data, medical records, and observations of significant others.

TESTS OF PERSONALITY/EMOTIONAL ADJUSTMENT

MINNESOTA MULTIPHASIC PERSONALITY INVENTORY (MMPI)

Description

The MMPI is the most widely used personality inventory to assess the patient's level of adjustment, personality dynamics, and attitude toward self and world. It contains 566 (MMPI) and 567 (MMPI-II) true or false items.

Strengths

1. MMPI has built-in validity scales to determine whether the patient is malingering or denying psychological problems.
2. Presents a profile of the patient's scores for each clinical scale.
3. Sensitive to a variety of personality disorders and psychiatric problems.
4. Adequate reliability and validity.

Limitations

1. Never designed to evaluate brain-damaged patients.
2. Cannot be used to diagnose brain damage.
3. Interpretations of profiles vary according to background, training, and expertise of the examiner.

MILLON CLINICAL MULTIAXIAL INVENTORY (MCMI)

Description

The MCMI is a 175-item personality inventory which requires the patient to respond in a true/false format.

Strengths

1. It attempts to directly assess pre-existing personality traits or disorders.
2. Computerized interpretations are available.
3. Research studies have demonstrated its validity and reliability.

Limitations

1. Test was never designed to diagnose brain damage.
2. May not accurately assess pre-existing personality traits or disorders.
3. The patient's profile should be corroborated by significant others and behavioral observations.

Chapter 8

Neuropsychological Test Scoring and Analysis

After the neuropsychological testing has been completed, the neuropsychologist must score and analyze the tests that have been administered. In most cases, test scoring is fairly straightforward and requires simply counting the correct items or errors made by the patient on a particular test. In such cases, the neuropsychologist typically refers to a specific test manual that provides a scoring key and which lists the correct answers for each test item. In other cases, the psychologist must compute the patient's correct performance in terms of the amount of time it took for the patient to obtain the correct answer or by the quality of the answer. For example, several of the subtests on the Wechsler Adult Intelligence Scale (WAIS-R) allow the examiner to give the patient bonus points (either 1 or 2), if the correct response is provided within a specified period of time. In other instances, the examiner must assign a specific numeric score to the patient's response based either on the amount of time taken or the relative proximity of the patient's response to the correct answer according to guidelines set forth in the test manual. In many cases, the test manual will provide actual examples of patients' responses so that the examiner can judge the patient's response in terms of its similarity to sample responses and assign a particular score. In other cases, however, the patient's response may not be easily categorized by the test manual, which places the burden of assigning a numeric score to the patient's response on the psychologist's understanding and interpretation of the test manual, as well as his or her training, background, and experience with this particular test.

Mean and Standard Deviation

After the patient's score on a particular test has been determined, the psychologist typically tries to calculate the statistical significance of that score. This is usually done by comparing the patient's score on a particular test to normative data which has been compiled by either the test's author or by subsequent research studies. Normative data usually consists of the mean (average score) and standard deviation, which is a statistical measure of variability from the mean based upon a normal distribution of test scores. The size of the standard deviation determines the degree to which any obtained score is likely to vary from the mean for a particular group of individuals or patients. For example, if a person scores 100 on an IQ test and the standard deviation is 15, then approximately two-thirds or 68.27% of the people who are given this test should fall within one standard deviation of the mean, that is, one standard deviation below and one standard deviation above the mean. Thus, if a person who is given this test scores 93, their score falls within one standard deviation of the mean and is generally consistent with scores obtained from the majority of individuals who take this test. On the other hand, if a person scores 40 on a particular test and the mean for this particular test is 50 and that the standard deviation is 3, then the person's score falls 3.33 standard deviations below the mean. Thus, this person's score on this particular test is quite rare, in that it would be seen in only one individual out of 1,000. This means that if we were to randomly select 1,000 people and give them all this particular test, 999 of these people would be expected to score better than this person. Thus, through the use of comparison means and standard deviation scores, the neuropsychologist can determine precisely how poorly or how well a particular patient scored on a particular test.

Determining the Relative Severity of the Patient's Cognitive Impairments

Many psychologists and neuropsychologists typically base the relative severity (e.g., slight, mild, moderate, marked, severe, profound) of the patient's cognitive impairments on the degree to which the patient's score on a particular test or set of tests deviates statistically in terms of standard deviation units from the mean of the normal controls. If the patient scores two standard deviations below the mean, the psychologist is likely to infer that the patient is moderately impaired. Unfortunately, in many cases, this practice is idiosyncratic to the psychologist or neuropsychologist making this determination. The author has seen some neuropsychologists conclude that a particular patient is mildly impaired in a specific cognitive ability, such as speed of cognitive processing, because their score on a particular test, like the Symbol Digit Modalities test, placed them one standard deviation below the mean of the control group. Another neuropsychologist may interpret the patient's score on this test as indicative of "minimal or no impairment." Thus, one can easily see that while there may be relatively little dispute regarding the magnitude of the patient's score from a particular mean, the clinical significance given by many neuropsychologists often varies considerably. For example, the author vividly recalls examining the test scores of a patient who had been examined by a particular psychologist. The psychologist reported that the patient had exhibited evidence of marked impairment in her conceptual thinking and problem solving skills. This was based on the patient's score of 45 on the Category test. The author noted that the norms for normal controls reported a mean of 32.38 and a standard deviation of 12.62 (Reitan 1955). Thus, this patient's score tested at only 1.0 standard deviations below the mean for normal controls. Yet, the psychologist had concluded in his report that the patient's score on this particular test revealed evidence of marked impairment in the patient's conceptual thinking and problem solving skills as determined by this particular test. The psychologist's opinion taken to its illogical conclusion suggests that 16% (e.g., the percentage of normal controls whose scores fall below one standard deviation) of most people are markedly impaired in their conceptual thinking and problem solving skills.

Unfortunately, many psychologists and neuropsychologists tend to look at a patient's test scores in an absolute manner. In other words, a poor score on a particular neuropsychological test, such as the Category test, indicates brain damage, and the severity of the patient's brain damage is in direct proportion to the severity of the patient's score. While in some cases this may be true, in many legal cases, however, poor scores on a particular test indicate poor performance, but may not necessarily indicate brain damage. Also, the severity of a patient's score, that is its magnitude in terms of standard deviation units below the mean, may not necessarily reflect the severity of a brain injury or even its presence!

Poor Performances on Tests

Poor performances on neuropsychological tests can reflect a number of factors which may be unrelated to brain injury. For example, if the patient has sustained a low back injury and orthopedic injuries to both legs and admits that he is unable to sleep at night and is in constant pain and discomfort, then these are strong indications that he will perform poorly on any test which requires sustained attention or concentration. If we also assume that he has been taking several pain medications each day and finds that the only relief he can get from his pain is to drink one quart of whiskey each night before retiring, then the likelihood of him scoring poorly further increases. The patient is seen at 8:30 a.m. in the examiner's office and is given the Category test at 8:45 a.m. The patient completes the test by 10 a.m. The patient knows that any type of prolonged sitting for more than 10 minutes results in intense pain and discomfort, which affects his concentration skills. Prior to testing, he has been informed by the psychologist's secretary that he may be required to sit for prolonged periods of time. The patient decides that he does not wish to cry in front of the doctor and takes four pain medications which produce blurred vision and mental confusion when taken at once. During testing, however, the patient still experiences rather severe pain in his low back and decides that he wants to get the test over with as quickly as possible so that he can leave the psychologist's office and go home to lie flat on his back. The patient decides to simply press the Number 4 button each time a stimulus picture is presented to him. This dramatically speeds up the time taken to complete the test and allows the patient to leave the doctor's office as quickly as possible. The psychologist calculates the patient's score, which indicates that the patient has made 144 errors on this test. The psychologist concludes that the patient shows evidence of severe impairment and has sustained a severe diffuse brain injury since the cut-off score used by Reitan is 51 errors for brain-damaged patients. However, because of the various extraneous factors described above, it is not possible to draw any conclusions regarding brain damage on the basis of the patient's score or performance on this particular test.

Comparison Groups: Are They Really Representative?

The comparison group to which the patient's scores are compared may not be representative of the patient's background, skills, or abilities. For example, if a Hispanic patient who has only completed three years of formal education and speaks little English is given this test and achieves a score of 55 (which exceeds the cut-off score used to categorize individuals as either brain-damaged or normal), then the psychologist must decide that if the patient had never been involved in the accident of record, would his or her score on this particular test be any different? Unfortunately, psychologists who treat scores in an absolute sense frequently ignore this issue and consequently are likely to reach erroneous conclusions about the presence or absence of brain injury. The author has frequently observed that such psychologists typically spend little, if any, time with the patient and utilize technicians or psychological assistants to administer neuropsychological tests to the patient. Such individuals rarely obtain a clinical or background history from the patient and rarely, if ever, interview significant others. The case example provided below illustrates this point.

CASE STUDY

The patient is a 45-year-old male who had been involved in an automobile accident in which he was not rendered unconscious and there was no physical evidence of head trauma. He was able to provide an excellent recall of all the events that occurred immediately prior to, during, and following the accident. He had no trouble recalling detailed conversations that were held with drivers of the other vehicles, the paramedics at the scene of the accident, and doctors in the emergency room. He was noted by the paramedics and emergency room physicians to be alert, oriented, and cognitively and neurologically intact. Shortly after his accident, he began experiencing nightmares and began to complain of concentration and memory difficulties consistent with a post-traumatic stress disorder. He was referred, however, by his neurologist for neuropsychological testing, which was done by a clinical psychologist whose background and training consisted of taking a three-day workshop in the administration and scoring of the Luria-Nebraska Neuropsychological Battery.

The patient complained to the psychologist of frequent headaches, numbness in his head, arm, and hand, concentration difficulties, dizziness, balance difficulties, occasional double vision, memory difficulties, difficulties understanding others, slurred speech, deteriorated handwriting, sexual difficulties, nightmares, irritability, fatigue, confusion, and feelings of disorientation. In response to the patient's complaints, the psychologist stated in his report that, "The symptoms that he offers are all ones which are associated with brain insult. The purpose of neuropsychological testing today is to provide corroboration for the patient's complaints."

The history obtained by the psychologist from the patient indicated that the patient had been involved in an automobile accident that was the fault of the other party. The patient informed the psychologist that he was unconscious for at least 24 hours following his accident and that his memory of the events over the next two weeks was spotty. (This information was contradicted by his medical records.) He presented as a physically small individual who looked older than his stated age. He was appropriately dressed with appropriate personal hygiene and grooming. He was examined over four two-hour sessions. He appeared cooperative and pleasant.

The psychologist's description of his neuropsychological test data were as follows: "The results of neuropsychological testing indicate that this patient has suffered brain damage and consequent cognitive, tactile, and verbal impairments. He also demonstrated a generalized slowness, difficulties in receptive and expressive speech, perceptual difficulties, attention and concentration difficulties, problems in abstract thinking, learning difficulties, and problems dealing with complex relational concepts. The patient also demonstrates problems in learning which are common among people who have suffered frontal lobe damage."

The psychologist concluded, "On the basis of neuropsychological testing, this patient appears to be suffering from brain damage which is diffuse and bilateral and is most prominent in his left and right frontal lobes, left and right temporal lobes, and right occipital/parietal areas. His brain deficits are of mild to moderate severity but still render him occupationally disabled."

Comment

This psychologist appears to have based his conclusions entirely on the history of unconsciousness with which the patient provided him (the patient was never rendered unconscious according to the paramedics and emergency room records) and his interpretation of the neuropsychological test data. The psychologist also appears to have relied on the patient's numerous complaints in reaching his conclusions of brain injury, since he states, "ones which are associated with brain insult." Unfortunately, there is no mention in this psychologist's report of ever observing such problems while the patient was in his office for a total of eight hours over four sessions. Additionally, such complaints are rarely provided by patients who have sustained traumatic brain injuries. Careful examination of the psychologist's test data, however, contradict his conclusions, in that only two of the clinical scales exceeded the critical level on the Luria-Nebraska Neuropsychological Battery. Three or more scores exceeding the critical level are necessary to infer the presence of brain injury on the test data alone. The psychologist makes no mention in his report of such factors as depression, fatigue, nervousness, or anxiety which had been noted by each of the patient's previous examiners and by his own treating doctors in their reports which the psychologist had never bothered to review. There is no mention whatsoever of the possible confounding influence of these factors in his report, even if the test scores had suggested the possibility of brain impairment. The psychologist also did not administer any tests of emotional functioning to determine whether the patient had any personality or emotional problems which could have influenced his test performance or caused him to complain of so many somatic problems. When the MMPI was later administered by another psychologist, it revealed a long history of exaggerated physical complaints and strong needs for secondary gains. It also indicated that this patient is likely to use his somatic complaints as a means of manipulation and deceiving others for purposes of secondary gain.

Does the Normative Data Fit the Patient?

While it is generally assumed that the means and standard deviations of normal controls are representative of that population, this assumption has recently been challenged by Fromm-Auch and Yeudall (1983). These investigators found that the mean and standard deviations for normal controls based on a number of validation studies of the Haltead-Reitan Battery showed a wide range of variability. Thus, one psychologist using one set of norms and analyzing test data could conclude that a particular patient's score on one of the Halstead-Reitan tests was impaired, while another using a different set of norms might conclude that there was no impairment in this patient's cognitive functioning as determined by that particular test. The psychologist or neuropsychologist using a certain set of norms should be able to justify his or her choice for using that set of norms as well as how a particular patient "fits" the normative control group in terms of their attributes, such as sex, age, occupation, educational achievements, intellectual functioning, cultural and linguistic background, etc. When a particular patient does not fit a particular normative group, then the use of the mean and standard deviations of this group to judge whether the patient is impaired or not on a particular test is likely to result in spurious conclusions.

Normative data exists for "brain-damaged" patients. Thus, a particular patient's score can be compared to the test scores of patients who have been diagnosed as brain-damaged to determine if any similarities exist. For example, if a particular patient achieves a score of 65 errors on the Category test, his or her scores can be compared to the mean and standard deviations of "brain-damaged" patients. For example, based on the norms obtained by Reitan (1955), the patient's score (65) would be slightly higher than the mean of approximately 62, which is for brain-damaged patients. Since the standard deviation for the brain-damaged group was 21.82, the patient's score appears consistent with scores obtained from brain-damaged patients. However, without looking at the other factors, one should not simply conclude that the patient is brain-damaged. For example, if the patient had only completed the seventh grade and had worked as a dishwasher for most of his life, then his relatively poor score on this test could reflect the fact that he may have been borderline retarded in his intellectual functioning prior to his injury. Since patients with low IQ's tend to score poorly on this test in the absence of brain damage, the patient's score on this test could simply reflect his low premorbid IQ score.

Does the Patient Behave Like They Have a Brain Injury?

The real issue, however, is whether or not this patient behaves like he is brain-damaged. In other words, does this patient exhibit the types of symptoms, behaviors, and neuropsychological test performances which are generally seen in patients who have sustained brain injuries? Thus, even though his score on a particular test from a quantitative perspective may categorize him as brain-damaged or indicate that his performance on this particular test is similar to brain-damaged patients, does this hold up from a qualitative and ecological perspective? In other words, does he exhibit behaviors inside and outside of the examiner's office that are generally consistent with brain-injured patients? For example, a patient has been referred for neuropsychological testing by the patient's treating physician, who asks the neuropsychologist to "rule out brain damage." The patient is taken to the neuropsychologist's office by his wife. When the patient is asked if he or she has any problems or difficulties, the patient states, "No, I don't think so." The patient appears confused and bewildered and does not know the correct day of the week or the month. The patient is a poor historian, in that his memory for events that have occurred since the accident appears very spotty and fragmented. He has no recollection of the accident, even though his medical records indicate that he was rendered unconscious for approximately 30 minutes. His wife was interviewed. She informed the neuropsychologist that she had observed a dramatic change in her husband's behavior in that he is now absent-minded, irritable, oblivious to what's going on around him at home, and displays impulsive behavior and poor judgement whenever they go shopping. The neuropsychologist, over the six hours the patient spends in his office, observes evidence of these problems. The patient performs poorly on neuropsychological tests that are sensitive to frontal lobe pathology but does well on neuropsychological tests that are sensitive to posterior lobe pathology. The patient goes to the bathroom but later is found wandering up and down the hallway appearing confused and bewildered. The patient's wife explains that she must leave and pick up their children from school. Later, when the patient is asked, "When did you last see your wife?", he indicates, "Yesterday." When he is then asked how he got to the examiner's office that morning, he states, "I drove here alone this morning." Later, on tests of memory, the patient exhibits evidence of severe memory impairment for recent events and confabulation, such as filling in the gaps in his memory for certain events with fantasized versions of these events. The patient also demonstrates impulsivity, distractibility, and perseverations during the interview and neuropsychological testing. Whenever he makes an error, he is not observed to become upset but appears instead to be quite indifferent. His affect appears flat. He also talks in an almost robotic monotone fashion.

From this example, one can see that this patient acts like he is brain-damaged without giving the impression that he is "acting." Thus, from a qualitative and ecological perspective he appears to be brain-damaged. If this is supported by the clinical history, interviews with significant others, medical records, and neuropsychological test data, then there is a very strong likelihood that this patient is brain-damaged.

Most neuropsychological tests allow the experienced clinician to perform a qualitative analysis of the patient's performance. For example, the Trail Making Test (Parts A and B) is a quantitative measure of the patient's visual-motor tracking skills. Scoring consists of the time required for the patient to complete Parts A and B. On the other hand, if the psychologist observes the patient taking the test, then he or she has additional qualitative information to rely on in determining whether the patient's performance was impaired. For example, if the patient is given this test and achieves quantitative scores which are consistent with brain-damaged patients but fails to make any errors or require any cues or prompts from the examiner similar to normal controls, then the neuropsychologist must decide on which set of data to rely on in reaching any conclusions about the patient's performance on this test and about whether or not this patient's performance is consistent with brain damage.

In most cases, however, the patient will exhibit a relatively consistent pattern of behavior during testing which provides the examiner with consistent and reliable qualitative information about the patient. For example, the examiner notices that the patient has no difficulty following the test instructions (which are often complicated) and requires no assistance, cues, or prompts during testing. The patient was never observed to be confused, bewildered, or to exhibit any evidence of gross neuropsychological impairments outside of formal testing. For example, the patient had no difficulty recalling what the examiner had discussed with him prior to going to the restroom and appeared abreast of current and local news events. The patient had no trouble recalling the doctor's name and arrived for her scheduled appointment alone at the designated time. The neuropsychologist noted, however, that during testing, the patient appeared quite nervous and began sweating profusely. The neuropsychologist also observed that the patient's hands during testing began trembling and that the patient began to draw attention to her poor performance. From a quantitative perspective, the patient's performance was found to be consistent with severe traumatic brain damage, however, from a qualitative perspective, the patient's behavior was inconsistent with brain damage and was consistent with emotional problems which had persisted throughout the majority of this patient's life. Many neuropsychologists will include both quantitative and qualitative information about the patient's behavior in their reports.

Chapter 9

Test Interpretation

The interpretation of neuropsychological test data is difficult because of the numerous factors that must be considered to arrive at valid conclusions about whether a patient has brain damage. For example, after each of the patient's test scores are analyzed in terms of their statistical significance, the neuropsychologist must then decide whether the pattern of the patient's test scores is consistent with a well-recognized neurobehavioral disorder, such as hypoxic encephalopathy, cerebral concussion, Alzheimer's Disease, etc. For this to be done effectively, the neuropsychologist must understand the expected cognitive, behavioral, and emotional sequelae of specific neurological disorders or diseases. Thus, if the results of neuropsychological testing do not fit a well-recognized neurological disorder or disease, then the neuropsychologist must ask, "What other explanations are there to explain this data?" In a surprising number of cases, this question is not answered, which results in the neuropsychologist reaching inaccurate conclusions or diagnoses. In the author's opinion, this is most likely to occur when the neuropsychologist is either incompetent, in the sense of lacking sufficient background in behavioral neurology and, thus, fails to recognize the consistencies or inconsistences between the test results and a specific neurological disorder, or basically dishonest. To illustrate this point, the author presents a case involving a 40-year-old female who claimed brain damage secondary to exposure to industrial solvents during her employment at a film studio. She was seen by six psychologists, who examined her and based their respective interpretations on her neuropsychological test data. The name of the applicant and names of the psychologists have been changed to protect their identities.

Dr. Rube

Dr. Rube examined the applicant on 2/15/84 after she had been referred by Dr. Jones, a neurologist, to determine whether and to what extent she might be intellectually or emotionally impaired due to a suspected "organic brain syndrome." Dr. Rube noted that the patient presented as an alert, outgoing, and personally engaging lady. Despite her numerous complaints, she appeared unusually cheerful and optimistic. She also appeared voluble and was responsive to questions. She indicated that she had won a National Merit scholarship and that both her SAT and IQ scores had been exceptionally high prior to her employment. She also indicated that there were no other apparent causes of her complaints except for possible exposure to industrial solvents during the course of her employment at a film studio. She denied a history of any serious illnesses, head trauma, or seizures. She also denied a family history of psychiatric problems. She had participated in group therapy from 1970 through 1973 at the request of a boyfriend. She was seen by a psychologist for counseling in 1980 stemming from interpersonal problems and irritability. At the time she had been seeing Dr. Rube, she had been in individual psychotherapy for several months.

The applicant complained of the following problems to Dr. Rube:

1. Impaired balance and gross motor coordination difficulties. She claimed that she was "extremely clumsy" and sometimes fell.

2. Impaired fine motor coordination. She indicated that since 1980, she could no longer keep her fingers coordinated. She also indicated that her handwriting is "terrible." She also complained that at work "she is clumsy with tools and drops them."

3. Impaired pronunciation. She indicated that she has difficulty pronouncing some words correctly and sometimes felt that she was saying familiar words for the first time.

4. Sexual impairment. She indicated that she had experienced no sex drive since 1980. She claimed that this was "highly unusual" because she used to enjoy sex several times weekly. She claimed that she no longer achieved orgasm except with considerable effort, a problem which she claimed she did not have prior to 1980.

5. Impaired memory and concentration. She indicated that she could not account for significant periods of time and had difficulty recognizing persons she once knew well. She indicated, however, that her memory for material that she read was somewhat better than it was when she was working.

6. Impaired mathematical ability. She claimed that at the beginning of 1980 she "lost the ability to manipulate fractions or calculate percentages." Although she indicated that this problem had improved somewhat, she had continued to experience difficulties in this area.

7. Impaired geographic orientation. She claimed that early in 1983, there was a period when she could not tell directions. She indicated that she got lost getting in and out of the city, but noted some improvement in this area since then.

8. Impaired visual-spatial abilities. She claimed that she now draws "terribly" and had "given up drawing."

9. Emotional difficulties. She claimed that she had become more irritable and had a shorter temper than she previously had. She also stated that she was very sensitive to "slights," and began psychotherapy about one year ago because of these emotional problems.

Dr. Rube indicated, "The above pattern of emotional and cognitive impairments is consistent with psychological impairment due to an organic brain syndrome." He then indicated in his report that he carried out "diagnostic, psychological testing to evaluate these complaints to determine as reliably as possible whether and to what extent the applicant may be intellectually or emotionally impaired due to an organic brain syndrome."

Dr. Rube then stated that the applicant's test performance implied a pattern of impairment that is "consistent with organic brain syndrome," in that she showed evidence of impaired visual-spatial (constructional) abilities, impaired concentration and tracking, and impaired arithmetic reasoning. Dr. Rube based this on the applicant's ability to draw or assemble three-dimensional objects and on her performance on the tactual performance test. Careful review, however, of Dr. Rube's test data revealed that the applicant's drawing of a cross was performed quite well and revealed no evidence of impairment. Dr. Rube contended that her "low" block design subtest score on the WAIS-R was "inconsistent with the level of accuracy which would reasonably be expected for a person who has had a career as a graphic artist." (Author's note: Careful analysis of Dr. Rube's test data indicated that the applicant rotated one of the blocks 45° on Design 4 and apparently failed to recognize this discrepancy. As a consequence, she did not receive any points on this item. It should be noted, however, that the applicant was able to complete the remaining five designs, which were more difficult, without error. Thus, this oversight on her part may have been caused by anxiety which apparently served as the basis for Dr. Rube's contention that the applicant's visual-spatial abilities were impaired. However, had she not made this one error, she would have most likely received five points of credit, which would have increased her overall score on this subtest to 35, and given her an age-corrected scaled score of 12, which would have been identical to her digit symbol subtest score [12]. Since the digit symbol subtest is generally regarded as the most sensitive subtest on the WAIS-R to the presence of organic brain dysfunction, the lack of any difference between these tests indicates that Dr. Rube's interpretation of the applicant's test data is unwarranted.)

Dr. Rube reported that the applicant's performance on the tactual performance test was impaired and suggested that her impairment on this test was "probably caused by an impaired sense of spatial relations." (Author's note: Dr. Rube's interpretation of her test findings is unwarranted, since careful analysis of the test data revealed that her performance on the localization component of the tactual performance test was actually higher than the mean for normal controls. The applicant's performance on this test would indicate that her spatial relationships and tactile learning skills are intact. Furthermore, the applicant's spatial memory score, which is a measure of her tactile learning abilities, also fell within the normal range. Dr. Rube's interpretation of the test data appears to be based entirely on the length of time the applicant took to complete this test, which fell outside the cut-off score developed by Reitan. However, this cut-off score has been found by researchers [Lezak, 1983], to be "questionable when applied to persons over the age of 40." In addition, a blindfold was placed over the applicant's eyes during the test. Some individuals become quite anxious when this occurs and typically require more time to complete the test than usual.)

Dr. Rube reported finding evidence of "impaired concentration and tracking." He based this on his interpretation on the applicant's performance on the Trail Making test and her difficulties on the arithmetic subtest of the WAIS-R. The applicant required 26 seconds to complete Part A and 65 seconds to complete Part B. However, her performance on both of these tasks placed her within the normal range for persons her age. Dr. Rube contended that the applicant's performance on the arithmetic subtest of the WAIS-R indicated that she is "somewhat distractable; that is, that she is having some difficulty keeping her mind on problem solving when it requires going through a series of mental steps." (Author's note: Dr. Rube's conclusions are contradicted by the fact that the applicant obtained an age-corrected scaled score of 13 [above average performance] on the digit span subtest, which is a more sensitive test of distractibility than the arithmetic subtest. Thus, her score on this test contradicted Dr. Rube's interpretation.)

Dr. Rube concluded that the applicant's test performance was consistent with organic brain syndrome. (Author's note: Dr. Rube's conclusions are strongly contradicted by the applicant's excellent performance on memory testing. For example, she was able to learn all 15 words on the Rey-Auditory Verbal Learning test by the end of the third trial, which placed her 1.14 standard deviations above the mean for professionals, typically individuals of generally superior intellectual functioning. The applicant was also able to recall 13 out of 15 words when she was given a second list after only the first presentation of these words. It should be noted that brain-damaged patients typically perform significantly poorer when they are given a new list of words after having learned a previous [different] list of words. In this applicant's case, however, her performance was in the exact opposite direction than would be expected if she were brain-damaged, in that she was able to learn more words on the first trial of the second list than on the first trial of the first list. This finding suggests that the applicant was most likely anxious on the first trial of the first list. A review of Dr. Rube's test data also revealed that the applicant's ability to learn a list of 10 paired associates on the Wechsler Memory Scale was also excellent, in that she was able to recall all 10 paired associates after the first trial. The author has never seen anyone perform better on memory testing than this applicant who was claiming to be brain-damaged. In addition, there is no indication that this applicant had ever undergone any type of psychological or neuropsychological testing prior to being examined by Dr. Rube. Furthermore, her performance on the logical memory test of the Wechsler Memory Scale indicated that she was able to recall an average of 14 bits of information from each story, which placed her 3.4 standard deviations above the mean of what would be expected from a 40-year-old woman. Since memory impairment is typically the most commonly observed symptom in patients with organic brain syndromes, the applicant's exceptional performances on tests involving recent memory strongly contradict Dr. Rube's conclusions.)

Dr. Rube administered the Minnesota Multiphasic Personality Inventory to the applicant. (Author's note: Dr. Rube, however, did not discuss the applicant's profile on this test in his report. The applicant's MMPI profile indicated evidence of "la belle indifference," which is typically the hallmark of a conversion neurosis or hysterical conversion disorder. This indicated that her symptoms would be at least partially psychological in origin, in that patients with similar profiles typically have a history of hypochondriacal complaints and that such patients frequently dramatize their complaints for purposes of secondary gain. Her profile also suggested that if this applicant were to be involved in any legal action or compensation procedure, she would most likely unconsciously manipulate the situation. Finally, her profile suggested that the precipitating circumstances in her complaints are likely to involve the loss of a significant interpersonal relationship.)

Dr. Rube concluded in his report that, "The pattern of impairments seen on neuropsychological testing is generally consistent with the applicant's complaints." (Author's note: It should be noted that Dr. Rube found no evidence of impaired fine motor coordination, pronunciation, memory, concentration, mathematical abilities, geographic orientation, or visual-spatial abilities which are commonly observed in patients who sustain brain damage as a result of chronic exposure to industrial solvents with neurotoxic properties.) Dr. Rube also felt that the applicant's neuropsychological impairments were "slight to moderate." (Author's note: There is nothing in Dr. Rube's data that suggests any evidence of impairment which could not be explained by simple test anxiety. Dr. Rube also failed to comment that the applicant's overall pattern of performance across the different neuropsychological tests she was administered did not fit any known organic brain syndrome, but instead revealed an individual whose attention-concentration, recent memory, language, judgement, visual-spatial, abstract thinking, and judgement skills were intact.)

Dr. Rube further concluded that "the pattern of impairments seen on neuropsychological testing is consistent with reports in the literature about the neurotoxic effects of exposure to a volatile organic substance and psychological sequelae." (Author's note: Dr. Rube's conclusions are highly inconsistent with recent reviews of this literature by Spencer [1984] and Hartman [1988].)

Comment

Dr. Rube's interpretations and conclusions are not even remotely supported by his own test data. What he finds is a bright, articulate woman who exhibits numerous complaints in a histrionic fashion. His own test data actually contradicts the applicant's complaints and finds her cognitive functioning to be intact. He ignores her exceptional memory and MMPI profile, which strongly contradict his interpretations and opinions, and concluded that the applicant has an organic brain syndrome which he described as ranging from slight to moderate. He concluded that the applicant's "impairments" are consistent with the literature on the neurotoxic effects of exposure to volatile organic substances, even though this opinion is strongly contradicted by two recent reviews of this literature.

Though Dr. Rube found evidence of a hysterical neurosis on psychological testing, he apparently chose to ignore this to conclude that the applicant has had an organic brain syndrome which he attributed to organic solvent exposure. Dr. Rube said that there is no other possible explanation of his test findings other than that of brain damage. Dr. Rube failed to mention in his report that the applicant had a long-standing history of hypothyroidism and had sustained a cerebral concussion in 1979 as a result of a motor vehicle accident.

Dr. Smith

The applicant informed Dr. Smith that while working for a film studio from 1979 to 1983, she was subjected to "supervisory harassment," as well as exposure to a variety of chemicals in a poorly ventilated room during the course of her employment. She indicated that her initial symptomatology began approximately six months after she commenced her employment, which included "flu-like symptoms consisting of sore throat, headaches, and a sensation of feeling fuzzy." She also began experiencing "impaired equilibrium," which consisted of tripping without falling or sustaining head injuries. She also stated that she developed an "almost electronic stutter" and reading difficulties. She indicated that her memory for recent events was poor and that she was no longer able to draw. She continued to experience headaches on a weekly basis. The applicant also informed Dr. Smith of a history of "depression with suicidal ideation and anxiety" which preceded her employment.

Dr. Smith indicated that the applicant presented as a casually but neatly dressed female who appeared her stated age. He found no evidence of attention-concentration impairments or distractibility during his interview. He also found no evidence of language difficulties or stuttering. He found her abstract thinking skills to be "quite good." Her affect was described as "pleasant." He also noted that her performance on the digit span test improved with repeated trials. He found that her speech was within normal limits for rate, content, and pressure. He found no evidence of tangential thinking, paraphasic errors, word finding difficulties, or looseness of associations. The applicant denied experiencing any hallucinations.

Dr. Smith saw this applicant on 7/15/85 and reported evidence of impaired memory, which is exactly the opposite of what Dr. Rube had found. Dr. Smith's interpretations were contradicted by the applicant's performance on the Wechsler Memory Scale, in which she obtained a memory quotient of 135, which was significantly higher than her full-scale IQ score of 118. (Author's note: It is generally accepted among neuropsychologists that patients with memory impairment typically score significantly lower on the Wechsler Memory Scale than on the Wechsler Intelligence Scale. In this applicant's case, she scored significantly higher.)

Dr. Smith reported that the applicant's performance IQ was 119, while her verbal IQ tested at 113. (Author's note: Patients who sustain brain damage secondary to industrial solvent exposure typically do much worse on the performance subtests. In this applicant's case, the applicant did better on the performance subtest. It should also be noted that the applicant obtained an age-corrected digit symbol subscale score of 14, which was only one point less than her highest performance subtest score. Thus, her performance on the Wechsler Adult Intelligence Scale reveals no evidence of any type of brain dysfunction or impairment. Furthermore, this is exactly opposite to what one typically finds following chronic exposure to industrial solvents.)

Dr. Smith reported that the applicant's full-scale IQ was 118 and reported that her intelligence quotient in school was once tested at approximately 130. He concluded that her present IQ score represented a mild decline in her intellectual functioning from her premorbid levels. Dr. Smith was unaware that Dr. Rube had previously found the applicant to have a full-scale IQ of 127.

Dr. Smith reported that the applicant tested as mildly impaired on the Wisconsin Card Sorting test in that "she was only able to develop five of the six necessary hypotheses." He concluded that her performance revealed that she had "exceptional difficulty" on this test. (Author's note: Dr. Smith's conclusions are unwarranted, since a normative study published by Heaton [1981] indicates that the average number of categories obtained by normal controls, whose average full-scale IQ was 114, was only 5.4. Thus, the applicant's score falls within the normal range and is consistent for persons of her intellectual functioning.)

Dr. Smith found no evidence for any type of expressive or receptive language difficulties, dyscalculia (arithmetic difficulties), dyslexia, or spelling or writing difficulties. He also found that the applicant had no difficulty replicating a three-dimensional cube without the model and found no evidence whatsoever of word finding difficulties. His test results in these areas are corroborated by his observations of her behavior during his interview with the applicant.

Dr. Smith reported evidence of mild impairment in the patient's motor functioning. He found, for example, that her grip strength was mildly impaired in her left hand in comparison to her right hand. (Author's note: Careful examination of her test data revealed that the difference between her grip strength was only 10.8%. Thus, Dr. Smith apparently based his conclusion on the generally accepted rule that the difference in performance between the left and right hands should not be more than 10%. However, Bornstein [1986] reported that a significant proportion of females with no history of brain damage show differences of greater than 10% between their left and right hands. Dr. Smith also reported that the patient's performance on the finger tapping test was impaired. When the applicant's performance on this test was compared to normative data which has recently been published by Fromm-Auch and Yeudall [1983], her performance with both hands fell within the normal range for persons of her age.)

Dr. Smith concluded that the applicant tested as impaired on approximately 20% of the key tests on the Halstead-Reitan Neuropsychological Test Battery. When the applicant's test scores were compared to persons her age, each of her scores were within the normal range. Dr. Smith concluded that "the impairments demonstrated by this applicant on neuropsychological testing are consistent with exposure to toxic chemicals." (Author's note: Dr. Smith's interpretations of her neuropsychological test data appear to be based on his failure to use age-corrected norms. As a consequence, his conclusions are highly inaccurate, since her neuropsychological test performances do not suggest any known neurological disorder. It should also be further noted that while the applicant informed Dr. Smith of her history of hypothyroidism, Dr. Smith made no attempt in his report to correlate the applicant's complaints to this chronic medical condition, even though patients with this condition frequently report similar complaints.)

Dr. Crook

Dr. Crook saw the applicant on 2/6/86. The applicant informed Dr. Crook that during the course of her employment between 1979 and 1983 she had experienced many acute symptoms which included loss of balance, memory lapses, changes in depth perception, acute respiratory problems, and psychological symptoms. Dr. Crook reported that the applicant presented as an attractive, lively, and talkative person who appeared warm and responsive to questioning. The applicant stated that she thought testing would be fun and indicated that some of her "previous psychological testing" had been disturbing to her because "she was not able to perform as well as she wished." Dr. Crook reported that the applicant obtained a full-scale IQ on the WAIS-R of 135 and a verbal IQ of 129, with a performance IQ of 135. The applicant's performance on this test not only contradicts her complaints but also is highly inconsistent with brain damage secondary to industrial solvent exposure. Dr. Crook reported that the applicant's scores on the WAIS-R subtest showed considerable variability, which he interpreted as evidence of organic brain damage. (Author's note: Dr. Crook fails to point out that previous testing by Drs. Rube and Smith revealed no such variability on this test. Careful observation of Dr. Crook's test data indicate that he failed to utilize age-corrected scaled scores when interpreting the results of the applicant's test scores. Had Dr. Crook done this, the applicant's variability on this test would have been significant reduced and would not have been an issue.)

With respect to the applicant's test scores on the WAIS-R, Dr. Crook stated in a cavalier fashion that "the applicant's lowered score on the arithmetic subtest suggests a 'loss in her formerly excellent ability to perform mathematical calculations.' Her impairment in this function indicates a loss in her capacity to sustain the mental tracking necessary to perform sequential reasoning tasks." (Author's note: It should be noted that the applicant achieved a scaled score of 13 on the arithmetic test when she was tested by Drs. Rube and Smith, which indicated that the applicant had tested in the above-average range and that her score did not indicate cognitive impairments in this area. This is corroborated by the applicant's excellent score of 15 on the picture arrangement subtest, which is essentially a task of mental sequencing.)

Dr. Crook reported that the applicant's performance on the receptive and expressive speech skills on the Luria-Nebraska Neuropsychological Battery, while placing the applicant within normal limits, revealed some "significant errors." Dr. Crook strongly argued that "these errors are highly reflective of brain damage." (Author's note: Dr. Arnold Purisch, one of the developers and authors of the Luria-Nebraska Neuropsychological Battery [and the author's associate], was consulted with respect to Dr. Crook's statements. Dr. Purisch concluded that after carefully reviewing the test data, there was "no evidence whatsoever of brain damage," and "the applicant's performance on these specific items reflected test anxiety.")

Dr. Crook reported that the applicant's visual-spatial ability was the applicant's weakest skill. He based this on the fact that the applicant's score on the block design subtest of the WAIS-R fell "into the average range." Dr. Crook argued that this most likely "represented a significant drop" from the applicant's previous level of functioning, in light of the fact that the applicant was a successful graphic artist. (Author's note: It is interesting to note that when age-corrected norms are utilized, the applicant's score on this test fell into the above-average range. Also, Dr. Crook's assumption that the applicant should have performed much better on this test is unwarranted, since the applicant's work history did not involve the manipulation of small blocks which contain colors and geometric designs.)

Dr. Crook indicated that the applicant's total time on the Tactual Performance test was 16.5 minutes and indicated that her score on this test indicated that she was brain-damaged. (Author's note: Dr. Crook made no mention whatsoever that utilizing the cut-off criteria of 15 minutes incorrectly misclassifies over 25% of normal controls as brain-damaged. Using normative data recently published by Dodrill [1988], the applicant's overall score on this test placed her within the normal range as determined by a mean of 13.65 with a standard deviation of 7.21. Dr. Crook also makes no mention whatsoever in the patient's report that the mere condition of placing a blindfold on an anxious individual would be expected to significantly increase test anxiety. This is corroborated by the applicant's poor performance on the localization component of this test, in which she made a score of only two even though she had obtained a score of six when previously tested by Dr. Rube. Rather than addressing the issue of test anxiety and failing to note the discrepancy between prior testing, Dr. Crook stated, "This score demonstrates that the applicant has not recovered her abilities to orient herself in space and that she will continue to have difficulty remembering where she has placed items and finding her way around the city." Dr. Crook's explanation is not only unwarranted but is also contradicted by the applicant's excellent performance on the memory component of this test.)

Dr. Crook indicated that the applicant's performance on the tactual performance test revealed evidence of "right hemisphere damage." (Author's note: Dr. Crook apparently chose to ignore the prior test data of Drs. Rube and Smith, who found no evidence whatsoever of any visual-perceptual difficulties or anything that could be construed as evidence of right hemisphere brain damage or dysfunction. By way of contradiction, Dr. Crook stated, "The applicant's visual scanning ability is excellent and her visual memory and ability to associate verbal stimuli with visual stimuli was also intact." However, it should be noted that these functions are primarily mediated in the right hemisphere of the brain, and that they are typically impaired if a person has sustained right hemisphere brain damage.)

Dr. Crook indicated that the applicant's short-term verbal memory was significantly impaired, in that she had "significant difficulty retaining information when supplied with additional material to memorize." (Author's note: Dr. Crook's finding contradicted previous testing by Drs. Rube and Smith, who found the applicant's memory across all spheres to be outstanding. Unfortunately, Dr. Crook makes no mention in his report of their findings or this discrepancy. It should be noted that Dr. Crook based his conclusions on the applicant's performance on the memory scale of the Luria-Nebraska Neuropsychological Battery, which fell within the normal range, well below the cut-off point that would even be suggestive of even slight impairment.)

Dr. Crook indicated that the applicant exhibited severe problems in thinking, planning, and concept formation skills based on her performance on the Categories test. (Author's note: The applicant obtained a score of 59, which falls within the normal range based on normative data published by Dodrill [1988] and Fromm-Auch Yeudall [1983]. Dr. Crook stated that the applicant's score on this test provides "clear evidence that she has sustained a loss in her ability to engage in abstract thinking." Dr. Crook's conclusion is strongly contradicted by the applicant's performance on both the similarities and comprehension subtests of the WAIS-R and by previous testing by Drs. Rube and Smith, who found that her abstract thinking skills were excellent. It is also contradicted by Dr. Crook's clinical interpretation of the applicant's Rorschach Test, which demonstrated "flexibility in thinking in a rich, intellectual life.")

Dr. Crook administered the MMPI to the applicant and reported that her profile on this test indicated "considerable denial and a lack of awareness of her own contributions to the difficult circumstances that she gets into, as well as a tendency to externalize blame and to rationalize her own behavior." Dr. Crook also indicated that the applicant's MMPI Profile "showed a strong somatic focus and a tendency to convert her repressed emotional feelings into somatic complaints." (Author's note: Dr. Crook made no mention of the fact that this patient had been previously administered this test by Dr. Rube, nor does he mention Dr. Rube's interpretation. He also fails to examine the possibility that the applicant's complaints are excessive and most likely reflect long-standing emotional problems.) Finally, Dr. Crook stated in his report that the applicant's neuropsychological test data was consistent with previous psychological testing by Drs. Rube and Smith. (Author's note: Dr. Crook apparently chose to ignore the numerous inconsistencies between his data and that of Drs. Rube and Smith to reach this conclusion.)

Dr. Oar

The applicant was seen by Dr. Oar on 9/17/87. The applicant indicated to Dr. Oar that she stopped working on 11/17/83 because of "severe memory problems, stuttering, severe attention and concentration difficulties, disorientation to time, person, and place, falling episodes, and numerous cognitive and psychological problems. Dr. Oar indicated that at the time the applicant was seen in his office, she was working as a real estate agent for a large real estate firm and had earned over $75,000 during the past year. She also indicated that she had received extensive psychotherapy in the past and had attempted suicide on two occasions after her relationships with two different men had ended. Dr. Oar noted that the applicant appeared outgoing, pleasant, and was able to provide a very detailed, chronological history in a "understandable and coherent fashion." He observed that the applicant did not tire during her eight-hour testing session. He also noted that her speech was unremarkable and exhibited no evidence of word finding difficulties, dysfluencies, or any aphasic difficulties. In fact, Dr. Oar noted that the applicant spoke with complex sentences and utilized a very sophisticated vocabulary and spoke in a very articulate manner. Dr. Oar indicated that the applicant obtained a full-scale IQ of 127, a verbal IQ of 119, and a performance IQ of 132. (Author's note: Dr. Oar made no mention of this 13-point difference between the applicant's verbal and performance IQ, which is highly inconsistent with brain damage secondary to toxic solvent exposure. Instead, Dr. Oar argued that the applicant's performance on this test demonstrated that "her verbal abilities and skills are impaired," which contradicts his behavioral observations of the applicant's behavior during the interview.)

Dr. Oar reported that the applicant tested as significantly impaired on tests of short-term verbal memory and abstract thinking. (Author's note: The applicant's performance on three different memory tests administered to her by Dr. Oar was outstanding. In addition to this, the applicant completed all six categories on the Wisconsin Card Sorting test, which is a test of problem solving skills. Her performance on this was excellent in that she was able to complete all six categories and made a total of only 11 errors.)

Dr. Oar indicated that the applicant tested as having rather significantly impaired constructional skills. (Author's note: This was contradicted by the fact that the applicant's drawings on the Bender Gestalt test were excellent and the applicant's drawing of a triangle and skeleton key, Greek cross, and bicycle were performed adequately with no evidence of any distortions of shape or size.)

Dr. Oar stated that the applicant's "impaired visual memory rendered her completely incapable of returning to any field which requires that she keep track of visual stimuli." (Author's note: Dr. Oar's highly irresponsible statement completely contradicts all of the previous neuropsychological test data obtained by Drs. Rube, Smith, and Crook, not to mention his own findings, in which he found that the patient's delayed visual recall was virtually perfect. His statement also contradicts the applicant's ability to complete all six categories on the Wisconsin Card Sorting test, which involves visual stimuli and relies heavily on the patient's visual memory. His statement also ignored the applicant's excellent performances on tests of visual-motor tracking [Trail Making test] and visual processing [Picture Arrangement subtest].)

Dr. Joke and Mr. Butt

Dr. Joke, a psychiatrist, saw the applicant on 2/5/88. Dr. Joke referred the applicant to his psychological assistant, Mr. Butt, for neuropsychological testing. The applicant complained to Dr.

Joke of balance difficulties, severe memory loss, severe headaches, burning eyes, sore throat, dyslexia, hair loss, ulceration of her thumb, frequent urination, a dramatic loss of her intellectual functioning, and of being unable to speak. There was no mention in Dr. Joke's report of when these problems initially began or their relationship to her exposure to industrial solvents. She indicated to Dr. Joke that she was currently employed as a real estate agent. (Author's note: She did not indicate that she had earned $75,000 during the past year as a real estate agent. There was no mention in Dr. Joke's report of the discrepancy between the applicant's successful real estate practice and her numerous complaints.)

Mr. Butt administered a variety of psychological tests, which are typically utilized to test the psychological rather than neuropsychological functioning of patients. His choice of tests revealed that he had received very little training in the field of neuropsychology. Mr. Butt found the applicant to be very attractive, well-dressed, extremely articulate, and appearing younger than her stated age. Mr. Butt indicated that he gave the applicant the MMPI to bring home with her. (Author's note: This technically violates the rules of testing, because when patients take tests home there can be no guarantee that they have not consulted with others, or referred to textbooks to help them answer specific questions. Thus, the results of the applicant's MMPI profile cannot be considered valid.) Mr. Butt reported that the applicant attained a memory quotient of 137 on the Wechsler Memory Scale (which is extremely good and strongly contradicts her claim of recent or remote memory difficulties). Mr. Butt reported that the applicant's profile on the MMPI revealed long-standing histrionic tendencies and the likelihood to convert her repressed emotional feelings into a variety of cognitive and somatic complaints.

Even though the applicant admitted to having a 20-year history of hypothyroidism and stated that she frequently forgot her medications (Premarin and Synthroid), Dr. Joke failed to see any relationship between the applicant's complaints and hypothyroidism. (Author's note: Drs. Jefferson and Marshall in their textbook, *Neuropsychiatric Features of Medical Disorders* [1983], state that the most frequently reported symptoms of hypothyroidism are forgetfulness, concentration difficulties, difficulty performing simple arithmetic, anxiety, hair loss, fatigue, diminished appetite, disorientation, and emotional conflicts.) Dr. Joke concluded that the results of his psychiatric examination, combined with neuropsychological testing, revealed that the patient had a "Mixed Organic Brain Syndrome, with bilateral cerebral dysfunction and cerebellar dysfunction." (Author's note: Dr. Joke's conclusions are unwarranted and strongly contradicted by Mr. Butt's test findings, which reveal no evidence whatsoever of any cognitive, speech, memory, attention-concentration, or visual spatial difficulties. In addition, there was no mention whatsoever in Dr. Joke's report of the possibility that all or some of her complaints could be due to her long-standing hypothyroid disorder and her history of relatively poor medication compliance.)

Dr. Hunt

Dr. Hunt administered an extensive battery of psychological tests to the applicant on 6/25/89. He reported that the applicant obtained a full scale IQ of 132, with a performance IQ of 135, and a verbal IQ of 126. He found that the applicant's arithmetic scaled score was 15 and, with the exception of her score of 11 on the Digit Span subtest, there was no evidence of scatter of her verbal subtest scores. The applicant obtained a score of 71 on the Digit Symbol subtest, which gave her an age-corrected scaled score of 16, which is two standard deviations above the mean and consistent with her overall intellectual functioning. She obtained an age-corrected scaled score of 19 on the Object Assembly subtest, which indicated that her visual, spatial, and constructional skills were outstanding. Dr. Hunt reported that the applicant made a total of 31 errors on the Category test. He reported that the applicant's performance on the Trailmaking test was excellent, particularly with respect to her performance on Part B, which she was able to perform in only 37 seconds. (Author's note: Part B is considered to be a highly sensitive test of brain damage. Her performance on this test placed her approximately two standard deviations above the mean for persons her age.) Although Dr. Hunt reported that the applicant's performance on virtually all of the neuropsychological tests he administered to her was intact, he concluded that the applicant had "evidence of borderline organic impairment." (Author's note: Dr. Hunt's conclusions are strongly contradicted by the applicant's excellent performance on virtually every neuropsychological test she was administered. Dr. Hunt made no mention whatsoever of the patient's MMPI profile in his conclusion and that her profile on this test revealed her to be highly manipulative, have a poorly developed conscience, and to have a history of perverse sexual tendencies and underachievement.)

Comment

The above case study demonstrates the problems which a significant number of psychologists have in interpreting neuropsychological test data. It should be noted that three of the six psychologists identified themselves as neuropsychologists on their letterhead stationery. None of these individuals, however, had ever been granted diplomate status by either the American Board of Clinical Neuropsychology or the American Board of Professional Neuropsychology. None of the six psychologists had ever published any studies in the area of neuropsychology, industrial solvent, or toxic exposure. None of the psychologists had ever completed a post-doctoral training program in neuropsychology. Only one of the psychologists had ever received supervision by a qualified neuropsychologist. It should also be noted that only two of the six psychologists obtained a history of the applicant's background. None of the psychologists interviewed any significant others, nor mentioned the marked discrepancy between the patient's behavior during the interview and numerous and exaggerated complaints. Only one of the psychologists even bothered to mention or list the various industrial chemicals and solvents, the applicant claimed she had been exposed to during her four-year employment. Only one of the six psychologists asked the applicant to describe her work duties to determine the nature and extent of her alleged exposure to toxic and industrial chemicals. None of the psychologists asked the applicant if any of her coworkers had developed similar symptoms, particularly coworkers who performed many of the same duties and functions.

Chapter 10

Reaching Conclusions Regarding Brain Damage and/or Cognitive Impairment

Conclusions regarding the presence or absence, severity, location, or type of brain injury, such as diffuse, focal, subcortical, etc., must be made in conjunction with the patient's complaints, history of injury, background information, medical/psychological records, interviews with significant others, and behavioral observations. In other words, it should not be based entirely on the results of a particular neuropsychological test or battery. While studies have shown that the Luria-Nebraska or Halstead-Reitan Neuropsychological Batteries can discriminate between the performance of brain-damaged and nonbrain-damaged patient groups with over 90% accuracy (Golden, Hammeke, and Purisch, 1978; Wheeler and Reitan, 1974), it should be recognized that neuropsychological tests can only provide information about cognitive impairment, but their etiology must be inferred by careful examination of the pattern of behavioral impairments and comparing this pattern to characteristic patterns commonly found in various types of brain disorders (Sbordone and Purisch, 1987). If neuropsychological testing should reveal a pattern of behavioral impairments that is uncharacteristic or inconsistent with well-recognized brain injury syndromes, then the likelihood of brain damage or dysfunction, as well as the validity of the neuropsychological test data, is most likely poor.

The patient's impairments should be generally consistent with the neurobehavioral sequelae expected from a particular type of brain injury. Conversely, the patient's strengths should generally be consistent with the neurobehavioral sequelae expected from the patient's injury, based on a review of the patient's medical records and an interview with the patient and significant others. This principal of what has been described as "double dissociation" was originally proposed by Teuber (1959). Unfortunately, many psychologists lack an adequate understanding of behavioral neurology or brain-behavior relationships and may not recognize the inconsistency between the patient's performance on neuropsychological tests and expected neurobehavioral sequelae stemming from the patient's injury. When inconsistencies occur, the psychologist should carefully review the patient's neuropsychological test data and carefully evaluate the conditions under which the data were obtained, as well as the adequacy of the neuropsychological tests that were administered to the patient.

Strict reliance on test data can have serious shortcomings. For example, Damasio (1979), stressed that neuropsychological testing is relatively insensitive to orbital frontal lobe damage. Since Alexander (1984) reported that this region of the brain is most vulnerable to traumatic brain injuries, conclusions based solely on the neuropsychological test data may be misleading and inaccurate. For example, orbital frontal lobe damage typically produces a pattern of behavioral and emotional disinhibition characterized by inappropriate social comments, inappropriate or antisocial behavior, dramatic changes in personality, poor judgement, impulsivity, marked egocentricity, loss of sexual libido, and poor emotional control (Cummings, 1985; Sbordone, 1990). Psychologists assessing patients who have sustained cerebral contusions resulting in prominent orbital frontal lobe damage, should avoid placing heavy emphasis on their neuropsychological test data and instead should rely heavily on the observations of significant others, the patient's behavior in relatively unstructured situations and a qualitative neuropsychological assessment approach.

CASE STUDY

For example, the author was asked to consult on a case in which the patient, a 45-year-old male, sustained a head trauma in a motor vehicle accident. According to the patient's medical records, it was not clear whether or not he had actually lost consciousness, but he was observed to be combative at the scene of the accident and confused. He was given a Glasgow Coma Scale score of 13. He underwent a CT scan and an EEG, both of which were negative. Neuropsychological testing was requested because his employer and family noticed a dramatic change in his personality following the accident. When the patient was seen approximately nine months post-injury, he denied any cognitive, emotional, or behavioral problems. A background history revealed that he had only completed the ninth grade and had a history of dyslexia. He came from a broken home and had an unhappy childhood. His grades in school were generally poor, which reflected his emotional problems, dislike of school, and dyslexia. He had worked continuously for 15 years as a bus driver and had been described as a very courteous and responsible driver.

Neuropsychological testing revealed only slight impairments on cognitive tasks mediated by his frontal lobes. The neuropsychologist then interviewed the patient's spouse, children, parents, employer, supervisor, coworkers, and family physician. Even though none of these individuals were aware of what others had discussed with the neuropsychologist, or had any real knowledge that the patient had sustained a traumatic brain injury, they consistently reported a dramatic change in the patient's personality since his injury, poor frustration tolerance, impatience, marked egocentricity, impulsivity, poor judgement, coarse and vulgar language, poor social graces, and an inability to regulate his emotions and behavior since his motor vehicle accident. These descriptions were consistent with orbital frontal lobe damage, which was supported by the patient's medical records (e.g., the patient had been diagnosed as having a cerebral contusion when he was seen in the emergency room and had a Glasgow-Coma Scale score of 13).

This example illustrates the importance of not strictly relying on the neuropsychological test data in reaching conclusions about the presence or absence of brain damage and its probable role in causing changes in the patient's behavior. While it is clear that this patient had cognitive difficulties prior to his accident, based on his academic records and a history of dyslexia, each family member and significant other who was interviewed described him as courteous and responsible prior to his motor vehicle accident. He had worked for 15 years as a bus driver, had never been given any form of disciplinary action. A review of his employment records revealed that his supervisors consistently rated him as an excellent employee, who was patient, understanding, and diligent in his work responsibilities and interactions with customers. His wife indicated that prior to his accident they engaged in sexual intercourse approximately three times per week and thoroughly enjoyed it. The patient had always been a considerate father, and had always been fair and understanding to both of his children. After the patient's accident, he no longer showed any interest in sex and had stopped having sexual intercourse with his wife. His wife no longer found him to be the patient and understanding husband that he had once been. Instead, he had become impatient, impulsive, and frequently used vulgar and profane language at the dinner table. He no longer seemed concerned about the welfare of his family. He no longer spent any time with his children or wife and spent virtually all of his time watching cartoons on television. He no longer acted mature and responsible. Since returning to work, several of his customers had phoned his employer and had complained about some of the insulting remarks that he had made toward them, his irresponsible behavior, and dangerous driving. There was little question that this patient's behavior had changed dramatically since his closed head injury. While everyone around him recognized the dramatic changes in his behavior and personality, neuropsychological testing showed evidence of only slight impairment of his cognitive functions.

Many psychologists and neuropsychologists erroneously assume that complex processes, such as the patient's attentional skills, can be adequately assessed by administering one or two neuropsychological tests, such as the Digit Span, Trailmaking, or Symbol Digit Modalities tests, to the patient. In actuality, the patient's attentional skills can be broken down into such skills as alertness, stimulus reactivity, concentration, freedom from distraction, vigilance, flexibility, capacity, speed of processing, resistance to fatigue, resistance to emotional factors, resistance to interference from stimulus overload, and resistance to contiguous stimuli. Neuropsychological tests such as the Digit Span, Trailmaking, or Symbol Digit Modalities tests, may only measure some of these abilities. Thus, "normal" scores on these tests may not rule out that a particular patient may have a number of significant attentional impairments, secondary to their traumatic brain injury (Sbordone, in press).

NEUROPSYCHOLOGICAL TEST PERFORMANCE OF PATIENTS WITH FOCAL BRAIN DAMAGE

Patients who sustain focal brain damage have typically sustained a cerebral contusion. In most cases, these individuals are either rendered briefly unconscious, or not rendered unconscious at all. However, these patients usually show evidence of physical trauma to the head and are typically seen as combative, disoriented, or confused after their accident, and have no recollection of the accident or event that produced their injury. Neuropsychological testing will usually demonstrate impairments on tasks mediated by the site of injury. For example, if a patient has sustained a focal injury involving the left frontal lobe, the patient often exhibits difficulties on tasks involving logical reasoning, grammatical analysis, and problems with organization, mental sequencing, mental arithmetic, and verbal memory. In addition, the strength of their right hand will typically be weaker than expected and their performance on higher order motor tasks with this hand will also be impaired. On the other hand, these patients will typically not demonstrate impairments on tasks involving visual perception or visual organization, speed of cognitive processing, or left-sided motor weakness or impairment.

NEUROPSYCHOLOGICAL TEST PERFORMANCE OF PATIENTS WITH DIFFUSE BRAIN DAMAGE

Patients who sustain diffuse brain damage are normally rendered unconscious for prolonged periods of time. Their neurological examinations are usually abnormal. Neuropsychological testing, in most cases, reveals a wide range of neuropsychological impairments. Anterior or posterior brain damage can be inferred from the neuropsychological test data combined with the patient's complaints (or lack thereof), interviews with significant others, and the behavioral observations of the patient. Patients who sustain anterior brain injuries will typically be significantly impaired in the ability to plan, initiate, execute, and regulate behavior. These patients are frequently unable to follow through on tasks and require considerable cues and prompting from others. These patients generally test poorly on tasks which are heavily mediated by the frontal lobes, but generally show little or no impairment on tasks involving language and perception. Patients who sustain posterior brain injuries typically have not been involved in motor vehicle accidents and are most likely to have sustained hypoxic encephalopathy or strokes. They have difficulty perceiving or identifying specific objects and familiar persons or places. Unlike patients with anterior brain damage, patients with posterior brain damage show a fairly good awareness of their impairments. They perform poorly on perceptual tasks, but usually do not demonstrate impairment on tasks involving planning, organization, or initiation.

Inferring the laterality of the patient's brain damage can usually be accomplished by careful review of the patient's neuropsychological test data. For example, patients who sustain prominent left hemisphere damage, are likely to exhibit significant difficulties in communication, sequential organization, mental sequencing, word finding, and right-sided motor tasks. Patients who exhibit right hemisphere damage are likely to have difficulties understanding and comprehending the nonverbal aspects of language on tasks involving visual perception, and will typically show left-sided motor impairments. Corroboration with neurodiagnostic tests such as the EEG, and the patient's neurological examination can also be helpful.

NEUROPSYCHOLOGICAL TEST PERFORMANCE OF PATIENTS WITH SUBCORTICAL BRAIN DAMAGE

Most neuropsychologists generally have a poor understanding of subcortical brain damage, which is typically seen following diffuse brain damage, post-concussive syndromes, hypoxic encephalopathy, and exposure to a variety of toxic or industrial substances. To illustrate this, a case will be presented that describes a 28-year-old male, who was employed as a pipeline worker in the North Sea, when a fire ignited while he was working inside a large pipe. He inhaled noxious fumes, consisting of carbon monoxide and hydrochloric acid, from the burning insulation material and lost consciousness. He was removed from the pipe, in a comatose state, that lasted three days. A CT scan and EEG's, taken shortly after, were reported to be within normal limits. After he returned home, the patient began exhibiting severe depression, headaches, sexual impotence, and mental lethargy. He also exhibited spells of uncontrolled crying and complained of recent memory difficulties. He was hospitalized for depression and headaches and was placed on several different antidepressant medications during his hospitalization, with mixed results. After his discharge, he began seeing a psychiatrist for outpatient psychotherapy and medication follow-up. The patient was seen by three neuropsychologists, whose results, interpretations and conclusions will carefully be reviewed.

Dr. A.

Dr. A. reported that the patient, in addition to his severe depression and headaches, complained of difficulty in thinking, forgetting his train of thought, word finding difficulties, and decreased ability to manipulate numbers as well as spelling difficulties. He also complained of brief episodes of loss of consciousness, with occasional urine and bowel incontinence. He also reported smelling unusual odors, occasional vomiting, increased temper outbursts, and continued sexual impotence. The patient had no previous history of psychiatric problems, alcohol, or drug abuse, or major medical illnesses.

Dr. A. reported that the patient achieved a verbal IQ of 95, a performance IQ of 94, and a full scale IQ of 88 on the WAIS-R. On verbal subtests, he showed strength in mental calculation skills, in spite of his complaints of decreased ability to perform arithmetic. His abstract reasoning skills were intact. However, he tested as severely impaired, in terms of his ability to recall digits backward and forward. He could only recall three digits forward and two digits backward. On nonverbal subtests, he demonstrated above average ability and visual-spatial organization and conceptual skills. However, his visual scanning skills, ability to attend to details, and visual-motor coordination and speed, were significantly impaired. He obtained a memory quotient of 81 on the Weschler Memory Scale, indicating mild to moderate impairment. He demonstrated a good fund of current information. His recall of two verbally presented stories was slightly impaired. However, he showed more impairment in his recall of geometric designs.

The Halstead-Reitan Battery yielded an impairment index score of 0.4 (normal range), although he was markedly impaired on his performance on the Speech Sounds Perception and Seashore Rhythm tests. However, his performance on the Category test fell within the normal range. His motor tapping speed was markedly impaired bilaterally, however, his left arm was significantly slower than his right. He was able to execute simple psychomotor tasks (Trails-A) and was able to alternate between numbers and letters without error (Trails-B), but performed both of these tasks extremely slowly. His performance on the Wisconsin Card Sorting test, a test of mental flexibility and problem solving, was within normal limits.

Dr. A. diagnosed the patient as having sustained a Post-Traumatic Stress Disorder and felt that the patient's left-sided perceptual and motor difficulties were secondary to organic brain dysfunction.

Dr. B.

Dr. B. administered the verbal fluency (FAS) test which the patient performed in a severely impaired manner. When he was given a more difficult task, which required him to name as many items as possible belonging to specific categories (animals, fruits and vegetables, and first names), his performance was generally intact. He could only recall two digits forward and two digits backward, on a digit span test. Dr B. observed that the patient had no difficulty copying drawings and found that the patient demonstrated good comprehension of speech from others, both in testing and in nontesting situations. His ability to communicate was excellent. He exhibited no evidence of word retrieval difficulties and appeared to be quite intelligent. On the Weschler Adult Intelligence Scale, he had a verbal IQ of 79, a performance IQ of 83, and a full scale IQ of 80. He was able to complete all six categories on the Wisconsin Card Sorting test and made a total of only 22 errors. He also tested well within the average range on the Category test. He demonstrated good abstract reasoning skills and obtained a Weschler Memory Scale quotient of 103. He was able to recall only five out of 12 words on the Buschke Selective Reminding test, however, on the Recognition test, he obtained a score of nine out of 12.

His performance on the WAIS-R indicated average to very superior performances on visual organization, higher order spatial perception, temporal sequencing, and visual discrimination tests. On the Trail Making test, he took an extremely long time to complete Parts A and B, but performed them without error. On the Finger Tapping test, he obtained a mean score of 51.3 taps with his right hand and a score of only 20 taps with his left hand. His profile on the MMPI was valid and revealed significant depression with some symptom exaggeration.

Dr. B. felt that the patient's numerous inconsistencies in his cognitive functioning ruled out an underlying organic etiology. Dr. B. questioned the patient's performances and felt that they were highly suggestive of a functional disorder and raised the possibility of malingering.

Dr. C.

Dr. C. reported that the patient obtained a verbal IQ of 79, a performance IQ of 75, and a full scale IQ of 76. He reported considerable variability among the subtest scores, ranging from a scaled score of two on the Digit Span and Digit Symbol subtests to an eight on the Similarities and Information subtests, and a nine on Object Assembly subtest. He obtained an impairment index score of 0.6 on the Halstead-Reitan Neuropsychological Battery in that he scored in the impaired range on four of the seven tests, which comprised this index. He exhibited evidence of severe impairment in his motor speed with his left hand on the Finger Tapping test, severe impairment of his manipulative dexterity when using his left hand, and when using both hands simultaneously on the Purdue Pegboard test. He also demonstrated severely impaired performance on the Seashore Rhythm and Speech Sounds Perception test. His ability to recognize learned words was much greater than his free recall skills. He performed Trails A and B extremely slowly, but failed to make any errors. On the positive side, he performed in the normal range on both the Category and Wisconsin Card Sorting test. He exhibited no evidence of aphasia or word finding difficulties.

Dr. C. felt that the inconsistencies seen in the patient's intact performances on more complex and difficult tasks of problem solving, such as the Category and Wisconsin Card Sorting test, and the patient's poor performance on the Trail Making tests, Digit Symbol and Digit Span tests, most likely represented malingering. He felt that it was highly unusual for a patient to fail relatively simple tasks, yet perform more difficult tasks correctly. This, in Dr. C.'s opinion, most likely reflected motivational factors.

Conclusion

While each of the three neuropsychologists observed inconsistencies between the patient's performance on very simple and complex tasks, several consistent findings were contained in each of the examiner's reports. For example, the patient's auditory and coding skills, particularly with respect to the amount and rate of information processed, were markedly impaired. By way of contradiction, the patient appeared to have little difficulty comprehending spoken language. The patient's ability to process information was markedly impaired, yet he made few errors on complex cognitive tasks. In other words, the patient was observed to have considerably more difficulty with lower order attentional tasks and little, if any, difficulty with higher order attentional tasks. Tasks which contained a speed component were performed very slowly, but generally were done accurately. His speed of cognitive processing, as well as his speed of motor movements, were abnormally slow. This was particularly true when the patient was tested with his left hand. The patient's ability to learn new information was seen as markedly impaired on tasks requiring free recall, but only slightly impaired on tasks involving recognition. Thus, taken together, the results of the three examiners showed evidence of dramatic consistencies when they are examined within these dimensions. It is interesting that in spite of being aware of the patient's etiology, none of the examiners felt that the neuropsychological test results warranted the diagnosis of subcortical brain damage.

CORTICAL VS. SUBCORTICAL BRAIN DAMAGE

Cortical brain damage typically affects the accuracy or effectiveness of the patient's behavioral responses. For example, patients with right posterior cortical brain damage will exhibit prominent inaccuracies in their drawing skills or be unable to read a road map, while patients with left hemisphere cortical brain damage typically display marked impairments in their ability to understand or use language. Patients with subcortical brain damage, on the other hand, typically exhibit impairments in the amount and speed at which information can be processed and their ability to perform relatively automatic or lower order attentional tasks. While both patients with cortical and subcortical brain damage will be impaired in their ability to retrieve new information, the patient with subcortical brain damage will typically be far less impaired on recognition tasks. At the emotional level, patients with cortical brain damage often display euphoria or flat affect, while patients with subcortical brain damage often complain of depression or anxiety, which often does not respond well to antidepressant or antianxiety medications. Patients with subcortical brain damage are also likely to show more evidence of episodic outbursts of anger. Many patients with subcortical brain damage will also complain of fatigue, headaches, vomiting, and "seizure-like events." At the social level, these patients typically become emotionally withdrawn and avoid the company of others (Sbordone, 1986).

IMPORTANCE OF INTEGRATING INFORMATION ABOUT THE PATIENT'S BEHAVIOR AND NEUROPSYCHOLOGICAL TEST DATA

The importance of integrating the information of the patient's behavior and neuropsychological test data prior to reaching conclusions about the patient's impairments and their causation or etiology, cannot be overemphasized.

CASE STUDY

To illustrate this point, the author selected a case involving an 18-year-old female who was struck by an automobile while walking in a crosswalk as a pedestrian in January 1987. She was immediately rendered unconscious and has no recollection of the accident. She was taken to a trauma center, where she was intubated. She had a Glasgow Coma Scale Score of eight, which improved to 12 over the next two weeks, at which time she began to localize all four limbs. She continued to show improvement, but was observed to have problems with blurred vision and to be highly distractible, tangential, somewhat irrational, and impulsive. She also exhibited evidence of left-sided hemiparesis and was quite moody. With respect to fine and gross motor coordination of her upper extremities, she exhibited slowing and slight incoordination on finger-to-nose testing in her left upper extremity. When she was asked to perform fine motor movements with her left hand, she was observed to be very slow, awkward, and somewhat dysfunctional. She was discharged in March 1987, and was transferred to a rehabilitation center, where she was observed to be distractible, tangential, and impulsive. She was discharged from this program in July 1987. Shortly after returning home, she developed significant psychiatric problems consisting of severe mood swings, depression, and suicidal behavior. The patient returned to school in September, but dropped out shortly after due to her lack of motivation and depressed mood. In May 1988, she was caught shoplifting by store personnel at a local department store. Fortunately, the criminal charge against her was dropped due to the interventions of her treating physician and attorney.

The patient was admitted to a residential head injury program for extensive cognitive rehabilitation in July 1988. At the time of her admission, she was noted to have problems with her recent memory, residual left hemiparesis, poor coordination, and visual disturbances. While in this program, she had staring spells lasting six to seven seconds, which increased in frequency to five to six times per day. During these spells, the patient claimed she stopped hearing what was going on around her. She was also observed to have significant problems in her abstract or complex reasoning, as well as behavioral and emotional disinhibitory tendencies. She cursed at her family and punched her mother in the face. She was also seen as having significant impairments on tasks involving the integration or organization of information, manipulating materials, completing complex and varied tasks (particularly under time pressure) recalling critical day-to-day or work-related information, sustaining energy or endurance over time, and maintaining thought organization under stress or in the face of social demands. The patient was discharged from this program in January 1989, to the care of her family.

After returning home, the patient began attending classes at a local junior college, where she was earning credits to complete her high school equivalency examination. The patient indicated that she wanted to become an attorney and had been seeing a clinical psychologist for psychotherapy every two weeks since her discharge from the residential brain injury rehabilitation program.

The patient was sent to a psychiatrist and clinical psychologist by the defense, who examined her. Neither of them had expertise in the field of traumatic brain injuries or rehabilitation. To illustrate this, portions and excerpts of their respective reports will be reviewed. Their names have been changed to protect their identities.

Dr. White (Psychiatrist)

Dr. White indicated that he reviewed this applicant's various medical records prior to seeing the patient in his office. The patient was seen in his office in April 1989. Dr. White initiated his interview by asking the patient if she had any complaints about her health. She said, "My back is bothering me. I have to sit up straight. It hurts if I don't. This has been true since the accident." She volunteered that she had headaches and rated them three on a scale of one to five. She complained of neck pain in the left side and on the right side, adding that it hurts all over. Spontaneously, she said, "If I walk three or four blocks, then the next day my left knee hurts. My left ankle bothers me. I go running in the evening a quarter of a mile, sometimes four or five blocks. My chest hurts a lot. I have stabbing pains in my chest on both sides." She also complained of blurred vision which used to occur frequently and generally lasts about 10 seconds. She estimates that these episodes occur two to three times an hour."

The patient indicated that, "I eat a lot. I never get full. I keep on eating, especially very often. I get depressed a lot. I will be sitting and I start thinking. Then I get depressed. I'm not the same person inside." She added that she had gained 40 pounds during the past year. She then indicated, "When I get depressed, I look for food for comfort."

Dr. White asked, "Are you nervous?" The patient indicated, "Yeah, I get frustrated a lot. I like to play volleyball and swim, but I can't swim on top of the water. I try to go swimming once a week.

I try to use both arms. I just can't keep my head up. I enjoy swimming."

Dr. White asked her if she had had any fights with her parents or family members since her accident. She indicated that she would become upset easily and frequently assaulted her parents and other family members because, "I wanted my way." She indicated that over the past year, however, she no longer strikes her parents, but still hits her brothers and sisters.

Dr. White noted that the applicant was fully conscious and oriented to time, place, and person. He saw no evidence of a thought disorder. Her speech was coherent. The patient had no difficulty with word selection and her speech was well-articulated. Dr. White noted that the patient soon became irritated by his questions. She then freely admitted that she was frustrated and that she often reacted with violence when she felt frustrated. Dr. White noticed a lack of self-criticism. He also observed that her long-term plans were unrealistic.

Dr. White concluded that on the basis of his psychiatric interview and review of her records, that, "The patient's level of adaptive functioning, as measured by her vocational functioning and social functioning, together with her use of leisure time, indicates strongly that she is carrying on at the present time as effectively as she did prior to her motor vehicle accident."

Dr. Clark (Clinical Psychologist)

Dr. Clark indicated that he had reviewed the applicant's academic and rehabilitation records. He indicated that she presented as an impatient and variably cooperative woman. He determined that she had no recollection of the accident. He had difficulty obtaining a clear and consistent chronological history from her, since her accident two years earlier.

Dr. Clark found the patient to have a full scale IQ of 85, with a verbal IQ of 91, and a performance IQ of 83. He found the patient's motivation was variable and noted that the patient became easily frustrated and irritable. He also observed that while she was taking the Block Design subtest of the WAIS-R, she became so frustrated, she actually threw the blocks at him, and stated, "This is making me mad." On the Bender-Gestalt Test, he felt that the patient's performance was due to insufficient attention to detail. He administered the Halstead-Reitan Neuropsychological Battery, which revealed an impairment index which ranged from 0.71 to 0.87, which he felt was at least consistent with moderate impairment of her adaptive abilities dependent on organic brain functions. He felt, however, that her poor performance on this test was largely attributable to her poor frustration tolerance, irritability, and impatience. He administered the MMPI. While taking this test, the patient indicated that it was taking too long and that she had started guessing so that she could get home.

Dr. Clark indicated that his review of the patient's academic records indicated that she was experiencing some difficulty in school prior to her accident. He concluded that there had been little change in her academic performance since her accident and that all of her treatments had "in all probability, contributed to a role assumption of being disabled." He concluded that her current problems reflected long-standing personality tendencies that were not related to her brain injury.

Comment

It seems quite obvious that neither Dr. White nor Dr. Clark possessed an adequate understanding of traumatic brain injuries and attributed the patient's behavioral disinhibition to her pre-existing personality, although there had never been any evidence that she had ever behaved in this manner prior to her motor vehicle accident according to her academic records and interviews with significant others. Neither Dr. White nor Dr. Clark interviewed the patient's family.

PATIENT'S COMPLAINTS

The patient was seen by a neuropsychologist in May 1989. The neuropsychologist obtained the following complaints from the patient:

1. Headaches that were described as constant and ranged from one to four on a 10-point scale of severity. They were usually aggravated by stress, performing housework, and frustration, and were partly relieved by the medication Tegretol.
2. "Blurred vision" that the patient indicated having brief episodes of lasting eight to 10 seconds, usually two to three times per day. She indicated that during these episodes, she lost touch with her surroundings and was seen by her family as staring off into space. She is presently taking Tegretol, 100 mg t.i.d., which has reduced the frequency of this problem.
3. Low back pain, which occurred four to five times per week and typically lasted between 30 and 60 minutes. This problem usually started at the base of her neck and continued downward into her lower back.
4. The patient complained of clicking sounds in her jaw.
5. Weakness in her left lower extremity after extended walking. This was often accompanied by uncontrolled tremors and shaking of her left lower extremity.
6. Retro-orbital pain which occurred two to three times per week and usually accompanied her headaches.
7. "Deja vu" experiences (a feeling that a particular event has occurred before), which occurred two to three times per week.

PROBLEMS OBSERVED BY PATIENT'S FATHER

The patient's father was interviewed. He indicated that he had recently observed the following problems in his daughter:

1. She frequently complained of headaches.
2. She exhibited frequent mood swings, often without any obvious external precipitants.
3. She had angry outbursts consisting of throwing objects, breaking things, yelling, and striking members of her family, followed by extreme remorse.
4. Increased religiosity since her accident.
5. The patient's thinking had become more "black vs. white" since her injury. She also appeared to have become morally inflexible since her injury.
6. Paranoia. The patient often complained that someone was "watching her."
7. Excessive guilt and remorse since her injury.
8. The patient complained of feelings of "impending doom."
9. She had become increasingly dependent on others since her injury.
10. She had exhibited a marked increase in philosophical interests since her injury and often stated, "What is the purpose of life?"
11. Tangential thinking.

12. Memory difficulties for recent events.
13. The patient's interest in dating or sex appeared to have diminished since her accident.
14. The patient frequently exhibited evidence of suicidal ideation which tended to come on very quickly and often without external precipitants. The patient slashed her wrists and took an overdose of medications in July 1987.
15. The patient tended to make rapid decisions about her likes and dislikes of others, based on her nonverbal perceptions.
16. She was frequently impulsive and exhibited poor judgement and control over her emotions and behavior.

REVIEW OF PATIENT'S MEDICAL RECORDS

The neuropsychologist's report contained a review of this patient's medical and psychological records, as follows:

Initial neuropsychological testing was performed on 9/5/87 and revealed evidence of significant attention-concentration, memory, word finding, problem solving, higher level executive, left-sided motor and emotional problems which were felt to be secondary to her traumatic brain injury. These findings were considered consistent with a frontal lobe syndrome, organic personality syndrome, and residual left-sided hemiparesis.

Follow-up neuropsychological assessment on 6/15/88 indicated that the patient continued to exhibit evidence of markedly compromised neuropsychological functioning, which was manifested on a wide range of cognitive, social, emotional, and behavioral tasks. The neuropsychologist also felt that this patient was desperately in need of immediate placement in a residential brain injury rehabilitation program.

The patient was admitted to a residential treatment program in July 1988. At the time of her admission, she was noted to have problems with recent memory, residual left hemiparesis, poor coordination and visual difficulties. It was also noted that she had a variety of problems with respect to her inability to regulate her emotions and behavior. She had significant problems integrating and organizing information, performing complex tasks, recalling recent events, and organizing her thoughts, particularly under conditions of stress or social demands. While at this center, she underwent a neurological examination which revealed evidence of very mild increased tone in her left upper and lower extremities. Rapid alternating movements were reduced in her left upper and lower extremities. When she increased her walking speed, or when she attempted to run, she showed evidence of slight dyscoordination of the left foot. She was able to hop on her right foot, but had difficulty on her left foot. She was unable to walk on her left heel or toe. Tandem walking revealed evidence of mild ataxia. She was diagnosed as having a closed head injury with left hemiparesis, impaired coordination, memory loss, and emotional lability.

A chart note by her treating neurologist, dated 12/16/88, indicated that the patient had been observed having staring spells lasting six to seven seconds, which have been increasing in frequency. During these spells, she could not hear what was going on around her.

A review of her chart notes indicated that while she was in the residential head injury program, there was evidence of frequent maladaptive verbal behaviors and physical actions that were noted by the staff on virtually a daily basis. She was also noted to be verbally abusive toward others, excessively argumentative and oppositional, verbally disruptive through the use of excessive swearing or profanities, physically belligerent, physically assaultive, and exhibited evidence of hyper-agitated behaviors and inappropriate touching of others in a sexually offensive or aggressive manner.

BEHAVIORAL OBSERVATIONS OF PATIENT

The neuropsychologist recorded the following behavioral observations during his interview with the patient:

The patient presented as an 18-year-old, right-handed female. She presented as alert and oriented and did not appear to be in any type of acute distress. She was accompanied by her father, who appeared to be a reliable historian. She was casually dressed in appropriate attire. She spoke fluently, without evidence of word finding difficulties, dysphasia, or dysarthria. Her mood fluctuated considerably during the clinical examination and interview, as well as during neuropsychological testing. It ranged from euphoria to rather severe depression and did not appear to be due to external factors. Her attention also varied considerably. At times, she appeared distractible and would often speak in a garrulous and complaining fashion. On one occasion during neuropsychological testing, she appeared to stare off in space for several seconds and appeared oblivious to her surroundings. After this event, she appeared somewhat confused and had difficulty explaining what had occurred. Her attention and concentration was also compromised by her poor frustration tolerance and her difficulty regulating her emotions and behavior. Her recent memory appeared mildly impaired with respect to recent events. Her remote memory seemed intact. Her thinking was often tangential, which necessitated this examiner to provide her with cues to redirect her train of thought back to the topic of conversation. There was no evidence of hallucinations, delusions, loose associations, or bizarre thinking. During her examination, she confessed that she had fallen while riding her bicycle and showed the examiner her left arm which was quite bruised. She indicated that she had fallen during one of her episodes of "blurred vision" and had not revealed this incident to anyone for fear it would keep her from getting her driver's license. Her motivation to perform to the best of her ability waxed and waned as a function of her poor frustration tolerance and difficulty regulating her emotions and behavior.

NEUROPSYCHOLOGICAL TESTING

The neuropsychologist indicated that the following neuropsychological tests had been administered to this patient:

Tests Administered

The Raven Progressive Matrices Test
The Sbordone Attention Battery
The Symbol-Digit Modalities Test
Trail Making Test (Parts A and B)
The Stroop Test
The Logical Memories Test
The Rey Auditory Verbal Learning Test

Non-Standardized Tests of Memory
The Boston Naming Test
The Controlled Word Association Test
The Hooper Visual Organization Test
The Grip Strength Test
The Finger Tapping Test
The Grooved Pegboard Test
Luria's Motor Examination
Test of Executive Function
The Millon Clinical Multiaxial Inventory

Test Results

Intelligence

The patient was administered the Raven Progressive Matrices Test to assess her intellectual functioning. Her performance on this test placed her in the 15th percentile with respect to persons of her age, and gave her an IQ of 84, which placed her in the low-average range of intellectual functioning.

Attention

She was administered several different tests to evaluate her attentional skills. Her performance on the Sbordone Attention Battery revealed evidence of moderate impairment on tasks involving serial seven subtraction, serial 13 subtraction, and alternating three and five subtraction. She also exhibited evidence of moderate impairment when she was asked to indicate which letters of the alphabet rhyme with the word "tree." She was observed to lose her attentional set several times during these tasks and had to be redirected back to the task by the examiner.

She was administered Parts A and B of the Trail Making Test to assess her ability to connect circles containing either numbers or letters. This required a total of 24.3 seconds to complete Part A. Her performance, based on age corrected norms, revealed that she tested as 0.25 standard deviations below expectancy. She required 53.56 seconds to complete Part B, which placed her 0.15 standard deviations below expectancy. It should also be noted that while her performance placed her within normal range on both of these tasks, she indicated that she had taken these particular tests several times in the past. She was administered the Symbol Digit Modalities Test to assess her speed of cognitive processing and obtained a score of 48, which placed her 0.96 standard deviations below expectancy. Finally, she was administered the Stroop Color Word Naming Test to assess her ability to name words, identify colors, and inhibit distracting stimuli. Her performance on this test revealed evidence of overall moderate impairment in that it placed her between 1.8 and 2.0 standard deviations below expectancy.

Memory

The patient was administered a variety of different tasks to assess her memory. She was initially given the Rey Auditory Verbal Learning Test, but indicated after completing the first trial that she had been given this test several times in the past and had memorized most of the answers. In an attempt to assess her ability to learn new information, she was orally presented with a list of 12 words. On each of three learning trials, she was asked to recall as many of these words as possible. By the end of the third trial, she was able to recall 10 of the 12 words. Immediately following this, she was presented with a different list of 12 words for three trials. She was able to recall 11 of the 12 words of the second list by the end of the third trial. Following this, she was asked to recall as many words as she could remember from the first list. She was able to recall only six of the 10 words she had recalled only a few minutes earlier, but made three errors. Thus, she exhibited a retroactive interference memory loss of 40%. Then she was asked to recall the second list of words and was only able to recall seven of the 11 words she had recalled only a few minutes earlier, but made a total of six errors. A careful analysis of her errors on both lists revealed numerous errors of contamination and confabulation. (Author's note: These errors are typically made by patient's with prominent frontal lobe pathology.) Since the patient indicated that she had been previously given the Rey-Osterrieth figures on numerous occasions, and had made a deliberate effort in the past to memorize this figure, she was given two tests in which she was asked to copy complex geometric figures. While her drawing of both figures revealed no evidence of constructional dyspraxia (distortion), her ability to draw these figures from memory approximately 30 minutes later was found to be markedly impaired.

Language

She was administered the Boston Naming Test to assess her ability to name pictures of familiar objects. She obtained a score of 45 out of a possible 60, which placed her 2.43 standard deviations below educational expectancy. A careful analysis of her errors revealed a strong indication of word finding difficulties. She was administered the Controlled Word Association Test in which she was asked to generate as many words as possible, beginning with specific letters of the alphabet (FAS). Her overall score, which was corrected for her educational background, placed her between the 85th and 89th percentile. (Author's note: The striking discrepancy between her performances on these tests are indicative of right hemisphere dysfunction.)

Perception

She was administered the Hooper Visual Organization Test to assess her ability to recognize pictures of objects which had been cut up and placed in different positions. While her overall score (25.5) placed her within the normal range, qualitative analysis of errors on specific items revealed errors which are typically made by patients with prominent right frontal lobe pathology.

Motor

She was administered the Grip Strength Test to evaluate the strength of her left and right hands. The strength of her right hand was tested at 40.5 kilograms, while her left hand tested at only 19 kilograms. Thus, a difference of 213% was found between her left and right hands. Similarly, on the Finger Tapping Test, she was able to tap 51.8 times with her dominant right hand, but only 25.6 times with her nondominant left hand. Thus, testing revealed a difference of 202.3% between her dominant and nondominant hands. Similarly, her performance on the Grooved Pegboard Test revealed that the manual dexterity of her nondominant left hand was severely impaired in comparison to her dominant right hand. Immediately following this, she was given Luria's Motor Examination to assess her ability to perform complex movements with one or both hands. On tasks involving parallel motor processing, she exhibited a pronounced impairment as the tempo of the task increased. At this point, she was noted to lose her motor set and perform the task with two separate movements, which indicated that she was no longer capable of maintaining reciprocal motor control. On tasks involving touching her fingers with her thumbs, she was unable to perform this sequence correctly, even though she had been given extensive practice and cues from the examiner. This was observed on both hands separately. On tasks involving three-stage motor movements, she was observed to have considerable difficulty performing this task and was noted to make frequent loss of set errors, which increased dramatically as the tempo of the task increased. On tasks which involved programmed tapping of both hands, she was observed to have difficulty performing this task without relying on verbal cues. Her performance with her left hand, however, was ataxic (characterized by jerky movements). She was also given tasks of motor sequencing on which she exhibited evidence of moderate impairment.

Executive Functions/Problem Solving

Her responses to a variety of different tasks involving problem solving, interpretation of proverbs, and judgement, were compromised by her admission that she had been given these tests before on numerous occasions. She even stated, "I have memorized the right answers." She was then given a variety of orally presented problem solving tasks to assess her logical-grammatical and reasoning skills. Her performance on these tasks was moderately impaired. An initial attempt was made to give this patient the Wisconsin Card Sorting Test, however she indicated that she had been given this test several times in the past and had memorized the correct solution.

Personality/Emotional

She was administered the Millon Clinical Multiaxial Inventory to assess her current emotional functioning and long-standing personality characteristics. Her profile on this test revealed that she is likely to exhibit variable moods, unpredictable outbursts of anger and rage, and to have a low frustration tolerance. Her insight into these problems appeared generally poor. She showed evidence of variable and brittle control over her emotions and is likely to act impulsively and in an unpredictable fashion. Her self-esteem was seen as being low. At one moment, she is likely to appear euphoric, which may be followed by depression and suicidal thoughts and behaviors.

IMPRESSIONS AND CONCLUSIONS REACHED BY THE NEUROPSYCHOLOGIST

The patient is an 18-year-old, right-handed female who was struck by a car while walking in a crosswalk on the evening of January 3, 1987. She was immediately rendered unconscious and has no recollection of the accident. She was immediately taken to a trauma center in a comatose state. Her initial Glasgow Coma Scale Score was eight, which improved to 12 in approximately two weeks. She was diagnosed as having sustained a moderately severe concussion. A CT scan revealed no evidence of intracranial shifting or hemorrhages. Her accident left her with a left hemiparesis.

After her discharge from the hospital, she was transferred to an acute rehabilitation center, where she was observed to be distractible, tangential, somewhat irrational, and impulsive, secondary to her brain injury. She was also observed to have significant neurological impairments.

She was discharged from this program in July 1987, and returned home. Shortly after she arrived home, she attempted suicide by slashing her wrists and taking an overdose of pills. While at home, her family noticed that her personality had changed dramatically in that she began to exhibit frequent aggressive outbursts in which she would physically attack her parents and siblings. She was also observed by her family to exhibit frequent mood swings, impulsive behavior, memory loss, and significant difficulties regulating her emotions and behavior. She was admitted to a residential head injury rehabilitation program in July 1988. Throughout her stay in this program, she was observed to exhibit almost daily evidence of significant problems regulating her emotions and behavior, which resulted in frequent episodes of physical, assaultive, and inappropriate behavior, which were noted by the treatment staff. She was discharged from this program in January 1989, to the care of her parents. Presently, the patient has been attempting to complete her educational requirements to obtain her high school diploma. She has also been receiving supportive counseling from a clinical psychologist on a regular basis.

When she was seen by this examiner, she complained of headaches, frequent episodes of blurred vision, low back pain, weakness of the left lower extremity after extended walking, retro-orbital pain, and deja vu experiences. Her father indicated that since her injury he observed frequent mood swings, angry outbursts, and physical violence followed by extreme remorse, changes in thinking (e.g., hypermorality and hyper-religiosity), paranoia, feelings of impending doom, increased dependency on others, increased philosophical interests, tangential thinking, memory difficulties of recent events, frequent suicidal ideation, decreased interest in sex or dating, and impulsive behavior. He also observed frequent staring spells which lasted several seconds, during which time she appears oblivious to her surroundings. He indicated that he had not observed any of these problems prior to his daughter's injury, particularly with regard to her aggressive behavior toward he and his wife and other family members.

Behavioral observations of this patient during the clinical examination revealed evidence of significant difficulties regulating her behavior and emotions. Her mood frequently changed dramatically from euphoria to depression without any obvious external precipitants. Her mood changes and behavioral disinhibition significantly interfered with her performance on neuropsychological testing. She was also observed to stare for several minutes and appeared oblivious to her environment during these episodes.

Neuropsychological testing was compromised by her rapid mood swings and difficulty regulating her emotions and behavior. It was also compromised by her familiarity with several of the neuropsychological tests, which she indicated had been given to her on several occasions. In an effort to evaluate her cognitive functioning, she was administered three nonstandardized tests to assess her memory. Her performance on these tests revealed serious impairment of recent memory, particularly under conditions of interference and temporal delays of 30 minutes or longer. On tests of serial mental processing, she exhibited evidence of a variety of pathognomic errors consistent with bilateral frontal lobe and right frontotemporal lobe pathology. This was further corroborated by a variety of motor, perceptual, and problem solving tests.

These findings, combined with a review of her medical and rehabilitation records, indicate that this patient suffers from a variety of significant cognitive, behavioral, social, and emotional problems as a direct consequence of her traumatic brain injury. Her neuropsychological test performances, combined with the behavioral observations of this examiner and her father, are highly consistent with frontal lobe pathology, and an Organic Personality Syndrome. The behavioral observations of this examiner, her father, and the complaints of this patient, are also highly consistent with temporal lobe epilepsy and are supported by her neuropsychological test findings.

The frequency and severity of these above problems will, in all probability, significantly affect this patient's ability to care for children, cope with the demands of marriage, work in a competitive job environment, and operate a motor vehicle. While this patient may make some mild improvement in her cognitive functioning over the next several years, this will most likely be foreshadowed by significant emotional, behavioral, and psychiatric problems. In addition, she would be expected to require psychiatric treatment/hospitalization in the future for these problems.

Comment

This patient sustained a severe traumatic brain injury as a result of being struck by a motor vehicle while walking in a crosswalk. She most likely sustained a cerebral contusion and concussion resulting from the acceleration and deceleration forces caused by being struck by a moving vehicle and striking her head to the ground. As mentioned earlier, patients who sustain injuries to the orbital frontal lobes frequently exhibit no evidence of abnormalities on CT scans and EEG studies, even though there was no dispute that she had ever sustained a traumatic brain injury since she was found to have a Glasgow Coma Scale of eight and exhibited positive findings on a clinical neurological examination, particularly left hemiparesis. Shortly after her accident, she began exhibiting marked difficulties regulating her behavior and emotions, as well as cognitive difficulties consistent with her traumatic brain injury. She also began exhibiting psychiatric problems consisting of rapid mood swings, suicidal attempts, rage and assaultive behavior, and severe interpersonal difficulties. These behaviors were consistently observed by all of her treating doctors and rehabilitation specialists, as well as her family. The development of her psychiatric difficulties at six months post-injury is significant, since Sbordone and Eames (1985) previously described this phenomenon in patients who sustain prominent right frontal temporal lobe brain damage. She also exhibited antisocial behavior (being arrested for shoplifting), poor judgement, impulsive behavior, and poor planning and organizational skills.

This patient was seen by a defense psychiatrist who failed to recognize the neurobehavioral sequelae of her traumatic brain injury. This is not unusual since the psychiatric examination is typically unable to detect such problems, as the patient's language functioning is generally intact and they fail to exhibit psychiatric difficulties during examination. The patient was also seen by a clinical psychologist who failed to recognize the organic basis for the patient's behavioral outbursts, her aggressive behavior, distractibility, and mood swings. He based his conclusions on a lack of change in the patient's grades since her accident, but ignored changes in this patient's emotionality and behavior since her accident. None of these doctors interviewed the patient's family even though they were both aware that the patient had physically assaulted each family member on numerous occasions since her injury. One can also clearly recognize a dramatic inconsistency between their conclusions, their behavioral observations, and the various medical records describing her hospitalization, treatments, and rehabilitation since her injury. Consequently, their conclusions were inaccurate and misleading.

The neuropsychologist, on the other hand, attempted to integrate a variety of different sources of information about the patient. He interviewed the patient and her father. He reviewed all of the various medical, psychological, psychiatric, and rehabilitation records pertaining to her treatment. He also carefully observed her behavior during both the clinical interview and during neuropsychological testing. He inquired whether the patient had been given particular tests before, knowing that she had been seen by several psychologists and neuropsychologists prior to his examination. Rather than giving neuropsychological tests which the patient admitted that she had taken several times before and had memorized the answers, he decided to administer several informal neuropsychological tests based on his experience, background, and training. While this is somewhat unorthodox, each of these tests were similar in format to the tests the patient had taken several times before but contained different items. Although there were clearly no norms available, the neuropsychologist decided to perform a more qualitatively oriented examination to investigate the types of problems and difficulties the patient would most likely encounter, given the cognitive demands of these tests. In addition to a quantitative description of the patient's scores in comparison to normative data, the neuropsychologist also performed a qualitative analysis of the particular errors made by the this patient which further corroborated her impaired brain-behavior relationships and was consistent with her medical history, his behavioral observations, and the reports of significant others.

The neuropsychologist obtained a description from the patient's father of behaviors and problems which are highly descriptive of temporal lobe epilepsy. While a neuropsychologist cannot formally diagnose a patient as having temporal lobe epilepsy, he suggests in his report that the patient shows strong evidence of neuropsychological test findings and behavioral problems consistent with temporal lobe epilepsy. It should be noted that none of the prior doctors who had examined this patient recognized these symptoms which are classic descriptors of patients with temporal lobe epilepsy (Benson and Blumer, 1975).

The neuropsychologist indicated that based on his review of the patient's medical records, interviews with the patient and the patient's father, his behavioral observations, and the neuropsychological test data, it was his opinion that the frequency and severity of the patient's problems (listed in his report) would be expected to significantly affect this patient's ability to care for children, cope with the demands of marriage, work in a competitive job environment, as well as operate a motor vehicle. Based on his experience, background, and training, he felt that while the patient would most likely show evidence of some improvement in her cognitive functioning, he felt that this would be foreshadowed by her psychiatric difficulties that would most likely require psychiatric treatment and/or hospitalization in the future. This case later went to trial. The jury agreed with the opinion of the neuropsychologist and awarded a large sum of money to the patient which was placed in a structured settlement.

Chapter 11

Determining the Prognosis of the Patient's Impairments Following Brain Damage

Neuropsychologists are frequently asked to determine the prognosis of the patient's impairments following brain injury. In other words, "Is the patient's condition permanent and stationary? Will the patient improve? Will the patient be able to return to work, school, or their household responsibilities? Will the patient's condition ever return to normal? Will the patient ever lead a normal life again? Will the patient's condition deteriorate? Will the patient develop any additional problems which might require hospitalization or treatment? If the patient receives treatment or rehabilitation, will they ever be able to work, enjoy life, or be as they were before their accident?" These are some of the questions that are frequently asked of neuropsychologists by the patient's family, employer, physicians, and attorneys. Obviously, to answer these questions the neuropsychologist must understand what has been termed "the natural history" of a particular psychological and neurological injury, disease, or disorder. With few exceptions, psychological and/or neurological injuries are dynamic processes, which change over time. For example, a patient who sustains a traumatic brain injury typically passes through six discrete stages from the time the injury first occurred. A description of these stages can be seen in Table 9. Sbordone (1989) found that these patients continue to improve cognitively, emotionally, socially, and behaviorally at a fairly steady rate from one year post-injury to at least 10 years post-injury. This research challenges the widely held assumption that patients improve for only one or two years post-injury. In 1989 the author reported that a 10-year retrospective study of 20 patients, who averaged 9.8 years post-injury, made gradual and continuous improvement in virtually all areas of functioning from one year post-injury. In fact, in many cases, the majority of the improvement occurred after the first two years.

According to Sbordone's model (1990), the first stage of recovery begins with the injury and the patient's coma. The second stage begins when the patient first opens his or her eyes. The third stage begins when the patient becomes oriented to place, but continues to be disoriented to time. During this stage, the patient exhibits marked denial of any cognitive, social, or behavioral deficits. Patients during this stage exhibit severe cognitive impairments. When the patient becomes oriented to place and time and begins to complain of cognitive deficits, they have entered the fourth stage. During this stage, the patient's cognitive functions have improved significantly from the previous stage, and are now moderately impaired. During this stage, the patient is likely to become depressed, and has also tried to return to work or school (usually unsuccessfully). Patients during this stage appear relatively "normal," but continue to exhibit significant cognitive, emotional, or behavioral difficulties.

During the fifth stage of recovery, the patient's depression and emotional problems have increased. The brain-injured patient is either working or attending school, but has been given reduced work responsibilities or is taking a reduced academic load. These patients have lost most of their friends. During the sixth and final stage of the recovery process, the patient typically has resumed most, if not all, of their pre-injury responsibilities. Their self-image has improved considerably. While they continue to exhibit relatively mild cognitive difficulties, they have usually developed compensatory behaviors and coping strategies that permit them to function effectively in their environment.

TABLE 9
STAGES OF RECOVERY IN TRAUMATIC BRAIN INJURY

Stage 1	Injury
Stage 2	Opens eyes Severe agitation-restlessness or vegetative state Severe confusion Disoriented to place and time
Stage 3	Oriented to place, but not time Moderate confusion Denial of cognitive deficits May complain of somatic problems Fatigues very easily Poor judgement Marked to severe attention deficits Severe memory deficits Severe social difficulties Severe problem solving difficulties
Stage 4	Oriented to place and time Becoming aware of cognitive deficits May appear relatively normal Mild confusion Mild to moderate attention difficulties Marked problem solving difficulties Moderate to marked memory deficits Early onset of depression-nervousness Unsuccessful attempts to return to work or school Poor endurance Moderate to marked social difficulties
Stage 5	Significant depression-nervousness Mild to moderate memory deficits Mild to moderate problem solving difficulties Frequent comparison to premorbid self Given little hope of further recovery Has returned to work or school Mild to moderate social difficulties
Stage 6	Mild memory impairment Mild problem solving difficulties Acceptance of residual deficits Improving social relationships Return of most premorbid responsibilities Generally positive self-image

Reprinted with permission of Paul H. Brooks Publishing Company. Sbordone (1990) Psychotherapeutic Treatment of the Client with Traumatic Brain Injury. In J.S. Kreutzer and P. Wehman (Eds.), *Community Integration Following Traumatic Brain Injury.* pp. 139-156.

At this point, the reader must be asking, "Well, if this is true, why do physicians keep telling us that these patients will not improve after one or two years post-injury?" There are several reasons for this. Neurologists and/or neurosurgeons only see brain-injured patients who require ongoing medical care or surgical intervention. Patients who improve have no need to see their doctor and are usually not motivated to do so. Thus, the physician's perception that the brain-injured patient does not improve after one year is most likely based on a relatively small number of patients whose neurological problems continue to hinder their recovery or create secondary brain damage, such as post-traumatic seizures or patients requiring a ventroperitoneal shunt, etc. Some physicians will frequently cite studies by Bond (1975) and Bond and Brooks (1976), which studied the "recovery" of patients with severe traumatic brain injuries. In Bond's first study, he examined 56 patients, whose ages ranged from 15 to 64. Fifty-two percent of these patients had post-traumatic amnesia for more than four weeks and had been referred to a neurosurgical treatment unit for examination. (Author's note: This suggests that they may have required a ventroperitoneal shunt or were continuing to have seizures.) Bond grouped these patients according to their duration of post-traumatic amnesia and time since injury. He then administered the Wechsler Adult Intelligence Scale and compared the IQ scores of the patients in these groups. He found that the patients who were at six months, 12 months, and two years post-injury, had roughly the same IQ's. He therefore argued that because of this finding, patients with traumatic brain injuries made most of their improvement during the first six months and very little improvement following this.

A careful analysis of Bond's rationale and conclusions reveals that he may not have studied a representative sample of brain-injured patients, since these patients had been referred for neurosurgical treatment service some time following their accident. Since the IQ is relatively insensitive to brain injury, administering an IQ test to three groups of patients will most likely result in the mean IQ (average score) of the three groups being roughly the same even in the absence of brain damage. Bond did not utilize any sensitive neuropsychological tests or measures, nor did he have access to the premorbid (prior to their injury) IQ scores of these patients to determine whether any changes had occurred. He also did not utilize any suitable control groups and ignored the possible influence of such factors as age, sex, education, employment status, medications, physical disabilities, or emotional factors. In short, this study appears to have been plagued by serious methodological problems and fallacious assumptions.

In addition to the author's research, which is discussed above, there are several other studies which have also reported that patients who sustain traumatic brain injuries continue to show improvement in their cognitive functioning after two years post-injury. For example, Klonoff, Low, and Clark (1977) found that 76.3% of brain-injured children and adolescents exhibited a marked improvement in their cognitive functioning during a five-year follow-up study. The investigators also reported that these patients made significant improvement in their cognitive functioning between the fourth and fifth years post-injury. These improvements were seen both on neuropsychological testing and on neurodiagnostic tests such as the EEG. Miller and Stern (1965) followed 92 patients who had sustained severe head injuries. At 11 years post-injury only five were unemployed, even though their physicians had predicted at three years post-injury that nearly 75% of them would never be able to return to work. Thomsen (1981) reported a case involving a 44-year-old male, who was seen 12 years after he sustained severe brain damage. She reported that virtually all of his improvement occurred after the first two years of his injury.

While patients with severe traumatic brain injuries typically show evidence of gradual improvement in their cognitive functioning over time, a significant number of these patients may develop psychiatric or neurologic problems several months or years post-injury. Sbordone (1987) reported that patients who sustain severe traumatic brain injuries are likely to become depressed after six or 12 months post-injury. This has also been reported by Lezak (1987), who found that patients with traumatic brain injuries show anxiety, depression, and significant problems with others, between six and 12 months post-injury. In addition to this, Sbordone (1985, 1988), and Shukla, Cook, Mukherjee, Goodwin, and Miller (1987) have reported that patients who sustain right frontal temporal lobe injuries, are likely to develop an "atypical bipolar depression," or organic affective disorder characterized by rapid mood swings, grandiose thinking, irritability, impulsive and often violent behavior, pressured speech, and hyperactivity. In the Shukla et al. study, the onset of these symptoms did not occur until an average of 2.8 years post-injury. With this in mind, attorneys representing the plaintiff should avoid rapidly settling cases involving traumatic brain injury when a patient has sustained prominent right frontal temporal lobe damage. The author sadly recalls a case involving a severe traumatic brain injury, in which the patient's attorney settled at one year post-injury for $90,000. Approximately six months after the case was settled, the patient, a 17-year-old girl, developed an atypical bipolar depression which necessitated repeated hospitalizations, costing more than $400,000 over the next five years. Her family was forced to sell their home and virtually all of their possessions to pay for their daughter's psychiatric care.

Unlike traumatic brain injuries, patients who sustain brain injury as a result of hypoxic encephalopathy, particularly if the patient is in a coma for more than 48 hours, typically show little recovery. The reasons for this are not fully understood, but most likely involve the destruction of brain tissue (necrosis) when the brain is deprived of oxygen for substantial periods of time (usually five minutes or longer). A notable exception to this, however, can be found in young children, who after drowning in icy water, frequently show a complete recovery of their neurological functioning after they are resuscitated. This happens because the icy water slows down the brain's metabolic activity and considerably diminishes the brain's need for oxygen. Patients who develop cerebrovascular disorders, such as strokes, frequently demonstrate a recovery in their cognitive and behavioral functioning but are at considerable risk for having another stroke if the stroke was caused by a history of hypertension or coronary disease.

Psychological problems, in general, have a much brighter prognosis than neurological disorders. For example, depression is typically a self-limiting condition, which resolves over time (usually in two or three years) without treatment or psychotherapeutic intervention. This is particularity true if the depression was the result of a grief reaction, caused by the death of a loved one, divorce, or loss of employment. Post-traumatic stress disorders will gradually improve over time, however the litigation process will often prolong, and sometimes even reinforce, the patient's symptoms and complaints. For example, the patient is usually compelled to discuss the painful traumatic event with their treating and examining doctors, their attorney, the defendant's attorney (during depositions), and in court. In addition, the defense psychiatrist, psychologist, or attorneys may dredge up painful experiences of the past, which may be emotionally upsetting, or imply that the patient is either malingering, crazy, or hysterical. For example, the author recalls treating a large number of these patients in the past, who had been undergoing litigation. Each time one of these patients was seen by a psychiatrist or psychologist or was deposed by opposing counsel, their nightmares, flashbacks, sleep difficulties, and symptoms associated with their post-traumatic stress disorder markedly increased.

Many psychologists or neuropsychologists have never had the opportunity to treat or follow patients who have sustained brain damage over time. This will often be reflected by such statements as, "It has been over a year and a half since this patient's traumatic brain injury, therefore no further improvement is expected." Clinicians who have had the opportunity to follow such patients over time will rarely say this since they typically observe these patients improve over time. Therefore, the accuracy of a particular doctor's prognosis is no better than the doctor's experience with such patients. Therefore, attorneys should carefully evaluate the experience a neuropsychologist or physician has with regard to how many of these patients they have actually followed over time. The attorney might also wish to ask the "expert" if he or she is aware of any research on recovery following brain damage, what it demonstrates, and whether or not he or she has ever done any research on the recovery process.

REFERRING THE BRAIN-INJURED CLIENT TO A BRAIN-INJURY REHABILITATION PROGRAM

The attorney should consider referring his or her severely brain-injured client to a brain injury rehabilitation program. (Author's note: The cost of the average residential brain injury treatment program is $17,000 per month. Brain-damaged patients usually require from three months to two years in such programs. Some of these programs are willing to accept the patient on a lien if there is a good chance of obtaining a substantial financial recovery.) The chief advantage of sending a brain-injured patient to a rehabilitation program is that the program will dramatically improve the quality of that patient's life. For example, these programs will usually improve the patient's interpersonal and social skills, teach them to be more self-reliant, improve their self-confidence, help alleviate their depressed mood, improve their endurance and physical appearance, and provide them with a greater sense of mastery over their environment by teaching them compensatory skills and techniques to minimize their cognitive deficits. Brain-damaged patients who are not referred to a brain injury rehabilitation program will often drive their families "crazy" and are eventually rejected and scorned by their family because of their disruptive and inappropriate behavior at home. Consequently, many of these patients are forced to live a pitiful life and lose all of their pre-injury friends. Therefore, it should come as no surprise why they become depressed, sad, and contemplate or attempt suicide. To make matters even worse, many of these patients often associate with social "misfits" because of their poor judgement and become involved in criminal activity, usually as a patsy or fall guy, or engage in heavy alcohol or drug use.

The reader might, at this point, ask, "If these patients improve in their cognitive functioning, why do they have these problems or often end up this way?" The reason for this is that a brain-injured patient's cognitive and behavioral functioning is usually determined by their emotional state, environment, and the types of stress that they have been placed under. This phenomenon has been termed the "principal of a conditional neurological lesion" (Sbordone 1988). Thus, when brain-injured patients become depressed, anxious, or are placed in an environment which is critical of them or deprives them of their sense of worth, their cognitive and behavioral functioning will deteriorate. On the other hand, if a brain-injured patient is placed in a structured rehabilitation environment that treats them with dignity and respect, their cognitive functioning will significantly improve. The following case study illustrates this:

CASE STUDY

A 24-year-old female suffered a brain injury at work, when she fell on a slippery floor and struck her head on metal pipe. She was rendered unconscious for approximately 10 minutes. She had amnesia for approximately 24 hours following her accident and was hospitalized for three days. She was placed on medical leave for three weeks, after which she tried to return to her job as a manager of a fast food restaurant. She found herself unable to cope with the cognitive and emotional demands of her job and became very depressed and anxious. She was placed on medical leave and spent most of the day home alone watching television, which only caused her to feel more depressed. She was referred for neuropsychological assessment. During the interview, it was discovered that she had graduated from college with a 3.5 GPA and had prided herself in her athletic and academic achievements.

Neuropsychological testing revealed moderate impairments in her recent memory and problem solving skills. She was referred to a residential brain injury program. The patient spent six months in this program, during which time her self-esteem and mood brightened considerably. Because of the cognitive training she had received and the compensatory skills she had learned, she was able to successfully return to her job. Had she not been sent to this program, she most likely would have either attempted suicide (she later admitted that she had actually made plans to commit suicide and would have done so had she not been sent to the rehabilitation program) or would still be unemployed and severely depressed.

Chapter 12

Determining the Type of Treatment and/or Rehabilitation Services Needed for the Brain-damaged Patient

Over the past several years, there has been a growing realization that brain-damaged patients are more handicapped by their emotional and personality problems than by their cognitive or physical disabilities (Lezak, 1987). Brain-damaged patients frequently exhibit emotional changes which are often characterized by either apathy, silliness, rapid mood swings, irritability, euphoria, depression, or altered sexual libido. The social behavior of the brain-damaged patient is often characterized by egocentricity, insensitivity to the needs of others, inappropriate and impulsive behavior, a lack of tact and self-control, poor frustration tolerance, impatience, irritability, use of coarse or foul language, angry outbursts, and impaired communication skills.

Patients who are found through neuropsychological assessment to have significant cognitive or behavioral impairments, are also likely to have marked emotional and social problems. The reason for this is that the brain is the major organ for cognitive, emotional, social, and behavioral functioning. For example, patients who sustain orbital frontal lobe damage, usually as a result of a cerebral contusion, typically display a striking inability to regulate their emotions and behavior. The primary reason for this is that this region of our brain exerts inhibitory control over our emotions. In the absence of this control, we typically see rapid mood swings and emotional lability consisting of excessive laughter, crying, angry outbursts, silliness, swearing, or inappropriate verbal statements and physical gestures. In other words, this part of the brain serves as the "brakes" for the emotional centers in the brain located within the limbic system. Injuries to the temporal lobes are likely to produce a variety of psychiatric problems including paranoia, depression, bizarre thinking, hallucinations, aggressive outbursts, excessive guilt, and rapid shifts in mood and behavior.

Environmental Modification

Patients who have sustained severe brain injuries generally require what has been termed "environmental modification" (Sbordone, 1990), usually consisting of placing them in a carefully structured environment designed to maximize their functioning. Such environments have been shown to significantly reduce the patient's confusion and anxiety (Howard, 1988). Eames (1988) has also stressed the importance of environmental modification to manage the cognitive, social, and emotional behavior of the brain-damaged patient during the early stages of recovery by eliminating environmental precipitants such as pain, alien surroundings, or insensitive authoritarian handling of the patient. Unfortunately, this type of environment is not typically found in psychiatric hospitals or nursing homes, but usually is only found in specially designed brain injury rehabilitation units in either hospitals or residential settings. For example, during the first six months post-injury, patients with severe brain damage exhibit severe attentional problems and are unable to comprehend environmental stimuli or are unable to organize this information. As a consequence, their behavior is poorly organized. These patients frequently exhibit emotional outbursts which have been described as "catastrophic reactions" (Goldstein, 1942). Placing a severely brain-damaged patient in a highly controlled and structured environment will allow them to become accustomed to its demands and eventually learn its daily routine. Environmental modification within this environment, which includes consistent communications to patients from each member of the treatment team allow the patient to encode and process information accurately. Thus, the environmental modification may actually serve as an "ancillary cortex" since it serves to regulate and filter out irrelevant, ambiguous, and competing stimuli which are likely to impinge on the patient.

Behavior Modification

Patients who have sustained severe brain injuries, who are between one and two years post-injury, typically exhibit a variety of significant cognitive, emotional, and behavioral problems. Such patients are able to function fairly well in concrete or highly structured settings. However, if these patients are placed in relatively unstructured or ambiguous settings, they become easily confused and may exhibit a number of significant behavioral and emotional problems. During this stage of recovery, behavior modification programs are highly effective in minimizing their cognitive impairments and alleviating their impaired social and emotional functioning. Such programs are typically found in community re-entry programs for brain-injured patients. These programs serve to increase the patient's sense of independence, mastery over his or her environment, responsibility, communication, and interpersonal and social skills.

Psychotherapy/Counseling

Brain-damaged patients who have reached the sixth stage of recovery (see previous chapter) require psychotherapeutic treatment usually consisting of counseling and/or family therapy. If these patients acquire compensatory skills and strategies as a result of cognitive rehabilitative training, they are usually able to compensate for their brain injury and adjust to their residual cognitive impairments if they undergo psychotherapy or counseling.

Cognitive Rehabilitation

Cognitive rehabilitation is the most likely type of psychological treatment a brain-injured patient is likely to receive, since their behavioral and social difficulties largely stem from their cognitive impairments. Cognitive rehabilitation frequently improves the patient's ability to communicate, comprehend, recall important information, perceive the environment accurately, and engage in effective problem solving. Cognitive rehabilitation is most commonly provided by rehabilitation professionals such as speech pathologists, occupational therapists, and neuropsychologists. It typically consists of improving the patient's attentional, memory, perceptual, language, conceptual, and problem solving skills through a series of cognitive exercises, such as games, computer programs, simulated activities, etc. Treatment usually consists of daily sessions which focus on specific cognitive functions, such as recent memory. During the sessions, patients will be given specific tasks to teach them various strategies, like repetition of recently learned material, verbal mediation, visual imagery, etc., to improve their ability to recall recent information. Computers are frequently used to improve the impaired cognitive skills of the brain-damaged patient. Over the past several years, there has been a growing abundance of computer software specifically designed for the brain-damaged patient. Because cognitive rehabilitation often requires lengthy and repetitive drills, not to mention an exceedingly high degree of patience, microcomputers have certain advantages in that they can patiently monitor the patient's progress and performance, as well as provide cues to facilitate the patient's performance. Computer programs have been written to improve the reaction time, attention and concentration skills, visual scanning, memory impairments, frustration tolerance skills, comprehension, and problem solving skills (Story and Sbordone, 1988). The use of microcomputers and specific software programs can be used within the patient's home and can provide a relatively inexpensive means of cognitive rehabilitation training.

Predictors of Rehabilitation Potential

Sbordone (1987), in collaboration with Dr. Michael Howard, developed a set of pre-injury, neurological, behavioral, and environmental predictors to determine the brain-damaged patient's rehabilitation potential. They based their predictors on their experience treating thousands of brain-injured patients and a careful review of the brain injury rehabilitation literature. With respect to pre-injury predictors, patients with a pre-injury history of good achievement, high IQ scores (120 or higher), good academic history, good relationships with their families and significant others, and who were considered strong-willed and determined, were felt to have the best rehabilitation potential when all other factors could be put aside. On the other hand, patients with a pre-existing history of poor achievement, poor social relationships, low intelligence (IQ below 80), poor grades and academic performance, history of substance abuse, criminal behavior, or who grew up in a cold and rejecting family, are not usually considered good candidates for cognitive rehabilitation. The rationale used by these investigators is that it is much easier to return a patient to his or her pre-injury skills and abilities rather than to habilitate them (i.e., to make an individual better than what they were prior to a brain injury). Thus, if a patient had a history of poor grades, was unable to maintain a job, was irresponsible, had significant drug and alcohol problems, gave up easily, and had considerable difficulty coping with stress or frustration prior to their brain injury, then our best rehabilitation efforts would most likely be wasted trying to overcome the patient's pre-existing characterological problems. These patients are unlikely to be sufficiently motivated to participate in a rehabilitation program or would be unable to cope with the demands of the program.

From a neurological perspective, patients who sustain hypoxic or anoxic brain damage, develop intracranial infections, have post-traumatic epilepsy, or continue to demonstrate abnormal EEG and evoked potential studies, typically have less rehabilitation potential than patients who do not have these problems. Patients who exhibit persistence, an ability to recognize their errors, mental flexibility, and intact perceptual skills following brain injury, tend to be better-suited for cognitive rehabilitation than patients who are unable to recognize their errors or deficits. It is also important to recognize that specific environmental variables are important in terms of the patient's rehabilitation potential. For example, if there are no rehabilitation professionals or programs in the patient's community, or the patient does not have adequate financial or insurance resources to pay for rehabilitation, then the patient will be deprived of the opportunity to benefit from rehabilitation even when their potential to benefit from such treatment may be considerable. In addition to this, it is important that the patient's family be involved in the brain-damaged patient's treatment and rehabilitation. In the absence of this, the patient's chances for successful rehabilitation are significantly reduced.

The following case study illustrates the importance of using these predictors as guidelines in determining whether a particular patient is a good candidate for cognitive rehabilitation or placement in a brain injury program.

CASE STUDY

The author was asked to evaluate the rehabilitation potential of a 17-year-old male patient who lived in a small midwestern town by his speech pathologist. The patient was two and a half years post-injury and was unable to walk, talk, and was functionally triplegic (i.e., the patient had only limited use of his left hand). He also had severe ataxia. The patient's cognitive functioning was profoundly impaired. He had been involved in a motor vehicle accident that had rendered him comatose for nine months. He had been hospitalized for over two years. His treating physicians recommended that he be placed in a nursing home, since they felt that the severity of his injuries had rendered him a "vegetable." They also felt that since it had been over two years since his brain injury that no further recovery or improvement could be expected.

The patient had a premorbid IQ of 140 and had, just prior to his injury, been awarded an academic scholarship to a well-respected midwestern university. He had excelled in creative writing and desired to become a professional writer. He had never used drugs and did not have any significant emotional or personality problems. His family was intact and generally supportive. The author felt that, based on this patient's pre-injury intellectual skills, combined with his supportive family and excellent health and medical coverage, he was a good candidate for cognitive rehabilitation. As a result, an intensive cognitive rehabilitation program was set up in his home with the assistance of his speech pathologist. Computer programs were developed by the author and his associates to improve his attention and concentration skills. At the end of one year, (Author's note: Three and one-half years post-injury.) the patient's cognitive skills improved dramatically. Given this success, the intensity of the cognitive rehabilitation efforts increased and now included his physical skills and abilities. Five years later, the patient's cognitive skills had progressed to the point where he was capable of writing short stories on a word processor, some of which were actually published. He still, however, could not ambulate. Consequently, he was referred to a rehabilitation program in Texas, where he currently resides. As a result of receiving approximately five hours a day of physical therapy, he can now walk with some assistance and continues to write short stories on his word processor. While he still has a variety of significant residual cognitive and behavioral problems, he is happy and lives in an environment that provides him with a sense of dignity and worth. He spends most of his time writing short stories.

Determining the Effect of Brain Damage on the Patient's Family and/or Significant Others

When someone in the family becomes brain-damaged, it markedly disrupts normal family communication patterns and creates serious emotional problems for each family member. The families of brain-damaged patients typically have a high divorce rate (Thomsen, 1974), and experience a great deal of psychological stress, as determined by their need of sleeping pills and tranquilizers (Panting and Merry, 1972). These families, however, are likely to exhibit what has been termed as a "command performance syndrome" in that they appear relatively normal, and are able to mask their emotional distress and create the spurious impression that they are coping well and do not require psychological or psychiatric intervention (Sbordone, Kral, Gerard, and Katz, 1984). Family members try to cope with the brain injury by denial (e.g., "My son is doing fine. He doesn't have any problems."), avoidance (e.g., staying away from or avoiding the patient), projection (e.g., "He's been very upset lately and is very depressed."), rationalization (e.g., "He'll be able to go back to work when he wants to go back to work. The reason why he can't go back to work is he doesn't feel like it."), or somatization (e.g., complaints of physical problems and discomfort secondary to repressed feelings).

Family members are ill-equipped to manage the brain-injured patient's behavior at home as a result of their own emotional problems, grief, and poor understanding of brain injury. In addition, their own demands frequently exceed the brain-injured patient's ability to comprehend or accept their suggestions or directions. Some members of the family may experience excessive guilt and even become martyrs, saying, "If I could die to make my son better I would do it in a second." Or they might quit their job and devote their entire life to getting the brain-injured patient well. Some family members may even scapegoat other members of the patient's immediate family, saying, "It's all your fault." The family also tends to become socially withdrawn and isolated from the community. Additionally, the family is likely to become extremely critical and demanding of the patient.

Family Counseling and Psychiatric Treatment

Families require psychotherapeutic intervention from professionals who understand these issues. In the absence of such treatment, the family system is likely to disintegrate, leaving more vulnerable and sensitive members of the family without a viable support system. As a consequence, some members of the family may actually require psychiatric hospitalization and/or treatment to help them cope with the brain-damaged patient, as well as their feelings of guilt and ambivalence.

Unfortunately, many family members do not receive any counseling or psychological/psychiatric treatment. Instead, they are expected to care for the brain-damaged patient, who is generally insensitive to their needs, frequently irritable and argumentative, and fails to acknowledge their kindness or concern. Some family members are also made to feel selfish and guilty if they complain about their own problems, since they are generally told how "lucky they are" not to have sustained a brain injury. Not infrequently, many family members will resort to drugs, alcohol, or extramarital affairs to help them cope with the enormous psychological pressures they have been placed under as a consequence of having to live with a brain-damaged family member. Unfortunately, very few neuropsychologists deal with these family issues and are often insensitive to them. This will often occur when the examining neuropsychologist fails to interview the patient's family or significant others. In other words, many neuropsychologists may fail to perceive the impact of the patient's brain injury on the family system and recognize the potential consequences of this problem. Thus, it is important that the patient's attorney insist that the neuropsychologist address some of these issues in his or her report, deposition, or during trial.

Determining Any Potential Problems

The neuropsychologist should discuss whether he or she anticipates that this patient will have any potential problems in the future. This should be based on the neuropsychological test data, interviews with the patient's family and significant others, the neuropsychologist's experience with similar patients, and an understanding of the vast medical and rehabilitation literature in this field. As mentioned previously, patients who sustain temporal lobe damage are at risk to develop psychiatric problems and/or temporal lobe epilepsy. Patients who sustain depressed skull fractures where the dura has been violated and severe brain damage, are at high risk for seizures. As patients who have sustained brain damage recover, they are likely to become anxious and depressed as they become more aware of their cognitive problems. Patients who have had a prior history of emotional problems and/or suicidal behavior, will clearly be at high risk for such problems following their head injury. Patients who were rigid prior to their brain injury or have a family history of psychiatric problems are likely to cope poorly with any type of perceived failure or rejection after they have sustained even relatively mild brain injuries. Patients who sustain prominent right frontal temporal lobe injuries are likely to develop a "atypical bipolar depression" or "secondary mania" characterized by euphoria, rapid mood swings, depression, grandiose thinking, angry outbursts, and even violence.

One of the advantages in taking a careful background history of the patient in the presence of other family members is that one will often obtain a history of how this particular patient coped with stress prior to his or her brain injury. This history, combined with a review of this patient's medical records, can provide valuable insights into this particular patient's vulnerability to potentially serious emotional and psychiatric problems. This, combined with the patient's neuropsychological test data, behavioral observations of the patient, an understanding of the patient's recovery process and external stressors, and the demands of the patient's environment, should help the neuropsychologist identify any potential psychological or psychiatric problems that are likely to occur in the future.

CASE STUDY

A 24-year-old woman was referred for neuropsychological assessment by her attorney approximately six months after she had been involved in a head-on collision with a pick-up truck. She was wearing her seat belt at the time of injury and was rendered unconscious for approximately 30 minutes. She was diagnosed as having a cerebral concussion and sustained some soft tissue injuries to her back, neck, and right elbow. When she was seen for neuropsychological assessment, she admitted to being sexually molested by her stepfather between the ages of five and 12 and as having an emotionally painful childhood after her father had been killed in an automobile accident when she was three. Her mother and stepfather were both alcoholics who enjoyed criticizing her and blaming her for all of their problems. She attempted suicide at age 15 and had been hospitalized for three weeks following this. When she was 18, she became depressed after she underwent an abortion at the insistence of her then boyfriend, who was a heroin addict. She was hospitalized for two months and was placed on antidepressant medications. She first married at the age of 20, but found her husband having sex with her best friend approximately six months after she was married. She felt betrayed and became extremely depressed and attempted suicide by overdosing on a bottle of aspirin. Fortunately, she was discovered by a friend who summoned the paramedics. She was hospitalized for two months and treated for severe depression. She divorced her husband, which was very stressful for her, during which time she saw her psychiatrist twice a week on an outpatient basis for emotional support. She married her current husband three months prior to her motor vehicle accident. Her husband was interviewed and indicated that he felt angry at his wife for the way she had been behaving since her motor vehicle accident. He felt that she was no longer the same person he had married and also stated that she no longer seemed interested in sex. He also indicated that he recently had begun having an affair with one of his secretaries to meet his sexual needs.

Neuropsychological testing revealed the patient to have poor frustration tolerance, attentional problems, and difficulties with her recent memory. She also appeared mildly impulsive and exhibited impaired judgement. She only seemed partially aware of her cognitive problems and difficulties. Her family indicated that only three weeks earlier she had denied having any problems or difficulties and stated, "I'm doing fine." (Author's note: This indicated that she had recently entered into the fourth stage of the recovery process.) Psychological testing revealed evidence of borderline personality traits which suggested that her ability to cope with stress in the past had been poor and that she was most likely to have a history of suicidal behavior.

The neuropsychologist phoned the patient's attorney and informed him that given this patient's history and her current neuropsychological impairments, she would be at extremely high risk for psychiatric problems and/or suicide over the next three to six months, particularly as she became more aware of her cognitive problems. The neuropsychologist also indicated that any significant emotional trauma could easily precipitate these problems. Approximately four months later, the patient began acting bizarre and reported hearing voices (probable auditory hallucinations), which informed her that she must hurt others to make the world a better place. When she was interviewed at that time, the patient indicated that she had recently purchased a handgun and had planned on killing the driver of the pick-up truck and his family. She was immediately taken to a psychiatric hospital, where she remained hospitalized for the next six months, during which time she continued to hear voices (auditory hallucinations) and behave irrationally. The neuropsychologist informed the plaintiff's attorney that his client would most likely require some form of psychiatric treatment for the remainder of her life or could possibly spend the rest of her life in a psychiatric institution.

Chapter 13

Sample Neuropsychological Reports

This section presents two neuropsychological reports which illustrate the concepts discussed in the preceding chapters. The first report was written for the plaintiff's attorney and deals with a patient who sustained a mild head injury (a post-concussional syndrome). The second report was written for the defendant's attorney and concerns a claim of brain damage as a result of a motor vehicle accident. The names, dates, and identifying information contained in both reports have been changed to protect the identities of all parties involved. Any resemblance to any actual persons, places, or hospitals, is coincidental.

Neuropsychological Assessment of Dawn Smith

AGE:	39 (8/18/49)
HANDEDNESS:	Strongly Right- Handed
HIGHEST GRADE COMPLETED:	14
OCCUPATION:	Job Recruiter
EMPLOYER:	Stone Recruiters
MARITAL STATUS:	Divorced
CHILDREN:	2
PATIENT'S ADDRESS:	25 Main Street Middletown, Texas
REFERRED BY:	Robert B. Jones Attorney at Law 10 Honest Street Suite 10 San Antonio, Texas
DATE OF INJURY:	12/5/86
DATE OF ASSESSMENT:	6/20/89

Chief Complaints as Obtained from Patient

1. Cognitive difficulties consisting of forgetfulness and difficulty processing more than one event at time.
2. Problems with mental arithmetic.
3. Extreme mood swings.
4. Becomes frustrated easily, particularly towards her mother.

History of Injury as Obtained from Patient

The patient was driving home in her 1986 Camaro after dropping off her daughter at a slumber party on 12/5/86. She was planning to make a lane change from the number one to the number two lane when the driver of an oncoming vehicle crossed over the center divider and made an improper left-hand turn directly in front of her car, which resulted in her car broadsiding the other vehicle. The patient indicated she was wearing a shoulder harness at the time of the accident, but it apparently came loose, causing her to strike her forehead on the windshield. This resulted in a broken windshield. Her knees also slammed into the dashboard. She was rendered unconscious for an unspecified period of time. Her first recollection of the events following the accident began shortly after the paramedics arrived. She was able to recall conversations with the paramedics who removed her from the car. After she was removed, she felt nauseated. She was placed in a cervical collar and taken by ambulance to the emergency room of Valley Hospital in San Antonio, where she underwent x-rays of her cervical spine and skull. The x-rays were negative. After her discharge, she was driven home by a neighbor who is a registered nurse.

At the time of her injury, the patient was employed as a leasing agent for Johnson Properties. The day prior to her accident, she had completed a business deal to begin a telemarketing company and was in the process of closing another business deal to start a restaurant. She returned to work three days after the accident to attend a meeting, but went home shortly after the meeting when she began feeling extremely fatigued. She returned the next day, but was only able to work a few hours before she felt extremely fatigued and nauseous. She also began experiencing headaches. She then saw her family physician who informed her that she had sustained a cerebral concussion. She spent two to three days at home at the request of her physician and then returned to work. Within a week of returning to work her boss informed her that her behavior had changed dramatically and that she had gone from being a very aggressive person with considerable energy to someone who appeared apathetic. Two weeks later she was fired.

The patient was referred to Dr. Zebra, a clinical psychologist, in late January 1987. Prior to seeing Dr. Zebra, she had been experiencing episodes of disorientation, stuttering, poor frustration tolerance and stress management skills, irritability, forgetfulness, episodes of poor judgement, and attentional-concentration difficulties. She informed Dr. Zebra that her father had recently died, but denied that her father's death, after a prolonged illness, depressed her. Instead she claimed that her father's death actually eased her burden because her mother moved in with her and contributed $1,000 per month to her finances. She also received a substantial part of her father's $25,000 insurance death benefit. These monies, eased the financial burdens she had been under since being fired from her job.

In January 1988, she began working for Stone Recruiters. When she first came to work she appeared "off the wall" to her coworkers and acted in a defensive and paranoid manner. In April 1988, she was advised to seek psychiatric help because of continuing episodes of confusion and emotional problems. She was seen by Dr. Freud who diagnosed her as having a mild head trauma and referred her for outpatient occupational, physical, and speech therapy in May 1988, which continued until September.

Review of Medical Records

The Paramedic Report, dated 12/13/86, indicates that the patient was involved in a motor vehicle accident and was rendered unconscious for a couple of minutes. The patient complained of headache and mild chest pain. She was observed to be confused and nauseous at the scene of the accident.

The Trinity Ambulance records, dated 12/5/86, indicate that the patient was unconscious for "a couple of minutes." These records also note that the patient was observed to be confused, nauseated, and complained of headache and mild chest pain.

The State of Texas investigating officer's report of the traffic accident, dated 12/5/86, indicates that a 1984 Cadillac cut in front of the patient's vehicle. Apparently the driver and the passenger in this vehicle were talking and not paying much attention. The patient's vehicle collided into the right side of the other vehicle causing extensive damage to both vehicles. A witness informed the officer that he was driving directly behind the patient's vehicle and saw the approaching vehicle (the 1984 Cadillac) turn directly in front of the patient's vehicle.

The records of Valley Hospital indicate that the patient struck her head on the windshield causing the windshield to shatter. The patient sustained multiple superficial lacerations of her forehead. Her neurological exam was intact. X-rays of the cervical spine and thoracic spine were negative. She was diagnosed as having sustained facial lacerations and a cervicothoracic strain.

The Nursing Care record of the emergency department of Valley Hospital, dated 12/5/86, indicates the patient was involved in a motor vehicle accident and was wearing a seatbelt at the time. The windshield of her car was broken. These records indicate that the patient briefly lost consciousness, but bystanders state she was "out-of-it" following this.

The report of Dr. Dole, dated 8/12/87, indicated that he had examined the patient on 4/25/87. She had just returned from Texas and complained of back pain. At that time, she informed Dr. Dole that she had been involved in an automobile accident in December 1986. Her complaints were sinusitis, fatigue, and back pain. On examination, she was found to have a chronic yeast infection, which she felt may have contributed to her fatigue. Dr. Dole also indicated that he had seen the patient in 1984 regarding a chronic sinus condition. At that time she had no previous complaints of back pain or discomfort. It was Dr. Dole's impression that her back pain may have been precipitated by the automobile accident.

The report of Dr. Zebra, the clinical psychologist, indicated that he saw the patient on several dates during January and March 1987. His report, dated 5/6/87, indicated that the patient complained of cognitive difficulties explaining that she will "think a thought" but was unable to connect it with her speech. She also complained of memory difficulties. She stated that she was forgetting appointments. She also complained of difficulties with locations, directions, and dizziness. Her greatest concern was that her accident had produced changes that had made it difficult for her to perform her various occupational responsibilities. Dr. Zebra interviewed the patient's 15-year-old daughter and asked what it was like living with her mother. Her daughter stated that her mother had become cranky and blamed her children for some of her own mistakes since her accident. Her daughter gave some examples that illustrated her mother's memory difficulties. She also stated that her mother fatigued very easily and has considerable difficulty controlling her temper. Her daughter stated that her mother did not have these problems prior to her motor vehicle accident.

Dr. Zebra also interviewed the patient's mother who stated her daughter had become more irritable since her accident and indicated that she had observed periods in which her daughter had considerable difficulty maintaining her emotional composure. She also observed that her daughter became fatigued easily since her motor vehicle accident.

Dr. Zebra indicated that the patient denied a past psychiatric background and criminal history. Dr. Zebra examined the patient's high school transcripts which indicated that she ranked 25th out of a class of 116 and had a 3.2 GPA. Her transcript also indicated that she had taken the Harmon-Nelson IQ test in 1966 and obtained an IQ of 122. She also took the Otis-Gamma IQ test in April 1967 and obtained an IQ of 122. According to Dr. Zebra, her IQ test scores indicated that the patient was functioning within the superior range of intellectual functioning prior to her injury. Dr. Zebra also examined her academic transcript from West Texas University for the 1969-70 academic year, and noted that she obtained a 2.8 GPA while majoring in business administration.

Dr. Zebra administered the WAIS-R and obtained a verbal IQ of 115 and a performance IQ of 117, which yielded a full scale IQ of 116. Dr. Zebra reported that her score on the Digit Span Test, which is highly sensitive to impairments in attention and immediate memory, was impaired. Difficulties in attention and concentration were also observed on the Arithmetic subtest. The patient's attention and concentration skills were also noted to be somewhat impaired on the Picture Completion Test in which she was asked to identify the missing part of a picture. Her performances on the Sentence Repetition, Controlled Oral Word Association, and Wisconsin Card Sorting Tests were within normal limits. On the Benton Visual Retention Test she made four errors, three of which were perseverative. On the Neurological Symptom Checklist, she complained of a change in her sense of smell, blurred vision, coordination difficulties, headaches, periods when she loses time, forgetfulness, an inability to think clearly, difficulty being able to tell left from right, difficulty following conversations, and difficulty with anger and temper control. On the Personal Problems Checklist, she indicated that she felt uncomfortable in social settings and was experiencing difficulties as a result of not having a job, as well as financial difficulties. She also complained of feeling anxious, having difficulty concentrating, and being influenced by others. On the Medical Problems Checklist for Women she complained of a stiff neck, swollen eyelids, bone and joint pain, and having trouble because she dropped things.

Her profile on the MMPI indicated her concern of a number of psychological and organically based problems. Her profile on the validity scales indicated that she may have been crying out for help for many of the psychological and cognitive difficulties that she was experiencing. Her profile on the clinical scales indicated that she was becoming upset and angry easily, feeling confused and misunderstood by others. She was also seen as being anxious, but operating at lowered levels of efficiency. She also expressed concern about the integrity of her body. Dr. Zebra felt that the patient's history and performance on the psychological tests satisfied the diagnostic criteria of an Atypical or Mixed Organic Brain Syndrome secondary to her motor vehicle accident. He recommended that she receive counseling and psychotherapy from a psychologist who was well-versed with head injuries and that she be re-evaluated in six months.

Dr. Zebra's report, dated 1/5/88, indicated that in November and early December 1987, he re-administered the Wechsler Adult Intelligence Scale and the MMPI. On the former he found evidence of mild improvement which was particularly evident on her performances on the Digit Span and Similarity subtests. On the MMPI, she presented as more depressed than previous testing indicated. Dr. Zebra concluded that, while she was making some improvement in her neuropsychological functioning, her psychological functioning had deteriorated since her injury. He recommended weekly visits with a psychologist and biweekly and monthly visits with a psychiatrist.

The Neuropsychological Evaluation report of George Black, Ph.D., the defense psychological expert, dated 1/15/88 indicated that her childhood was fairly happy. She described her father as successful. She was very involved in extracurricular activities in high school. She first married at age 19 and remained married for four years. She left her husband because he joined an occult religious sect. About one year later, she married her second husband. This marriage lasted only five years and did not produce any children.

Dr. Black noted that the patient had a mildly dysphoric mood and was somewhat hesitant in her speech, although she had no difficulty in forming sentences or expressing herself. She showed strong needs to be successful in her work. She complained of becoming tired easily and having feelings of inadequacy. She complained that her productivity had diminished as a result of these problems and concentration difficulties. She complained of increased irritability and anger since her injury. She also complained of occasional crying spells and headaches. She seemed preoccupied with her financial difficulties, as she was ready to default on loans and faced the possibility of bankruptcy. She also exhibited evidence of anxiety and had difficulty trusting others.

Dr. Black administered the Halsted-Reitan Neuropsychological Battery. She obtained an average impairment rating of .91, which placed her within the average range of neuropsychological functioning. He indicated that on measures which evaluated frontal lobe functioning, her test performances fell within the normal range. On the Wechsler Adult Intelligence Scale she obtained a verbal IQ of 119 with a performance score of 119 and a full scale IQ of 119. Her performance on this test was similar to previous testing by Dr. Zebra. On the Wechsler Memory Scale, she obtained a verbal memory index of 83, a visual memory score of 103, and a general memory index of 87. On attention and concentration, her score was 100 with a one hour delayed recall index of 79. The areas where she showed her lowest levels of functioning included logical memory, delayed logical memory, and delayed visual memory. Her profile on the MMPI was valid. She showed a personality pattern with strong histrionic features. Such individuals are likely to be childish, suggestible, egocentric, and psychologically naive. Such individuals also have difficulty dealing with hostility and expressing their anger.

Dr. Black indicated that the patient had sustained an apparent closed head injury, although he stated that there was "no significant loss of consciousness, no amnesia, nor any other usual significant predictors of major injury residuals." (Author's note: This is contradicted by this patient's medical records.) While Dr. Black found that she performed less than expected on tasks involving delayed recall, he did not feel that this was a compelling finding. He felt instead that her personality style, as well as stressors in her life at the time of her injury, were responsible for her current complaints and difficulties.

Comment

In reviewing Dr. Black's raw test data, he apparently failed to recognize that Ms. Smith's performance on Trails B placed her 2.0 standard deviations below expectancy and that her drawing of a complex figure (The Rey-Osterrieth Visual Figure Test) after a delay of one hour, was performed poorly and showed evidence of perseverations. He also failed to note that Ms. Smith made three sequencing errors on Part B of The Trail Making Test which is pathognomic for individuals who have sustained significant brain trauma. Dr. Black also appeared to place minimal significance on Ms. Smith's performance on The Tactual Performance Test, parti- cularly with her low scores on the memory and localization components of this test. Based on age-corrected norms, Ms. Smith's performance on the localization component placed her 1.8 standard deviations below expectancy, while her performance on the memory component placed her 2.4 standard deviations below expectancy. Finally, Dr. Black noted that Ms. Smith was impulsive and exhibited poor frustration tolerance while taking many of the tests. However, Dr. Black apparently placed minimal importance on these behaviors even though they are some of the more commonly observed problems seen in patients who have sustained closed head injuries.

The Occupational Therapy records of Valley Hospital, dated 6/9/88 through 6/15/88, indicated that the patient complained of decreased endurance, decreased memory, decreased organization, increased irritability, decreased frustration tolerance, increased emotionality, increased disorientation, inability to tolerate stressful situations, and a desire to avoid people and complex environments as she becomes easily over-stimulated. Her evaluation consisted of administering a variety of neuropsychological and occupational tests. These records note that, while she appeared punctual and diligent, unless she was in a quiet and isolated environment, she became distractible and her concentration skills became impaired. Testing also revealed deficits in her ability to process verbal information, attention, memory, speed and efficiency, organizational skills, and comprehension of complex or abstract material. These deficits were considered consistent and predictable for an individual who had sustained a mild head injury.

The Outpatient Communication Assessment of the Speech-Language Pathology and Audiology Department of Valley Hospital, dated June 1988, indicated that language testing revealed areas of deficits which were felt to significantly interfere with her ability to function in her day-to-day life. Specific testing revealed decreased verbal fluency resulting in delays for word retrieval and the ability to formulate her thoughts into ongoing conversation. She also showed a need for increased processing time during her comprehension of written material. Her ability to deal with multiple stimuli for problem solving was found to be reduced. She was seen as having difficulty developing alternative solutions while problem solving. She was also easily distracted by excessive stimuli, as a result of difficulty focusing her attention. Testing for written language showed decreases in consistency of spelling with the need for frequent self-correction. These deficits were considered consistent with predicted problems that are typically seen following a mild head injury.

The Outpatient Conference of the Clark Rehabilitation Institute of Valley Hospital, dated 7/15/88, indicated that the patient had been making steady progress in her therapy and had reached her potential for recovery from her mild head injury.

The report of Harry Flake, M.D., dated 4/19/88, indicated that Ms. Smith did not sustain a loss of consciousness or retrograde of post-traumatic amnesia. (Author's note: This is contradicted by this patient's medical records. Dr. Flake indicated that the patient's neurological examination was negative when she was seen in the emergency room. Dr. Flake makes no mention in his report of the fact that published studies have found that the neurological examination is typically negative over 95% of the time in cases involving mild head trauma.) Dr. Flake also indicated that the patient reported that she did not notice any problem with her memory until one month after her accident. (Author's note: Dr. Flake makes no mention that patients who sustain closed head injuries typically do not begin complaining of cognitive difficulties, such as memory problems, until several weeks or even months following their injury.) Dr. Flake concluded that the patient's "minimal head trauma" was very unlikely to produce closed head injury with neuropsychological sequelae. Dr. Flake also stated that there was no evidence of improvement characteristic of the recovery process from head injury. (Author's note: This is contradicted by Dr. Zebra's follow-up neuropsychological testing and by the records of the rehabilitation program of Valley Hospital. Dr. Flake's statement suggests that he had never reviewed these records.) Dr. Flake's conclusions were similar to those of Dr. Black, in that he attributed Ms. Smith's complaints and difficulties to her personality makeup, current emotional problems, and environmental stressors.

The Speech Pathology and Audiology Outpatient Evaluation report of the Clark Rehabilitation Institute of Valley Hospital, dated 5/20/89, indicated no notable changes in the patient's performance from previous testing. She continued to be easily distracted from tasks and demonstrated difficulty in concentrating for extended periods of time. Her primary deficit area appeared to be on tasks involving attention and concentration. This could partially account for difficulties in auditory memory.

The report of Sandra Acres, M.S., a clinical audiologist, dated 5/25/89, indicated the results of the P300 study show an abnormal delay of the P300 latency which is indicative of delayed cognitive functioning. (Author's note: It should be noted that abnormal P300 studies are frequently seen in patients who have sustained significant closed head injuries.)

The Occupational Therapy Re-evaluation report, dated 5/29/89, indicated that while this patient demonstrated improvements in her verbal fluency and in her ability to formulate her thoughts into conversation, she continued to demonstrate deficits when dealing with multiple stimuli while solving problems and developing alternative solutions. Her continuing deficits were felt to be consistent with a mild head injury.

The report of Stanley Waddle, M.D., dated 6/2/89, indicated that the patient's clinical neurological examination was normal. Her EEG was abnormal, based on abortive sleep spindles and focal driving. Her EMG was abnormal, based on the Hallpike positionals accentuated with hyperventilation. Pure tone audiometry showed a 10 to 15 decibel loss on the right in the conversational ranges and a 10 to 25 decibel loss in the 750 to 1,500 cycles per second range on the left. Dr. Waddle concluded that the patient had sustained a cerebral concussion with loss of consciousness in her motor vehicle accident and had experienced headaches and problems with her memory, energy, balance, and neck.

The Neuropsychiatric Evaluation report of Norman Fisher, M.D., dated 6/29/89, indicated that from a neuropsychiatric perspective, this patient presents a classical clinical picture of a continuing post-concussive syndrome and closed head brain injury. She continued to have problems in cognitive, intellectual, emotional, social, personal, and job-related areas. This has been documented by interviews with significant others. Not only do her complaints and clinical picture include problems in her thinking, memory, conceptual ability, organizational ability, judgement, language, hearing, emotional control, sleep, energy, and interpersonal areas, but have been documented through a variety of neurodiagnostic tests of the brain.

Dr. Fisher's addendum report to his neuropsychiatric evaluation report of 6/29/89 indicated that Ms. Smith was started on Tegretol, 100 mg daily, which was increased on 7/13/89 to 100 mg twice daily. He felt that the physiological effects of this small dosage of Tegretol had been generally positive and would be predicted by the findings on her EEG study. He felt that Ms. Smith's improvement in her functioning following Tegretol gave further support for the brain injury she suffered as a result of her closed head trauma.

Behavioral Observations

Ms. Smith presented as a 38-year-old, right-handed white female in no acute distress. She arrived at 8:30 a.m. for her scheduled appointment and indicated that she had been driven to the appointment by a close family friend. During the clinical interview she spoke fluently and exhibited no gross evidence of word finding difficulties, paraphasia, or dysarthria. She did not appear depressed or significantly anxious. Her recent and remote memory appeared grossly intact. Her thinking appeared slightly tangential at times, particularly when she felt stressed. She made good eye contact and did not appear evasive or manipulative. There was no evidence of any gross neurologic abnormalities in her speech, gait, or behavior. There was no evidence of hallucinations, paranoia, or bizarre thinking. Her affect tended to be somewhat bland. She did not exhibit emotional lability or perseverative thinking. She appeared to be trying to the best of her ability on each of the neuropsychological tests which were administered to her. At no time did she exhibit any evidence of malingering or factitious behavior.

Neuropsychological Testing

Tests Administered

The Raven Standard Progressive Matrices Test
The Sbordone Attention Battery
The Trail Making Test (Parts A and B)
The Symbol Digit Modalities Test
The Sbordone-Hall Memory Battery
The Boston Naming Test
The Controlled Word Association Test
The Grip Strength Test
The Finger Tapping Test
The Grooved Pegboard Test
Luria's Motor Examination
Test of Executive Functions
The Millon Clinical Multiaxial Inventory
The Millon Behavioral Health Inventory
The Minnesota Multiphasic Personality Inventory

Tests Results

INTELLIGENCE

She was administered The Raven Standard Progressive Matrices Test to assess her current level of intellectual functioning. (Author's note: This is an untimed nonverbal test of intellectual functioning which relies almost entirely on the individual's perceptual and problem solving skills.) She obtained a score of 52 out of a possible 60 which placed her at the 93rd percentile with respect to persons her age. Her score on this test gave her an IQ of 123.

ATTENTION-CONCENTRATION

She was administered The Sbordone Attention Battery to assess her ability to perform a variety of different arithmetic and non-arithmetic tasks. While she generally performed well on virtually each of these tasks, she took substanially longer than expected to complete each task. (Author's note: This finding suggests that she sacrificed speed for accuracy, which is a compensatory device frequently used by brain-injured patients.) Her visual motor tracking skills were assessed by The Trail Making Test. She required 34.34 seconds to complete Part A, which placed her 0.82 standard deviations below expectancy. She required 68.04 seconds to complete Part B, which placed her 0.34 standard deviations below expectancy. In comparison to previous testing, her performance on Part B, which is a task that involves cognitive flexibility, improved significantly. However, little improvement was seen in her performance on Part A. Her speed of cognitive processing was assessed by The Symbol Digit Modalities Test. She obtained a score of 50, which placed her 0.14 standard deviations below expectancy. (Author's note: While her scores on the above tests place her within the normal range, it should be recognized that her IQ, as determined by The Raven Standard Progressive Matrices Test, predicts substantially higher scores on the above tests.)

MEMORY

She was administered The Sbordone-Hall Memory Battery to provide an assessment of her memory. Her ability to learn new information was assessed by the Alpha-Numeric Free Recall Test. Testing revealed that she was only able to learn a maximum of eight out of 15 possible alpha-numeric stimuli by the end of the fifth trial. Her score on this subtest placed her 1.54 standard deviations below age expectancy. Her ability to recognize 12 words she had been shown over the three consecutive trials was also found to be impaired. Similarly, her ability to recognize geometric figures after a delay of between 16 and 23 seconds was also impaired. When she was shown multiple geometric figures and asked to identify them after a delay of only six seconds, she also tested as impaired. A discriminant function statistical analysis, based on 60 test scores on the battery, indicated that her overall performance was found to be 243.1 times more likely to be obtained from an individual with brain damage than from an individual without any history of brain damage.

LANGUAGE

She was administered The Boston Naming Test to assess her confrontational naming skills. Testing revealed that she was able to name 56 out of 60 objects which placed her within the normal range. Her ability, however, to generate as many words as possible, beginning with specific letters of the alphabet for one minute each, was found to be mildly impaired. Thus, when contrasting her performance on timed and untimed tests, her performance on timed tests is seen as mildly impaired in comparison with her performance on untimed tests. (Author's note: This finding is frequently seen in patients who have sustained subcortical or brain stem injuries. It should also be noted that these results are consistent with the results obtained at the Clark Rehabilitation Institute at Valley Hospital.)

MOTOR

She was administered The Grip Strength Test to assess the strength of her dominant and nondominant hands. Testing revealed intact strength bilaterally without any significant lateralizing differences. She was also administered The Finger Tapping Test to assess her motor speed. Testing revealed that the motor speed of her nondominant (left) hand was 25.1% slower than her dominant (right) hand. (Author's note: This finding, in light of her performance on The Grip Strength Test, suggests evidence of right subcortical dysfunction.) She was also administered The Grooved Pegboard Test to assess the speed of her fine motor movements and manual dexterity. Testing revealed that the speed of her nondominant left hand was 26.6% slower than her dominant right hand. (Author's note: This finding is consistent with her performance on The Finger Tapping Test and further corroborates the likelihood of right subcortical dysfunction.)

She was also administered Luria's Motor Examination to evaluate her ability to perform a wide variety of complex movements with one or both hands. Testing revealed that on tasks involving parallel motor processing with both hands, her left hand appeared to lag behind. Her ability to perform programmed tapping movements with both hands was also found to be mildly impaired, however, when she was permitted to utilize verbal mediation, her performance became intact. (Author's note: This finding indicates that when this patient was given the opportunity of utilizing her relatively intact higher cortical skills, she was able to compensate for her subcortical brain dysfunction.)

EXECUTIVE FUNCTIONS/PROBLEM SOLVING

Her responses to tasks involving verbal similarities, the interpretation of proverbs, judgement, and problem solving revealed that her abstract and conceptualization skills are relatively intact. This finding corroborates her performance on The Raven Standard Progressive Matrices Test. However, when she was given a number of orally presented questions to evaluate her problem solving skills, her response tended to be impulsive. Whenever this occurred, her responses were inaccurate. However, when she permitted herself the opportunity to spend more time thinking about the problem, her responses were accurate. These results are consistent with previous testing performed at the Clark Rehabilitation Institute of Valley Hospital.

PERSONALITY/EMOTIONAL

She was administered The Millon Behavioral Health Inventory to assess long-standing traits that most likely characterize her personal, social, and work relationships, as well as the manner in which she is likely to relate to health personnel services and treatments. Her profile on this test indicated that under duress she is likely to maintain an image of cool strength, self-confidence, and independence. She takes pride in being self-reliant, capable of taking care of herself without any help from others. However, illness is not an experience that this patient is likely to accept easily since the role of the patient is seen as being weak and vulnerable. Thus, it is important that when working with this patient, that health care professionals be open and frank with her and provide her with clear explanations as to why certain steps and treatments are necessary.

She was administered The Millon Clinical Multiaxial Inventory to assess her long-standing personality traits and current emotional problems. Her profile on this test indicated that she is likely to have long-standing needs to seek affection, attention, and security. Thus, she may act in a socially gregarious and superficially charming manner, yet may be quite naive about interpersonal matters. When faced with interpersonal tension, she may maintain an air of buoyancy and deny disturbing emotions and inner discomforts. When faced with the possible loss of security or support of significant others, she may openly, if not dramatically, solicit their reassurance. Her profile on this test indicated that she was experiencing feelings of weakness and tiredness, diminished social interests, and emotional lability. She also saw herself as having difficulty regulating her emotions.

She was administered The Minnesota Multiphasic Personality Inventory to assess her current emotional problems and personality traits. Her profile on this test was found to be valid. Her profile indicated that she is experiencing episodic cognitive difficulties and is likely to have problems maintaining control over her emotions. Consequently, she is likely to be seen by others as impulsive, irritable, and as having a poor frustration tolerance. She is likely to react to relatively minor frustrations and have difficulty on tasks requiring thinking or concentrating. She is also likely to be suspicious, moody, emotionally labile, likely to ruminate about her problems, and see herself as inadequate.

Summary and Impression

The patient is a 39-year-old, right-handed white female who was involved in a motor vehicle accident on 12/5/86 during which she struck her forehead on the windshield, the force of which caused her head to break the windshield. She was rendered unconscious for appoximately two minutes. She appeared confused and bewildered following this. Her first clear memory following her accident begins after the paramedics arrived. She was taken by ambulance to the emergency room of Valley Hospital, in San Antonio, where x-rays were taken and found to be negative. She began experiencing a headache and felt nauseated shortly after her accident. She was seen by her family physician who informed her that she had sustained a cerebral concussion and recommended bed rest. After two or three days, she returned to work. After she had been working for some time, her boss informed her that her personality had changed and that she had gone from being a very aggressive individual with considerable energy to someone who appeared apathetic and unmotivated. Therefore, he felt it necessary to terminate her because she was not the same person he had hired prior to the accident. As a consequence of her tendency to fatigue quickly, attention-concentration difficulties, emotional lability, diminished frustration tolerance, difficulty processing more than one event at a time, and the relative slowness of her cognitive processing skills, not to mention her impaired judgement, she was not able to find work as a leasing agent and encountered financial difficulties.

She was referred to a clinical psychologist, Dr. Zebra, in late January 1987, whose psychological and neuropsychological testing of her revealed a variety of cognitive difficulties consistent with organic brain dysfunction secondary to her motor vehicle accident. Subsequent testing by Dr. Zebra in late November 1987, revealed that while Ms. Smith had improved in her cognitive functioning with respect to her recent memory, she had become more depressed. Ms. Smith was referred to Dr. Black, who performed a neuropsychological evaluation of Ms. Smith. His report concluded that her complaints were caused by psychological rather than organic factors. Careful analysis, however, of Dr. Black's raw test data contradicts his conclusions and indicates that he apparently failed to recognize the severity of Ms. Smith's difficulties, particularly on tasks involving attention, concentration, and recent memory. Over the next two months, Ms. Smith was referred to the Clark Rehabilitation Institute of Valley Hospital, where occupational and language testing revealed strong evidence of cognitive deficits consistent with mild head trauma. Ms. Smith entered into this program on an outpatient basis and received approximately four months of cognitive rehabilitation which helped her considerably. Follow-up testing and evaluations by the clinical staff found that, while Ms. Smith improved in her cognitive functioning, she still continued to demonstrate a number of significant cognitive difficulties.

Extensive neurological and neuropsychiatric evaluations by Dr. Waddle and Dr. Fisher revealed neurologic abnormalities consistent with cerebral concussion and post-concussive syndrome. Neuropsychological testing by this examiner revealed a number of residual cognitive difficulties which were generally consistent with patients who have sustained cerebral concussion. These findings were also consistent with the test results of the Clark Rehabilitation Institute and corroborate this patient's persistent cognitive, behavioral, and emotional difficulties secondary to her traumatic brain injury.

On the basis of the above information and test findings, it is the opinion of this examiner that Ms. Smith sustained a traumatic brain injury in her motor vehicle accident of 12/5/86 which produced significant cognitive, behavioral, and emotional impairments consistent with the diagnoses of a post-concussion syndrome, closed head injury, or mild head injury which have been given by many of her treating and examining doctors. Because of the severity of these impairments, it is expected that she will continue to experience these impairments over the next 5 to 10 years. The author also anticipates that she will continue to require psychiatric treatment and cognitive rehabilitation over this time, particularly if she attempts difficult or novel activities.

Diagnosis

Axis I:	Organic Mental Disorder (post-concussion syndrome)
Axis II:	None
Axis III:	Closed head injury as per medical records
Axis IV:	Severity of psychosocial stressors: mild
Axis V:	Highest Level of Functioning Since Injury: GAF = 63 Current: GAF = 63

Comments

The above neuropsychological report demonstrates the importance of the neuropsychological expert carefully reviewing all of the patient's hospital, medical, psychological, and rehabilitation records. Fortunately, these records are consistent in that they demonstrate that she was rendered unconscious, appeared bewildered, confused, and became nauseated shortly after her accident, and had been diagnosed by the treating doctors as having sustained a cerebral concussion. She was fired by her employer, who noticed a rather dramatic change in her behavior and personality after she returned to work. Initial psychological and neuropsychological testing detected this patient's cognitive difficulties which were correctly attributed to her traumatic brain injury. The defense neuropsychologist, Dr. Black, concluded that the patient's complaints were caused by psychological rather than organic factors. However, when Dr. Black's neuropsychological test data was carefully reviewed, it became apparent that his interpretation and conclusions were based on an inaccurate analysis of his own test data. In fact, his test data actually showed evidence of cognitive impairment and corroborated the diagnosis of brain damage.

The patient was referred to a rehabilitation institute which specializes in the assessment, treatment, and rehabilitation of brain-injured patients. Their assessment revealed numerous cognitive difficulties consistent with brain injury. Extensive neurological and neurospychiatric evaluations also revealed abnormalities consistent with brain damage. Finally, neuropsychological assessment found evidence of cognitive impairments consistent with the observations of her examining and treating doctors.

The report of the defense psychiatrist contained numerous historical inaccuracies which were contradicted by the patient's medical records. The defense psychiatrist's report suggested that the doctor lacked expertise in the field of traumatic brain injuries. The defense neuropsychologist and psychiatrist had also not reviewed the patient's rehabilitation records which documented her cognitive impairments. Their reports focused on this patient's personality characteristics and generally ignored the patient's medical and rehabilitation records.

The next report stresses the importance of taking a careful background history, reviewing prior medical records, and making a qualitative interpretation of the plaintiff's neuropsychological test data.

Neuropsychological Assessment of Sarah Stark

AGE:	38 (6/5/51)
MARITAL STATUS:	Divorced
CHILDREN:	None
OCCUPATION:	Physical therapist
EMPLOYER:	Highland Community Hospital
DATE OF INJURY:	3/6/83
DATE OF ASSESSMENT:	2/15/89
REFERRED BY:	John Jones, Attorney at Law Law Offices of Jones and Smith 10 Main Street Small Town, Wisconsin

Current Complaints

1. Attention-concentration difficulties. The patient indicated that conversations with others tend to become vague and distant. These episodes can last for a few moments to as long as several hours. This problem, however, can be overcome by conscious effort, stimulants, such as coffee, and the use of the medication Tegretol. This problem is minimal when there is little activity or competing stimulation or noise in the background or when she is rested. This problem typically occurs on a daily basis and can vary in severity. The patient denied ever being prescribed Cylert, Ritalin, or any CNS stimulants.
2. Left-sided weakness. The patient denied any clear difference between her upper and lower extremity with respect to this problem. The problem was greatest shortly after her motor vehicle accident and caused her to fall down. She also experienced a foot drop in her left

leg at that time. She described the severity of this problem as mild to moderate for normal activity, such as activities of daily living, but severely impaired for work-related activities. This problem affected her ability to lift patients and was particularly severe when helping patients transfer to the left. This was stated while the patient was laughing and exhibited a bland affect. This problem was most severe during the first year post-injury, but has improved considerably due to therapy and the "natural healing process."

3. Memory difficulties under conditions of "stimulus complexity." The patient indicated that "if there is too much competing information during the memory and encoding process, I have difficulties retaining this information." Coffee and rest minimize this problem, whereas factors such as fatigue and stress maximize it. The severity of this problem could not be assessed during the first two and one-half years following her injury because of the severity of other problems, such as left-sided weakness, mental confusion, and a feeling of "being overwhelmed." Since that time, she observed a significant improvement in this problem.
4. Depression secondary to "losses," which she described as her friends, job, home, and stressors (she defined this as having to live with her mother following her accident). She indicated that she did not have a good relationship with her mother in the past and described her mother as "always right and unwilling to compromise." Her mother was described as very domineering, controlling, and rigid. She also said her mother was cold and uncomfortable with children. The patient indicated that harsh corporal punishment was frequently administered for minor infractions while she was growing up. Her parents were highly prejudiced. Sex was also never discussed at home. She also recalled that her parents denied her any opportunity to date or have fun. She described other stressors such as major financial difficulties stemming from the cost of her medical and rehabilitation treatments, physical weakness, difficulty with ambulation, frequent falls, and feeling overwhelmed by the accident. The patient believed that she was placed on some medications by her neurologist for her depression; however, they produced bad side effects consisting of syncopal episodes, falling, being "out of touch with her surroundings," dysphoria, etc. The patient denied receiving any formal psychotherapy, although this was recommended by her neurologist and psychologist. (Author's note: This was contradicted by records of Union Medical Center reviewed later in this report.)

   The patient indicated that she had received counseling through the student health center while she was in college to cope with the advances of a married man. She also received counseling and psychotherapy from a Christian psychotherapist/minister after she went to live with her mother after her injury, which she stated was "under protest."
5. The patient is not able to drive because of "absence spells" which can last up to several hours. As a consequence, the patient must take the bus or ride her bicycle. The patient indicated that she has few friends because of her inability to drive. She admitted that she has not dated a man for several years and typically spends her weekends going to movies alone. She claimed that it takes her much longer to do things now as a result of the necessity of riding the bus. She tried to keep busy to avoid feeling lonely. She did admit, however, that she owns a car but does not drive it because of her seizures.

History of Accident as Described by Patient

The patient indicated that she was driving her car up a hill in the physical vicinity of several large trucks. She recalled that her car was struck on the left side when a semi-trailer/truck changed lanes.

She indicated that she was wearing a seat belt and shoulder harness at the time the accident occurred. She remembered feeling scared when the truck suddenly came into her lane and that she began shaking. She then recalled that she struck the left side of her head on the metal doorpost located on the driver's side. She also recalled that her car spun around and hit a guard rail and bounced back into a traffic lane. She indicated that she then got out of the car "in a state of shock" and noticed that she was shaking. Her recall of the events preceding, during, and following the accident is excellent. She remembered that she was driven home by a highway patrol officer. After she got home, she felt like "the wind had been knocked out of me" and that "my stomach felt queasy-upset" and that "I felt pins and needles all over my body." She also felt a strange sensation of numbness in her left temple and stated, "It felt like it wasn't there." She recalled that this sensation of numbness began to creep into the back of her neck. She stated that she started becoming afraid and then phoned a female friend who drove her to the emergency room at the Union Medical Center. While she reported that her memory for events which occurred while she was in the emergency room is generally poor, she did recall that "they made the point that the accident was an insurance case and would be paid by the insurance company."

After she got home from the emergency room, she began experiencing a sudden and painful sensation of "white light." Her next memory was that of waking up the next morning. She indicated that she felt like dialing "911" to summon the police, but she did not. She then began experiencing a sensation of "freezing of my limbs." Later she called her physician and tried to get his secretary to summon an ambulance and set up an appointment for her to be immediately seen. It should be noted that the patient's affect appeared bland and inappropriate while discussing these events.

The patient indicated that later that day she began experiencing a sharp knife-like pain on the left side of her head, which also, paradoxically, felt numb in the area surrounding this. She went to see her physician, demanding an x-ray. Her physician, however, refused to x-ray her head. She then claimed that her physician "placed his hand into her head." When she was asked to describe what she meant by this, she indicated that "it (her physician's hand) went through the bone." She recalls that the pain was very severe and that she was told that she was "seriously hurt" and required immediate medical attention but that she needed money to receive treatment, and that the hospital would not treat her unless she had money. The patient claimed that she had an insured motorist's policy on her motor insurance and had adequate financial resources to pay for treatment. The patient claimed that this did not seem right to her and later sought out legal representation to resolve this issue. She also indicated that she had a prior attorney who did not agree with her regarding her condition.

The patient indicated that at the time of her injury she was employed as a physical therapist in private practice and had recently formed her own company and that her business had been doing well. She indicated that she billed $75 per hour for private paying patients but that she had started her private practice only two months prior to her accident. She admitted that she had been under "a lot of stress" due to the rapid rise and physical demands of her business. She claimed that her motor vehicle accident prevented her from developing her company. She indicated that she was currently employed as a physical therapist for Highland Community Hospital but was negotiating the details of her hours and salary arrangements with the administrative staff at the hospital.

Pre-existing Difficulties According to this Patient

The patient indicated that as a child, she would often ignore many of the statements or conversations held with her mother, particularly when her mother became upset, and recalled that she would "tune out" what her mother was saying to her because it was repetitive and "I had heard it before." She denied any subsequent instances of attention-concentration difficulties of the type she described since leaving home. She also denied a prior history of left-sided weakness, memory difficulties, depression (except for specific times during her adolescence, particularly when her grandmother died, since she indicated that she was very close to her grandmother), absence spells, seizures, and episodes of confusion and disorientation. She also denied any significant cognitive or emotional difficulties prior to her motor vehicle accident except for relatively mild spelling and language difficulties during her childhood in comparison to her science and mathematics skills.

Background

DEVELOPMENT

The patient was born in Newark, New Jersey, as the oldest of four children. Although she could not recall her birth weight, she believed that she was the product of a full-term, uncomplicated delivery. She denied any hospitalizations or medical problems other than having the usual childhood diseases while growing up, although she reported that she had pneumonia at age 14. She denied a history of fractures, head trauma, neurological illnesses, or seizures during her childhood and adolescence. She also denied a history of emotional or physical abuse, although she reported that her parents frequently inflicted harsh corporal punishment whenever she committed any minor infractions of their rules. Later she indicated that she had visual difficulties during the first grade, which caused her to have reading problems and fall academically behind her peers. This problem was rectified after she was prescribed glasses.

CHILDHOOD

Both parents were described as very rigid, controlling, domineering, and as having strong prejudices. Her mother wanted her to be a schoolteacher. The patient, however, wanted to be a physical therapist. Her parents would not allow her to express any negative thoughts or feelings in their presence and would send her to her room whenever this occurred. Her parents also denied her any opportunities to have fun or date. She recalled that she was forced to act in a very docile and quiet manner at home and had to be extremely diplomatic when dealing with her mother.

The patient left home at age 17, shortly after graduating from high school. She went to live in Madison, Wisconsin, where she attended the University of Wisconsin for one year. She recalled that her family rejected her after she left home. While living in Madison, she recalled that she tried to live a "more normal existence," but her parents actually tried to influence her dorm mother to instill their values on her.

MARITAL

The patient was married for the first time in 1979. Her husband was a 25-year-old physicist. They were married for four years and did not have any children. She indicated that their marriage dissolved as the result of a "mutual growing apart," which stemmed from frequent quarrels around control issues. She indicated that she tried dating after her divorce but felt ill at ease with the expectations of men, particularly regarding sex.

CHILDREN

The patient became pregnant when she was 18. She gave birth to a boy but put the child up for adoption. She indicated that she continues to feel guilty for giving up her child. She denied any other pregnancies.

SEXUAL

The patient denied any sexual difficulties or loss of sexual libido since her accident. She indicated that her sexual libido became extremely low after her marriage terminated. She denied any significant change in her sexual libido since that time. She gave up romantic dating about 10 years ago and denied any sexual relationships since that time.

MEDICAL HISTORY

The patient underwent a tonsillectomy at age seven. She was hospitalized for pneumonia at age 14. She underwent childbirth at age 18, and had an appendectomy at age 24. She became ill during a hike in the mountains in 1980, but reports that this illness lasted only one month. She also indicated that between 1978 and 1983, she developed some allergies to meat and dairy products which eventually cleared up. She claimed that the allergies produced nausea, vomiting, and diarrhea. She claimed that this problem resolved after she modified her diet; however, she later admitted that she went off her diet one year prior to her accident, but denied experiencing any difficulties.

PSYCHIATRIC

The patient denied a family history of substance abuse or psychiatric illness.

Behavioral Observations

The patient presented as an alert and oriented attractive 38-year-old, right-handed white female who appeared five to 10 years younger than her stated age. She arrived for her scheduled appointment approximately 30 minutes late. She was neatly dressed and well-groomed with good personal hygiene. She appeared to be an excellent historian and exhibited no gross evidence of language, motor, cognitive, or perceptual difficulties. Her affect was bland with evidence of "La Belle Indifference" while she described her symptoms and provided a detailed chronology of her accident. Her thinking at times appeared bizarre, particularly when she described her physician's examination of her following the accident. She did not seem anxious, but appeared generally pleasant. There was no evidence of hallucinations, frank paranoia, perseverations, or ataxia. She did not appear to be experiencing any significant physical pain or discomfort. She had no difficulty moving her extremities. Her attention, concentration skills, and recent memory seemed excellent. For example, she was able to provide an excellent chronological history of her accident, and had no difficulty describing recent events. She did not seem guarded or apprehensive. At no time did she exhibit emotional lability, poor impulse control, or behavioral evidence of frontal lobe pathology. On one or two occasions, her superficial "nice" facade gave way to some feelings of depression which she seemed to be repressing. She also exhibited strong feelings of anger and rage toward her parents, particularly her mother, which she also tried to suppress and rationalize.

She was seen for a total of nearly seven hours. Approximately four and one-half hours were spent obtaining a clinical and background history. The remainder of the time was spent administering neuropsychological tests. She had considerable difficulty completing the Millon Clinical Multiaxial Inventory and required nearly an hour and a half to complete it. The inventory is normally completed in 20 to 25 minutes.

Review of Medical Records

The report of Dr. Coffee, dated 4/5/78, indicated that the patient had a history of menstrual pain and excessive bleeding. These records indicated that the patient was afraid to take pills because she knew a young woman who had had a stroke while taking birth control pills. She also indicated that she did not want to use condoms. On 5/30/78, Dr. Coffee indicated that the patient had been adamant in preferring to use an I.U.D. as a birth contraceptive device, even though it had been explained to her that this device was likely to cause menstrual pain and discomfort and had resulted in a history of uterine infections in the past. She also stressed to the patient that these infections could cause infertility.

The records of the Medical Health Plan (undated) indicated that the patient completed a health history, wherein she indicated that she had been hospitalized for five days in July 1969, as the result of injuries stemming from an automobile accident. She also reported a past history of pneumonia, urinary difficulties, back problems, and anemia.

A review of Dr. Storm's records indicated that the patient completed an adult health history on 6/11/82 that reported a prior history of headache, dizziness, sinus difficulties, stuffy nose, visual and auditory difficulties, pneumonia, loss of appetite, indigestion, heartburn, nervous stomach, vomiting blood, passing blood, dark stools, abdominal pain, diarrhea, constipation, changes in bowel habits, anemia, low thyroid, physical weakness, nervousness, irritability, depression, tiredness, sleeping difficulties, and urinary difficulties.

Dr. Storm's records indicated that when the patient was seen on 6/18/82, she complained of episodes of weakness and mental confusion associated with a loss of energy. She also indicated that she thought she may have "passed out" at times and could not recall where she was or what she was doing. She also complained of headaches and visual and hearing difficulties, as well as severe and multiple allergies causing nausea, vomiting, and diarrhea. She indicated that these symptoms were triggered by foods such as wheat, meat, eggs, fish, chicken, soybeans, oats, barley, and also by insecticides and weed killers. She said that she could eat very few things, such as rye, millet, corn, and potatoes in small amounts. She expressed concern about her nutritional state and had been seeing a homeopath for several years. She attributed her above symptoms to an accident four years ago while hiking with a party of other people, during which time they were sprayed by an airplane. All of the individuals suffered skin, eye, and nose irritation, irritability, gastrointestinal problems, and weak muscles. She was diagnosed as having episodes of mental confusion; rule out seizures and migraine, as well as gastrointestinal difficulties; and rule out infectious and inflammatory diseases.

When the patient was seen on 7/31/82, she complained of mental confusion and headaches, as well as gastrointestinal difficulties. She had also had another episode of severe gastrointestinal distress and diarrhea, as well as headaches and mental confusion the previous week. At times her symptoms were associated with changes in her visual fields, as well as an occasional inability to speak. Lesser episodes were associated with a feeling of fogginess, as well as mental symptoms. She indicated that these mental symptoms were occurring on almost a daily basis. She was diagnosed as having probable migraine headaches with associated gastrointestinal symptoms.

Dr. Storm referred the patient to Midwest Medical Center, where she was seen by Dr. Chance, a neurologist, on 7/27/84. Dr. Chance's report indicated that the patient had a four-year history of episodes of dizziness, loss of coordination and disorientation which periodically was followed by a loss of consciousness for periods up to several hours. On one occasion, disorientation followed for about three days. The patient had associated these spells with the ingestion of high protein foods and grains. Since she stopped eating these foods, she had not had a spell in six months. Her EEG showed minimal alterations over the temporal areas of both hemispheres which were felt to be of questionable clinical significance. There was no evidence of specific epileptiform patterns. She also underwent a sleep EEG which was found to be normal.

The patient was referred for a CT brain scan which was performed at Standard Medical Center on 8/7/82, and found to be normal.

The patient was seen again by Dr. Storm on 8/24/82. He indicated that she had undergone some respiratory and gastrointestinal symptoms while eating in a restaurant, but indicated that she had stopped eating in restaurants. Dr. Storm discussed the possibility of a sulphur allergy.

Dr. Storm's notes, dated 11/4/82, indicated that the patient's migraines had reduced in frequency to about two per week after she bought a migraine cookbook and eliminated all suspected foods which had been contributing to this problem. She also had eliminated numerous foods from her diet because of gastrointestinal difficulties. The patient indicated that she had requested an IUD insertion even though she had been advised by her previous treating physician that IUD's caused her menstrual pain and the development of infections.

Dr. Storm's chart note, dated 2/15/83, indicated that her abdominal symptoms improved, providing she did not eat too much protein at one sitting. The patient's only sources of proteins were sesame seeds, garbanzo beans, peas, lentils, peanuts, and pinto beans combined with oats, rice, rye, or corn. Dr. Storm felt that the patient's headaches and gastrointestinal distress were being successfully controlled by careful attention to her diet.

The emergency room record of Sick Medical Center indicated that the patient was involved in a motor vehicle accident on 3/6/83, during which time she had a questionable loss of consciousness. She complained of headache involving her left side, numbness of her left temporal area, strain involving the left side of her neck, and mental confusion. Her greatest concern was that of numbness in her left temporal area. A neurological exam performed on this date was found to be essentially normal. The patient returned again on 3/16/83 complaining of increased neck pain and aching pain down both arms. She complained that two days earlier she had developed paresthesias and numbness of both hands, occipital and nuchal headaches, and diarrhea. A neurological examination was performed on this date and was found to be normal. She was placed on Dolobid and was provided a soft collar restraint. On 3/18/83, she complained of neck pain and numbness in her left hand, although her physical exam was reported as negative. She was reported to have inconsistent hypesthesia in her left parietal area which was not associated with any neurological abnormality other than her neck pain. Her hypesthesia was felt to be under conscious control since it was not observed when she was distracted. She was informed that she should recover in two weeks. She was encouraged to continue taking Dolobid and Aspirin and wear her cervical collar when necessary. X-rays of her cervical spine were performed on 3/18/83 and were interpreted as normal.

The patient was seen by Dr. Mottle on 5/13/83 who reported that her mental symptoms dramatically improved. She continued to show improvement when she was seen on 7/14/83, although Dr. Mottle reported mood instability which had persisted to some extent. In a letter dated 7/15/83, Dr. Mottle indicated that he expected the patient's problems to "resolve completely." When Dr. Mottle saw the patient again on 10/31/83, he noted that the patient's description of her motor vehicle accident was "contradictory." At that time the patient complained of increasing weakness and numbness in both hands and complained of dropping things which she stated "comes and goes." She also complained of a "burning sensation in her hands," word finding difficulties, attention-concentration difficulties, balance difficulties, dizziness, mental confusion, being unable to do several things at once, diarrhea, and constipation. Although Dr. Mottle reported some weakness in the patient's left side, the remainder of the neurological examination was normal.

A psychological evaluation on 11/27/83 by Dr. Swift, an unlicensed psychologist, reported that neuropsychological testing revealed evidence of attention-concentration difficulties, mental confusion, memory difficulties, mild dysarthria, an adjustment reaction characterized by depression, anxiety, and diminished self-esteem, and social withdrawal. Dr. Swift indicated that the patient's symptoms suggested the presence of a head injury and felt that this patient's cognitive difficulties had prevented her from functioning independently in her vocation.

In a letter to the patient's attorney on 11/29/83, Dr. Swift indicated that the patient had continued to experience gastrointestinal difficulties from an incident whereby she was sprayed with chemicals from an airplane. He indicated that her physical symptoms had resolved and that her mental/cognitive difficulties stemming from this incident had much cleared up. He also felt that these problems stemming from this prior incident were of a generalized nature, whereas her neuropsychological symptoms stemming from an automobile accident suggest a more focal left-sided weakness and focal cognitive difficulties.

The patient underwent an EEG study on 2/18/84 which was interpreted by Dr. Mottle as essentially within normal limits. There was no evidence of epileptiform seizure activity. She underwent a CT scan on the same date, which was also interpreted as normal. She underwent an awake and sleep EEG on 2/20/84, which was interpreted as normal without evidence of any epileptiform activity. The patient underwent an EMG study on 3/5/84; however, the results were felt to be either due to the presence of diffuse polyneuropathy or most likely due to the fact that the patient had large hands, resulting in an artifact in the test data.

Dr. Mottle's notes, dated 4/31/84, indicated that the patient still was complaining of memory difficulties and had been placed on Tegretol, which resulted in a clearing up of her cognitive confusion. She reported that she still had episodes of staring, accompanied by pressure in her head. The patient also complained of visual disturbances and headaches.

The records of Dr. Reeves were reviewed. Dr. Reeves' undated assessment report indicated that the patient had been seen on 6/1, 6/2, and 6/15/84 for evaluation. He indicated that the patient was having difficulty in organization, memory, and stamina, which interfered with her ability to function as a physical therapist in private practice, and was experiencing confusion in all aspects of her life following a motor vehicle accident on 3/6/83. She received counseling with Dr. Swift but discontinued it as a result of her dissatisfaction of Dr. Swift's treatment, which consisted of hypnosis, rather than cognitive rehabilitation to improve her organization, memory, and problem solving skills. Dr. Reeves notes in his report that the patient may have sustained a loss of consciousness in her motor vehicle accident but did not seek medical attention until later in the day. The patient reported a series of problems consisting of difficulty in language processing, impaired concentration, organization difficulties, memory impairment, confusion, fatigue, reduced frustration tolerance, poor self-esteem, impaired interpersonal relationships, and physical symptoms which included pressure sensations, left-sided weakness, and an inability to maintain her past level of physical activity. She also reported that she was experiencing some secondary life stressors stemming from some long-unresolved issues related to her mother. These stressors had been activated by the accident, and stemmed from her having to move in with her mother, whom she described as controlling and demanding. She also indicated that she found herself presently operating under her mother's control and direction in ways that were disturbing to her. She also indicated that her mother had taken over some aspects of organizing the patient's home without her consent to do so.

Dr. Reeves administered a wide variety of psychological and neuropsychological tests to this patient. He found that the patient had a full-scale IQ of 124 with a performance IQ of 117. With respect to the patient's verbal subscale scores, he found that the patient's performance on the Digit Span subtest was more than one standard deviation below the mean for other test scores. Dr. Reeves indicated that this is suggestive of "neurogenic interference" of her previous abilities. (Author's note: Unfortunately, a relatively low score on the Digit Span subtest, in comparison to other verbal subtests, usually is indicative of emotional problems resulting in concentration difficulties. This was corroborated by the fact that the patient complained quite extensively to Dr. Reeves of having been under a great deal of stress as a result of having to live with her mother, with whom she had had a very poor relationship in the past as a result of her mother's attempts to dominate and control her.)

Dr. Reeves evaluated the patient's nonverbal abilities and felt that the patient's performance on the Picture Arrangement subtest was suggestive of "neurogenic interference" in her pre-existing intellectual abilities and suggested that such findings are likely to show evidence of right anterior temporal lobe dysfunction. (Author's note: Dr. Reeves, however, made no mention of the fact that this particular subtest reflects socially appropriate thinking and social perceptiveness. Since this patient came from a socially dysfunctional family whose childhood and adolescent friendships and social relationships were restricted and as an adult has led a largely solitary existence with relatively few social interactions, her score on this test most likely reflects social deficiencies stemming from her limited social experiences, rather than from a brain injury. Dr. Reeves also failed to mention in his report that the patient's performance on the Digit Symbol subtest, which is regarded as the most sensitive WAIS-R subtest to brain damage, was intact and consistent with her scores on the remaining performance subtests. In fact, the patient's performance on the Block Design and Object Assembly subtests, which are highly sensitive to right hemisphere brain damage, were intact and revealed no evidence of brain dysfunction.)

Dr. Reeves evaluated the patient's executive functions, specifically her ability to initiate, control, and monitor her behavior, as well as to generate plans and change them to fit external circumstances. Dr. Reeves indicated that the patient "had some evidence of difficulty in maintaining a mental set once it had been established." He then further stated, "On the Wisconsin Card Sorting test, Ms. Stark exhibited difficulty in decision making and in the maintenance of mental set." (Author's note: Careful examination, however, of the patient's raw test data revealed virtually no support whatsoever to corroborate Dr. Reeves' claim of impairment. For example, the patient completed all six categories on the Wisconsin Card Sorting test in only 70 trials and made only seven errors, which is the best performance the author has ever seen on anyone taking this test for the first time. Dr. Reeves also administered the Category test, which is also quite sensitive to executive functions. This patient made only 15 errors on this test. This is an excellent performance, which like her performance on the Wisconsin Card Sorting test, is highly inconsistent with frontal lobe impairment or brain damage.)

Dr. Reeves claimed that the patient had difficulty initiating and sustaining a mental focus and was readily distracted by irrelevant stimuli, such as external noises or competing information. He further stated that "as tasks become more complex, she has greater difficulty in maintaining a mental set." (Author's note: Dr. Reeves' statements are contradicted by this patient's excellent performances on both the Category and Wisconsin Card Sorting tests, as well as her performance on the Stroop Color Word Naming test, in which the patient failed to show any evidence of impaired performance under conditions of competing information or irrelevant stimuli.)

Dr. Reeves indicated that the patient had "difficulty in the acquisition of immediate memories for unrelated stimuli, such as digits or words." (Author's note: Dr. Reeves' statement is strongly contradicted by the fact that this patient was able to learn 14 out of 15 possible unrelated words on the Rey Auditory Verbal Learning test by the end of five consecutive trials. Her performance on this test was consistent for performances obtained from college students and reveals no evidence of impairment. In fact, the patient was able to recall all 14 words under conditions of interference and following a 30-minute delay, which demonstrates that her memory for verbal material is excellent. It should be known that patients with traumatic brain injuries, particularly frontal lobe injuries, do poorly on this test under such conditions. Thus, this patient's performance on this test is highly inconsistent to patients who have sustained traumatic brain injuries.) Dr. Reeves also reported that while this patient had no difficulty recalling two short stories immediately after they were both presented to her, her ability to recall these stories after a delay of 30 minutes was found to be impaired, in that the patient could only recall 59% of the originally learned information. (Author's note: It should be noted that this particular finding is highly inconsistent, in light of the fact that this patient exhibited 100% recall of verbal material in a previous test after a delay of 30 minutes. Since it has been the author's experience that it is easier for patients to recall more meaningful information, such as short stories, rather than unrelated words, this patient should have performed much poorer on the Rey Auditory Verbal Learning test than on the Logical Memories test [recall of short stories], as the latter information is typically easier to learn since it contains much more meaningful information.)

Dr. Reeves then pointed out that the patient's visual memory tested as impaired, particularly with her reproduction of visual (geometric) information. (Author's note: Careful observation of Dr. Reeves' raw test data revealed that the patient's drawing of this figure from memory after a 30-minute delay was not significantly impaired, since using scoring criteria published by Lezak (1976), the patient's original copying of this figure placed her at the 62.5 percentile, while her drawing from memory placed her at the 35th percentile, which represents a difference of less than one standard deviation, which falls within the normal range.)

Dr. Reeves indicated that the patient exhibited significant difficulties in comprehending instructions and frequently failed to comprehend the nuance of questions. She also, according to Dr. Reeves, "tended to become confused and befuddled by test demands." (Author's note: It is interesting to note that the patient's performances on the Verbal subtest of the Wechsler Adult Intelligence Scale revealed no such impairments, since the patient demonstrated evidence of intact performance on verbal subtests that examined her verbal comprehension, abstract thinking, and her ability to comprehend fairly detailed questions of verbal tasks. Thus, Dr. Reeves' statements contained in his report, such as, "Ms. Stark had extreme difficulty in prioritizing her verbalizations. She tended to over-elaborate on answers without any awareness when the answer had been completed. All bits of information seemed to be equally important to her," are contradicted by his test data, as well as by this patient's performance on the Wechsler Adult Intelligence Scale, in which she demonstrated a verbal IQ of 124, which places her in the top five percent of the population. It is also contradicted by her performance on a variety of other neuropsychological and psychological tests which place a high premium on understanding complex instructions.)

Dr. Reeves reported that sensory-perceptual testing revealed a mild decrease in sensation on the left to light touch, pain, and weight discrimination. He also reported that the patient's performance on the tactual form perception test demonstrated some evidence of impairment with the left hand. On the Tactual Performance Test, he noted that the patient was "far clumsier" in using her left hand as compared to her right hand. He also noted that the patient's left hand, on tasks involving sequencing and organizing motor movements, was somewhat disorganized. (Author's note: It is highly unusual that this patient's impaired motor performances involving her left hand are unaccompanied by any impairment on tasks that are highly sensitive to right hemisphere dysfunction. For example, the patient's performance on tasks involving right frontal lobe dysfunction was intact. The right frontal lobe controls the motor activities of the left hand. Patients who typically demonstrate left-sided weakness, slowness, or impairment are usually found to have evidence of right frontal lobe impairment. For example, the patient's performance on both The Wisconsin Card Sorting and Category Test, which are highly sensitive to right frontal lobe pathology, were performed extremely well and revealed no evidence of impairment. The patient's performance on the Tactual Performance Test revealed that her memory and localization scores were intact, suggesting that her visual memory and right hemisphere functions were also intact. This was corroborated by the patient's excellent performances on the Block Design and Object Assembly Tests, which are highly sensitive to posterior right hemisphere functioning. Thus, without evidence of right hemisphere damage, it would appear that the patient's performances with her left hand could represent some form of peripheral neuropathy, injury to her left arm or hand, or conscious efforts to simulate such difficulties. Thus, Dr. Reeves' findings cannot simply be the result of a brain injury, since they are not corroborated by other neuropsychological test data or neurological tests, such as electroencephalographic and CT brain scan studies, which were essentially normal.)

Dr. Reeves, in discussing the patient's higher cognitive functions, indicated that "Ms. Stark's strategies for problem solving are disorganized, non-hierarchical, and highly inefficient. She seems to get the right answer more by serendipity than by design." (Author's note: Dr. Reeves' statements are strongly contradicted by his own test data, in which the patient's performance on several problem solving tasks was in fact excellent, if not outstanding. For example, the patient made only seven errors on the Wisconsin Card Sorting Test, which is the best performance this examiner has ever seen from anyone being given this test for the first time. The patient's performance on the Category, Object Assembly, and Block Design subtests of the WAIS were all performed well. Thus, Dr. Reeves' statement, "It is unlikely that she would be able to maintain sufficient goal direction in order to participate in an academic class or perform rudimentary work over the course of a day," is strongly contradicted by his test data.)

Dr. Reeves indicated that the patient was "unable to engage in serial addition by threes or alternating threes and fives." (Author's note: Careful review of Dr. Reeves' raw scores indicated that while the patient had some initial difficulty performing serial three and five addition, which most likely reflects some initial misunderstanding of test instructions, she was able to perform this task without error following this.) Dr. Reeves also stated that the patient's performance on serial subtraction by sevens was significantly impaired. (Author's note: However, the patient's performance on this task, while initially confused on the first trial, had responses on the second trial of "93, 86, 79, 72, 65, 58, 51, 44 and 40." Thus, she made only one error (40), which suggests that her initial difficulties encountered on the first trial were most likely due to the effects of anxiety.)

Dr. Reeves also indicated that the patient's arithmetic skills on the Wide Range Achievement Test "left something to be desired" in that her score placed her more than one standard deviation below her current intelligence scores. (Author's note: Dr. Reeves' statement is misleading, since it suggests that there should be a high correlation between an IQ score and arithmetic skills and ignores the fact that this patient had a pre-existing history of arithmetic difficulties throughout school. Thus, based on this information, this patient's performance on this test appears consistent with her background and pre-existing skills in this area.) Dr. Reeves also indicated that the patient's reading scores placed her only in the 75th percentile with her ability to comprehend what she had read. He pointed out that the patient exhibited disorganization in reading and a need to go back and re-read items. (Author's note: He attributed this to the patient's complaints about disorganization and impaired reading comprehension, rather than attributing this to emotional factors, since complaints of concentration are more likely to be made by patients with emotional rather than neurologic difficulties.)

Dr. Reeves, in discussing the patient's emotional functioning, indicated that, based on his interaction with the patient, it is clear that "she is having difficulties in emotional adjustment." Dr. Reeves also stated, "She appears to have little insight of how her behavior affects other people and some of the rudiments of social perception which she clearly exhibited in the past." (Author's note: While Dr. Reeves acknowledged that this patient has had difficulties in her social perception, he failed to recognize that this patient's performance on the Picture Arrangement subtest (which he attributed to brain damage), most likely reflected this problem. For example, Dr. Reeves stated, "Whenever it was suggested that she might perform a task or behave in a slightly different manner in order to be more cooperative in some aspect of the task demands, Ms. Stark was both startled and hurt. She tends to be overly sensitive and expects social sanctions. She is cognizant of her premorbid tendency to be harsh in judging herself and presently expects others to judge her in the same way." Thus, Dr. Reeves further elaborates on this patient's emotional difficulties, as well as drawing attention to her long-standing tendencies to misperceive social cues based on her troubled childhood and dysfunctional family.)

Dr. Reeves reviewed the results of the patient's MMPI Profile, which showed evidence of a moderately severe distress disorder consisting of depression, nervousness, tension, and feelings of helplessness. Her profile on this test showed evidence of long-standing emotional problems which most likely began in this patient's childhood, as well as marked tendencies to behave in a self-defeating manner. (Author's note: It should also be noted that her profile on this test is atypical for patients who have sustained traumatic brain injuries and it is clearly the profile of an individual with long-standing emotional problems who is likely to deny the above emotional problems and convert them into numerous physical and cognitive complaints, for which no organic basis can usually be found. Thus, there is strong evidence, based on this patient's MMPI profile, that her complaints and symptoms are most likely functional in their etiology and utilized to meet her long-standing dependency needs, thus reinforcing her self-defeating behavior and attitudes.)

Dr. Reeves concluded that while this patient's brain impairment falls within the mild end of the spectrum, she had become "severely debilitated by her cognitive abnormalities." (Author's note: Dr. Reeves' statement is strongly contradicted by his own test data, which showed that this patient's cognitive functioning was intact and that her complaints most likely reflected long-standing emotional problems and current emotional stressors, such as living with her mother. In fact, Dr. Reeves even stated that "she is far more depressed than test results indicate.")

Dr. Reeves stated that the patient's deficits are "consistent with the classical syndrome of closed head injury. These findings tend to be primarily referable to disruption of some frontal lobe functions. Additionally, Ms. Stark exhibits symptomatology referable to her right hemisphere." (Author's note: Dr. Reeves' statements are strongly contradicted by the literature on closed head injuries which suggest that there is no such thing as a "classical syndrome of closed head injury." His statement of frontal lobe dysfunction is strongly contradicted by the patient's excellent, if not outstanding, performance on two of the most sensitive neuropsychological tests ever developed to assess the integrity of the frontal lobes (The Wisconsin Card Sorting Test and the Halstead

Category Test). Dr. Reeves further stated that the patient exhibited symptomatology referable to her right hemisphere; yet, as previously pointed out, there was no indication of any evidence of right hemisphere impairment when the patient's performance on these tests were carefully analyzed.)

Dr. Reeves concluded that the pattern of deficits was "consistent and could not be feigned." (Author's note: The author strongly disagrees with Dr. Reeves, since there is overwhelming evidence to the contrary. While Dr. Reeves stated, on one hand, that the patient is far more depressed than the tests themselves indicate (moderately severe depression), her depression or emotional problems, in Dr. Reeves' mind, could not account for the degree of disorganization and fragmentation in her performance, for which there is virtually no support based on careful examination of this patient's test data.) Dr. Reeves further concluded that this patient should apply for disability insurance since she is "incapable of gainful employment at this point in time." (Author's note: It is hard to imagine that this patient could be conceived as incapable of gainful employment on the basis of her neuropsychological test data. It should be noted that patients with similar MMPI profiles are quite adept at getting mental health professionals to rescue them and further reinforce their long-standing dependency needs, as well as their tendencies to become chronic medical invalids and behave in highly self-defeating ways. Dr. Reeves' recommendations for cognitive rehabilitation are not supported by his test data, since this patient showed intact cognitive abilities, but on the other hand, displayed evidence of moderately severe emotional problems for which Dr. Reeves made no recommendation for psychotherapy or counseling.)

Dr. Reeves' clinical notes, dated 8/14/84, indicated that the patient demanded that she review the neuropsychological report that was scheduled to be sent to her attorney and insisted on the right to change it if she disagreed with it. In a handwritten letter addressed to Dr. Reeves dated 8/17/84, Ms. Stark expressed her disappointment and distress with Dr. Reeves, as well as her anger at her perception that Dr. Reeves was trying to kid her out of her problems by adopting the attitude of "you can do it." Ms. Stark admits in her letter that she had lost touch with reality while she was in treatment with Dr. Reeves, which apparently prompted Dr. Reeves to issue a letter dated 8/30/84 addressed to Ms. Stark. He apologized for the misunderstanding and difficulties encountered on 8/17/84 regarding Ms. Stark's demands to review her report and make changes on information that she did not agree with. Dr. Reeves suggested that in light of this disagreement, Ms. Stark should seek the services of another neuropsychologist since, "It was apparent to me (Dr. Reeves) that you are highly distrustful of my behavior and my ethics." Dr. Reeves also pointed out that he was not trying to throw her (Ms. Stark) out, but stressed the importance of her working with a clinician in whom she would have greater trust and confidence. Dr. Reeves also mentioned in his letter the necessity to return a present which had been sent to him by Ms. Stark, since it was not his policy to accept gifts of any sort.

A review of Dr. Reeves' clinical notes regarding his treatment sessions with Ms. Stark reveals a number of emotional problems stemming from her family and childhood. He also listed the patient's financial difficulties as being very stressful. In a letter dated 6/15/84, written by Ms. Stark entitled, "Major Problem Areas," she indicated that with respect to her physical health, her doctor had just diagnosed her as having cancer. (Author's note: If this is true, it would certainly constitute a major stressor for this patient, which is unrelated to her motor vehicle accident.)

In a letter dated 6/19/84 to her attorney, Ms. Stark severely criticized her attorney when he questioned her complaints and etiology of her symptoms. Much of the anger at her attorney, expressed in her letter, seems to involve control issues which were also demonstrated in her conflicts with Dr. Reeves. In a note written by Dr. Reeves, dated 7/20/84, he indicated that the patient's organizational skills have been lost secondary to her head injury and emotional problems. In a note dated 7/28/84, Dr. Reeves wrote that the patient keeps changing her mind about her issues and does not follow through on assignments they had agreed upon. He also noted that the patient frequently says that the issue is different than what they had previously agreed upon.

A report of Drs. Matson and White, dated 1/15/86, indicated that the patient was referred for cognitive rehabilitation by her attorney. The patient was initially seen on 3/25/85. At that time, her major complaints were that of being unable to work, keep up with conversations, or to exercise. At that time, it was felt that these problems reflected an underlying attentional problem. It was agreed then that Ms. Stark would attend 10 one-hour sessions with Dr. White starting on 4/15/85. The first four sessions were used for baselining purposes to gain a measure of her attentional functioning and could subsequently be used to evaluate her treatment progress. On the fifth session, she was given feedback about her baseline performance, and treatment was begun. She was very concerned with the way her attentional problems were affecting her everyday life. The session focused on finding strategies that she could apply to such situations. While Ms. Stark gave every indication of understanding what was happening and being motivated to continue during the first five sessions, she seemed to have difficulty staying on track during interview conversations and seemed vague and inappropriate in her responses to questions. She did respond to restructuring and was able to stay on target sufficiently for therapeutic purposes. She canceled what would have been her sixth session and subsequently wrote a letter of criticism which bore no relationship to what actually occurred during the first five treatment sessions. The patient was then contacted and an interview with Drs. Matson and White was arranged to sort out this "extreme misunderstanding." This interview occurred on 5/25/85. Drs. Matson and White felt that the psychiatric difficulties exhibited by this patient neccesitated psychiatric treatment from a psychiatrist who specialized in biochemical approaches to psychiatric treatment. Ms. Stark, however, was resistant to this idea, since it suggested to her that she had serious emotional problems. Drs. Matson and White also felt that the patient's psychiatric problems did not appear to be entirely attributable to her closed head injury and felt that she had a prior history of psychiatric difficulties following her reported exposure to insecticide spray in 1978, but that these problems did not incapacitate her for working purposes.

The records of Brooks Medical Center indicated that the patient was admitted on 3/12/86 for partial hospitalization (day hospitalization) for treatment of the patient's depressed mood and for a clinical trial of antidepressants. The patient's attitude was noted to be unresponsive to group and individual psychotherapy. The patient received a medication trial with Nortriptyline which was stopped at 20 mg q h.s. because the patient complained of dizziness and a feeling as "though a seizure was about to begin." The patient had a spontaneous feeling which she associated with seizures since before admission to the day hospital program. Because of this feeling, she was frightened about the continued use of this antidepressant or any other ones; therefore, she elected not to continue trials with antidepressant medications. The patient was much improved at the time of discharge, in that she had no suicidal thoughts and was more responsive to group and individual psychotherapy. She was diagnosed as having an adjustment disorder with depressed affect; rule out affective disorder secondary to head injury.

In her admission records, she indicated that she had been involved in a car accident in March 1983. She indicated that after the accident she began feeling "electric-like shocks" down her left side. She said that this pain involved her arm and leg on the left and then began noticing some arm and leg weakness and began limping and stumbling. She also noted that her right hand was weak and that she couldn't grasp as well as before her accident. She indicated that over the past several years her symptoms had gradually improved. Her friends had told her that "sometimes she is spaced out." She thought this was because she was having mild seizures. Her mood had been down and her appetite decreased and then increased. She had lost interest in some of the things she liked to do in the past, although she was sleeping "O.K." The patient was a vegetarian and ate few dairy products, although she occasionally ate eggs. She was not involved in any love relationship at that time and had not been sexually active for a number of years.

During her history and physical examination, she was noted to be preoccupied with the fear that she had a seizure disorder. The patient also expressed concern over periods of "mood lability and belligerence." She noted that these periods were very much "out of context" in terms of her baseline personality. She also realized that she was under a great deal of stress. Her affect was noted to be limited to the depressive realm. A review of her day hospital notes dated 4/19/86 revealed that the patient attributed "all of her current difficulties to a motor vehicle accident three years ago which resulted in a closed head injury." Before that she described herself as "a high-functioning, high-energy person working full-time." Later that day, she appeared extremely fearful of expressing her own feelings. It was noted that "she does appear to have a great deal of anger and hurt underlying her superficially bright presentation."

On 4/31/86, it was noted that the patient was able to identify feelings of anger, sadness, and hurt in regard to the people she worked for and her mother. She described how it was unacceptable to have feelings of pain and that as a child she was sent to her room until she could "put on a happy face." On 5/5/86, the patient admitted that she shuts off her feelings when she becomes scared and was critical of this. She also admitted that she had always been in a "caretaker role" throughout much of her life and may not nurture herself as well as she nurtures others. This suggests that her self-esteem is too poor for her to accept her own dependency needs; thus, her current complaints provide her with the necessary rationale she needs to have her long-standing dependency needs met.

The patient was administered the MMPI while she was a patient at Brooks Medical Center. Her MMPI profile was interpreted by Dr. Smith, the clinical psychologist, as showing evidence of a considerable degree of repressed anger and resentment, the awareness of which was highly threatening to her. Her profile also suggested that she was likely to convert many of the emotional problems she experienced as a result of not getting her own (dependency) needs met into somatic complaints. Her profile indicated that she was likely to project her anger onto others in such a way which allows them to feel justified in displaying some hostility. Her profile also indicated that interpersonal relationships in such individuals are typically disturbed. Patients with similar profiles typically do not benefit from insight-oriented psychotherapy, since they tend to utilize repression and denial as a way of coping with their problems. Dr. Smith concluded that it was unlikely that her continuing pursuit to identify the underlying physical cause for her somatic complaints was likely to yield her a solution that will also remedy her characterological issues. Thus, her MMPI profile report suggested a past history of seeking out external causes for her various complaints, rather than addressing her own repressed and denied emotional problems and angry feelings.

Neuropsychological Testing

Because of the limited time available for testing, the patient was given an abbreviated neuropsychological test battery consisting of the following:

The Sbordone Attention Battery
The Trail Making Test (Parts A & B)
The Symbol Digit Modalities Test
The Stroop Test
The Logical Memories Test (Part B)

The Grip Strength Test
The Finger Tapping Test
The Grooved Pegboard Test
Luria's Motor Examination
Test of Executive Functions
The Millon Clinical Multiaxial Inventory

Test Results

ATTENTION-CONCENTRATION

She was administered The Sbordone Attention Battery to assess her ability to perform a variety of serial arithmetic and non-arithmetic tasks. She exhibited no evidence of significant impairments on tasks involving counting backwards, serial three addition, alternating serial three and five addition, serial seven subtraction, serial 13 subtraction, alternating three and five subtraction, or indicating which letters in the alphabet contain only straight lines. She was administered the Trail Making Test to assess her ability in her visual-motor tracking skills. She took 28.8 seconds to complete Part A, which required her to connect circles containing numbers ranging from 1 through 25. Her performance on this test placed her within the normal range and revealed no evidence of qualitative errors. She needed 58.66 seconds to complete Part B, which required her to connect circles containing either numbers or letters in alternating sequence. Her performance on this test placed her within the normal range. She started making one error but quickly caught herself and was able to correct the error without any cues or prompting from the examiner. She was administered The Symbol Digit Modalities Test to assess her speed of cognitive processing. She obtained a written score of 42, which placed her 1.12 standard deviations below expectancy. Her performance on this test revealed evidence of slight impairment. Finally, she was administered The Stroop Test to assess her ability to rapidly name words, identify colors, and inhibit competing stimuli. Her performance on this test was confounded by the fact that she used her finger to point at stimuli while performing this task, which typically requires more time than visually inspecting the stimuli. This most likely contributed to her relatively impaired performance on the first two parts of this test. However, her ability to inhibit competing or distracting stimuli tested within the normal range. (Author's note: Testing revealed that while this patient's speed of cognitive processing appeared somewhat impaired, she exhibited no signs of impairment on tasks that place considerable emphasis on concentration, such as mental arithmetic, mental sequencing, visual-motor tracking, and inhibiting competing stimuli. Thus, her speed of cognitive performance most likely reflected emotional factors such as depression.)

MEMORY

She was administered The Logical Memories Test (Form II) to assess her immediate verbal memory, as well as her ability to retain this information after delays in excess of 30 minutes. Testing revealed that her immediate memory for two orally presented stories was intact and consistent for persons her age. Her ability to recall these stories after delays of over 30 minutes was excellent, in that she demonstrated a 91.3% retention of the previously recalled information.

MOTOR

She was administered The Grip Strength Test, which demonstrated that the strength of her nondominant left hand was slightly weaker than expected, based upon the strength of her dominant right hand. Her performance on The Finger Tapping Test was highly inconsistent and suggestive of functional impairment, since her scores varied considerably across trials. Her manual dexterity and fine motor coordination skills were assessed by The Grooved Pegboard Test. Testing revealed that the performance of her nondominant left hand was mildly impaired in comparison to her dominant right hand. She was then administered Luria's Motor Examination to assess her ability to perform a variety of complex movements with one or both hands. She exhibited virtually no difficulty performing any of these tasks and did them correctly on the first trial with virtually no practice or time to rehearse them. (Author's note: It should be noted that this is extraordinarily unusual in patients who have allegedly sustained traumatic brain injuries. Additionally, there was no evidence of any pathognomonic findings in that the patient always knew whenever she had made an error and was able to correctly rectify the error without any cues or prompting from the examiner.)

HIGHER COGNITIVE FUNCTIONS

Her responses to the Verbal Similarities and Interpretation of Proverbs Tests revealed intact conceptual and abstract thinking. Her responses to hypothetical situations to evaluate her judgement were generally intact. Her problem solving skills for both tasks involving logical grammatical analysis and arithmetic problem solving were found to be intact.

PERSONALITY-EMOTIONAL

She was administered The Millon Clinical Multiaxial Inventory to assess her current emotional problems and long-standing personality traits. Her profile on this test revealed a distinct tendency toward avoiding self-disclosure, which may signify a characterological evasiveness or an unwillingness to divulge matters of a personal nature, problematic or not. Her profile also suggested the possibility of broad deficits, introspectiveness and psychological mindedness, owing to either emotional impoverishment or thought vagueness. Her profile on this test also indicated that she was submissively dependent, self-effacing, and noncompetitive. She was likely to lean on others for guidance and security and assume a passive role in relationships with others. She was seen as having a striking lack of initiative and a general avoidance of autonomy. She was also exceedingly dependent and vulnerable if separated from those who provide support. She also resented those upon whom she must depend, since in the past they have often been critical and disapproving of her. Although infrequent minor displays of anger are likely to be directed towards those who fail to appreciate her intense need for attention and nurturance, her need for security is threatened when angry impulses are felt or expressed by her. Fearful of being criticized, she may withdraw from social relationships in an effort to moderate her anxiety and her sensitivity to rejection. As a consequence, depressive feelings of loneliness and isolation have most likely been increasingly experienced, although she was not inclined to publicly divulge her mood.

While this patient tried to appear calm and pleasant on the surface, she was likely to have an underlying tension and emotional dysphoria comprised of disturbing mixtures of anxiety, sadness, and guilt. She was likely to feel insecure and have fears of abandonment. Except for infrequent displays of irritability, she was likely to be conciliatory, placating, and even ingratiating. By acting weak, expressing her complaints and self-doubts, as well as communicating her needs for assurance and displaying a willingness to submit and comply, she was likely to evoke nurturance and protection from others. By submitting to the wishes and needs of others, she helped to avoid the abandonment she dreads. Her frequent complaints of weakness, fatiguability, and physical ailments most likely represent the somatic expression of her underlying depressed mood. Presently, her life may be experienced as empty with a persistent feeling of wariness or apathy. By withdrawing and restricting her social contacts and emotional involvements, however, she may limit the possibilities of new sources of needed support in a self-defeating manner.

Treatment efforts for this particular patient are best directed toward countering her strong dependency behaviors. A primary therapeutic task would most likely prevent her from becoming totally ineffectual as she relies increasingly on the support of a benign environment. She not only observes deficits in her competence but also depreciates the virtues and talents she possesses. Trapped by her own persuasiveness, she further reinforces her belief in the futility of standing on her own and, therefore, is less likely to overcome her inadequacies. Thus, she has created a vicious circle of increased helplessness and dependency, making herself inaccessible to growth opportunities. This effectively makes her increasingly dependent upon others.

She strongly desires a dependent therapeutic relationship and is likely to resist efforts to assume a measure of autonomy. Persuading her to forego her long-standing habits of dependency and the use of her symptoms to obtain secondary gains is likely to be difficult. Efforts should be expended to build an image of confidence and self-esteem but must be preceded slowly through a program concentrated on strengthening her attributes and dislodging her habit of leaning on others. Environmental changes may be introduced to maximize growth and to minimize continued dependency. Psychopharmacologic treatment, most likely antidepressants and anti-anxiety agents, may prove useful in increasing her alertness and vigor, since she is so often plagued by complaints of fatigue, lethargy, and diffuse anxieties. Nondirective and humanistic therapeutic approaches are more likely to foster the growth of autonomy and self-confidence than directive or cognitive reorientation methods. Group therapy may also be utilized as a viable means for her to learn autonomous skills as a means of increasing her social skills and confidence.

Impression

The patient is a 38-year-old, divorced Caucasian female whose automobile was sideswiped by a truck on 3/6/83. The patient was wearing a seat belt and shoulder harness at the time of the accident. She recalled striking the left side of her head on the metal doorpost adjacent to her head. She recalled that her car spun around and hit a guard rail, bouncing back into the traffic lane. She then remembered that she got out of her car and was extremely nervous and in "a state of shock." Her recollection of the events that occurred immediately prior to, during, and following her accident is excellent. She was then driven home by a highway patrol officer. After she arrived home, she began experiencing a variety of odd musculoskeletal sensations, including a strange sensation of numbness over her left temple. She became frightened and phoned a female friend, who drove her to the emergency room at the Union Medical Center. When she was seen at the medical center, she was able to provide a detailed description of the accident and stated that at the time of the accident she did not feel that she lost consciousness, but later thought that she might have lost consciousness. At that time she complained of left-sided headaches, numbness in her left temporal area, neck strain, and confusion. Her neurological examination was normal except for diminished strength in her left trapezius. She was diagnosed as having no apparent intracranial (brain injury) problems.

The patient returned to the emergency room 10 days later complaining of increased neck pain and aching pain down both arms. She indicated that two days earlier she had developed paresthesias and numbness of both hands, occipital and nuchal headaches, as well as diarrhea. She returned two days later complaining of neck pain and numbness in her left hand, although her physical examination was negative. She was reported to have inconsistent hypesthesia in her left parietal area; which was felt to be under her conscious control since it was not observed when she was distracted. She was informed that she should recover in two weeks and was encouraged to take Dolobid, Aspirin, and wear a cervical collar when necessary.

She began seeing Dr. Mottle, a neurologist, who over the next several months, reported that the patient's symptoms were slowly improving. In a letter dated 7/15/83, Dr. Mottle indicated that he expected the patient's problems to "resolve completely." When the patient was seen again by Dr. Mottle on 10/31/83, Dr. Mottle noted that the patient's description of her motor vehicle accident was contradictory. The patient, at that time complained of increasing weakness and numbness in both hands, as well as of dropping things which she stated "comes and goes." She also complained of a number of other bizarre symptoms, such as a "burning sensation in her hands." She also began complaining of a number of cognitive difficulties. Although Dr. Mottle reported some weakness in her left side, the remainder of her neurological examination was normal.

Psychological testing by Dr. Swift, an unlicensed psychologist, on 11/27/83, reported evidence of cognitive difficulties, as well as an adjustment reaction characterized by depression, anxiety, diminished self-esteem, and social withdrawal. The patient began seeing Dr. Swift for psychotherapy but, at some point, became dissatisfied with Dr. Swift's treatment, which shifted to a more psychological than cognitively oriented approach. She then began seeing Dr. Reeves, a clinical psychologist, for psychotherapy. Dr. Reeves' clinical notes mention this patient's emotional problems and difficulties with her mother, with whom she had been forced to live with since her injury.

Dr. Reeves performed neuropsychological testing which was completed on 6/15/84. Testing indicated that Ms. Stark complained of difficulties in language processing, impaired concentration, organizational difficulties, memory impairment, mental confusion, fatiguability, reduced frustration tolerance, diminished self-esteem, difficulty in interpersonal relationships, and physical symptoms that included pressure sensations, as well as long-standing, unresolved psychological conflicts relating to her mother. Overall, Dr. Reeves reported evidence of generally mild neuropsychological impairments that were contraindicated by a careful review of Dr. Reeves' raw test data. This data, instead, demonstrated that this patient exhibited inconsistent and often contradictory test results that appeared to be secondary to emotional rather than to neurological factors. Personality testing revealed evidence of a somatization disorder, as well as a depressed, anxious, and highly dependent female who appeared adept at getting others to rescue and take care of her. Dr. Reeves' conclusions were strongly contradicted by this patient's medical records which revealed no evidence that this patient had sustained a brain injury in her motor vehicle accident. While Dr. Reeves indicated that he did not attribute his findings to psychological or motivational factors, he refused to continue treating her after the patient had demanded the right to critically review Dr. Reeves' neuropsychological test report before it was sent to her attorney and make any changes she deemed necessary. While this examiner respects Dr. Reeves' professional ethics, this patient's demands appear to contradict Dr. Reeves' previous assertion that the patient's test performance did not appear to reflect psychological or motivational factors.

The patient was seen by Drs. Matson and White, who had accepted this patient in their outpatient cognitive rehabilitation program to improve her attentional difficulties (complaints). It seems clear that they relied heavily on the neuropsychological test report of Dr. Reeves, without critically examining his raw data. They reported in a discharge summary dated 1/5/86 that the patient exhibited emotional difficulties of sufficient magnitude to require psychiatric treatment which she resisted at that time. They concluded that her cognitive difficulties and confusion did not appear to be entirely related to her closed head injury. Drs. Matson and White suggested that there had been some indication in the past of psychiatric difficulties and mental confusion stemming from a reported exposure to insecticide spray in 1978 which did not incapacitate her at that time for working purposes. They stressed that it was essential that her psychiatric problems be treated by a psychiatrist.

On 3/12/86, the patient was admitted to Brooks Medical Center, where she was noted to be depressed and preoccupied with the fear that she had a seizure disorder. The patient also expressed concern over periods of mood lability and belligerence. At that time, it was unclear whether the patient had an organic mood disorder, based on her history of an alleged closed head injury, or an adjustment disorder with depressive features of a prolonged nature. Psychological testing during her hospitalization revealed that this patient had considerable repressed anger and resentment, the awareness of which was highly threatening to her. As a result of placing considerable energy into decreasing awareness of her underlying anger and resentment, the patient was seen as converting her feelings of anger and resentment into somatic complaints. She was also seen as projecting her anger onto others in a way that allowed her to feel justified in displaying some hostility. As a consequence of these problems, the patient would typically experience disturbed interpersonal relationships and would likely be seen as odd and peculiar and to have impaired social perceptions. Testing further indicated that this patient was on a continual pursuit to identify the underlying physical cause for her somatic complaints while using repression and denial as defense mechanisms to prevent her from recognizing her long-standing feelings of resentment and anger.

The patient underwent a neuropsychological evaluation on 2/15/89. She was interviewed for four and one-half hours, during which time she discussed an extremely painful and unhappy childhood in which her parents were described as very domineering, controlling, rigid, and cold. The patient was denied any opportunity to have fun and was given frequent corporal punishment for slight infractions of her parents' numerous rules and regulations. The patient was never allowed to express her anger or feelings or any negative emotions in the presence of her family. Whenever she did this (according to the records of Brooks Medical Center), she was immediately sent to her room and not permitted to come out until she had a smile on her face. Because she was the oldest of four children, she was assigned a caretaker's role to these children. This was a role she clearly did not enjoy, but because she was not allowed to complain in any way or display any negative emotions, she had to suppress her feelings of anger and resentment at her mother and at that of being in a caretaker's role. The patient left home shortly after graduating from high school and attended several colleges to keep as much distance as she could from her parents, who tried spying on her and controlling her by influencing others. Her parents also refused to help her out financially, which forced her to work half or full-time while attending school. The patient eventually graduated from college in 1973 and was married shortly thereafter. Her marriage proved to be an unhappy one since she constantly fought with her husband over control and domination issues. The patient began working as an physical therapist but, according the records of Brooks Medical Center, apparently did not enjoy this type of work since it reminded her of the caretaker role she experienced as a child.

The patient began experiencing a variety of odd muscular sensations, OB-GYN problems, food allergies, neck pain, physical weakness, mental confusion, memory difficulties, syncopal episodes, visual difficulties, auditory difficulties, irritability, gastrointestinal difficulties, migraine headaches, and a variety of neurological-like symptoms that persisted for four years after she claimed she and her companions were sprayed with insecticide by an airplane in 1978. In fact, this patient was seen for these problems only one month prior to her motor vehicle accident of 1983. Prior to her accident, she had also undergone extensive neurological testing for these problems which failed to reveal any clear organic basis for them.

The patient's description of her automobile accident is highly inconsistent with brain injury. For example, she exhibited an excellent memory for the events immediately preceding, during, and following the accident, which indicated that she did not lose consciousness or sustain any post-traumatic amnesia. There was no evidence that she exhibited any type of bewilderment or mental confusion of the type which is typically seen following traumatic brain injuries when she was seen in the emergency room later that day. Her description of her symptom development strongly suggested conversion of her feelings of anxiety and nervousness following her accident into a variety of odd, if not bizarre, somatic complaints. While this patient has been suspected of having a seizure disorder resulting from this accident, review of her medical records indicated that she reported similar episodes prior to her motor vehicle accident which were most likely dissociative episodes secondary to her pre-existing emotional difficulties and use of repression and denial. This is supported by the fact that this patient had never been observed to a seizure and EEG studies failed to detect evidence of epileptiform discharge activity. While the patient reported improved mental confusion after taking Tegretol, a review of the notes of Dr. Mottle, her treating neurologist, indicate that Dr. Mottle suspected that the improvement of the patient reported while taking Tegretol was most likely due to the antidepressant effects of this medication.

This examiner strongly feels that this patient, in all medical probability, never sustained any type of brain injury in her accident of 3/6/83. Her complaints are histrionic and present as a somatoform disorder. They appear to have been utilized as a means of fostering her dependency needs and provide her with an effective means to control her environment and secondary gains. Such efforts are, unfortunately, highly self-defeating and rob her from living a satisfying and rewarding life. Her current problems appear to be a functional manifestation of pre-existing emotional conflicts with her parents and her difficulty in handling and accepting her pent-up feelings of rage toward her mother and authority figures, who have tried to dominate and control her in the past.

Diagnosis

Axis I:	1. Somatization disorder
	2. Dysthymic disorder, chronic
Axis II:	Mixed personality disorder with dependent, histrionic, and schizoid features
Axis III:	Deferred
Axis IV:	Severity of psychosocial stressors: Severe
Axis V:	Highest level of adaptive functioning during past year: GAF = 70

Comment

This report demonstrates that when a careful history of the accident was taken from the plaintiff, she was able to provide a very detailed, rich description of the events that occurred immediately prior to, during, and following the accident, which is highly inconsistent with patients who sustain traumatic brain damage. This plaintiff's family background, combined with her mixed personality disorder, predicts that she is likely to use her complaints to control her environment, meet her dependency needs, and seek out secondary gains.

A review of her prior medical records indicated that she was predisposed to convert her repressed emotional problems into a variety of pseudoneurological and somatic complaints. Her disturbed interactions with her treating doctors corroborate her pre-existing history of emotional problems. Her own treating neurologist (Dr. Mottle) did not regard the plaintiff's problems as serious and questioned the plaintiff's description of her accident and some of her complaints. The plaintiff's psychological expert's (Dr. Reeves) interpretations of his test data appear to have been heavily influenced by the plaintiff's complaints and manipulative behavior. When these inconsistencies were pointed out in the above report, the credibility of Dr. Reeves' opinions lost considerable ground. The report also suggested that the patient had a history of "doctor shopping" before her motor vehicle accident, which persisted after this accident. The report of Drs. Matson and White subtly concluded that the plaintiff's complaints were of a psychiatric nature and recommended psychiatric treatment. The plaintiff's psychiatric records discussed her troubled childhood and life and her tendency to repress her feelings of rage and anger. The above report highlighted the numerous discrepancies between the plaintiff's complaints, medical records, psychiatric records, and observed behavior. It also pointed out that many of her present complaints were similar to her pre-existing complaints in that in both instances no organic basis was found for either.

Chapter 14

How to Select a Neuropsychological Expert

While many psychologists offer neuropsychological testing, very few of these individuals are qualified neuropsychologists. For example, at the time of this writing, approximately 150 neuropsychologists have been granted a Diplomate (the highest certification possible) by the American Board of Clinical Neuropsychology. This diplomate status is granted upon successfully completing a rigorous examination process by acknowledged experts in the field of neuropsychology. This should not be construed that individuals who do not possess such certification are incompetent. Regardless of whether an attorney decides to utilize a neuropsychologist who has or has not achieved diplomate status, the attorney should be aware that a jury may give more weight to the opinion of a board-certified neuropsychologist than a neuropsychologist who is not board-certified.

Where might an attorney locate such neuropsychologists? The attorney can either write to the American Board of Professional Psychology, 2100 E. Broadway, Suite 313, Columbia, Missouri 65201-6082, or telephone (314) 875-1267 and ask for the names of Diplomates of the American Board of Clinical Neuropsychology. This organization also publishes a directory listing the names of each diplomate and their area of specialty. Appendix A presents a directory of the names of neuropsychologists who have been granted diplomate status in the field of neuropsychology from the American Board of Clinical Neuropsychology.

The attorney may also consult the latest issue of *The Clinical Neuropsychologist*, published each month by Swets Publishing Service, located at Heereweg No. 347, 2161 CA LISE, The Netherlands. This journal publishes a cumulative list of all of the psychologists who have been awarded a Diplomate from the American Board of Clinical Neuropsychology. This list is presented in the last issue of each volume. A review of the psychologist's curriculum vitae or business card should indicate whether the psychologist is a Diplomate of the American Board of Clinical Neuropsychology.

The neuropsychologist should have extensive background, experience, and expertise in the particular area in which damages are claimed by the plaintiff's attorney. Unfortunately, the author has seen numerous cases where the attorney representing the plaintiff or defendant utilized the services of a psychologist who had little expertise in either neuropsychology or brain damage. Thus, the expert lacked sufficient expertise to document or refute brain damage in his or her report. When some of these attorneys were later questioned by the author, they admitted they did not know the difference between a psychologist and a neuropsychologist and naively assumed that it was all a matter of simply giving a patient a particular test battery and looking at the test results. Unfortunately, their expert's lack of expertise hurt their case, and several times resulted in a victory for the other side.

A review of a prospective neuropsychological expert's curriculum vitae will typically indicate where their experience and competence lies. For example, if the psychologist's expertise is in the area of biofeedback and behavioral medicine (based on the psychologist's publications and presentations as contained within the curriculum vitae), then the attorney should have doubts about whether this particular psychologist possesses the necessary expertise to serve as an expert in his or her brain injury case. The attorney should also determine where the psychologist received his or her training and supervision in the field of neuropsychology. In most cases, however, the psychologist's training will have consisted of one or two workshops dealing with the administration, scoring, and interpretation of a particular neuropsychological test battery (e.g., Halstead-Reitan or Luria-Nebraska Psychological Battery). As mentioned in earlier chapters, many psychologists never receive supervision on a regular basis from a qualified neuropsychologist after completing these workshops. The attorney should also attempt to determine whether the psychologist has ever taken any courses in neuroanatomy, behavioral neurology, neurophysiology, or any courses dealing with brain-behavior relationships taught at either a medical school or within a graduate psychology program.

The attorney should inquire as to whether or not the prospective expert spends any time interviewing the patient and/or significant others prior to the administration of neuropsychological tests. Psychologists who de-emphasize the importance of this, or who indicate that they spend little time since this is "not important," should be carefully questioned about the extent of their medicolegal or litigation experience, since the failure to obtain such information generally indicates that the psychologist has had little experience in the medicolegal area and is likely to base his or her conclusions entirely on the neuropsychological test data. Opposing counsel will typically have little or no difficulty impeaching these psychologists when they ask, "Would it change your opinion, Doctor, if you knew that this patient had sustained a previous brain injury two years ago?" Or, "Would it change your opinion, Doctor, if you learned that this patient had broken his left hand three months prior to your examination and had a 30-year history of heavy alcohol abuse?" Thus, as discussed earlier in this book, the importance of a careful background history allows the neuropsychologist to carefully weigh the possible contaminating effects of confounding variables in his or her assessment of the patient's damages.

Attorneys should beware if the prospective expert suggests that he or she need not review the patient's medical, psychiatric, educational, or vocational records prior to preparing his or her report. Once again, this may reflect the theoretical biases of the psychologist, but is likely to create serious difficulties when the psychologist is later asked by opposing counsel why he or she failed to do this. Jurors are likely to get the impression that the psychologist was being less than objective in reaching his or her conclusions regarding brain damage and its probable causation.

The attorney should inquire as to the types of cases generally seen by the psychologist or neuropsychologist within their practice. Psychologists whose practices consist of treating patients with sexual disorders or marital difficulties, are more than likely to be a dilettante in the area of neuropsychology or brain damage. Opposing counsel will often have a "field day" with these individuals, particularly when they point out to the jury that the patient did not have any of these problems before he began seeing the doctor for his brain injury. The jury will get the impression that the doctor's skill is making his patients fit his practice and is good at manufacturing problems when no such actual problems exist.

Attorneys should look for psychologists who hold teaching positions at universities or medical schools, since this implies that the individual is knowledgeable, scholarly, and is a teacher of other doctors. Such appointments also imply that the psychologist's expertise has been recognized by members of his or her profession, or by medical doctors. It also suggests that this individual has been active in research studies with an institution of higher learning that is far removed from the "slime" which is frequently associated with experts whose entire practice consists of courtroom testimony or examining clients referred by one particular side. Attorneys should also ask if the perspective psychologist has ever conducted any research or studies in the area involved in the case. If so, then the attorney should inquire as to what particular findings or conclusions the psychologist reached.

This author has found that very few attorneys ask prospective neuropsychological experts how many cases they have actually seen with this particular problem (e.g., hypoxic encephalopathy). The author recalls a recent case in which the plaintiff's neuropsychologist, who had seen quite a number of brain-injured patients of traumatic etiology, admitted during his deposition that he had never previously seen a patient who had sustained hypoxic encephalopathy. The plaintiff's attorney had never bothered to ask this psychologist whether he had ever seen a patient with this disorder and naively assumed that "all brain damage is alike."

The author has reviewed the depositions of so-called "experts" and discovered that even though they had been named as experts and had been scheduled to testify in court for the plaintiff or defendant, they had never seen more than five brain-damaged cases because their practice consisted primarily of assessing and treating patients with emotional problems. While it is obviously difficult to specify how many cases a prospective expert should have seen to possess expertise in a particular area, common sense dictates that the more cases seen the better. Jurors, based on this author's experience, are much more likely to give more weight to the testimony of an expert who has seen 500 cases than an expert who has seen only five.

In summary, attorneys should seek out neuropsychologists whose competence has been established by a formal examining board and who have been granted certification based on a rigorous examination of their training, background, and competence. The attorney should review the curriculum vitae of the prospective expert to determine if the prospective neuropsychological expert has the necessary training, publications, background, and expertise to qualify as an expert in the field of neuropsychology. The attorney should also determine if the prospective neuropsychologist has expertise in a specific area (e.g., post-concussive syndrome, anoxic encephalopathy, etc.), by carefully questioning his or her training, background, and experience. The time spent questioning the prospective psychologist may later prove to be invaluable in that it may eliminate prospective experts who lack the necessary qualifications to serve as an effective expert. It may also spare the attorney potential embarrassment which could possibly jeopardize the outcome of the case, or result in a malpractice case being brought against him or her if the case is lost because of failing to choose an appropriate neuropsychological expert.

Chapter 15

How to Utilize the Services of a Neuropsychologist

The neuropsychologist, because of his or her expertise in brain-behavior relationships, can be of invaluable assistance to attorneys representing the plaintiff or defendant. Because of their rich background in psychology, research design, statistics, psychometric testing, understanding behavioral, emotional, and social manifestations of brain damage, as well as the effects of such problems on the patient's spouse, family, and significant others, the neuropsychologist can play a pivotal role in either Workers' Compensation, personal injury, wrongful death, job termination, or criminal and medical malpractice cases. Listed below are some ways the neuropsychologist can assist the attorney with his or her case:

1. Interviewing Clients

The neuropsychologist has typically received extensive training in interviewing patients, taking careful histories, detecting emotional problems, and recognizing psychological defense mechanisms and resistance in dealing with painful and emotional issues. The attorney may not recognize some of the client's problems and, therefore, may not adequately state the client's damages in a manner likely to gain the sympathy and understanding of jurors.

CASE STUDY

The author was recently asked to interview a 26-year-old woman who had been involved in a car accident approximately one year ago. She sustained a closed head injury and was rendered unconscious for approximately 30 minutes. She was hospitalized one day for observation and then discharged. At the time of her injury, she had been one semester short of completing her bachelor's degree in nursing and had been employed as a registered nurse. Her attorney phoned the author and indicated that he was considering settling her case. He indicated that her medicals amounted to nearly $4,000 and that from all accounts she appeared to be doing quite well. The attorney indicated that she had recently undergone neuropsychological testing that had failed to reveal any evidence of "organic impairment" and that her family had said she was "doing fine." Her attorney thought, however, that it might be a good idea to have the author spend an hour or two with her and her family to see if "she was all right." Before interviewing his client and her family, the author asked to review her medical records and the results of previous neuropsychological testing. These records indicated that she had struck her forehead and had been rendered unconscious for approximately 30 minutes. When the paramedics arrived, she was noted to be combative, agitated, and confused. She was given a Glasgow Coma Scale score of 14. She was taken to the emergency room where a CT scan was performed that was interpreted as normal. She remained hospitalized for 24 hours to observe her neurological status, since she had been diagnosed as having a closed head injury and cerebral concussion. Her cognitive status improved, and she appeared neurologically intact at the time she was sent home. She stayed home for one week and returned to work as a nurse, working in a nursing home. She continued to work and did not seem to be having any particular problems.

Her family was interviewed. They appeared overprotective of their daughter and had had only seven years of formal education each. They lived in a rural community and were both retired. They admitted that they had seen little of their daughter since her injury, because she lived in an apartment approximately 30 miles away. Initially they stated that she had been doing fine and that she had made an excellent recovery. However, when they were asked if they had observed any changes in her behavior since her injury, they stated, "Actually, yes. We've noticed that she seems to get upset easily." This led to a series of questions which revealed that they had each recognized that their daughter's behavior and personality had changed dramatically since her accident. They observed that she had become impatient, exhibited rapid mood swings, did not appear as sharp intellectually as she had been before, was forgetful and irritable, appeared insensitive to their feelings and the needs of others, and often acted irresponsibly.

When their daughter was interviewed, she admitted that she had recently loaned a man she just met over $4,000, and had failed to take any precautions against becoming pregnant, even though her sexual appetite had increased dramatically since her accident. She admitted that she had been having sex with as many as 10 different men a week. She had gotten three speeding tickets during the past year for reckless and irresponsible driving, and had lost virtually all of her friends. She also indicated that she had recently purchased a handgun and admitted that she had given some serious thought to committing suicide or harming others. She also admitted that during the last month she had given three patients incorrect medications and that one of them became seriously ill and nearly died. Because she had been so well-liked by her supervisor prior to her injury, the supervisor had successfully covered up this incident. The author then phoned her attorney and indicated that this client had most likely sustained a significant frontal lobe injury during her accident, had been having a number of significant problems in all aspects of her life, and that she required immediate hospitalization because of the likelihood of committing suicide or harming others.

2. Reviewing Records

Neuropsychologists are frequently asked to review the plaintiff's academic, vocational, medical, and psychiatric records. In most cases, the neuropsychologist can be of considerable assistance in identifying problems that may have been missed by other professionals.

CASE STUDY

The author was asked to review the records of a 24-year-old woman who had received a glancing blow to her head while attending a softball game when a disgruntled player had thrown his bat into the stands. The bat fractured her nose but did not render her unconscious. Her memory for the events that occurred immediately prior to, during, and following this event were excellent. According to her medical records, she had been complaining of concentration and memory difficulties and had been sent to a neurologist who ordered a CT scan of her brain which revealed marked cortical atrophy, which he attributed to her injury at the softball game. The author carefully examined her academic records and discovered that her IQ and grades had fallen dramatically between Grades 5 and 6. While in Grade 5, she had been a B+ student and had achieved an IQ of 123. In Grade 6, her IQ tested at only 87 and she received mostly D's and F's. The author then phoned the attorney and informed her that the academic records indicated that she most likely had undergone some type of traumatic event between the fifth and sixth grades. It was suggested by the author that the attorney subpoena the plaintiff's medical records for that time. These records were eventually obtained and revealed that she had sustained a head injury after she had fallen from her bicycle and had been rendered unconscious for several hours and was noted to be confused and disoriented when she was seen in the emergency room. A further review of her academic records indicated that her grades and IQ scores improved over the next few years and by the time she entered high school had returned to normal. When this information was provided to the attorney's neurological expert, he indicated that the patient's cortical atrophy most likely reflected her prior head injury and did not appear to be related to her recent injury.

3. Performing Neuropsychological Assessments

The principal role of the neuropsychologist in medicolegal cases is frequently to administer, score, and interpret neuropsychological tests and prepare a written report for the referring attorney. An example of such reports can be found in Chapter 13.

4. Educating Attorneys About the Effects of Brain Damage

This author has found that the vast majority of attorneys know very little about brain damage, particularly its effects on cognitive, emotional, social, and behavioral functioning; in other words, how a particular brain injury would be expected to effect a person's behavior, ability to work, perform household duties, return to school, activities of daily living, and live a fulfilling and successful life. While a neurologist or neurosurgeon may possess greater expertise in describing the neuropathological aspects of a brain injury, such as how the brain has been damaged or injured following secondary brain insults, the neuropsychologist possesses a greater understanding of how this specific injury is likely to effect this person's life and ability to function in society. The process of neuropsychological assessment, as described earlier in this book, typically involves spending anywhere from six to 10 hours with the patient and their family, during which time the neuropsychologist takes an extensive history of the patient's injury, particularly how it has effected their cognitive, behavioral, emotional, and social functioning. The neuropsychologist may administer as many as 25 to 30 different tests designed to assess different aspects of these areas. When the neuropsychologist has completed his or her assessment, the neuropsychologist generally possesses far more information about this patient than any other health professional. Consequently, the neuropsychologist can be an excellent resource for attorneys who wish to know more about the plaintiff or their client or how the person has been effected by brain injury.

While serving in the capacity of an educator, the psychologist may advise an attorney how to present his client's cognitive, social, emotional, and behavioral impairments to a jury so that they can fully appreciate his or her client's damages. It has been this author's experience that in the majority of brain-injured cases, the plaintiff appears "normal" and has no salient physical or behavioral stigmata that a juror or layperson would immediately recognize. This author has found that the common practice of putting the client on the stand or keeping the client in the courtroom during trial often creates serious problems in terms of the credibility of expert witnesses. For example, if a physically attractive and robust-looking young woman or man is put on the stand before the neuropsychologist can adequately describe to the jury how this person's brain injury has effected his behavior but has not effected the way he appears to others, jurors are likely to see "nothing wrong" with the plaintiff and become suspect of any expert who takes the stand later and describes this patient as having a number of significant problems as a result of their brain injury. It has been this author's experience that when this occurs, the outcome of the case is likely to favor the defendant rather than the plaintiff.

Chapter 16

How to Depose a Neuropsychologist

Many attorneys who are faced with the task of deposing a psychologist or neuropsychologist are often ill-equipped to perform this task in a manner which exposes the flaws or weaknesses of the neuropsychological expert's opinions. Some guidelines are presented below, as well as examples of psycholgist's depositions that this author has reviewed. The names of the attorneys and psychologists have been changed to protect their identity. Any resemblance to actual persons is purely coincidental.

Determine the Psychologist's Background, Experience, and Training

A significant number of psychologists have less than adequate training, experience, and background to qualify as experts in neuropsychology or brain damage. For example, Sbordone and Rudd (1986) found that approximately one-third of licensed psychologists were unable to recognize the existence of a neurological disorder when they were presented with clinical vignettes describing a particular patient and their presenting complaints and problems. This finding most likely reflects a lack of training in this area during their graduate education. For example, the graduate training of clinical psychologists typically fails to include courses in neurology, neuroanatomy, neuropathology, or neurophysiology. While psychologists usually take courses in physiological psychology at the graduate level, such courses focus primarily on animal research and generally spend little time discussing human neurological disorders. While courses in neuropsychological assessment have been rapidly gaining popularity at the graduate level, such courses typically focus on the administration, scoring, and interpretation of neuropsychological tests, rather than the underlying neurological mechanisms responsible for the behavioral impairments. Some psychologists are fortunate to do their pre-internship and internship training in medical centers where they may receive lectures or attend seminars on these topics taught by medical doctors. As described earlier in this book, the training of a clinical neuropsychologist primarily occurs after the psychologist has completed his doctorate (Ph.D.). Several formal post-doctoral training problems exist which provide training and course work in neuroanatomy, neuropathology, behavioral neurology, psychopharmacology, and neurophysiology for the trainee to understand the underlying physiological and pathological basis of brain dysfunction or damage. Unfortunately, few neuropsychologists have attended or completed such programs. Thus, the attorney may wish to determine as precisely as possible the psychologist's training in neuropsychology in terms of the courses, training, and supervision he or she has received. The attorney should expect that most of the psychologists deposed will only have taken one or two workshops in the administration, scoring, and interpretation of a particular test battery. While the psychologist may have done some additional reading or may have attended a few lectures, the psychologist's training will for the most part be quite limited.

EXAMPLE

Attorney: Doctor, can you describe the training you have received in your specialty (neuropsychology)?

Dr. Smith: I attended a seminar two years ago on the Halstead-Reitan Battery, during which time I learned how to administer, score, and interpret the battery. Since that time, I have attended some lectures and seminars given by neuropsychologists and neurologists on brain damage and neurological disorders.

Attorney: How long did this course take to complete?

Dr. Smith: The course lasted five days.

Attorney: These lectures and seminars that you indicated you have taken—can you describe what topics were addressed?

Dr. Smith: I attended a lecture by Dr. Jones, who is an expert on assessing traumatic brain injuries. I also attended a three-hour seminar on traumatic brain injury. I have attended neurology rounds once or twice at one of the hospitals where I am on staff. I believe that one of the lectures had to do with Alzheimer's disease and another had to do with brain tumors.

Attorney: Have you taken any other seminars or workshops other than those you just described?

Dr. Smith: No.

Attorney: Have you ever received supervision from any psychologist or physician when you were asked to test a patient suspected of having brain damage?

Dr. Smith: Yes. I have had occasions in the past to consult with another psychologist or physician.

Attorney: On how many occasions would you estimate, Doctor?

Dr. Smith: Approximately two or three occasions.

Attorney: Did these occasions involve someone who had brain damage?

Dr. Smith: Yes.

Attorney: Doctor, for what purpose did you seek this supervision?

Dr. Smith: I had some difficulty understanding why the test results came out as they did. On two occasions, I found a psychologist I know who has had more experience than I have. He was of considerable help to me. On another occasion, I spoke to a neurologist because I did not understand what a particular term meant that I found in the patient's medical records.

Attorney: What term was that?

Dr. Smith: I believe it was "hydrocephalus."

Determine the Psychologist's Knowledge of Brain-Behavior Relationships

Most psychologists have very limited knowledge of brain-behavior relationships which derives primarily from their educational background, theoretical orientation, training, type of practice, and patients seen. The attorney might wish to ask the psychologist specific questions to establish his knowledge and understanding of brain and behavioral relationships, particularly if the psychologist has written a report indicating whether or not a particular plaintiff has sustained brain damage.

EXAMPLE

Attorney: Doctor, can you tell me what would happen if someone sustained an injury to the left side of their brain?

Dr. Smith: Well, the patient would most likely have some problems understanding what was being said to them or might have difficulty speaking.

Attorney: Any other problems, Doctor?

Dr. Smith: Well, they might have some problems reading.

Attorney: Any other problems, Doctor?

Dr. Smith: I can't think of anything else.

Determine the Psychologist's Experience in Either Treating or Examining Patients with Brain Damage

Clinical psychologists who administer neuropsychological tests typically have relatively little experience in either treating or examining patients with brain damage, particularly if the bulk of their practice deals with treating patients having marital disorders, adjustment problems, depression, nervousness, anxiety, and tension-related disorders. Thus, it is not uncommon to find that a particular psychologist may have seen fewer than 100 patients who have some form of brain damage. However, only 20 of these patients may have sustained traumatic brain injury and none of these patients may have ever sustained hypoxic encephalopathy or brain damage secondary to industrial solvent exposure. This information should help determine if the psychologist has had sufficient experience with the type of neurological disorder or injury involved in the case.

EXAMPLE

Attorney: Doctor, what kinds of patients do you typically see in your practice?

Dr. Smith: Most of the patients I see have problems related to their marriage, work, or social relationships with others.

Attorney: Can you estimate what percentage of the patients you see, Doctor, that have some form of brain damage?

Dr. Smith: I would estimate that less than 5% of the patients I see have some type of brain damage.

Attorney: Could you be more precise, Doctor? Could you specify whether it's 1%, 2%, 3%, or 4%?

Dr. Smith: I would have to say that it's probably about 2%.

Attorney: Doctor, can you estimate for me how many patients you have seen in your practice who have had some type of brain damage?

Dr. Smith: I would probably estimate between 60 and 70.

Attorney: How many of these patients had ever sustained hypoxic encephalopathy?

Dr. Smith: None that I can recall.

Explore the Psychologist's Reasons for Accepting this Particular Case

Some psychologists operate on the assumption that it is not important what type of neurological or psychiatric problem a particular patient has, but only whether or not they can be tested. Thus, if a patient is not floridly psychotic, is cooperative, appears to follow the test instructions, and is able to complete all of the tests that have been administered to them, then the task of the psychologist is simply to score the patient's test and interpret the test results. The problem with this "psychometric mentality" is that it ignores a variety of factors that have been previously described in this book which may be of crucial importance when the psychologist tries to interpret the patient's test results. As a consequence, many of the interpretations that are often made by psychologists under these conditions are likely to be misleading and erroneous. The attorney should question the psychologist's motives or reasons for accepting to test a particular patient, as well as the psychologist's theoretical orientation to psychological and neuropsychological testing.

EXAMPLE

Attorney: Doctor, you indicated previously that you have never seen a patient who had sustained hypoxic encephalopathy?

Dr. Smith: Yes, that's correct.

Attorney: Doctor, did you know that the patient referred to you for assessment had sustained hypoxic encephalopathy?

Dr. Smith: I can't recall.

Attorney: If you were aware that a patient had sustained hypoxic encephalopathy, would that have made a difference? In other words, would you have agreed to test this person even though you had not previously seen a patient with this particular problem before?

Dr. Smith: No, I don't think it would have made a difference. I would have tried to test the patient if I found the patient to be reasonably cooperative.

Attorney: Doctor, can you tell me, if you know, what kinds of symptoms you would expect a patient with hypoxic encephalopathy to have?

Dr. Smith: I'm really not sure. I really don't know too much about that type of problem. I guess they might be depressed or act kind of funny. I really don't know.

Attorney: If I understand you correctly, Doctor, you wouldn't even be able to recognize one if one were standing next to you, aside from possibly being depressed or acting a bit strange?

Dr. Smith: That's probably true.

Attorney: Were you aware that one of the issues was whether this particular patient sustained brain damage as a result of hypoxic encephalopathy?

Dr. Smith: Yes.

Attorney: Why then did you agree to examine this patient when, Doctor, by your own admission you know virtually nothing about hypoxic encephalopathy?

Dr. Smith: Well, I don't think that really made any difference. I was asked to test this patient and I did that. I administered tests that have been designed to evaluate patients with brain damage. I gave the patient these tests and they indicated that he had brain damage.

Attorney: But Doctor, your report states that the probable cause of the patient's brain damage is hypoxic encephalopathy. How could you have reached such a conclusion when you have admitted that you know virtually nothing about hypoxic encephalopathy?

Dr. Smith: Well, I couldn't think of anything else to attribute his brain damage to.

Attorney: Doctor, did you review this patient's prior medical records or take a history of the patient's background to determine whether there were any pre-existing conditions that might have caused the patient to test poorly on the tests you administered?

Dr. Smith: No, I really didn't. I didn't think that was important, because all I was really asked to do was to administer neuropsychological tests to him to determine whether or not he had brain damage.

Determine the Rationale Used by the Psychologist to Arrive at His Particular Interpretations

The difficulty that many psychologists have interpreting their psychological and neuropsychological test data has been previously described. This is clearly an area of weakness for both psychologists and neuropsychologists, since a number of extraneous factors can result in poor performances on a variety of neuropsychological tasks. It is essential, therefore, that the neuropsychologist examine the pattern of performances across a particular set of tests and look for internal consistency, as well as rule out extraneous factors that might influence the patient's performance. The attorney should determine what particular rationale the psychologist utilized in interpreting the patient's neuropsychological test data.

EXAMPLE

Attorney: Doctor, you indicated in your report that Mr. Jones sustained severe brain damage?

Dr. Smith: That's correct.

Attorney: How, Doctor, did you arrive at this conclusion?

Dr. Smith: Well, I administered a number of neuropsychological tests and found that the patient scored in the brain-damaged range on each of the tests I gave him. I then concluded that the patient had severe brain damage.

Attorney: Doctor, if I took those tests and did poorly on them, would I have brain damage?

Dr. Smith: Well, it's possible.

Attorney: Thank you, Doctor. In other words, anyone who scores poorly on these tests is likely to have brain damage?

Dr. Smith: Yes, I would say so.

Attorney: Do these particular tests have the same accuracy as tests such as x-rays?

Dr. Smith: I'm not really sure if they do or not.

Attorney: If you obtained the same results from a 75-year-old man who had only completed three years of formal education, would you then conclude that this patient had brain damage?

Dr. Smith: Yes, I probably would.

Attorney: In other words, anyone who scores poorly on these tests regardless of their age, background, or events that may be going on in their lives would have brain damage if they scored poorly on these tests?

Dr. Smith: Yes, that's essentially correct.

Attorney: Doctor, do you know how Mr. Jones got to his appointment with you?

Dr. Smith: I believe he drove himself to the appointment.

Attorney: Was he accompanied by anyone?

Dr. Smith: No, he was alone.

Attorney: Did he arrive on time for his scheduled appointment?

Dr. Smith: Yes, I believe so.

Attorney: What kinds of problems did Mr. Jones complain of when you saw him at your office that day?

Dr. Smith: He complained of severe memory problems, concentration difficulties, severe headaches, low back pain, sleep difficulties, feeling tired, irritability, marital difficulties, and depression.

Attorney: Was he able to provide you with a history of what had happened to him in terms of his accident?

Dr. Smith: Yes.

Attorney: Exactly what did he tell you had happened to him?

Dr. Smith: Well, he said he had been involved in a terrible automobile accident and was rendered unconscious. He told me that he was taken to the emergency room and was discharged later that same day. He then went home and began to experience pain and discomfort in this lower back. The next day he tried to go to work and found himself having difficulty concentrating on what he was doing. About two days after the accident, he began noticing memory problems that kept getting worse. He then went to see Dr. White, who told him that he might have sustained a brain injury in his accident. He said that over the past six months his condition had been getting progressively worse and he now believes he has severe brain damage.

Attorney: Doctor, how did he appear to you? Did you make any notes or observations of his behavior when he came to your office?

Dr. Smith: Yes, I did.

Attorney: Can you tell me, Doctor, what you wrote down or recall about his behavior when he was seen in your office?

Dr. Smith: Well, he appeared depressed, in fact, very depressed. He also seemed very tired and to be in a great deal of pain and discomfort. He kind of walked in a bent-over fashion and frequently complained of severe pain in his lower back which radiated down his right leg. He indicated that he had not been able to sleep more than two hours a night because of this problem.

Attorney: Doctor, do you think that any of the problems you just described could have caused him to do poorly on the neuropsychological tests you administered to him?

Dr. Smith: Well, it's possible; however, I don't really think that they would have had a significant effect on him.

Attorney: Why is that, Doctor?

Dr. Smith: Well, these tests are sensitive to brain function. They are not really sensitive to physical pain or discomfort. These tests are very sensitive to brain injuries, and if a person tests poorly on them it means they have a brain injury, even though they may be in a lot of pain or discomfort.

Attorney: In other words, if somebody is in severe pain and has not slept for several nights as a result of a low back injury, their performance on these tests would not be significantly affected?

Dr. Smith: Yes, that's correct.

Determine Whether the Psychologist's Conclusions are Consistent with Other Sources of Data or Information

Many psychologists and neuropsychologists are prone to ignore the inconsistencies in the patient's behavior, medical records, complaints, and neuropsychological test data. They frequently focus on one specific set of data (e.g., neuropsychological test data) and use this information to formulate their conclusions. The attorney should inquire about the various sources of data and information that the psychologist relied on (or failed to rely on) in reaching his or her conclusions.

EXAMPLE

Attorney: Doctor, you indicated in your report that Mr. Jones sustained brain damage?

Dr. Smith: Yes.

Attorney: Did you find any inconsistencies among the neuropsychological tests you administered to this patient?

Dr. Smith: Not really. There was some variability, but they seemed to be pretty consistent.

Attorney: Doctor, I notice that the patient made 85 errors on the Category test but only made 15 errors on the Wisconsin Card Sorting test. Don't these tests measure brain damage?

Dr. Smith: Yes, they do. I am not sure why he scored poorly on the Category test and did very well on the Wisconsin Card Sorting test.

Attorney: Isn't it true that both of these tests require the patient to look at a particular figure and decide whether it fits one of four categories?

Dr. Smith: Yes, that's true, although they are not the same kinds of tests.

Attorney: Doctor, wouldn't you agree that they are similar and basically measure the same kinds of cognitive abilities?

Dr. Smith: Yes, that's generally true.

Attorney: You've indicated in your report that Mr. Jones' memory for recent information is severely impaired.

Dr. Smith: Yes, that's correct. He tested as severely impaired on the Wechsler Memory Scale.

Attorney: Doctor, was Mr. Jones able to provide you with a chronological history of the events and doctors he has seen since his accident?

Dr. Smith: Yes, that's true.

Attorney: Did you review the patient's medical records to determine if the information Mr. Jones provided you with was accurate?

Dr. Smith: Yes, I did.

Attorney: Did you find it to be essentially correct?

Dr. Smith: Yes.

Attorney: Doctor, how is it that someone whose memory is severely impaired is able to provide you with an accurate chronological history of the events that have occurred since the time of his accident?

Dr. Smith: Gee, I'm not really sure. It's possible that he's just been over this so many times that it's become old-hat for him.

Attorney: Doctor, according to Page 7 of your report, you state, "This patient's memory for recent events is so poor that he is unable to learn any new information since his injury."

Doesn't this strike you as being inconsistent—the fact that Mr. Jones was able to provide you with a detailed chronological history of the events that have occurred to him since his accident two years ago and your statement?

Dr. Smith: I really don't know how to answer that. What I do know is that Mr. Jones performed very poorly on formal memory testing.

Attorney: Doctor, I notice also that Mr. Jones provided you with a list of 14 complaints during his interview with you. Is that correct?

Dr. Smith: Yes, that's correct.

Attorney: Don't you find that a little bit unusual, Doctor, that someone who tests as having a severe impairment in recent memory can remember all of the problems he is having?

Dr. Smith: Not necessarily. These are problems that he has all the time, so therefore he is always aware of them.

Attorney: Didn't Mr. Smith arrive for his scheduled appointment at the designated time?

Dr. Smith: Yes, he did.

Attorney: Didn't you say earlier that he drove himself to the appointment and was not accompanied by anyone?

Dr. Smith: Yes.

Attorney: Doesn't there appear to be another inconsistency here?

Dr. Smith: I don't really see any. He knew he was supposed to come here and he showed up on time. That only goes to show you that he was motivated to undergo testing.

Attorney: Doctor, on Page 9 of your report, you state, "The patient's performance on neuropsychological testing indicates that he has lost his ability to initiate activities and no longer has any motivation."

Dr. Smith: Yes.

Attorney: I guess then, Doctor, that Mr. Jones was apparently not motivated to perform well during testing but was motivated to arrive at your office on time?

Dr. Smith: I'm not even sure if that's relevant here. It seems like we're really dealing with two different things.

Attorney: Doesn't the Wisconsin Card Sorting test involve recent memory? Doctor, isn't it true that the patient must remember the examiner's response and their previous responses to do well on this particular test?

Dr. Smith: Yes.

Attorney: Doctor, didn't Mr. Smith do well on this test?

Dr. Smith: Yes.

Attorney: Doctor, do you think Mr. Smith would have done well on this test if his recent memory were severely impaired?

Dr. Smith: No.

Determine Whether There are any Inconsistencies Between the Plaintiff's Past History and the Psychologist's Conclusions

Many psychologists do not take adequate or careful histories and are frequently unaware of any pre-existing conditions, neurological disorders, or problems that could traumatically effect their test interpretations and conclusions. The attorney should initially determine whether or not the psychologist took a detailed background history of the patient or reviewed the patient's prior records to determine if the patient has ever previously had similar problems.

EXAMPLE

Attorney: Doctor, you indicated in your report that you felt that the accident Mr. Jones sustained on October 25, 1986 caused him to sustain severe brain damage, is that right?

Dr. Smith: Yes.

Attorney: Doctor, did you take a history from this patient?

Dr. Smith: Sort of. I found out how many years of formal education he completed, whether or not he was married, what type of work he did, where he was born and raised, and whether he was primarily right-handed or left-handed.

Attorney: Did you inquire about his grades in school?

Dr. Smith: No.

Attorney: Doctor, wouldn't it be important for you to determine what kind of a student he was?

Dr. Smith: No, not really. He indicated he graduated from high school, so I assumed that he was probably a C student or better.

Attorney: Doctor, were you aware that Mr. Jones dropped out of school after completing only the ninth grade?

Dr. Smith: No.

Attorney: Would that change your opinion, Doctor, given this information about whether or not Mr. Jones sustained a brain injury?

Dr. Smith: No.

Attorney: Doctor, did you ask Mr. Jones whether or not he had ever had a prior history of dyslexia or hyperactivity?

Dr. Smith: No.

Attorney: Did Mr. Smith ever volunteer this information?

Dr. Smith: No.

Attorney: Doctor, did you ask Mr. Jones whether or not he had ever sustained a traumatic brain injury prior to the date of his accident?

Dr. Smith: No.

Attorney: Would it change your opinion to know that Mr. Jones was rendered unconscious for nearly 12 hours when he was 14 years old as the result of getting hit on the right side of his head with a baseball bat?

Dr. Smith: I'm not sure whether it would or not.

Attorney: Doctor, were you aware that following that injury, he developed seizures and was placed on Dilantin.

Dr. Smith: No.

Attorney: Doctor, did you inquire about Mr. Jones' past health history?

Dr. Smith: Yes.

Attorney: What specifically did you ask Mr. Jones?

Dr. Smith: I asked him if he had ever been hurt or injured.

Attorney: What did Mr. Jones say?

Dr. Smith: He denied that he had ever been involved in any accidents or had ever been hurt.

Attorney: Doctor, did you examine this patient's prior medical records?

Dr. Smith: No.

Attorney: In other words, you relied entirely on the information Mr. Jones provided you regarding his prior medical history?

Dr. Smith: Yes.

Attorney: Did Mr. Smith ever report a history of being sick or ill during his childhood or adolescence?

Dr. Smith: He said that he had never been sick or ill as a child and that the first time he ever had any problems was after he had his accident.

Attorney: In other words, you relied on the information that Mr. Jones provided you with during your examination?

Dr. Smith: Yes.

Attorney: You also relied on his test performances, Doctor, in reaching your opinions about this case?

Dr. Smith: Yes.

Determine if the Psychologist Interviewed the Plaintiff's Family and/or Significant Others

Many psychologists and neuropsychologists neglect to interview the patient's family and/or significant others. If a patient is living at home with his or her family, then they are in a position of being able to observe the patient's behavior for long periods of time each day, as well as to be able to contrast the patient's behavior since a particular injury to behavior prior to the injury. The attorney should inquire whether or not the psychologist interviewed the significant others and what types of questions he or she asked them, as well as what their responses were to those questions.

EXAMPLE

Attorney: Doctor, did you ever meet or speak to the patient's family, supervisors, or coworkers?

Dr. Smith: No.

Attorney: Did you feel that this information was unimportant?

Dr. Smith: I did not want to speak with them because I like to be objective and rely entirely on my neuropsychological test data to reach conclusions about whether or not a patient has developed a brain injury.

Attorney: Would it change your opinion if you interviewed the family and they indicated that they had not observed any changes in the patient's behavior since his head injury?

Dr. Smith: It's possible. I'd have to think about that.

Attorney: Doctor, if the patient's family informed you that they had not observed any changes in his behavior or psychological functioning since the accident, and you found evidence of brain damage based on his performance on neuropsychological testing, what would you then conclude?

Dr. Smith: I would conclude that the family's perceptions were biased and that they did not really understand brain injury.

Attorney: In other words, Doctor, regardless of what the family said to you, it would not have changed your opinion regarding his neuropsychological test data?

Dr. Smith: Yes.

Determine Whether the Psychologist Observed the Plaintiff's Behavior During Testing and Utilized a Quantitative and Qualitative Analysis of the Test Data

Approximately three out of four neuropsychologists utilize technicians or psychological assistants to administer tests to referred patients. The problem with this is that the technician or psychological assistant essentially serves as a psychometrist, in the sense that they simply give the test and record the patient's scores. Because of their limited education, poor understanding and background in behavioral neurology, and their tendency to focus on the quantitative aspects of the patient's behavior (e.g., test scores), they frequently ignore many aspects of the patient's behavior during testing. The attorney should determine how the neuropsychological tests were administered to the patient and the background and experience of this individual. The attorney should also inquire as to whether or not the psychologist utilized a qualitative approach in helping him or her interpret the neuropsychological test data and arrive at their conclusions.

EXAMPLE

Attorney: Doctor, who administered the neuropsychological tests to Mr. Jones that you described in your report?

Dr. Smith: My technician, Miss Johnson.

Attorney: Doctor, can you describe her educational background and training?

Dr. Smith: Miss Johnson is a college graduate and has taken some graduate courses in psychology and is currently working on her master's degree in this field. Two years ago, she took a workshop in the administration and scoring of the Halstead-Reitan Battery. I have also been her clinical supervisor and consult with her frequently.

Attorney: Doctor, did you observe her administering any of these tests?

Dr. Smith: No.

Attorney: In other words, you never saw her giving these tests?

Dr. Smith: That's correct.

Attorney: Was Miss Johnson given any specific instructions prior to her administration of these tests?

Dr. Smith: No.

Attorney: Did she take any notes that described how Mr. Jones went about taking the tests he was administered by her?

Dr. Smith: If by notes you mean his performances on these tests, yes.

Attorney: Did she take any notes on how he went about taking the tests from a qualitative perspective?

Dr. Smith: No.

Attorney: In other words, Doctor, Mr. Jones could have been deliberately performing poorly on these tests without their being any mention of that by Miss Johnson?

Dr. Smith: Well, I'm sure if she noticed him deliberately trying to score poorly on this test, she would have written something down to that effect.

Attorney: But Doctor, didn't you indicate that she is not usually required to take notes of the patient's behavior during testing?

Dr. Smith: Yes, that's correct.

Attorney: Therefore, Doctor, isn't it possible that Mr. Jones could have deliberately performed poorly on these tests without any written note or record of this fact?

Dr. Smith: Yes, that's possible.

Attorney: Doctor, didn't it strike you as being odd that Mr. Jones complained of severe problems with his recent memory and yet was able to provide you with a detailed chronological history of his accident and showed up on time for his scheduled appointment?

Dr. Smith: Well, I really didn't give it that much thought when I saw him.

Attorney: In other words, Doctor, you didn't think it important enough to alert Miss Johnson to this discrepancy and ask her to pay careful to Mr. Jones' behavior when she tested him?

Dr. Smith: No, I guess I didn't.

Determine How the Psychologist Established the Severity of the Plaintiff's Brain Damage

As previously mentioned in this book, there appears to be a wide range of differences among psychologists and neuropsychologists in terms of how they arrive at the severity of a patient's brain injury. The psychologist should carefully explore the psychologist's rationale for arriving at his or her conclusions.

EXAMPLE

Attorney: Doctor, you indicated in your report that Mr. Jones sustained severe brain damage?

Dr. Smith: Yes.

Attorney: How did you go about reaching this conclusion?

Dr. Smith: Well, he tested in the brain-damaged range on every test administered to him. He had a Halstead-Reitan Impairment Index of 1.0, which indicates severe brain damage.

Attorney: Did you rely on any other information to reach your opinion?

Dr. Smith: No.

Attorney: Doctor, did you ever review the records of the paramedics who examined Mr. Jones at the scene of the accident?

Dr. Smith: No.

Attorney: Would it change your opinion, Doctor, if you learned that there is no record, based on the paramedics' observations, that Mr. Jones had ever sustained any type of head injury or was rendered unconscious or appeared confused or bewildered shortly after his automobile accident?

Dr. Smith: No.

Attorney: Doctor, would it change your opinion if we assumed that the information I just gave you is accurate?

Dr. Smith: Well, it's possible, but he tested poorly on all of the neuropsychological tests administered to him.

Attorney: In other words, even though there is no indication in Mr. Jones' medical records that he ever sustained any type of head injury, you're telling me now that Mr. Jones has severe brain damage because he scored poorly on all of the neuropsychological tests he was administered?

Dr. Smith: Yes.

Attorney: Doctor, according to your report, you indicated that Mr. Jones sustained severe diffuse brain damage?

Dr. Smith: Yes.

Attorney: Doctor, do you find it unusual that a patient can sustain diffuse brain damage without ever losing consciousness or sustaining a head injury?

Dr. Smith: Yes, it seems unusual, but how do we explain his performance on each of the neuropsychological tests that were administered to him?

Attorney: Doctor, I notice that he did extremely poorly on each of these tests and even failed many of the simplest items on them?

Dr. Smith: Yes, that's true.

Attorney: Do you have any explanation for this, Doctor?

Dr. Smith: Only that he had sustained severe brain damage.

Attorney: Isn't it quite unusual, Doctor, that an individual who tested extremely poorly on even the simplest test was able to remember his scheduled appointment with you and drive some 14 miles to your office, a place he had never previously been to, and arrive on time for his appointment?

Dr. Smith: I'm really not sure how to answer that.

Attorney: Doctor, aren't there tests that have been specifically designed to detect malingering?

Dr. Smith: Yes.

Attorney: Did you ever administer any of these tests to Mr. Jones?

Dr. Smith: No.

Attorney: Given all of the inconsistencies we've discussed between Mr. Jones' behavior, his neuropsychological test performances, and his failure to provide you with an accurate history of his past medical problems, do you think it is possible that Mr. Jones may be malingering?

Dr. Smith: Well, it's possible.

Chapter 17

Malingering

Malingering refers to a deliberate attempt on the part of a patient to perform poorly on a specific test or set of tests to obtain financial compensation or secondary gains. Individuals who are malingering typically provide the examiner with inaccurate or misleading information regarding their past and deliberately withhold or conceal information from the examiner that could significantly influence the opinion or conclusions of the examiner. Malingerers typically display symptoms or behaviors in the presence of the examiner that are also designed to create the spurious impression that a serious problem exists that prevents them from returning to their previously held jobs, actively seek out other forms of employment or receive vocational training for a specific job or occupation.

The symptoms and behavior of the malingerer is under their conscious control and can be "switched on or off" at will. Behaviors that are typically observed in the examining doctor's office are virtually never seen outside the doctor's office or in the company of other family members or friends. Many malingerers have sociopathic personalities, that is, they are able to manipulate, lie to, or cheat others without any remorse or guilt. They typically have a long history of such behavior and have often been arrested for criminal or antisocial behavior. A surprising number of malingerers have deep-seated characterological and emotional problems that often "compel" them to deliberately exaggerate their symptoms in order to be hospitalized to avoid work, unpleasant tasks, or specific responsibilities. It is fairly easy to detect malingering in a person of below-average intelligence since their exaggerations typically lack sophistication and are easily recognizable by a skilled examiner. Malingerers who have superior or very superior intellectual functioning are more difficult to detect. Because of their high level of intellectual functioning, they often read textbooks and acquire a great deal of information about a particular sickness or type of injury. Hence, they often learn to provide the doctor with a set of complaints consistent with a specific neurological or medical disorder. Malingerers tend to focus on physical or neurological problems such as low back pain, memory difficulties, and inability to use a part of their body, etc. They are less likely to complain of hallucinations, bizarre thinking, feelings of anger and rage, and suicidal ideation or plans. When a specific treatment is proposed to them to alleviate one or more of their complaints, they typically refuse such treatment with rather flimsy rationalizations, such as, "I'm not taking those medications. I hate medications. Why should I put a foreign substance in my body?" after a physician informs them that a particular medication should alleviate their problems. This also includes surgery and compliance to a specific treatment regimen, such as attending physical therapy on a daily basis.

Malingerers tend to be guarded and suspicious when interviewed by an independent medical examiner retained by the defendant. They often refuse to answer specific questions regarding their accident or past history. Brighter and more sophisticated malingerers often state, "I can't remember," rather than stating, "I'm not going to answer that." They often inquire what the doctor hopes to gain by asking them a specific question or set of questions. They frequently try to manipulate the examination by providing rationalizations or excuses, like, "I'm just afraid that if I take this test, I'm liable to have another attack and pass out." While their performance on neuropsychological tests is typically poor from a quantitative perspective, they usually fail to exhibit errors that are typically made by patients with an organic or neurologic disorder. They often miss easy items on tests and get more difficult items correct in an inconsistent manner. They typically perform poorer than patients with legitimate neurological injuries or disorders, while at the same time displaying none of the characteristic errors that are typically made by brain-damaged patients.

Malingerers often carry their own medical records to the doctor's office when they are scheduled for an examination. They frequently provide the examiner with numerous complaints and exhibit behaviors that appear to be under their conscious control and are designed to deceive the examining doctor.

The author has found that the detection of malingering requires a careful examination of the patient's complaints, observations of significant others, the accuracy of the information provided by the "patient," a careful review of the pre-and post-accident medical records, legal history (e.g., previous claims or litigation, arrest history, and involvement with law enforcement authorities), educational records, prior employment records, observation of the "patient's" behavior when he or she is not aware that they are being observed, corroboration of the "patient's history of the accident" and background with educational, vocational, medical, and psychiatric records (if available), and a comparison of the patient's quantitative and qualitative performance during neuropsychological testing. An analysis of this information typically permits the examiner to detect malingering.

Malingering in its pure form tends to be less common than a combination of malingering and a somatoform disorder in which the patient may display both deliberate efforts to perform poorly and a psychological need to express complaints as a means of gratifying their long-standing dependency needs or in response to environmental stressors. The following case illustrates the points made above.

CASE STUDY

The patient is a 48-year-old male who was involved in a relatively minor motor vehicle accident in which his car was struck from the rear by another vehicle traveling less than five miles per hour. The patient was not wearing a seat belt at the time of his injury. While he reported that he struck his head on the visor, there was no evidence of physical trauma. He did not lose consciousness or experience post-traumatic bewilderment, confusion, or amnesia. His recollection of the events that occurred immediately prior to, during, and following the accident were excellent. He was not observed by the driver of the other vehicle or by the paramedics' report to experience a high level of anxiety. At no time did the patient ever develop a driving phobia, intrusive recollections of the accident, startle reactions to stimuli resembling the accident, recurrent nightmares or bad dreams about the accident, or symptoms consistent with either a post-concussive or post-traumatic stress disorder.

The patient complained to his family physician three days after his accident of pain and stiffness in his neck and left shoulder, sleep difficulties, and a burning sensation in his eyes. These problems eventually resolved over the next three months. He complained of fatigue and tiredness, however. A review of the patient's medical records indicated that the patient had been doing quite well during the next two months when he returned to see his family physician. He complained of weakness in his neck, however, as well as memory and sleep difficulties. He was diagnosed as depressed and placed on antidepressant medications. Over the next two months, the patient became more depressed and was then placed on a variety of different medications to treat his depression. Although he attributed his depression to his motor vehicle accident, a review of the handwritten notes of his treating physician indicated that the patient complained during this time of severe conflicts and problems with his daughter which have been "driving him crazy." His physician's chart notes reveal that the patient became increasingly depressed and continued to experience problems with his daughter during this time. He was placed on Norpramin and was referred for psychotherapy. A review of the handwritten notes of his treating psychotherapist indicated that his daughter had a severe drug abuse problem and had been acting belligerent toward the patient and other family members. The patient increased his dosage of Norpramin without consulting any of his physicians. This resulted in slurred speech and stuttering, which he attributed to his motor vehicle accident. However, a review of the handwritten notes of his treating physician indicated that he attributed these problems to excessively high dosages of this medication. While the patient continued to attribute his emotional problems, which had become worse over the past three months, to his motor vehicle accident, a review of the treating physician's handwritten notes indicated that the patient's wife had been diagnosed with cancer during this time. The patient also developed gastrointestinal and dermatological problems that he attributed to the accident but were most likely reactions to taking excessively high dosages of Norpramin. The patient was also taking Aldoril for hypertension, which his treating psychiatrist indicated in his handwritten notes had been causing him to become depressed. For example, when he was later taken off of this medication by his treating psychiatrist, his depressed mood improved considerably.

The patient continued to complain of a variety of somatic problems over the next several months and was placed on a number of different antidepressant medications. Approximately one year following his accident, he was referred to a neurologist who placed him on Dilantin, Tegretol, and Sinemet. (Author's note: Research studies have shown that Dilantin will produce cognitive impairments in 100% of the patients who take this medication.) After taking these medications, the patient's speech became more garbled. The patient was hospitalized with the admitting diagnosis of depression, which the patient attributed to his car accident. However, a careful review of his hospital records indicated that the patient admitted to one of his treating doctors that while he as hospitalized his daughter had embezzled over $25,000 from her employer and that they had to come up with this amount to reimburse her employer to prevent his daughter from being arrested and sent to prison. He also admitted that because of his wife's illness, she could no longer work and that these problems had seriously hurt his business. He was a self-employed auto mechanic. His treating neurologist had diagnosed him as having a post-concussive syndrome secondary to his motor vehicle accident based on the history he obtained from the patient. The neurologist hospitalized him and ordered neurodiagnostic tests. While hospitalized, he underwent several neurodiagnostic tests, including a brain CT scan, EEG, and evoked potential studies. All of which were all found to be normal. According to the patient's hospital records, his treating neurologist later changed his diagnosis to a post-traumatic stress disorder and referred him for neuropsycholgical testing.

The patient was seen by a clinical psychologist who administered the Wechsler Adult Intelligence Scale and the MMPI to evaluate his intellectual and emotional functioning. The psychologist concluded that the patient's MMPI profile was consistent with the diagnosis of depression but also revealed a highly manipulative and devious individual who is likely to have a history of past involvement with alcohol, drugs, or criminal activity. The patient attributed his depression to his motor vehicle accident and denied any current stressors in his life.

The patient was referred to a psychologist for neuropsychological testing because of his complaints of memory difficulties. The psychologist reported that the patient demonstrated significant impairments in attention-concentration, memory, and speed of cognitive processing on testing, which he felt was the result of a brain injury the patient had sustained in his motor vehicle accident. A careful review of the neuropsychologist's report indicated that the patient's motivation was "not very good throughout the testing" and that the "results should be viewed with caution, since the patient was not fully cooperative." Unfortunately, the psychologist ignored her own caveats and found evidence of brain damage, despite the fact that the patient was taking a wide variety of different medications which are well-known to produce significant cognitive effects, particularly in the area of attention-concentration, memory, and speed of cognitive processing. The psychologist was also unaware of the fact that the patient had been under severe emotional stress as a result of his daughter's drug problems and rebellious behavior, his wife's illness, and his financial difficulties. After the patient's treating neurologist received the psychologist's report, he changed his opinion once again and decided that the patient had really sustained a traumatic brain injury. The neurologist indicated that the probable cause of the patient's difficulties were due to the "acceleration/deceleration forces which occurred in his motor vehicle accident." However, there was no mention in this report that the patient's car had been rear-ended by another vehicle which was travelling an estimated three miles per hour, which would make such forces necessary to produce brain injury extremely improbable. In addition, the doctor's report also made no mention that there was no evidence that the patient had ever struck his head or sustained any type of whiplash injury.

A report by the patient's treating psychiatrist, whom the patient's attorney had referred him to, indicated that this patient had been in excellent emotional and physical health prior to his accident and did not have a prior history of emotional problems. Thus, his treating psychiatrist attributed all of his current problems to the brain injury he sustained in his motor vehicle accident. However, a careful review of the medical records of his family physician indicated that the patient had been seen 44 times during the 18 months prior to his motor vehicle accident for the following problems: throat swallowing difficulties, dermatitis, stiffness and soreness in his neck, visual difficulties, burning sensation in his eyes, nausea, lightheadedness, hypertension, difficulty controlling his weight, abdominal pain and discomfort, neck pain, stabbing pain in his right eye, vomiting and abdominal pain, depression, anxiety, tooth decay, paranoia, and head trauma as a result of a motor vehicle accident (during which he had struck his head six months prior to his motor vehicle accident), Achilles tendinitis, chest pain, difficulties with his right shoulder, pain in his right calf and ankle, an abscess in his nose, skin problems, abdominal pain, pain in his right buttocks secondary to a slip and fall injury which occurred only three months prior to his accident, financial difficulties, and concerns over his wife's failing health.

When the patient was seen for neuropsychological assessment, he reported a stable work history and denied that he had ever been terminated or asked to resign from any job he ever held. He also indicated that he had been honorably discharged from the Army and had achieved the rank of Staff Sergeant prior to his discharge. However, a review of his employment records indicated that he had held over 40 jobs during the 10-year period prior to his accident. These records also indicated that he had received a dishonorable discharge from the Army after being court-martialed for selling Army property. Even though the patient denied a history of prior arrests or ever filing a Workers' Compensation claim, or being involved in a lawsuit, a review of his records indicated that he had previously been involved in three personal injury cases as a plaintiff and had filed two Workers' Compensation claims during the past 15 years. The patient denied a history of alcohol or substance abuse; however, a careful review of the treating physician's medical records made numerous mentions of this patient's long-standing problems with alcohol and his frequent use of barbiturates.

Neuropsychological testing revealed that while the patient's quantitative scores were quite poor, he appeared to be deliberately trying to perform poorly and in several instances scored worse than chance, which indicates that he was deliberately trying to perform poorly. Personality testing revealed a highly manipulative, devious, and psychopathic individual who would be expected to have a history of irresponsible behavior, lying, and deceit, with little or no remorse. He also appeared guarded and paranoid during the interview and often refused to answer certain questions about his past, and claimed that he could "not remember anything about serving in the military" or any of the jobs he had held in the past.

It was the opinion of the neuropsychologist that while this patient had a long-standing history of psychosomatic difficulties secondary to external stressors, he had deliberately attempted to conceal information from his treating and examining doctors and had deliberately misrepresented his past medical and psychological functioning. The neuropsychologist also noted that the patient's performance on neuropsychological testing revealed a style of responding consistent with patients who deliberately simulate cognitive impairments and that his profile on the MMPI corroborated his prior history of irresponsible behavior, vocational difficulties, drug and substance abuse difficulties, manipulative behavior, and deceit. The neuropsychologist concluded that the automobile accident did not contribute to this patient's current complaints and that his symptoms, complaints, and behavior were a combination of external stressors and deliberate attempts to simulate neurological and cognitive difficulties which were consistent with the diagnosis of malingering and a somatoform disorder.

Comment

This case illustrates the importance of carefully reviewing the plaintiff's pre-existing medical records and corroborating the information he provides to his treating and examining doctors. Numerous inconsistencies were found when the patient's vocational, medical, and legal records were obtained. The patient's behavior during testing was very guarded and suspicious. He also made numerous attempts to control the examination by refusing to answer many of the examiner's questions or to complete the examiner's tests. Prior to taking each test, he would typically ask, "What does this test actually measure or examine?" His responses to the examiner's questions indicated that "the wheels were turning in his head," in that his responses were carefully selected and were under his deliberate, conscious control. He denied that any other factors could be responsible for his current problems, which he attributed to his motor vehicle accident of record. He denied a prior history of health problems, accidents, head trauma, or falls which were contradicted by his medical records. A qualitative analysis of his performance on neuropsychological testing revealed strong indications of deliberate attempts to perform poorly. In addition, he made none of the errors that are typically seen in patients with legitimate brain damage. He also denied that he had been taking any medications, even though a review of his medical records indicated that he had been taking at least eight different medications at the time he was seen for neuropsychological testing. He appeared manipulative and deceitful during the interview and testing, which was corroborated by psychological tests such as the MMPI. In other words, all of the "vectors" were consistent and revealed overwhelming evidence of malingering.

Appendices

Appendix A

Diplomates of The American Board of Clinical Neuropsychology

as of June 30, 1990.[1]

Kenneth M. Adams Ph.D.
2464 Newbury Court
Ann Arbor, Michigan 48103
USA
Work Phone: 313-761-7935

Russell L. Adams Ph.D.
Dept. of Psychiatry & Behavioral Science
P.O. Box 26901
Oklahoma City, Oklahoma 73190
USA
Work Phone: 405-271-5639

Lydia Artiola Ph.D.
5930 East Pima Street
Suite 208
Tucson, Arizona 85712
USA
Work Phone: 602-290-1700

Lyle E. Baade Ph.D.
Department of Psychiatry
University of Kansas School of Medicine
1010 North Kansas
Wichita, Kansas 67214
USA
Work Phone: 316-261-2647

Gale W. Bach Ph.D.
1945 Second Avenue
San Diego, California 92101
USA
Work Phone: 619-239-2021

Russell A. Barkley Ph.D.
Department of Psychiatry
University of Massachusetts Medical Center
55 Lake Avenue North
Worcester, Maine 01655
USA
Work Phone: 414-778-4588

Augustine Baron Jr., Psy.D.*
2507 Rae Dell Avenue
Austin, Texas 78704
USA
Work Phone: 512-471-3515

Ida S. Baron Ph.D.
10116 Weatherwood Court
Potomac, Maryland 20854
USA
Work Phone: 202-687-4954

Edwin T. Barrett Jr., Ph.D.*
8948 Hollyhock Drive
Cincinnati, Ohio 45231
USA
Work Phone: 513-559-5013

[1]Published with permission of The American Board of Clinical Neuropsychology.

Jeffrey T. Barth Ph.D.
465 Ivy Farm Drive
Charlottesville, Virginia 22901
USA
Work Phone: 804-924-2718

Bruce C. Becker Ph.D.
9508 Newbold Place
Bethesda, Maryland 20817
USA
Work Phone: 301-365-9109

James T. Becker Ph.D.
Suite 400, Iroquois Building
3600 Forbes Avenue
Pittsburgh, Pennsylvania 15213
USA
Work Phone: 412-647-2569

Thomas E. Beniak Ph.D.
Mincep Epilepsy Care, PA
Park Place Office Center
5775 Wayzata Boulevard, Suite 200
Minneapolis, Minnesota 55416
USA
Work Phone: 612-331-4477

Arthur L. Benton Ph.D.
504 Manor Drive
Iowa City, Iowa 52240
USA
Work Phone: 350-685-4261

Stanley Berent Ph.D.
Department of Psychiatry
University of Michigan Medical Center
1500 East Medical Center Drive
Ann Arbor Michigan 48109-0840
USA
Work Phone: 313-763-9259

Larry C. Bernard Ph.D.
Psychology Department
Loyola Marymount University
Loyola Boulevard at West 80th Street
Los Angeles, California 90045
USA
Work Phone: 213-338-4592

Linas A. Bieliauskas Ph.D.
Psychology Service (116B)
VA Medical Center
215 Fuller Road
Ann Arbor, Michigan 48105
USA
Work Phone: 313-761-7936

Erin D. Bigler Ph.D.
Department of Psychology
Brigham Young University
1086 SWKT
Provo, Utah 84602
USA
Work Phone: 801-378-4289

Laurence M. Binder Ph.D.
2636 Southwest 64th Place
Portland, Oregon 97221
USA
Work Phone: 503-273-5187

H. Daniel Blackwood Ph.D.
133 East Harmont
Phoenix, Arizona 85020
USA
Work Phone: 602-285-3838

Joseph Bieiberg Ph.D.
National Rehabilitation Hospital
102 Irving Street, N.W.
Washington, D.C. 20010
USA
Work Phone: 202-877-1121

Thomas J. Boll Ph.D.
University Station
P.O. Box 109
Birmingham, Alabama 35294
USA
Work Phone: 205-934-8723

Robert A. Bornstein Ph.D.
Department of Psychiatry
Ohio State University
473 West 12th Avenue
Columbus, Ohio 43210-1228
USA
Work Phone: 614-293-8847

Joan C. Borod Ph.D.
Department of Psychology
Queens College
NSB-E318
Flushing, New York 11367
USA
Work Phone: 718-520-7930

Jason Brandt Ph.D.*
Johns Hopkins Hospital, Meyer 218
600 North Wolfe Street
Baltimore, Maryland 21205
USA
Work Phone: 301-955-2619

Alan E. Brooker Ph.D.
Department of Mental Health
David Grant USAF Medical Center
Travis AFB, California 94535-5300
USA
Work Phone: 707-423-5149

Gregory G. Brown Ph. D.
38719 Yale Court
Northville, Michigan 48167
USA
Work Phone: Unavailable

Ernest T. Bryant Ph.D.
#9 Meadowlark Court
Novato, California 94947
USA
Work Phone: 415-372-1960

Nelson M. Butters Ph.D.
Psychology Service (116B)
San Diego VA Medical Center
3350 La Jolla Village Drive
La Jolla, California 92161
USA
Work Phone: 619-552-7561

Bruce M. Capian Ph.D.
Rehabilitation Medicine
Thomas Jefferson University
11th and Walnut Streets
Philadelphia, Pennsylvania 19107
USA
Work Phone: 215-928-6571

Gordon J. Chelune Ph.D.
Department of Psychiatry
Cleveland Clinic Foundation
9500 Euclid Avenue
Cleveland, Ohio 44195
USA
Work Phone: 216-444-5984

Mitchell I. Clionsky Ph.D.
Six Crescent Hill
Springfield, Massachusetts 01105
USA
Work Phone: 413-734-3331

Louis D. Costa Ph.D.*
Department of Psychology
University of Victoria
P.O. Box 1700
Victoria, British Columbia V8W 2Y2
Canada
Work Phone: 604-721-7066

Lloyd I. Cripe Ph.D.
P.O. Box 2257
Sequim, Washington 98382-2257
USA
Work Phone: 206-683-7883

Bruce A. Crosson Ph.D.
Dept. of Clinical & Health Psychology
University of Florida
Box J-165, Health Sciences Center
Gainesville, Florida 32610
USA
Work Phone: 904-392-4551

Herman M. Davidovicz Ph.D.
931 East 84th Street
Brooklyn, New York 11236
USA
Work Phone: 516-562-3054

Richard C. Delaney Ph.D.
Psychology Service (116B)
VA Medical Center
West Haven, Connecticut 06516
USA
Work Phone: 203-932-5711

Leonard Diller Ph.D.
400 East 34th Street
New York, New York 10016
USA
Work Phone: 212-340-6161

Carl B. Dodrill Ph.D.
Epilepsy Center
Harborview Medical Center, AZ-50
Seattle, Washington 98104
USA
Work Phone: 206-223-3557

Richard G. Doiron Ph.D.
86 Dartmouth Street
Portland, Maine 04103
USA
Work Phone: 207-773-1790

Robert W. Elliott Ph.D.
629 27th Street
Manhattan Beach, California 90266
USA
Work Phone: 213-545-6400

George M. Faibish Ph.D.
Psychology Service (116B)
VA Medical Center
2002 Holcombe Boulevard
Houston, Texas 77030
USA
Work Phone: 713-795-7444

Deborah A. Fein Ph.D.
Eight Front Street
South Natick, Massachusetts 01760
USA
Work Phone: 617-638-4850

Eileen B. Fennell Ph.D.
Department of Psychology
University of Florida
Box J-165, JHMHC
Gainesville, Florida 32610
USA
Work Phone: 904-392-6860

Susan B. Filskov Ph.D.
Suite 205
3333 West Kennedy Boulevard
Tampa, Florida 33609
USA
Work Phone: 813-876-7191

Mariellen Fischer Ph.D.
Section of Neuropsychology
Medical College of Wisconsin
1000 North 92nd Street
Milwaukee, Wisconsin 53226
USA
Work Phone: 414-778-4588

Francis J. Fishburne Ph.D.
20 Pitt Court
Rockville, Maryland 20850
USA
Work Phone: 301-656-5291

John L. Fisk Ph.D.
Division of Neuropsychology (K-11)
Henry Ford Hospital
2799 West Grand Boulevard
Detroit, Michigan 48202
USA
Work Phone: 313-876-2526

Jack M. Fletcher Ph.D.
Department of Pediatrics (MSB 3.136)
University of Texas Medical School
6431 Fannin
Houston, Texas 77030
USA
Work Phone: 713-792-5464

David Freides Ph.D.
Psychology Department
Emory University
Atlanta, Georgia 30322
USA
Work Phone: Unavailable

Charles J. Furst Ph.D.
1100 Glendon Avenue, Suite 1614
Los Angeles, California 90024
USA
Work Phone: 213-824-0092

David C. Garron Ph.D.
Dept. of Psychology & Social Science
Rush-Presbyterian St. Luke's Medical
1753 West Congress Parkway
Chicago, Illinois 60612
USA
Work Phone: 312-942-6652

Eikhonon Goldberg Ph.D.*
Division of Neuropsychology
Medical College of Pennsylvania
3200 Henry Avenue
Philadelphia, Pennsylvania 19129
Work Phone: 215-842-4032

Gerald Goldstein Ph.D.
6943 Reynolds Street
Pittsburgh, Pennsylvania 15208
USA
Work Phone: 412-363-4900

Harold Goodglass Ph.D.
150 South Huntington Avenue
Boston, Massachusetts 02130
USA
Work Phone: Unavailable

John E. Gordon Ph.D.
Architects Building, Suite 1700
Clinical Neuropsychology Association
117 South 17th Street
Philadelphia, Pennsylvania 19103
USA
Work Phone: 215-864-9444

Wayne A. Gordon Ph.D.
Department of Rehabilitation Medicine
Box 1240
One Gustave Levy Place
New York, New York 10029
USA
Work Phone: 212-241-7917

Ruben C. Gur Ph.D.*
815 St. Geroge's Road
Philadelphia, Pennsylvania 19119
USA
Work Phone: 215-662-2826

Kathleen Y. Haaland Ph.D.
Psychology Service (116B)
VA Medical Center
Albuquerque, New Mexico 87108
USA
Work Phone: 505-265-1711

Thomas A. Hammeke Ph.D.
Neuropsychology Clinic
1000 North 92nd Street
Milwaukee, Wisconsin 53225
USA
Work Phone: 414-778-4588

Kerry DeS. Hamsher Ph.D.
Department of Neurology (R480)
University of Wisconsin Medical School
P.O. Box 342, 950 North 12th Street
Milwaukee, Wisconsin 53201-0342
USA
Work Phone: 414-289-8218

Milton E. Harris Ph.D.
95 Montgomery Drive, Suite 102
Santa Rosa, California 95404
USA
Work Phone: 707-579-3140

Robert P. Hart Ph.D.
Department of Psychiatry
Medical College of Virginia
P.O. Box 268
Richmond, Virginia 23298
USA
Work Phone: 804-786-0762

Mary E. Hayden Ph.D.
Suite 201
3801 Gaston Avenue
Dallas, Texas 75246
USA
Work Phone: 214-821-2511

Robert K. Heaton Ph.D.
Neuropsychology Laboratory
University of California, San Diego
3427 Fourth Avenue
San Diego, California 92103
USA
Work Phone: 619-497-6644

Edward T. Heck Ph.D.
28 Church Street
Winchester, Massachusetts 01890-2590
USA
Work Phone: 617-729-8311

Bruce P. Hermann Ph.D.
6384 Richfield
Bartlett, Tennessee 38134
USA
Work Phone: 901-522-5854

Roy E. Hollis Ph.D.
P.O. Box 929
East Hampstead, New Hampshire 03826
USA
Work Phone: 603-329-5311

Stephen Honor Ph.D.*
222 Middle Country Road
Smithtown, New York 11787
USA
Work Phone: Unavailable

C. Alan Hopewell Ph.D.
2010 Fair Meadow
Arlington, Texas 76012
USA
Work Phone: 817-265-3236

Diane B. Howieson Ph.D.
Psychology Service (116B)
VA Medical Center
P.O. Box 1034
Portland, Oregon 97207
USA
Work Phone: 503-273-5187

Theresa M. Incagnoli Ph.D.*
240 Central Park South, 24C
New York, New York 10019
USA
Work Phone: 516-261-4400

Robert J. Ivnik Ph.D.
Department of Psychiatry & Psychology
Mayo Clinic
Rochester, Minnesota 55905
USA
Work Phone: 507-284-3985

Judy W. Johnson Ph.D.
10 Office Park Drive
Little Rock, Arkansas 72211
USA
Work Phone: 501-224-0416

Barbara P. Jones Ph.D.
Suite 20
4601 Connecticut Avenue, N.W.
Washington, D.C. 20008
USA
Work Phone: 202-362-7882

Robert L. Kane Ph.D.
54 Sunset Road
Winchester, Massachusetts 01890
USA
Work Phone: 201-676-1000

Edith F. Kaplan Ph.D.
P.O. Box 476
Lexington, Maine 02173
USA
Work Phone: 617-862-1207

Peter Karzmark Ph.D.
1281 Shasta Avenue
San Jose, California 95126
USA
Work Phone: 408-299-5116

Alfred W. Kaszniak Ph.D.
Department of Psychology
University of Arizona
Tucson, Arizona 85721
USA
Work Phone: 602-621-5149

Mark P. Kelly Ph.D.
Montebello Rehabilitation Hospital
University Maryland Medical System
2201 Argonne Drive
Baltimore, Maryland 21218
USA
Work Phone: Unavailable

Robert M. Knights Ph.D.
52 Hopewell Avenue
Ottawa, Ontario K1S 2Y8
Canada
Work Phone: 613-231-5587

Sandra P. Koffier Ph.D.
Neuropsychology Laboratory, M.S. 341
Hahnemann University Hospital
230 North Broad Street
Philadelphia, Pennsylvania 19102
USA
Work Phone: 215-448-4956

Richard Kovner Ph.D.
Six Birch Grove Drive
Armonk, New York 10504
USA
Work Phone: 212-920-5482

Robert T. Kuriychek Ph.D.
132 East Broadway, Suite 700
Eugene, Oregon 97401
USA
Work Phone: 503-686-7044

Robert Lapiant Ph.D.
Department of Neurosciences
Marshfield Clinic
Marshfield, Wisconsin 54449
USA
Work Phone: 715-387-5366

Glenn J. Larrabee Ph.D.
112 83rd Street Northwest
Bradenton, Florida 33529
USA
Work Phone: 813-365-6463

Gregory P. Lee Ph.D.
Department of Surgery/Neurosurgery
Medical College of Georgia
Augusta, Georgia 30912
USA
Work Phone: 404-289-8218

Dano A. Leli Ph.D.
Florida Medical Plaza
2501 North Orange Avenue, Suite 509
Orlando, Florida 32804
USA
Work Phone: 407-894-4947

Harvey S. Levin Ph.D.
Division of Neurosurgery (D73)
University of Texas Medical Branch
Galveston, Texas 77550-2777
USA
Work Phone: 409-761-2057

Maureen J. Levine Ph.D.
Department of Psychology
Central Michigan University
Sloan Hall 226
Mt. Pleasant, Michigan 48859
USA
Work Phone: 517-774-3001

Muriel D. Lezak Ph.D.
1811 S.W. Boundary
Portland, Oregon 97201
USA
Work Phone: 503-279-7772

Patrick E. Logue Ph.D.
14 Harvey Place
Durham, North Carolina 27705
USA
Work Phone: 919-684-6908

I. Barry Lorinstein Ph.D.*
155 Stratton Road
New Rochelle, New York 10804
USA
Work Phone: 914-328-0090

Joan A. Lorr Ph.D.
11521 Erskine Street
Takoma Park, Maryland 20912
USA
Work Phone: 202-745-8174

Sandra Lundgren Ph.D.
4229 Dupont Avenue South
Minneapolis, Minnesota 55409
USA
Work Phone: 612-725-2073

George W. MacDonald Ph.D.
Department of Psychology
Iwk Hospital for Children
P.O. Box 3070
Halifax, Nova Scotia B3J 3G9
Canada
Work Phone: 902-424-6055

James L. Mack Ph.D.
Department of Neurology
2074 Abington Road
Cleveland, Ohio 44106
USA
Work Phone: 216-844-3188

Lawrence V. Majovski Ph.D.
130 South Euclid, Suite #1
Pasadena, California 91101
USA
Work Phone: 818-397-5901

James F. Malec Ph.D.
Dept. of Psychiatry & Psychology
Mayo Clinic
Rochester, Minnesota 55905
USA
Work Phone: 507-285-5199

Alexander A. Manning Ph.D.
P.O. Box 1725
Hickory, North Carolina 28603
USA
Work Phone: 704-433-2283

Wendy B. Marlowe Ph.D.
Cabrini Towers, Suite 610
901 Boren Avenue
Seattle, Washington 98104
USA
Work Phone: 206-623-5217

Joseph D. Matarazzo Ph.D.
Medical Psychology, L351
Oregon Health Sciences University
3181 S.W. Sam Jackson Park Road
Portland, Oregon 97201
USA
Work Phone: 503-225-8594

Ruth G. Matarazzo Ph.D.
Department of Medical Psychology
Oregon Health Sciences University
3181 S.W. Sam Jackson Park Road
Portland, Oregon 97201
USA
Work Phone: 503-494-8594

Catherine A. Mateer Ph.D.
Neuropsychological Services
Good Samaritan Hospital
1322 Third Street, Suite 250
Puyallup, Washington 98371
USA
Work Phone: Unavailable

Charles G. Matthews Ph.D.
Department of Neurology
University of Wisconsin Medical Center
600 North Highland Avenue
Madison, Wisconsin 53792
USA
Work Phone: 608-263-5430

Steven Mattis Ph.D.
RFD3
Indian Hill Road
Bedford, New York 10506
USA
Work Phone: 914-997-5944

Austin J. McSweeny Ph.D.
Department of Psychology
MCO
P.O. Box 10008
Toledo, Ohio 43699
USA
Work Phone: 419-381-3495

Manfred J. Meier Ph.D.
University of Minnesota Health Sciences
P.O. Box 390
Minneapolis, Minnesota 55455
USA
Work Phone: 612-624-2679

Fernando Melendez Ph.D.
2477 Congress Street
San Diego, California 92110
USA
Work Phone: 619-446-6474

John E. Mendoza Ph.D.
3928 South Inwood
New Orleans, Louisiana 70114
USA
Work Phone: 504-589-5235

Allan F. Mirsky Ph.D.*
Room 4C/110
NIMH/Building 10
9000 Rockville Park
Bethesda, Maryland 20205
USA
Work Phone: 301-496-2551

Steven F. Morgan Ph.D.*
Minneapolis Clinic of Neurology
4225 Golden Valley Road
Minneapolis, Minnesota 55422-4297
USA
Work Phone: 612-588-0661

James A. Moses Jr., Ph.D.
Psychology Service (116B)
VA Medical Center
3801 Miranda Avenue
Palo Alto, California 94304
USA
Work Phone: 415-493-5000

Robert F. Newby Ph.D.
628 Crescent Court
Wauwatosa, Wisconsin 53213
USA
Work Phone: 414-778-4588

James C. Norton Ph.D.
ACOSE (114)
Veterans Administration Medical Center
Lexington, Kentucky 40503
USA
Work Phone: 606-233-4511

Raymond A. Parker Ph.D.
14518 26th Avenue Court E
Tacoma, Washington 98445
USA
Work Phone: 206-627-8850

Rolland S. Parker Ph.D.
50 West 96th Street, #9C
New York, New York 10025
USA
Work Phone: 212-222-4543

Oscar A. Parsons Ph.D.
University of Oklahoma Health Science Ctr
P.O. Box 26901
Oklahoma City, Oklahoma 73190
USA
Work Phone: 405-271-5275

Marian B. Patterson Ph.D.
2520 Fairmont Boulevard
Cleveland Heights, Ohio 44106
USA
Work Phone: 216-459-4428

Edward A. Peck III, Ph.D.
31 Maxwell Road
Richmond, Virginia 21226
USA
Work Phone: 804-285-2555

Ralph J. Petrucci Ed. D.
Department of Psychiatry
Temple University Health Science Ctr
3400 North Broad Street
Philadelphia, Pennsylvania 15140
USA
Work Phone: 215-221-3357

George P. Prigatano Ph.D.
Barrow Neurological Institute
350 West Thomas Road
Phoenix, Arizona 85013-4496
USA
Work Phone: 405-271-6876

Arnold D. Purisch Ph.D.
Suite 750
7700 Irvine Center Drive
Irvine, California 92718
USA
Work Phone: 714-753-7711

Robert L. Pusakulich Ph.D.
313 Furnway Cove
Memphis, Tennessee 38117
USA
Work Phone: 901-523-8990

Stephen N. Rao Ph.D.
Section of Neuropsychology
Medical College of Wisconsin
1000 North 42nd Street
Milwaukee, Wisconsin 53226
USA
Work Phone: 414-778-4588

Helen R. Rausch Ph.D.
3464 Lisa Place
Sherman Oaks, California 91403
USA
Work Phone: 213-206-1220

Homer B. Reed Jr., Ph.D.
171 Harrison Avenue
Boston, Massachusetts 02111
USA
Work Phone: 617-956-5725

James C. Reed Ph.D.
83 Old Sudbury Road
Wayland, Massachusetts 01778
USA
Work Phone: 617-358-4691

John M. Rhodes Ph.D.
5801 Osula, N.E., #207
Albuquerque, New Mexico 87109
USA
Work Phone: 505-292-3776

M. Dougla Ris Ph.D.*
Department of Psychiatry/Psychology
Children's Hospital Medical Center
Elland and Bethesda Avenues
Cincinnati, Ohio 45220-2899
USA
Work Phone: 513-559-4336

Steven E. Rothke Ph.D.
Department of Psychology
Rehabilitation Institute of Chicago
345 East Superior Street
Chicago, Illinois 60611
USA
Work Phone: 312-908-6221

Byron P. Rourke Ph.D.
Department of Psychology
University of Windsor
Windsor, Ontario N9B 3P4
Canada
Work Phone: 519-253-4251

Joseph J. Ryan Ph.D.
Psychology Service (116B)
VA Medical Center
Leavenworth, Kansas 66048
USA
Work Phone: 913-688-2000

Paul Satz Ph.D.
4824 Oceanaire Street
Oxnard Shores, California 93035-2835
USA
Work Phone: 213-825-5360

Robert J. Sbordone Ph.D.
Suite 750
7700 Irvine Center Drive
Irvine, California 92718
USA
Work Phone: 714-753-7711

Jeffrey Schaeffer Ph.D.
3829 Benedict Canyon Drive
Sherman Oaks, California 91423
USA
Work Phone: 213-651-4281

Thomas Schenkenberg Ph.D.*
Psychology Service (116B)
VA Medical Center
500 Foothill Boulevard
Salt Lake City, Utah 84148
USA
Work Phone: 801-584-1269

Anne S. Schneider Ph.D.
Nine Ten Medical Place
Suite 210
910 East 26th Street
Minneapolis, Minnesota 55404
USA
Work Phone: 612-879-1660

Melvin L. Schwartz Ph.D.
3286 Villanova Avenue
San Diego, California 92122
USA
Work Phone: 619-455-6271

Rose L. Sherr Ph.D.*
Institute of Rehabilitation
New York University Medical Center
400 East 34th Street
New York, New York 10016
USA
Work Phone: 212-340-6164

Alan D. Shonkoff Ph.D.
Suite 102
2340 Ward Street
Berkeley, California 94705
USA
Work Phone: 415-848-0402

Aaron Smith Ph.D.*
3000 Glazier Way, #150
Ann Arbor, Michigan 48105
USA
Work Phone: 313-764-8445

William G. Snow Ph.D.
Department of Psychology
Sunnybrook Health Science Centre
2075 Bayview Avenue
North York, Ontario M4N 3M5
Canada
Work Phone: 416-480-4438

Walter L. Sobota Ph.D.
343 Tara Drive
Troy, Michigan 48098
USA
Work Phone: 313-493-6200

Gary T. Souheaver Ph.D.
15 Agate Cove
Little Rock, Arkansas 72212
USA
Work Phone: 501-661-1202

Frank J. Spellacy Ph.D.
Department of Psychology
University of Victoria
Victoria, British Columbia V8W 2Y2
Canada
Work Phone: 604-721-8590

Otfried Spreen Ph.D.
Psychology Department
University of Victoria
P.O. Box 1700
Victoria, British Columbia V8W 272
Canada
Work Phone: 604-721-7527

Donald T. Stuss Ph.D.
Rotman Research Institute of Baycrest Centre
3560 Bathurst Street
North York, Ontario M6A 2E1
Canada
Work Phone: 613-737-8179

Jerry J. Sweet Ph.D.
Department of Psychiatry
Evanston Hospital
2650 Ridge Avenue
Evanston, Illinois 60201
USA
Work Phone: 708-570-2686

Frederick W. Theye Ph.D.
Neurosciences Department
Marshfield Clinic
Marshfield, Wisconsin 54449
USA
Work Phone: 715-387-5366

Armin P. Thies Ph.D.
1395 Chapel Street
New Haven, Connecticut 06511
USA
Work Phone: 203-624-8959

Brenda D. Townes Ph.D.
Dept. of Psychiatry/Behavioral Science
University of Washington
Seattle, Washington 98195
USA
Work Phone: 206-223-5923

Daniel Tranel Ph.D.
Department of Neurology
University of Iowa Hospital & Clinics
Iowa City, Iowa 52242
USA
Work Phone: 319-356-2671

Robert G. Tureen Ph.D.
506 Oak Street
Cincinnati, Ohio 45219
USA
Work Phone: 513-221-1100

Robert L. Van Nastright Ph.D.
34 Grafton Crescent, S.W.
Calgary, Alberta T3E 4X1
Canada
Work Phone: 403-229-7959

Nils R. Varney Ph.D.
742 Varney Ph.D.
Iowa City, Iowa 52240
USA
Work Phone: 319-338-0581

Daniel J. Venezia Jr., Ph.D.
852 Bridle Court
Carmel, Indiana 46032
Work Phone: 317-355-5298

Preston J. Walker Ph.D.
c/o Psychology Service
P.O. Box 255
Newtown, Connecticut 06470
USA
Work Phone: 203-426-2531

Marc S. Walter Ph.D.
1480 East Bethany Home, #420
Phoenix, Arizona 85014
USA
Work Phone: 602-248-0019

Roberta F. White Ph.D.
Psychology Service (116B)
VA Medical Center
150 South Huntington Avenue
Boston, Massachusetts 02138
USA
Work Phone: 617-247-5172

Greta N. Wilkening Psy.D.
Department of Neurology
The Children's Hospital
1056 East 19th Avenue
Denver, Colorado 80218
USA
Work Phone: 303-861-6896

Barbara C. Wilson Ph.D.
70 Bayview Avenue
Great Neck, New York 11021
USA
Work Phone: 516-562-3054

Robert S. Wilson Ph.D.
Rush-Presbyterian St. Luke's Medical Ctr.
1653 West Congress Parkway
Chicago, Illinois 60612
USA
Work Phone: 312-942-8043

Ted W. Young Ph.D.
3825 Squaw Valley Circle
Reno, Nevada 89509
USA
Work Phone: Unavailable

James Youngjohn Ph.D.
Suite A202
7125 East Lincoln Drive
Scottsdale, Arizona 85253
USA
Work Phone: 602-948-4784

Allan Yozawitz Ph.D.
5170 Winterton Drive
Fayetteville, New York 13066
USA
Work Phone: 315-473-4980

Richard F. Zapf Ed.D.
25 East Main Street
Georgetown, Maine 01833
USA
Work Phone: 617-352-6135

Philip G. Zerfas Ph.D.
Marshfield Clinic
1000 North Oak Avenue
Marshfield, Wisconsin 54449
USA
Work Phone: 715-387-5366

Kenneth A. Zych Ph.D.
Psychology Service
Madigan Army Medical Center
Tacoma, Washington 88431-5008
USA
Work Phone: 206-967-6404

*Has not paid 1990 membership dues.

Appendix B

Glossary of Neurological and Neuropsychological Terms

A

Abnormal: Maladaptive behavior detrimental to the individual and/or the group.

Absence seizures: Petit mal seizures in children, characterized by brief altered states of consciousness.

Acalculia: Impaired calculation abilities, more often associated with left parietal or occipital lesions.

Achromatopsia: Impaired perception of colors due to cerebral dysfunction. Can be hemianopic or involve both entire visual fields.

Acute alcoholic hallucinosis: State of alcoholic intoxication characterized by hallucinations.

Acute paranoid disorder: Psychoses characterized by transient and changeable paranoid delusions, usually related to an identifiable stressor and transient in nature.

Acute post-traumatic stress disorder: Disorder in which symptoms develop within six months of an extremely traumatic experience instead of entering the recovery state.

Adipsia: A condition in which an individual refuses to drink fluids.

Adjustment disorder with depressed mood: Moderately severe affective disorder behaviorally identical to a dysthymic disorder or depressed phase of a cyclothymic disorder but having an identifiable, though not severe, psychosocial stressor occurring within three months prior to the onset of depression.

Afferent fibers/traits: Data going toward the brain through neuronal pathways from the peripheral area of the central nervous system.

Aggression: Behavior aimed at hurting or destroying someone or something.

Agitation: Marked restlessness and psychomotor excitement.

Agnosia: Defect in object recognition not due to primary sensory system dysfunction.

Agrammatism: Speech deficits characterized by language abbreviation, such as omission of articles, prepositions, and inflectional forms. Language is essentially reduced to substantives.

Agraphia: Disturbances in writing skills (not motor execution). Usually seen with aphasia.

Akathisia: A general motor restlessness together with elevated inner tension, subjectively reported by the patient.

Akinesia: Inability to move due to brain dysfunction.

Alien Hand Syndrome: Also termed the *"Dr. Strangelove effect,"* intermanual conflict between the two hands is seen, with patient's learning to use their "obedient" hand to control the alien hand. Contralateral supplementary motor area (SMA) and corpus callosum lesions have been implicated.

Alexia without agraphia: Inability to read in the absence of other language deficits.

Alexia: Inability to read due to brain dysfunction. Refers to total loss of disability due to a brain lesion, typically located in the posterior cerebral cortex.

Allesthesia: Sensation of being touched on the side ipsilateral to a lesion when contralateral stimulation was, in fact, presented.

Alpha rhythm: A brain potential that occurs during relaxed wakefulness, especially at the back of the head; frequency 8-12 Hz.

Alzheimer's Disease (AD): A degenerative disease characterized by the presence of neurofibrillary tangles and senile plaques. The disease is progressive in that it starts with memory and affect problems, then goes on to speech and motor problems, and eventually to an immobile and confused bedridden status. The disease typically first occurs in the late forties or early fifties and results in death.

Amblyopia: Reduced visual acuity not caused by optical or retinal impairment.

Amenorrhea: The absence of menses.

Amnestic Syndrome: Inability to remember events more than a few minutes after they have occurred coupled with the ability to recall remote events.

Amorphosynthesis: Loss of ability to synthesize more than a few properties of a stimulus. Multiple sensory stimuli cannot be processed simultaneously. Typically caused by parietal lobe dysfunction.

Amusia: A temporal lobe deficit associated with inability or reduced skill in perception of tonal patterns, individual tones, singing or humming to a rhythmical pattern, or even enjoying music.

Amygdala: A structure of the limbic system associated with flight/fight and other primitive responses. Located at the base of the temporal lobe.

Analgesia: Loss of sensitivity to pain.

Anarithmetria: Impaired primary calculation skills due to brain damage. Left hemisphere lesions are typically implicated.

Anergia: Decreased or absent motivation or drive.

Anesthesia: Loss of sensation.

Aneurysm: A dilation or bulging of a blood vessel which fills with blood.

Angiogram: A technique for examining brain structure in intact humans by taking x-rays after special dyes are injected into cerebral blood vessels. Inferences about adjacent tissue can be made by examining the outline of the principal blood vessels.

Angiography: X-rays of the head subsequent to injection of a radiopaque contrast material into a major artery. Designed to produce enhanced pictures of the cerebral vasculature.

Angular gyrus: A cortical convolution located in the parietal lobe, associated with speech functions.

Anomia: Inability to name objects due to brain dysfunction.

Anomic aphasia: A fluent aphasia characterized by difficulty in naming objects to confrontation. Comprehension and articulation may be unimpaired.

Anosmia: Loss of ability to smell.

Anosodiaphoria: Unconcern over, but admission of an actual neurological impairment. See also *Anton's Syndrome*.

Anosognosia: Denial of those effected with neglect syndrome that their paretic extremity belongs to them.

Anterior aphasias: Primarily indicating a left frontal lesion, these include Broca's aphasia, aphemia, transcortical motor aphasia, and supplemental motor area (SMA) disturbance.

Anterior cerebral artery (ACA): One of the two major vascular networks of the frontal lobes, the ACA and its branches feed the medial aspects of the anterior portion of the brain.

Anterior pituitary: The anterior lobe of the pituitary gland which secretes tropic hormones; also called *adenophpophysis*.

Anterograde amnesia: Inability to recall life events from the time of traumatic injury. Inability to learn and poor short-term memory are associated features.

Anton's Syndrome: See also *anosognosia*. Adamant denial of blindness often associated with bilateral posterior CVA.

Apathetico-akinetico-abulic behavior: Produced by massive damage to the prefrontal areas, among others. This syndrome is characterized by low drive and reduced motor output. Ongoing behavior may be disorganized. The effector aspect of action seems to be impaired producing what has been termed the "pathological inertia of existing stereotypes."

Aphagia: Refusal to eat, often related to damage to the lateral hypothalamus.

Aphasia: Impairment in language understanding and/or production due to brain injury.

Aphemia: A poorly articulated, slow, hypophonic, breathy speech with no syntax deficits. Usually follows initial mutism and is associated with Broca's area lesions, or a subcortical undercutting of Area 44.

Apoplexy: A sudden loss of consciousness, followed by paralysis resulting from cerebral hemorrhage, or blocking of an artery of the brain by an embolus or thrombus.

Apperceptive visual agnosia: The ability to synthesize or integrate visual input. Awareness of discrete parts may be intact.

Apraxia: Refers to impaired goal-directed motor behavior in individuals with unimpaired comprehension and primary motor skills (e.g., coordination, strength).

Apraxia of speech: Known also as *verbal apraxia* or *Broca's aphasia*. Speech movement/articulation problems may include (1) articulation errors, (2) phoneme substitution, (3) greater latency of response, (4) greater trouble with initial than subsequent phonemes, (5) no major vocal musculature problems (6) sparse output, (7) poor melody, and (8) articulation is with much effort.

Apraxic agraphia: Deficit in forming graphemes when writing to dictation or spontaneously. Lesions are in the parietal lobe contralateral to the dominant (writing) hand.

Apraxic agraphia without apraxia: Preserved oral spelling with illegible graphemes in spontaneous and dictated writing. Normal praxis is apparent including ability to hold/use a writing instrument. Typically associated with parietal lobe lesions.

Aprosodias: Deficits in the comprehension and expression of affect and emotion, traditionally associated with right hemisphere dysfunction.

Aqueduct: A canal for the conduction of a liquid; the cerebral aqueduct of Sylvius connects the third and the fourth ventricles of the brain.

Arachnoid space: Allows for cerebrospinal fluid to move about the cerebrum. Filled with fibroid matter and is considered one of the three layers of the meninges.

Arteriovenous malformation (AVM): Involving the frontal lobe preferentially and focally, AVMs are usually unrecognized until one or more episodes have occurred. Subsequent attacks by AVM hemorrhage widens the area of deficit.

Asphyxia: Unconsciousness owing to interference with the oxygenation of the blood.

Assertiveness training: A behavior therapy technique for helping individuals become more self-assertive in interpersonal relationships.

Association areas: Part of the cortex next to the motor or sensory cortex, involving an overlap of functions. Allows for integration of data; damage causes patterned rather than specific deficits.

Associative visual agnosia: Inability to visually recognize objects with ability to copy, draw, or match to sample intact.

Astereognosis: Inability to identify objects by touch in spite of intact appreciation of tactile sensation. Also called *tactile agnosia*.

Asthenia: Weakness.

Ataxia: Muscular coordination and balance problems due to brain dysfunction. A loss of the power of muscular coordination. Impairment in the direction, extent, and rate of muscular movement; often due to cerebellar pathology.

Athetosis: Slow, involuntary, twisting movements of the arms and legs. May occur either during movement or when at rest. Associated with lesions of the cortex and subcortex (especially globus pallidus and thalamus).

Atrophy: A wasting or diminution in the size of a part of the body or brain.

Attention deficit disorder: Maladaptive behavior in children characterized by impulsivity, excessive motor activity, and an ability to focus attention for appropriate periods of time; also called hyperactive syndrome or hyperkinetic reaction.

Auditory cortex: A region of the temporal lobe that receives input from the medial geniculate nucleus.

Auditory agnosia: Impaired hearing due to cerebral dysfunction with intact receptive abilities, as measured by audiometry or other means.

Auditory affective agnosia: Impaired ability to recognize or comprehend affectively intoned speech due to a cerebral disorder.

Auditory sound agnosia: Impaired ability to recognize nonspeech sounds due to cerebral dysfunction.

Automated assessment: Psychological test interpretation by electronic computer or some other mechanical means

Automatism: Producing without effort or delay material learned by rote in childhood or for a given temporal period (e.g., alphabet, number series). Errors reflect attentional disturbances; non-acute condition-related errors may indicate significant memory dysfunction.

Autonomic nervous system: Part of the peripheral nervous system that supplies neural connections to glands and to smooth muscles of internal organs. Composed of two divisions (sympathetic and parasympathetic) that act in opposite fashion.

Autotopagnosia: Disorientation of personal space. Typically associated with left frontal lesions and aphasic signs. The subject is typically assessed for ability to touch, name, or imitate the examiner in touching body parts. Typically associated with parietal lobe damage.

B

Balint's Syndrome: A syndrome consisting of (1) oculomotor apraxia, or difficulty shifting focus from a near to a distant stimulus, (2) optic ataxia, shown by impaired visually guided movements, and (3) impaired visual attention in the absence of general attentional deficits, with initial random gaze until a stimulus is fixated upon.

Ballism: Uncontrollable violent tossing of the limbs due to basal ganglia dysfunction.

Ballistic: Classes of rapid muscular movements thought to be organized or programmed by the cerebellum. Contrast with ramp.

Basal ganglia: Forebrain nuclei including those in the amygdala, caudate nucleus, claustrum, globus pallidus, and putamen.

Basilar artery: An artery formed by the fusion of the vertebral arteries; its branches supply blood to the brain stem and to posterior portions of the cerebral hemispheres.

Behavioral teratology: Impairments in behavior produced by early exposure to toxic substances.

Binocular disparity: The slight difference between the views from the two eyes, important in depth perception.

Bitemporal hemianopsia: Optic chiasm damage resulting in visual field loss in both temporal (as opposed to nasal) areas.

Blind spot: A place through which blood vessels enter the retina. Because there are no receptors in this region, light striking it cannot be seen.

Blindsight: Denial of recognition in the face of previous correct recognition and stimulus responses.

Blood-brain barrier: The mechanisms that make the movement of substances from capillaries into brain cells more difficult than exchanges in other body organs, thus affording the brain a greater protection from exposure to some substances found in the blood.

Body schema: Body image.

Bradycardia: Abnormal slowness of the heart or pulse.

Bradykinesia: Motor slowing.

Brain stem: Thalamus, hypothalamus, ganglia, midbrain, hindbrain, and associated structures.

Brain stem reticular formation: Part of the brain stem involved in arousal.

Broca's aphasia: An expressive speech disorder with relatively intact auditory comprehension. A nonfluent speech is exhibited that is slow, labored, dysarthric, incomplete, and concrete. Agrammatism consists of missing grammatical words and inflectional endings. Considered an anterior aphasia.

Broca's area: An area in the frontal region of the left hemisphere involved in the production of speech.

Brown-Peterson distractor technique: Counting backwards by twos or threes upon presentation of a verbal or nonverbal stimulus. Rehearsal is prevented by the counting.

Buccolinguofacial apraxia: An oral apraxia affecting voluntary movements of the larynx, pharynx, tongue, lips, and related suborgans in which simple, automatic movements are intact. Commanded tasks may yield deficits (e.g., no swallowing, laughing) in the presence of noncommanded, contextual responses (e.g., swallowing food after eating, smiling).

C

Capgras Syndrome: Involves the reduplication of relatives, friends, possessions, and the like, and is often viewed as a psychiatric, as opposed to neurological, problem. The target person, almost always a close relative, is considered an imposter.

Catastrophic reaction: Intensely negative but temporary emotional reaction, associated with left hemisphere lesions. Often occurs when subjects are informed of their limitations or shortcomings, in response to task demands. A heightened sensitivity to one's limitations.

Caudal: An anatomical term meaning toward the tail end. Opposed to rostral.

Caudate nucleus: One of the basal ganglia with a long extension or tail.

Central deafness: Hearing impairments related to lesions in auditory pathways or centers, including sites in the brain stem, thalamus, or cortex.

Central nervous system (CNS): The portion of the nervous system that includes the brain and the spinal cord.

Central sulcus: Known also as the *Fissure of Rolando*, this sulcus divides the anterior from the posterior areas of the brain (frontal and parietal).

Cephalic: An anatomical term referring to the head end. Also called *rostral.*

Cerebellar cortex: The outer surface of the cerebellum.

Cerebellar fits: Not true seizures, these movements consist of episodes of decerebrate rigidity. Typically associated with large midline cerebellar lesions.

Cerebellar Syndrome: Due to a lesion in the cerebellum, ambulation is unsteady with side-to-side swaying. The patient's equilibrium is adversely affected.

Cerebellum: A structure located at the back of the brain, dorsal to the pons; it is involved in the central regulation of movement.

Cerebral contusion: A brain bruise. Refers to superficial damage to gyri or other crests of the cortical convolutions.

Cerebral cortex: The outer (bark) cortex of the cerebral hemispheres which consists largely of nerve cell bodies and their branches.

Cerebral hemispheres: The right and left halves of the forebrain.

Cerebrospinal fluid: The fluid made and located in the cerebral ventricles.

Cervical: Pertaining to the neck region.

Cheiro-oral: Refers to the simultaneous twitching of the thumb and same-sided corner of the mouth. Occurs in epilepsy due to close proximity of motor execution zones for these body parts (i.e., the motor homonculus has its thumb in its mouth).

Chiasma: A crossing; specifically, the crossing of the optic nerve fibers from the medial halves of the retinae.

Chlorpromazine: An antipsychotic drug, one of the class of phenothiazines.

Cholinergic: Refers to the cells that use acetylcholine as their synaptic transmitter.

Choreic movements: Uncontrollable, brief, and forceful muscular movements related to basal ganglia dysfunction.

Cingulate bodies: Limbic system tissue above or superior to the corpus callosum.

Cingulum: A region of medial cerebral cortex lying dorsal to the corpus callosum. Also called *cingulate cortex.*

Circadian rhythms: Behavioral, biochemical, and physiological fluctuations during a 24-hour period.

Circle of Willis: A structure at the base of the brain formed by the joining of the carotid and basilar arteries.

Circulocution: Often seen in fluent aphasia, the substitution of an incorrect word for another word. The substitution may itself demand a specific but unobtainable word, thus producing a convoluted output.

Cistern: A closed space serving as a reservoir for fluid.

Cochlea: A snail-shaped structure in the inner ear which contains the primary receptors for hearing.

Coma: A state of profound unconsciousness from which one cannot be aroused.

Coma vigil: Immobility and unresponsiveness with eyes open and moving, associated with posteromedial-inferior frontal and/or hypothalamic damage.

Common carotid arteries: Arteries that ascend the left and right sides of the neck. The branch that enters the brain is called the *internal carotid artery*.

Complex cortical cells: Cells in the visual cortex that respond best to a bar of a particular width and direction anywhere within a particular area of the visual field.

Complex partial seizures: Epileptic seizures in which consciousness is altered (complex) and are restricted or at least arise from a circumscribed area of the brain (partial).

Computer axial tomogram: A technique for examining brain structure in intact humans through a computer analysis of x-ray absorption at several positions around the head. This technique affords a virtual direct view of the brain.

Conduction aphasia: A constellation of behaviors produced by a lesion in the white matter fibers connecting the posterior/anterior portions of the brain (near the arcuate fasciculus). A severe repetition deficit is apparent relative to good auditory comprehension and expression of speech.

Confabulation: Production of bizarre, false, or unverifiable verbal/written responses, usually in association with amnesia. A close correlation exists between confabulatory tendencies and impairment in self-correction.

Congenital: Existing at or before birth.

Consolidation: A state of memory formation in which information is short-term or intermediate-term memory is transferred to long-term memory.

Constructional disorders: Deficits in constructional tasks (e.g., drawing, assembling) in which the spatial form of the target object may be lost. Associated with pathology of the nondominant (nonspeech) hemisphere.

Contralateral: Situated on, or pertaining to, the opposite side.

Contrecoup: Refers to the contusion (bruise) in the area opposite the point of impact (coup).

Coronal (plane): The plane dividing the body or brain into front and back parts. Also called *frontal* or *transverse*.

Corpus callosum: Intracerebral white matter connecting the right and left cerebral hemispheres.

Cortical deafness: See also *cortical auditory disorder*. Difficulty recognizing both verbal and nonverbal stimuli due to cerebral dysfunction. Most often associated with a cardiovascular accident.

Cranial nerves: Originating from the brain, these are 12 pairs of nerves which transmit motor and/or sensory neuronal impulses to and from peripheral central nervous system sites.

Creutzfeldt-Jakob Disease: A rare, transmittable (i.e., through virus which has a two-year incubation) dementia with a relatively short clinical course (nine-month average). Ten percent of cases may be inherited. Anxiety and memory loss first appear. Myoclonic jerking appears in conjunction with motor neurocerebellar, basal ganglion, or pyramidal tract lesions.

Crossed aphasia: Aphasic symptoms occurring, usually temporarily, in right-handed person with a right hemisphere lesion.

Cyanosis: A dark, purplish coloration of the skin and the mucous membrane caused by deficient oxygenation of the blood.

Cyclothymic disorder: Mild affective disorder characterized by extreme mood swings of nonpsychotic intensity.

Cytoarchitectonics: The study of anatomical divisions of the brain based on the kinds of spacing of cells and distribution of axons.

D

Dacrystic epilepsy: Seizures where crying is the predominant ictal event.

Delirium tremens: Acute delirium associated with prolonged alcoholism; characterized by intense anxiety, tremors, and hallucinations.

Delusion: Firm belief opposed to reality but maintained in spite of strong evidence to the contrary.

Delusion of persecution: False belief that one is being mistreated or interfered with by one's enemies. Often found in schizophrenia.

Delusion system: An internally coherent, systematized pattern of delusional beliefs.

Dependent personality: A personality disorder marked by lack of self-confidence and feelings of acute panic or discomfort at having to be alone.

Depersonalization disorder: A dissociative neurotic disorder, usually occurring in adolescence, in which individuals lose their sense of self and feel unreal or displaced to a different location.

Depressive disorder: Neurotic reaction characterized by persistent dejection and discouragement.

Depressive neurosis: Depression of intermediate severity with little or no evidence of personality breakdown or loss of contact with reality.

Depressive stupor: Extreme degree of depression characterized by marked psychomotor underactivity.

Desensitization: Therapeutic process by means of which reactions to traumatic experiences are reduced in intensity by repeatedly exposing the individual to them in mild form, either in reality or in fantasy.

Dextral: Refers to right-handedness. Opposed to sinistral, or left-handedness.

Dialysis dementia: Chronic, degenerative intellectual problems (aphasia, memory difficulties), seizures, and motor signs (e.g., facial grimacing) seen occasionally as the result of long-term dialysis. The pathogenesis is unknown although the accumulation of aluminum in the brain has been implicated.

Dialysis disequilibrium syndrome: A consequence of the dialysis procedure itself, encephalopathy characterized by development of intermittent slowed speech, stuttering and word finding problems. Progression to dyspraxia, memory loss, concentration problems, and (occasionally) psychosis. Shifts in sodium and potassium are associated with the disorder.

Diaschisis: Reduction of neuronal activity in brain sites outside the immediate perimeter of the lesion. Associated with acute, focal conditions.

Diathesis: A predisposition or vulnerability toward developing a given disorder.

Diathesis-stress model: View of abnormal behavior as the result of stress operating on an individual with a biological, psychosocial, or sociocultural predisposition toward developing a specific disorder.

Dichotic: Refers to studies where different stimuli are simultaneously presented to both ears, eyes, or tactilely to the subject.

Diencephalon: The central core of the brain, which together with the telencephalon, forms the cerebrum. Consists of the thalamus, subthalamus, hypothalamus, and epithalamus.

Dilantin: An anticonvulsant medication often used in controlling epileptic seizures.

Diplopia: Double vision, due to eye muscle imbalance, metabolic disturbances, or other causes.

Disconnection syndromes: Disrupted neuronal transmission through the white matter that cut cortical pathways, thus disconnecting a cortical area from the rest of the brain. Corpus callosum disconnections are the most dramatic.

Disinhibition Syndrome: Inability to stop actions or impulses once initiated. Often attributed to frontal system deficits in exerting an inhibitory effect on on-going mental or behavioral processes.

Disorganized schizophrenia: Subtype representing most severe disintegration of personality and poor prognosis for recovery; characterized by marked incoherence, silly or inappropriate responses.

Dissociation: Separation or "isolation" of mental processes in such a way that they become split off from the main personality or lose their normal thought-affect relationships.

Dissociative disorder: Psychoneurotic disorder characterized by amnesia, fugue, somnambulism or multiple personality.

Distal: An anatomical term meaning toward the periphery or toward the end of a limb.

Diural: Daily. Divergence: A system of neural connections that allows one cell to send signals to many other cells.

Dopamine (DA): A neurotransmitter produced mainly in the basal forebrain and diencephalon that is active in the basal ganglia, the olfactory system, and limited parts of the cerebral cortex.

Dopaminergic: Refers to cells that use dopamine as their synaptic transmitter.

Dorsal: An anatomical term meaning toward the back of the body or the top of the brain; opposite of ventral.

Dorsal root: Root at the back of the spinal cord.

Double-dissociation: Differential effects of lesions, allowing for comparison of both independent and dependent variables. Lesion X causes X' but not Y, whereas lesion Y causes Y' but not X.

Double tracking: The simultaneous operation of two mental operations. Digits backward on the Wechsler Adult Intelligence Scale (WAIS), for example, calls for memory and reversing operations at the same time.

Down's Syndrome: A form of mental retardation associated with an extra chromosome.

Dura: First or outermost layer of the three layers of meninges which cover the brain.

Dynamic formation: An integrated evaluation of a patient's traits, attitudes, conflicts, and symptoms that attempts to explain the individual's problem.

Dysarthria: Refers to speech disorders based on peripheral motor deficits. The quality of speech is affected, as in hypernasality, breathy phonation, and stridor (flaccid paretic dysarthria), slow, low pitch, harsh and difficulty phonation (spastic paretic dysarthria) or explosive speech (ataxic or cerebellar dysarthria).

Dysfluency: Difficulty in generating words.

Dysmetropia: Defects in the visual appreciation of object size discrimination. Also called *past-pointing phenomenon* (i.e., in finger-to-nose exam). Typically associated with cerebellar lesions.

Dysnomia: Word-finding disability. Shown by failure to correctly name objects or by choosing words that are "off center."

Dysphagia: Difficulty swallowing.

Dysthymic disorder: Moderately severe affective disorder characterized by extended periods of nonpsychotic depression and brief periods of normal moods.

Dystonia: Prolonged abnormal posture as a consequence of involuntary muscle tension. Often a side-effect of antipsychotic (neuroleptic) medication.

E

Echopraxia: The mimicking of other's motor movements. Indicates that extant motor problems are not due to lack of inactivity.

Edema: An abnormal accumulation of clear, watery fluid in the lymph spaces of the tissues.

Electroencephalography (EEG): The recording and study of gross electrical activity of the brain recorded from large electrodes placed on the scalp.

Encephalitis: A generalized viral infection of the brain's neurons or glial cell bodies.

Encephalomalacia: Cerebral tissue softening.

Encephalopathy: Brain degeneration.

Encoding: A process of memory formation in which the information entering sensory channels is placed into short-term memory.

Episodic Dyscontrol Syndrome: Totally unprovoked violence associated with an aura, consisting of rising anxiety, headaches, illusions, numbness, drowsiness, and hyperacusis. The attack lasts 15 minutes to two hours and is very violent, often directed towards property or persons. May be due to temporal-limbic structure dysfunction. Associated features include hypersensitivity to alcohol, multiple traffic accidents, and sexual impulsiveness, the last rising to the level of forensic concern.

Episodic memory: Recall for events in one's life and experiences. It is therefore unique and anchored to distinct points in time and space.

Exner's area: Formally seen as a *frontal writing center*, located at the base of the second frontal convolution. Lesions in this area produce agraphia.

Extinction: One of a stimulus pair simultaneously presented to different parts of the body, visual fields, etc., is not perceived.

Extinction to double simultaneous stimulation: Failure to report the stimulus.

Extracerebral: Extrinsic or outside of the brain hemispheres, as for example, between the skull and the brain on one of the three layers of meninges.

Extrapyramidal system: A motor system that includes the basal ganglia and some closely related brain stem structures.

Extrinsic: Originating outside of the part where it is found or upon which it acts.

F

Face-hand test: Touching the fact simultaneously with another body part, particularly same-sided. Suppression or displacement of the more peripheral stimulus indicates possible parietal lobe dysfunction.

Finger agnosia: Inability to identify the fingers of one's own hand, or those of another person, due to brain damage.

Flaccid: Relaxed, flabby, soft.

Fluent aphasia: Speech difficulty with incomprehension, jargon speech, and other signs such as lack of awareness. Often associated with left posterior cerebral lesions. Non-fluent aphasia is associated with left anterior cerebral lesions and almost always involves expressive speech deficits.

Forebrain: The frontal division of the neural tube that contains the cerebral hemispheres, the thalamus, and the hypothalamus. Also called the *prosencephalon*.

Fornix: A fiber tract that runs from the hippocampus to mammillary bodies.

Frontal amnesia: Difficulty in switching from one set of memory traces to another in the face of intact operating memory. "Forgetting to recall," as in disregarding instructions is an illustration.

Frontal gait disturbance: See *magnetic apraxia* and *utilization behavior*.

Frontal psychosurgery: Includes leukotomies aimed at severing frontal-thalamic connections, orbital undercutting, for example, by placement of radioactive pellets in the orbital tissues, cingulomotomy, stereotactic destruction of focal sites, and topectomy, ablation of selected frontal areas.

Frontal "release" signs: These are primitive reflexes which long have been considered frontal signs. The grasp reflex is associated with midline frontal pathology. Frontal system problems are indicated by rooting, sucking, and snout reflexes indicating a brain stem-diencephalic lesion.

Fugue: A neurotic dissociative disorder which entails a loss of memory accompanied by actual physical flight from one's present life situation to a new environment or less threatening former one.

Functional psychoses: Severe mental disorders attributed primarily to psychological stress.

Fundus: The bottom of a sac or hollow organ; that farthest removed from the opening.

Future shock: A condition brought about when social change proceeds so rapidly that the individual cannot cope with it adequately.

G

Ganglion: A collection of nerve cell bodies. Also called a *nucleus*.

Ganglion cells: Cells in the retina whose axons form the optic nerve.

General paresis: A progressive mental deterioration due to syphilitic invasion of the central nervous system. Changes include deterioration of the entire range of mental functions due to brain atrophy. A loss of neurons with an increase in microglial cells and astrocytes is seen.

Generalized seizures: Epileptic seizures that arise from pathology at brain sites that project to widespread regions of the brain. These seizures involve loss of consciousness and symmetrical involvement of body musculature.

Gerstmann's Syndrome: The symptom cluster of acalculia, agraphia, left-right spatial disorientation, and finger agnosia. Traditionally considered to involve the left parieto-occipital region of brain.

Glabellar tap sign: The subject is tapped lightly just above and between the eyebrows in order to see whether blinking will normally and quickly habituate. Parkinson's patients will continue to blink with each tap.

Glial cells: Nonneural brain cells that provide structural, nutritional, and other supports to the brain. Also called *glia* or *neuroglia*.

Glioblastoma (multiforma): A neoplasm arising from the glial cells, characterized by high degree of lethality and malignancy.

Gliomas: Brain tumors resulting from the aberrant production of glial cells.

Global alexia: Inability to read letters of words.

Global aphasia: Severe comprehension and articulation deficits associated with a large lesion of the entire perisylvian area of the frontal, temporal, and parietal lobes. Prognosis is grim.

Global steropis: Depth perception in the presence of ambiguous stimulus forms. Presumed to be mediated by right hemisphere and is differentiated from a stereoacuity.

Glossopharyngeal nerve: A cranial nerve which serves taste receptors in the tongue.

Golgi tendon organs: Receptors located in tendons that send impulses to the central nervous system when a muscle contracts.

Grand mal seizures: A type of generalized epileptic seizure that involves nerve cells firing in synchrony. These seizures cause loss of consciousness and sudden muscle contraction.

Gyri: The ridged or raised portions of a convoluted brain surface. Contrast with *sulci*.

H

Hematoma: An accumulation of blood within the meninges of the brain. Most often caused by head trauma.

Hemiparesis: Weakness on one side of the body.

Hemiplegia: Weakness or paralysis of one side of the body.

Hemispatial neglect: Neglect of the hemisphere contralateral to a lesion. Also termed visuospatial agnosia or neglect, unilateral spatial neglect, or hemispatial agnosia.

Hippocampus: Actively concerned with memory consolidation functions, located in anterior temporal lobe.

Histrionic personality: Personality pattern characterized by excitability, emotional instability, and self-dramatization.

Homonymous hemianopsia: Loss of one half of the visual field in each eye, right or left sided (e.g., right temporal/left nasal; right nasal/left temporal).

Homonymous field cuts: Loss of vision in the same part of both visual fields.

Huntington's Disease: A progressive, hereditary, dementing condition that affects the basal ganglia with atrophy of the frontal lobes and corpus callosum. Involuntary and spasmodic movements are associated features, along with declining cognitive and personality/social skills.

Hyperacusis: The perception of sounds as abnormally loud.

Hypergraphia: Overwriting, as when too many words are written in response to task demands.

Hypnosis: Trancelike mental state induced in a cooperative subject by suggestion.

Hypnotherapy: Use of hypnosis in psychotherapy.

Hypnotic regression: Process by which a subject is brought to relive, under hypnosis, early forgotten or repressed experiences.

Hypochondriacal delusions: Delusions concerning various horrible disease conditions, such as the belief that one's brain is turning to dust.

Hypochondriasis: Condition dominated by preoccupation with bodily processes and fear of specific diseases.

Hypophonia: Lowered voice volume. Contrasted to aphonia, or total lack of voice. The most common cause of both disorders is laryngitis.

Hypothalamus: Involved in homeostatic, motivational activities such as sexual activity, eating, drinking, and emotions. This structure is located in the limbic system, dorsal to the thalamus.

Hypothermia: Low temperature; especially a state of low body temperature induced for the purpose of decreasing metabolic activities and need for oxygen.

Hypotonia: The state of muscles tiring easily. Typically associated with cerebellar lesions.

Hypoxia: Refers to insufficient blood oxygen to the brain. Contrasted to anoxia which refers to a total lack of blood oxygen to brain structures.

Hysterical amnesia: Loss of memory for emotional/psychological reasons without a organic basis.

Hysterical disorder: Disorder characterized by involuntary psychogenic dysfunction of motor, sensory, cognitive, or visceral processes.

I

Iconic memory: A very brief type of memory that stores the sensory impression of a scene.

Ideographic methodology: A method of study emphasizing the individual case and the uniqueness of each personality.

Ideomotor apraxia: Simple execution of motor responses (e.g., hitchhiking sign, salute, whistling) is impaired or absent in the presence of intact comprehension. Implies deficits in planning and initiation. Typically associated with left hemisphere lesions.

Idiopathic epilepsy: A seizure disorder of unknown origin. Opposed to symptomatic epilepsy whose cause is known.

Illusion: Misinterpretation of sensory data; false perception.

Inattention: Decreased/absent awareness of events occurring on the side of the body contralateral to the hemispheric lesion.

Indifference reaction: Denial, unawareness, or minimizing psychological/neuropsychological deficits, traditionally associated with right hemisphere lesions. Inappropriate elevated affect may be present.

Infarct: Impoverished or dead brain tissue associated with vascular occlusions.

Inferior colliculus: The auditory center in the midbrain; it receives input from the brain stem auditory nuclei and sends output to the medial geniculate nucleus.

Infundibulum: A funnel-shaped structure or passage. The stalk of the pituitary gland.

Intention tremor: Also called *kinetic tremor*, this anomaly occurs at the end of a movement. Contrasted to "resting" tremor which occurs when no movement is present.

Interictal: Refers to behaviors/events between the time seizures occur. Adversive personality traits (e.g., irritability, obsessional traits) are associated features.

Intermediate coup lesions: Scattered areas of focal tissue damage in line with the point of trauma impact (coup) and possible terminal point of the damage (countrecoup).

Intermediate-term memory: A form of memory lasting longer than short-term, and requiring no rehearsal, but not lasting as long as long-term memory.

Internal carotid artery: See *common carotid artery*.

Intracerebral: Intrinsic or inside of the brain hemispheres, usually referring to brain dysfunction caused by neoplasms or cardiovascular accidents.

Intracranial steal: Complicating the finding of an arteriovenous malformation (AVM) location, here blood is shunted away from normal brain tissue to the AVM site. Thus, the unaffected area may show evidences of neuropsychological deficit.

Intravascular: Within a vessel or vessels.

Ipsilateral: Same side; homolateral; opposed to contralateral (opposite side), bilateral (both sides), unilateral (one side).

Ischemia: Cut-off of blood flow to an area of the brain or body organ.

Ischemic infarction: A disruption of blood flow (infarction) creating dead or damaged tissue (infarct), resulting more from impaired or absent blood flow rather than from insufficient nutrients in the blood.

J

Jargon aphasia: A form of paraphasias which have no meaning to those who hear the sounds.

K

Kinesthetic: Pertaining to muscle sense, or to the sense by which muscular movement, weight, and position are perceived.

Kinesthetic afferentiation: Gathering data concerning one's own current muscle tone, body position, oral status, etc. Considered a function of the posterior cerebral association areas.

Kinetic afferentiation: Integration of input from parietal-occipital tertiary zones, basal ganglia, and premotor areas producing sequential and integrated actions. Depends initially on kinesthetic afferentiation.

Kinetic apraxia: Disorganized transition of single movements (see also apraxis, echopraxia, apraxia of speech). Associated with lesions in basal ganglia-premotor areas. Subordination of movements to intentions is impaired.

Kluver-Bucy Syndrome: A condition manifested by hyperorality, hypersexuality, labile emotions, and inability to form new memories. Associated with temporal lobe or limbic system lesions.

Korsakoff's psychosis: A progressive dementia considered subcortical in focus and associated with a nutritional deficiency of vitamin B1 (thiamine). The condition is considered secondary to alcohol abuse. This psychosis is usually characterized by disorientation, gross memory defects, and confabulation.

L

Labile memory: An early state of memory formation during which formation of a memory can be easily disrupted by conditions that influence brain activity.

Lacunar state: Multiple but small infarctions in the subcortical regions leaving lacunae. One of the end stages of hypertensive cerebrovascular conditions.

Lateral: An anatomical term meaning toward the side; opposite of medial.

Lateral hypothalamus (LH): A hypothalamic region involved in facilitating eating.

Lateral inhibition: A phenomenon produced by interconnected neurons that inhibit their neighbors, producing contrast at the edges of the stimulus.

Lexical agraphia: Impaired ability to spell irregular or unknown words with an intact ability to speak regular words. Associated with lesions in the parieto-occipital lobule.

Limb-kinetic apraxia: Complex/serial movement impairment in the presence of intact simple, repetitive movement. Brodmann areas 4 and 6 are implicated in almost all cases.

Limbic system: Interconnected and primarily subcortical structures which are involved in emotional responses and memory.

Literal paraphasia: Production of off-target sounds with effortless articulation. Associated with postrolandic lesions.

Localization of function: The concept that specific brain regions are responsible for various types of experience, behavior, and psychological processes.

Locked-in syndrome: Also known as de-efferentiation, this is due to bilateral pontine lesions and characterized by aphonia and quadriplegia. The patient is aware of his or her surroundings, but has no control of voluntary motor movements except for eyes.

Long-term memory: An enduring form of memory lasting for weeks, months, or years.

Lumen: The space in the interior of a tubular structure such as an artery or the intestine.

M

Magnetic apraxia: Compulsive exploration of the immediate environment in the usual presence of intact comprehension skills. Forced hand grasping with difficulty "letting go" is an example. Prefrontal, mesial, and contralateral lesions are implicated.

Major affective disorders: Category of affective disorders in which a biological defect or other aberration renders a person liable to experience episodes of a more or less severe affective disorder.

Major depression (unipolar disorder): A severe affective disorder in which only depressive episodes occur.

Malaise: A feeling of general discomfort or uneasiness; an out-of-sorts feeling, often the first indication of an infection.

Mammillary bodies: Paired nuclei at the base of the brain slightly posterior to the pituitary stalk.

Manic-depressive psychoses: Older term denoting a group of psychotic disorders characterized by prolonged periods of excitement and over-activity (mania) or by periods of depression and underactivity (depression) or by alternation of the two.

Masked fascies: An unblinking, bland, expressionless stare. Typically seen in Parkinson's Disease.

Masochism: Sexual variant in which an individual obtains sexual gratification through infliction of pain.

Medial: An anatomical term meaning toward the middle; opposite lateral.

Medial geniculate nucleus: A nucleus in the thalamus that receives input from the inferior colliculus and sends output to the auditory cortex.

Medulla: The lowest part of the brain stem, also called *myelencephalon*.

Melokinetic apraxia: Deficit in speech, skill, and coordination of movement, usually confined to a small muscle group. Unilateral and contralateral to lesion in premotor area.

Meninges: Thin membranes on the brain — dura mater, pia mater, and arachnoid, which provide a venous drainage system.

Meningioma: Neoplastic growth arising from the meninges.

Meningitis: Inflammatory disease of the meninges with associated signs of the fever, headache, and stiff neck.

Mesencephalon: The midbrain.

Metencephalon: A subdivision of the hindbrain that includes the cerebellum and the pons.

Midbrain: The middle division of the brain. Also called the *mesencephalon*.

Middle cerebral artery (MCA): The MCA and its branches is one of the two major vascular networks of the frontal lobes. The lateral convexity is fed by anterior branches of the MCA.

Misoplegia: A type of unilateral inattention where the lesioned individual, usually hemiplegic, exhibits a strong dislike for the affected limbs or portions of the body. Intense hatred resulting in self-mutilation may be expressed.

Motor aprosody: Inability to sing or to change pitch or voice tempo with intact ability to recognize melodies.

Motor cortex: A region of cerebral cortex that sends impulses to motor neurons.

Motor extinction: Increased contralateral limb akinesia when simultaneously using ipsilateral extremities, due to cerebral dysfunction.

Motor impersistence: Inability to maintain an initiate voluntary (motor) behavior chain. Implies distraction due to interference factors. Common impersistences include lack of tongue protrusion, eyelid closure, mouth opening, breath holding, hand-grip pressure, and central gaze.

Motor neuron: Spinal cord neurons involved in movement which extend to effector muscle sites.

Motor unit: A single motor axon and all the muscle fibers it innervates.

Multi-infarct dementia: A vascular disease that has a progressive, stepwise course caused by multiple strokes and arteriosclerosis. Cognitive symptoms usually precede personality problems. Motor anomalies are distinctive of this condition and reflect subcortical involvement.

Multiple personality: Type of dissociative disorder characterized by the development of two or more relatively independent personality systems in the same individual.

Multiple Sclerosis (MS): A degenerative condition involving deterioration of the myelin sheath on nerve fibers. This disease therefore affects primarily the white matter. Multiple cognitive and emotional deficits are noted. The rate of progression of MS is extremely variable.

Myasthenia gravis: A neurological disease characterized by easy fatiguability and weakness of muscles.

Myelencephalon: A subdivision of the hindbrain consisting of the medulla.

Myelin: The fatty insulation around an axon, formed by accessory cells; this improves the speed of conduction of nerve impulses.

Myelin sheath: A thin cover on the axons of many neurons.

Myelinization: The process of formation of myelin.

N

Narcolepsy: A disorder involving frequent, intense episodes of sleep, which last from 5 to 30 minutes, that can occur anytime during the usual waking hours.

Necker cube: An optical illusion using "rate of apparent change (RAC)" to differentiate normal from brain-injured. Fewer and slower reversals are reported by brain-injured, with damage associated with right hemisphere or frontal lobe lesions.

Necrosis: Local death of tissue.

Neocortex: The relatively recently evolved portions of the cerebral cortex.

Nerve impulses: The propagated electrical messages of a neuron which travel down from the axon to adjacent neurons. Also called action potentials.

Neural tube: A prenatal structure with subdivisions which correspond to the future forebrain, midbrain, and hindbrain. The cavity of this tube will include the cerebral ventricles and the passages that connect them.

Neurasthenic neurosis: Neurotic disorder characterized by complaints of chronic weakness, easy fatiguability, and lack of enthusiasm.

Neurofibrillary tangles: Abnormal whorls of neurofilaments within nerve cells that are especially apparent in people suffering from dementia.

Neuroglia: "Nerve glue" or glia, these cells make up about half the volume of the central nervous system and provide structural and metabolic support to neurons. See *glial cells.*

Neurological examination: Examination to determine presence and extent of organic damage to the nervous system.

Neuron: The basic unit of the nervous system, composed of a cell body, receptive extensions(s), and a transmitting extension (axon).

Neuron doctrine: A hypothesis which states that the brain is composed of separate cells that are structurally, metabolically, and functionally distinct.

Neuropathies: Peripheral nerve destruction.

Neurotic style: A general personality disposition toward inhibiting certain anxiety-causing behaviors; distinguishable from anxiety, somatoform, and dissociative disorders in that neurotic styles do not manifest themselves in specific, disabling neurotic symptoms.

Nigrostriatal bundle (NSB): A dopaminergic tract that runs from the substantia nigra of the midbrain to the lateral hypothalamus, the globus pallidus, caudate, and putamen.

Nihilistic delusion: Fixed belief that everything is unreal.

Nociceptors: Receptors that respond to stimuli that produce tissue damage or pose the threat of damage.

Nomadism: Withdrawal reaction in which the individual continually attempts to escape frustration by moving from place to place or job to job.

Norepinephrine (NE): A neurotransmitter produced mainly in brain stem nuclei, also called *noradrenalin*.

Normal pressure hydrocephalus (NPH): A reversible condition involving obstruction of cerebral spinal fluid (CSF). Increased pressure leads to ventricle enlargement with the primary lesion in the midbrain reticular formation.

Nosology: The classification of diseases, including mental diseases.

Nucleus: An anatomical collection of neurons, e.g., caudate nucleus.

Nystagmus: Abnormal to and fro movements of the eye during attempts to fixate. Rhythmic oscillation of the eyeballs, either horizontal, rotary, or vertical.

O

Occipital cortex: The cortex of the occipital (posterior) lobe of the brain.

Ondine curse: A type of sleep apnea where automatic breathing during sleep is disrupted. Lesions of the reticulospinal tract have been implicated in this condition.

Oneirism: Prolonged dream state despite wakefulness.

Optic aphasia: Inability to name visually presented objects with intact recognition. Spared recognition is shown by demonstration of use or matching (pointing) to the object when named.

Optic ataxia: Inability to localize objects in space by visual guidance. Difficulty in shifting (stimulus boundedness) is an associated feature.

Optic chiasm: The site where optic neurons from eye separate and cross over to the contralateral hemisphere. Located near the pituitary gland.

Optic radiation: Axons of the lateral geniculate nucleus that terminate in the primary visual areas of the occipital cortex.

Optic tract: The axons of the retinal ganglion cells after they have passed the optic chiasm; most terminate in the lateral geniculate nucleus.

Optokinetic system: A closed loop system controlling eye movement and keeping the gaze on target.

Osmoreceptors: Cells in the hypothalamus that were thought to respond to changes in osmotic pressure.

P

Paleocortex: Evolutionary old cortex, e.g., the hippocampus.

Papilledema: Edema of the optic disk, associated with increased intracranial pressure.

Paradoxical sleep: See *rapid-eye-movement sleep (REM)*.

Parallel processing: Using several different circuits at the same time to process the same stimulus.

Paralysis: A loss of power of voluntary movement in a muscle through the injury or disease of its nerve supply.

Paranoia: Psychosis characterized by a systematized delusional system.

Paranoid personality: Individual showing behavior characterized by projection (as a defense mechanism), suspiciousness, envy, extreme jealousy, and stubbornness.

Paranoid schizophrenia: Subtype of schizophrenic disorder characterized by absurd, illogical, and changeable ideas of hallucinations of grandeur and persecution.

Paranoid state: Transient psychotic disorder in which the main element is a delusion, usually persecutory or grandiose in nature.

Paraphasias: Errors in word usage associated with aphasia. Substitutions for a correct word may occur (e.g., "I ate night.") or substitution for syllables (e.g., "I ate rupper."). Neologisms may occur (e.g., "I ate ronks.").

Parasympathetic division: One of the two systems that composes the autonomic nervous system. The parasympathetic division arises from both the cranial and sacral parts of the spinal cord.

Paraventricular nucleus: A nucleus of the hypothalamus.

Parkinson's Disease: A degenerative neurological disorder involving dopminergic neurons of the substantia nigra.

Partial seizures: Epileptic seizures arising from pathological foci that do not have a widespread distribution. These include focal repetitive motor spasms and do not involve the loss of consciousness.

Perceptual defense: A process in which threatening stimuli are filtered out and not perceived by the organism.

Peripheral nerves: Neurons which lie outside the central nervous system.

Peripheral nervous system: The portion of the nervous system that includes all the nerves outside the brain and spinal cord.

Perseveration: Persistent continuation of a line of thought or activity once it is under way. Clinically inappropriate repetition.

Perseveration-consolidation hypothesis: A hypothesis stating that information passes through two stages in memory formation. During the first stage the memory is held by perseveration of neural activity and is easily disrupted. During the second stage the memory becomes fixed, or consolidated, and is no longer easily disrupted.

Personality disorder: A group of maladaptive behavioral syndromes originating in the developmental years and not characterized by neurotic or psychotic symptoms.

Petit mal seizures: A type of generalized epileptic seizure characterized by a spike-and-wave electrical pattern. During these seizures the person is unaware of the environment and later cannot recall what happened.

Phantom limb: The experience of sensory messages attributed to an amputated limb.

Phonological agraphia: Impaired ability to spell nonwords with intact ability for familiar words. Associated with lesions of the supermarginal gyrus or associated areas.

Phrenology: The belief that bumps on the skull reflect enlargement of the brain regions responsible for certain behavioral faculties.

Pick's Disease: Similar to Alzheimer's Disease, here neuronal damage is typically confined to the frontal and temporal lobes. Personality changes usually precede memory loss. Affects twice as many women as men.

Pitch: A dimension of auditory experience in which sounds vary from low to high.

Pituitary gland: A small complex endocrine gland located in a socket at the base of the skull. The anterior pituitary and the posterior pituitary are separate in function.

Planum temporale: A region of superior temporal cortex adjacent to the primary auditory area.

Plexus: A network or tangle of interweaving nerves, veins, or lymphatic vessels.

Pneumoencephalogram: A technique for examining brain structure in intact humans by taking x-rays after a gas is injected into the ventricles.

Pons: A portion of the metencephalon.

Positron emission tomography (PET) scan: A technique for examining brain structure and function in intact humans by combining tomography with injections of radioactive substances used by the brain. An analysis of metabolism of these substances reflect regional differences in brain activity.

Postcentral gyrus: Involved in sensory mediation, this cortical convolution is located just posterior to the Fissure of Rolando.

Posterior pituitary: The rear division of the pituitary gland. Also called *neurohypophysis*.

Post-traumatic stress disorder (PTSD): Category of disorder in which severe and residual symptoms occur following the traumatic experience.

Post-traumatic amnesia (PTA): A form of anterograde amnesia seen as a post-concussional effect of head trauma. Correlates well with the coma length and severity. Some retrograde amnesia may accompany PTA.

Postural tremor: A tremor that occurs when a person attempts to maintain a posture such as holding an arm or a leg extended, resulting from pathology of the basal ganglia or cerebellum.

Precentral gyrus: Involved in the mediation of motor activity, this cortical convolution is located just anterior to the Fissure of Rolando.

Prodrome: Behavioral/mood change preceding onset of a seizure. Prodromal signs may be apparent for several days before the seizure.

Progressive supranuclear palsy: An uncommon Parkinson-like condition that usually begins in the fifties with emotional lability, imbalance, and problems with downward gaze. A dementia develops with relative sparing of language and constructional abilities.

Prosody: Rhythm, pitch, and tempo characteristics of speech. Important in communication of affective content. Typically seen as a right hemisphere activity.

Prosopagnosia: Inability to recognize faces of those with whom one was previously familiar. Loss of ability to recognize unfamiliar faces is a variant of this disorder.

Proximal: An anatomical directional term meaning near the trunk or center; opposite of distal.

Pseudobulbar state: Strong affective expressions to include laughing and crying, often simultaneously but also incongruous to the stated feeling of the person. Associated with lesions of connecting pathways between the frontal lobes and lower brain structures.

Pseudodementia: A pattern of deficit behavior resembling organically produced dementia. Depression is the primary factor causing intellectual suppression.

Pseudodepression: Patient shows pattern of inactivity, flat affect, and diminished motor responses and initiative. The major pathology involves the dorsal-lateral frontal convexity, severe bilateral frontal pathology, or severing of frontal-thalamic pathways. This is a pathology of reduced/absent motor responses (e.g., mutism, inactivity, helpless unconcern). The subject may be aware of the deficit.

Pseudohemianopsia: Lack of attention to visual stimulation from the contralateral side despite intact visual fields.

Pseudopsychopathy: The major pathology involves the orbital frontal areas and reflect motor excess (e.g., puerile acts, restlessness, bursting into motion, impulsive antisocial acts). The subject knows but cannot control the motor behavior.

Psychomotor epilepsy: State of disturbed consciousness in which the individual may perform various actions of a repetitive nature, for which he or she is later amnesic.

Ptosis: Drooping eyelid caused by a lesion to the oculomotor cranial nerve.

Pure agraphia: Writing deficit caused by brain damage in the absence of other significant language disturbances.

Pure word deafness: Inability to understand spoken words with an intact ability to read, write, and speak. Usually does not occur in isolation of other defects and is typically associated with cerebrovascular accidents.

Purkinje cell: A type of large nerve cell in the cerebellar cortex.

Pyramidal cell: A type of large nerve cell in the cerebral cortex.

Pyramidal system: A motor system including neurons within the cerebral cortex and their axons which form the pyramidal tract.

R

Rapid-eye-movement (REM) sleep: A state of sleep characterized by small-amplitude, fast EEG waves, no postural tension, and rapid eye movements.

Reaction formation: Ego-defense mechanism in which the individual's conscious attitudes and overt behavior are opposite to repressed unconscious wishes.

Reality principle: Awareness of the demands of the environment and adjustment of behavior to meet these demands.

Receptor: Nerve ending that receives a stimulus.

Reduplicative paramnesia: Associated with right parietal and/or frontal damage. Involves relocating a place (e.g., hospital) to another place (e.g., one's hometown).

Reflex: A simple, highly stereotyped, and unlearned response to a particular stimulus (e.g., an eye blink in response to a puff of air).

Regression: Ego-defense mechanism in which the individual retreats to the use of less mature responses in attempting to cope with stress and maintain ego integrity.

Repression: Ego-defense mechanism by means of which dangerous desires and intolerable memories are kept out of consciousness.

Residual schizophrenia: Category used for persons regarded as recovered from schizophrenia but will manifest some residual symptoms.

Resistance: Tendency to maintain symptoms and resist treatment or uncovering of repressed material.

Reticular activating system: Brain stem area which mediates level of arousal.

Reticular formation: A region of the brain stem (extending from the medulla through the thalamus) which is involved in arousal.

Retrieval: A process in memory during which a stored memory is utilized.

Retroactive amnesia: A type of memory loss in which events just before a traumatic head injury are not recalled.

Retrograde amnesia: Inability to recall events previous to the onset of a trauma or condition. Recovery of remote events usually occurs first.

Rostral: An anatomical term meaning toward the head end; opposite of caudal.

S

Schizo-affective psychosis: Disorder characterized by schizophrenic symptoms in conjunction with pronounced depression or elation.

Schizoid personality: Personality pattern characterized by shyness, oversensitivity, seclusiveness, and eccentricity.

Schizophrenia: Psychosis characterized by the breakdown of integrated personality functioning, withdrawal from reality, emotional blunting and distortion, and disturbances in thought and behavior.

Schizophreniform disorder: Category of schizophrenic psychosis, usually in an undifferentiated form, of less than six months' duration.

Schizophrenogenic: Qualities in parents that appear to be associated with the development of schizophrenia in offspring; often applied to rejecting, cold, domineering, overprotective mothers or passive, uninvolved fathers.

Selective vigilance: A tuning of attentional and perceptual processes towards stimuli relevant or central to goal-directed behavior, with decreased sensitivity to stimuli irrelevant or peripheral to this purpose.

Semantic agraphia: Deficit or loss of ability to spell or write with meaning, produced by brain damage to various sites.

Semantic memory: Memory for what is learned as knowledge. This recall therefore is considered "timeless and spaceless" (e.g., a number system, a foreign language).

Senile dementia: A neurological disorder of the aged involving progressive behavioral deterioration including personality change and profound intellectual decline.

Sensorineural deafness: A hearing impairment originating from cochlear or auditory nerve lesions.

Septo-hypothalamo-mesencephalic (SHM) continuum: One of three limbic mechanisms, the SHM continuum has distinct circuitry connecting the hypothalamus, limbic midbrain area, and other sites. Only the prefrontal lobe has direct connections with the SHM continuum out of the entire isocortex.

Short-term memory: Memory that usually lasts only for seconds or as long as rehearsal continues.

Significant others: In interpersonal theory, parents or others on whom a person is a dependant for meeting physical or psychological needs.

Simultagnosia: The perception of one stimulus when two objects are presented. Often associated with inertia of gaze.

Sleep apnea: A sleep disorder that involves slowing or cessation of respiration during sleep, which wakens the patient. Excessive daytime somnolence typically results from frequent nocturnal awakening.

Slow-wave sleep: Stages of sleep including stages 1 through 4, defined by presence of slow EEG activity.

Somatosensory agnosia: Loss of tactile recognition due to cerebral dysfunction in the presence of intact somatosensory receptive functions.

Somatosensory modalities: Refers to different types of body sensations (e.g., touch, pain, pressure). Distinguished from auditory and visual senses.

Somesthetic: Pertaining to somatesthesia, or awareness of having a body.

Somnolent mutism: Immobility and unresponsiveness with eyes closed, associated with mesencephalic-diencephalic lesions. Intense stimulation yields minimal responses.

Spasm: An involuntary, convulsive muscular contraction.

Spatial acalculia: Spatial misarrangement of the numbers during arithmetic calculation with intact knowledge of the correct principle. Associated with right hemisphere lesions.

Spatial agraphia: Deficits in spatial-motor aspects of writing due to brain damage, located in the nondominant parietal lobe. Frequently associated with the neglect syndrome.

Split-brain: Individuals who have had the corpus callosum and other brain structures severed, halting communication between the right and left hemisphere.

Stage 1 sleep: The initial stage of slow-wave sleep involving small amplitude EEG waves of irregular frequency, slow heart rate, and a reduction of muscle tension.

Stage 2 sleep: A stage of slow-wave sleep defined by bursts of regular 14-18 Hz EEG waves that progressively increase and then decrease in amplitude (called spindles).

Stage 3 sleep: A stage of slow-wave sleep defined by the spindles seen in stage 2 sleep mixed with larger amplitude slow-waves.

Stage 4 sleep: A stage of slow-wave sleep defined by the presence of high amplitude slow waves of 1-4 Hz.

Statistical test of significance: A standard of probability stating that an experimental finding is significant if, by chance alone, it could have occurred fewer than one or five times in 100 occurrences. In the field of psychology, five times in 100 is usually the standard of acceptability for statistical significance.

Stenosis: Narrowing or contraction of a body passage or opening.

Stereoacuity: The ability to discriminate small differences in visual depth by point-by-point matching in the retinas.

Stereopsis: The ability to perceive depth, utilizing the slight difference in visual information from the two eyes.

Striate cortex: A portion of the visual cortex with input from the lateral geniculate nucleus.

Sulci: The furrows of convoluted brain surface. Contrast with gyri.

Superior colliculus: A structure in the midbrain that receives information from the optic tract.

Superior olivary complex: A brain stem structure that receives input from both right and left cochlear nuclei, providing the first binaural analysis of auditory information.

Supplementary motor area (SMA) location: Areas 6 and partially 7, anterior to paracentral lobule. Function: Volitional (self-initiated) movements; perineal and leg movements are found in the medial extension of the motor homunculus. Considered also to be a secondary speech area.

Supraoptic nucleus: A nucleus of the hypothalamus.

Synapse: An area composed of the presynaptic (axonal) terminal, the postsynaptic (usually dendritic) membrane, and the space (or cleft) between them. This is the site at which neural messages travel from one neuron to another. Also called the *synaptic region.*

Synaptic transmitter: The chemical in the presynaptic bouton that serves as the basis of neural-neural communication. It travels across the synaptic cleft and reacts with the postsynaptic membrane when triggered by a nerve impulse. Also called *neurotransmitter.*

Synaptic vesicles: The small, spherically shaped structures which contain molecules of synaptic transmitter.

T

Tactile: Pertaining to the sense of touch.

Tactile hallucination: Hallucinations involving the sense of touch, such as feeling cockroaches crawling over one's body.

Tardive dyskinesia: Abnormal involuntary movements involving the extremities or facial area (e.g., tongue, jaw, facial surface). Results as a late side effect of neuroleptic drug treatment and in many cases, is irreversible. Involuntary movements—especially those involving the face, mouth, lips, and tongue—related to prolonged use of antipsychotic drugs, such as chlorpromazine, or haloperidol.

Telecenphalon: Consists of the cerebral cortex, corpus striatum, and medullary center. The frontal subdivision of the forebrain which includes the cerebral hemisphere when fully developed.

Tetany: Intermittent tonic muscular contractions of the extremities.

Thalamic syndrome: Disturbance of the senses with the initial hemianesthia, followed by a raised threshold to touch, pain, heat, and cold on the side opposite the lesion. The sensations may be extremely adversive when reached. Typically due to a thalamic infarct.

Thalamus: The brain region that surrounds the third ventricle that serves to rely information to different parts of the brain.

Thrombotic strokes: Results from blockage or occlusion by blood or tissue particles or over-growth. Occur most often where blood vessels branch.

Thrombus: A clot of blood formed within the heart of the blood vessels, usually caused by slowing of the circulation of the blood or by alteration of the blood itself or the vessel walls.

Thyroxine: A hormone released by the thyroid gland.

Tinnitus: A ringing or singing sound in the ears.

Tomogram: See *computer axial tomogram*.

Transcortical motor (TCM) aphasia: Separation of general conceptual functions (posterior) from Broca motor output area (anterior). Lesions in the supplementary motor area (SMA) or in Broca's area. The patient can repeat words but has difficulty with comprehension and speech.

Transient global amnesia: A relatively brief (several hours to several days) amnestic condition with few neurological sequelae. Associated features include 1) a major symptom of anterograde amnesia, 2) some retrograde amnesia, 3) confusion and time/place disorientation, and 4) speech and orientation to person are unimpaired. There is usually a sudden onset and cessation with no prodromal symptoms or known cause.

Transient ischemic attacks (TIA): Neurological deficits of sudden onset; less intense and temporary strokes that may precede thrombotic strokes. Last less than 24 hours by definition. About half of those who experience TIA's will have a major stroke.

Tremor-at-rest: A tremor that occurs when the affected region, such as a limb, is fully supported.

Tremors: Rhythmic repetitive movement caused by brain pathology.

Trigeminal neuralgia: Intense and sudden pain in area of a trigeminal nerve lesion. The episodic pain may be set off by light stimulation such as touching the skin.

U

Unconscious motivation: Motivation for an individual's behavior of which he or she is unaware.

Undifferentiated schizophrenia: Subtype in which the patient either has mixed symptoms or moves rapidly from one type to another.

Unilateral apraxia: Apraxia affecting one side of the body. Sympathetic and callosal types have been postulated. The sympathetic aspect occurs when other functions are likewise impaired, (e.g., right hemiparesis, left-hand apraxia, and Broca aphasia produced by left motor association destruction of callosal fibers).

Unipolar disorder: A severe affective disorder in which only depressive episodes occur, as opposed to bipolar disorders in which both manic and depressive processes are assumed to occur.

Unmyelinated: Refers to fine diameter axons that lack a myelin sheath.

Unsocialized disturbance of conduct: Childhood disorder in which the child is disobedient, hostile, and highly aggressive.

V

Ventral: An anatomical term meaning toward the belly or front of the body or the bottom of the brain; opposite of dorsal.

Ventricles: Cavities in the brain which contain cerebrospinal fluid.

Ventromedial hypothalamus (VMH): A hypothalamic region involved in inhibiting eating, among other functions.

Verbal adynamia: Diminished speech spontaneity. There is slow speech initiation and/or reluctance to continue verbal output. Usually accompanies general apathy.

Vertigo: Dizziness, giddiness.

Viscosity: A behavioral pattern characterized by stickiness in interactional contexts. Associated with frontal system damage.

Visual anosognosia: Denial of blindness caused by brain lesions. The subject attempts to behave as if the deficit was not present. See *Anton's Syndrome*.

W

Wada technique: Designed to assess which hemisphere was language-dominant. Here, sodium amytal is injected into one carotid artery in order to deactivate an entire hemisphere. Changes in counting behaviors while the injection is in process indicate which hemisphere is dominant for speech and language.

Wernicke's area: A region of the left hemisphere involved in language comprehension.

Wernicke's aphasia: A fluent disorder with severe auditory comprehension and processing deficits. Empty speech, press for speech, and a moderate to substantial naming deficit is apparent. Considered a posterior aphasia.

White matter: Consists of densely packed conduction fibers that transmit neural messages between the cortex and lower centers (projection fibers), between the hemispheres (commissural fibers), or within a hemisphere (association fibers).

Word deafness: Also called *pure word deafness*. Here, nonspeech sounds are recognized but not spoken words. Usually produced by subcortical lesion disconnecting auditory input from auditory processing.

Bibliography

Alexander, M. P. (1984). Neurobehavioral consequences of closed head injury. *Neurology and Neurosurgery. Update Series. 20*, 1-8.

Astrup, J. (1989). Brain Injury: A pathophysiological basis for neuropsychological dysfunction. In D.W. Ellis and A. Christensen (Eds.) *Neuropsychological Treatment After Brain Surgery.* Boston: Kluwer Academic Press. 15-38.

Barth, J. T., Macciocchi, S. N., Giordani, B., Rimel, R., Jane, J. A., and Boll, T. J. (1983). Neuropsychological sequelae of minor head injury. *Neurosurgery, 15*, 529-533.

Bear, D., Levin, K., Blumer, D., Chetham, D., and Ryder, R. (1982). Interictal behavior in hospitalized temporal lobe epileptics: Relationship to idiopathic psychiatric syndromes. *Journal of Neurology, Neurosurgery, and Psychiatry, 45*, 481-488.

Bender, L. (1938). A visual motor Gestalt test and its clinical use. *American Orthopsychiatric Association Research Monographs, 3.*

Benson, D. F. (1978). Amnesia. *So. Medical Journal, 71*, 1221- 1227.

Benson, D. F., and Blumer, D. (1975). *Psychiatric Aspects of Neurologic Disease.* New York: Grune and Stratton.

Benton, A. L. (1974). *Revised visual retention test: Clinical and experimental applications.* New York: Psychological Corporation.

Benton, A. L. (1974). *The Revised Visual Retention Test (4th Edition).* New York: Psychological Corporation.

Benton, A. L., and Van Allen, M. W. (1968). Impairment in facial recognition in patients with cerebral disease. *Cortex, 4 (3)*, 44-358.

Benton, A. L., and Van Allen, M. W. (1972). Prosopagnosia and facial discrimination. *Journal of Neurological Sciences, 15*, 167-172.

Benton, A. L., Hamsher, K. D., Varney, N. R., and Spreen, O. (1983). *Contributions to Neuropsychological Assessment: A Clinical Manual.* New York: Oxford Press.

Benton, A. L., Varney, A. R., and Hamsher, K. D. (1978). Visual judgment: A clinical test. *Archives of Neurology, 35*, 364-367.

Berman, A., and Siegal, A. (1976). A neuropsychological approach to the etiology, prevention, and treatment of juvenile delinquency. In A. David (Ed.) *Current Perspectives in Child Personality and Psychopathology.* New York: Wiley. 259-294.

Binder, L. A. (1986). Persisting symptoms after mild head injury: A review of the post-concussive syndrome. *Journal of Clinical and Experimental Neuropsychology, 8 (4)*, 323-346.

Boll, T. J. (1982). Behavioral sequelae of head injury. In P. R. Cooper (Ed.) *Head Injury*. 363-375.

Bond, M. R. (1975). Assessment of the psychosocial outcome after severe head injury. *CIBA Foundation Symposium 34*, Outcome of severe damage to the central nervous system. Amsterdam: Elsevier/Excerpta Medica. 141-157.

Bond, M. R., and Brooks, D. N. (1976). Understanding the processes of recovery as a basis for the investigation of rehabilitation for the brain-injured. *Scandinavian Journal of Rehabilitation Medicine*, *8*, 127-133.

Boring, E. G. (1950). *A History of Experimental Psychology (2nd Edition)*. New York: Appleton-Century-Crofts, Inc.

Bornstein, R. A. (1986). Normative data on intermanual differences on three tests of motor performance. *Journal of Clinical and Experimental Neuropsychology, 8 (1)*, 12-20.

Broca, P. (1861). Perte de la parole. *Bull Soc Anthropol, 2*, 1.

Buschke, H., and Fuld, P. A. (1974). Evaluating storage, retention, and retrieval in disordered memory and learning. *Neurology, 11*, 1019-1025.

Chapman, L. F., and Wolf, H. (1959). The cerebral hemispheres and the highest integrative functions of man. *Archives of Neurology, 1*, 357.

Cummings, J. L. (1985). *Clinical Neuropsychiatry*. New York: Grune and Stratton.

Damasio, A. R. (1979). The frontal lobes. In K. M. Heilman and E. Valenstein (Eds.) *The Frontal Lobes*. New York: Oxford Press. 360-412.

Dodrill, C. B. (1981). Neuropsychology of epilepsy. In S. B. Filskov and T. J. Boll (Eds.) *Handbook of Clinical Neuropsychology*. New York: Wiley. 366-395.

Eames, P. (1988). Behavior disorders after severe head injury: Their nature and causes and strategies for management. *Journal of Head Trauma Rehabilitation, 3 (3)*, 1-6.

Filskov, S. B., and Boll, T. J. (1981). *Handbook of Clinical Neuropsychology*. New York: John Wiley and Sons.

Filskov, S. B., and Goldstein, S. G. (1974). Diagnostic ability of the Halstead-Reitan Neuropsychological Battery. *Journal of Consulting and Clinical Psychology, 42*, 382-388.

Filskov, S. B., and Goldstein, S. G. (1974). Diagnostic validity of the Halstead-Reitan Neuropsychological Battery. *Journal of Consulting and Clinical Psychology, 42 (3)*, 382-388.

Franzen, M. D. (1985). Luria-Nebraska Neuropsychological Battery. In D. J. Keyser and R. C. Sweetland (Eds.) *Test Critiques: Volume III*. Kansas City: Test Corporation of America. 402-414.

Fritsch, G., and Hitzig, E. (1870). Uber die Eleckatrische Erregebarkeit des grosshirns. *Arch. Anat. Physiol. Wisse. Med.*, *37*, 1.

Fromm-Auch, D., and Yeudall, L. T. (1983). Normative data for the Halstead-Reitan Neuropsychological Tests. *Journal of Clinical Neuropsychology*, *5 (3)*, 221-238.

Gennarelli, T. A. (1982). Cerebral concussion and diffuse brain injuries. In P. R. Cooper (Ed.) *Head Injury*. Baltimore: Williams and Wilkins. 83-97.

Golden, C. J. (1977). Validity of the Halstead-Reitan Neuropsychological Battery in a mixed psychiatric and brain-injured population. *Journal of Consulting and Clinical Psychology*, *45 (6)*, 1043-1051.

Golden, C. J. (1978). *Diagnosis and Rehabilitation in Clinical Neuropsychology*. Springfield Illinois: Thomas, C. C.

Golden, C. J. (1979). *Clinical Interpretation of Objective Psychological Tests*. New York: Grune and Stratton.

Golden, C. J. (1981). *Stroop Color-Word Test*. Chicago: Manual Stoelting.

Golden, C. J., and McFadden, J. (1983). Relationships between the Booklet Category Test and the Wisconsin Card Sorting Test. *International Journal of Neuroscience*, *21* 257-264.

Golden, C. J., and Moses, J. A., Jr. (1981). Objective clinical rules for interpreting the Luria-Nebraska Neuropsychological Battery: Derivation, effectiveness, and validation. *Journal of Consulting and Clinical Psychology*, *49 (4)*, 616-618.

Golden, C. J., Berg, R. A., and Graber, B. (1982). Test-retest reliability of the Luria-Nebraska Neuropsychological Battery in stable, chronically impaired patients. *Journal of Consulting and Clinical Psychology*, *50 (3)*, 452-454.

Golden, C. J., Fross, K. H., and Graber, B. (1981). Split half reliability and item-scale consistency of the Luria-Nebraska Neuropsychological Battery. *Journal of Consulting and Clinical Psychology*, *49 (2)*, 304-305.

Golden, C. J., Hammeke, T. A., and Purisch, A. D. (1978). Diagnostic validity of a standardized neuropsychological battery derived from Luria's Neuropsychological Tests. *Journal of Consulting and Clinical Psychology*, *46*, 1258-1265.

Golden, C. J., Purisch, A. D., and Hammeke, T. A. (1985). *Luria-Nebraska Neuropsychological Battery: Forms I and II*. Los Angeles: Manual Western Psychological Services.

Goldstein, H. (1942). *Aftereffects of Brain Injuries in Man*. New York: Grune and Stratton.

Graham, D. I., Adams, J. H., and Doyle, D. (1978). Ischaemic brain damage in fatal non-missile head injuries. *Journal of Neurological Science*, *39*, 213.

Gray, J. W., and Dean, R. S. (1985). Hooper Visual Organization Test. In D. J. Keyser, and R. C. Sweetland (Eds.) *Test Critiques: Volume III.* Kansas City: Test Corporation. 340-343.

Gronwall, D. (1977). Paced auditory serial-addition task: A measure of recovery from concussion. *Perceptual and Motor Skills*, *44*, 367-373.

Gronwall, D., and Wrightson, P. (1974). Delayed recovery of intellectual function after minor head injury. *Lancet*, *2*, 605-609.

Gronwall, D., and Wrightson, P. (1974). Recovery after minor head injury. *Lancet*, *2*, 1452.

Gronwall, D., and Wrightson, P. (1975). Cumulative effects of concussion. *Lancet*, *2*, 995-997.

Gronwall, D., and Wrightson, P. (1980). Duration of post-traumatic amnesia after mild head injury. *Journal of Clinical Neuropsychology*, *2*, 51-60.

Gronwall, D., and Wrightson, P. (1981). Memory and information processing after closed head injury. *Journal of Neurology, Neurosurgery and Psychiatry*, *44*, 889-895.

Guilmette, T. J., Faust, D., Hart, K., and Arkes, H. R. (1990). A national survey of psychologists who offer neuropsychological services. *Archives of Clinical Neuropsychology*, *5*, 373-392.

Halstead, W. C. (1947). *Brain Intelligence: A Quantitative Study of the Frontal Lobes.* Chicago: University of Chicago Press.

Halstead, W. C. (1950). Frontal lobe functions and intelligence. *Bulletin of the Los Angeles Neurological Society*, *15*, 205-212.

Hammeke, T. A., and Golden, C. J., and Purisch, A. D. (1978). A standardized, short, and comprehensive neuropsychological test battery based on the Luria Neuropsychological Evaluation. *International Journal of Neuroscience*, *18*, 135-141.

Heaton, R. K. (1981). *Wisconsin Card Sorting Test Manual.* Odessa, Florida: Psychological Assessment Resources.

Heaton, R. K., Smith, H. H., Lehrman, R. A. W., and Vogt, A. T. (1978). Prospects for faking believable deficits on neuropsychological testing. *Journal of Consulting and Clinical Psychology*, *46 (5)*, 892-900.

Howard, M. E. (1988). Behavior management in the acute care rehabilitation setting. *Journal of Head Trauma Rehabilitation*, *3 (3)*, 14-22.

Jefferson, J. W., and Marshall, J. R. (1981). *Neuropsychiatric Features of Medical Disorders.* New York: Plenum.

Jennett, W. B. (1975). *Epilepsy After Blunt Head Injuries, Second Edition*. London: Heineman.

Jones, B. P., and Butters, N. (1983). Neuropsychological psychological assessment. In M. Hersen, A. E. Kazdin, and A. S. Bellack (Eds.) *The Clinical Psychology Handbook*. New York: Pergamon Press. 377-396.

Klonoff, H., Low, M. D., and Clark, C. (1977). Head injuries in children: A prospective five-year follow-up. *Journal of Neurology, Neurosurgery and Psychiatry, 40*, 1211-1219.

Knippa, J., Golden, C. J., and Franzen, M. (1984). Interpretation and use of the Luria-Nebraska Battery. *Brain and Cognition, 3*, 343-348.

Koppitz, E. M. (1964). *The Bender-Gestalt Test for Young Children*. New York: Grune and Stratton.

Koppitz, E. M. (1975). *The Bender-Gestalt Test for Young Children Volume II: Research and Applications. 1963-1973*. New York: Grune and Stratton.

Leavitt, E. E., and Duckworth, J. C. (1984). Minnesota Multiphasic Personality Inventory. In D. J. Keyser, and R. C. Sweetland (Eds.) *Test Critiques: Volume I*. Kansas City: Test Corporation. 466-472.

Levin, H. S., Grossman, R. G., Rose, J. E., and Teasdale, G. (1979). Long-term neuropsychological outcome of closed head injury. *Journal of Neurosurgery, 50*, 412-422.

Lewis, G. P., Golden, C. J., Moses, J. A., Jr., Osmon, D. C., Purisch, A. D., and Hammeke, T. A. (1979). Localization of cerebral dysfunction with a standardized version of Luria Neuropsychological Battery. *Journal of Consulting and Clinical Psychology, 47 (6)*, 1003-1019.

Lezak, M. D. (1978). Living with the characterologically altered brain-injured patient. *Journal of Clinical Psychiatry, 39*, 592.

Lezak, M. D. (1981). *Neuropsychological Assessment*. New York: Oxford Press.

Lezak, M. D. (1983). *Neuropsychological Assessment*. New York: Oxford Press.

Lezak, M. D. (1983). *Neuropsychological Assessment: Second Edition*. New York: Oxford Press.

Lezak, M. D. (1987). Relationships between personality disorders, social disturbances and physical disability following traumatic brain injury. *Journal of Head Trauma Rehabilitation, 2 (1)*, 57-69.

Lishman, W. A. (1968). Brain damage in relation to psychiatric disability after head injury. *British Journal of Psychiatry, 114*, 373-410.

Lishman, W. A. (1973). Psychiatric sequelae of head trauma. *A Review of Psychological Medicine, 3*, 304-318.

Lishman, W. A. (1978). *Organic Psychiatry*. Blackwell: Oxford.

Llabre, M. M. (1984). Standard Progressive Matrices. In D. J. Keyser and R. C. Sweetland (Eds.) *Test Critiques: Volume I.* Kansas City: Test Corporation, 595-602.

Long, D. F. (1989). Issues in behavioral neurology. In D. W. Ellis and A. Christensen (Eds.) *Neuropsychological Treatment After Brain Injury.* Boston: Kluwer. 39-90.

Luria, A. R. (1966). *Human Brain and Psychological Processes.* New York: Harper and Row.

Luria, A. R. (1980). *Higher Cortical Functions in Man: Second Edition.* New York: Basic Books.

Marvel, G. A., Golden, C. J., Hammeke, T., Purisch, A., and Osmon, D. (1979). Relationship of age and education to performance on a standardized version of Luria's Neuropsychological Test in different patient populations. *International Journal of Neuroscience, 9,* 63-70.

McCabe, S. P. (1984). Millon Clinical Multiaxial Inventory. In D. J. Keyser and R. C. Sweetland (Eds.) *Test Critiques: Volume I.* Kansas City: Test Corporation. 595-602.

McCabe, S. P. (1984). Millon Clinical Multiaxial Inventory. In D. J. Keyser and R. C. Sweetland (Eds.) *Test Critiques: Volume I.* Kansas City: Test Corporation. 455-465.

McKinlay, W. W. (1981). The short-term outcome of severe blunt head injury as reported by relatives of the injured person. *Journal of Neurology, Neurosurgery and Psychiatry, 44,* 527.

McKinlay, W. W., Brooks, D. N., and Bond, M. R. (1983). Post-concussional symptoms, financial compensation and outcome of severe blunt head injury. *Journal of Neurology, Neurosurgery and Psychiatry, 46,* 1084-1091.

McLean, A., Temkin, N. R., Dikmen, S., and Wyler, A. R. (1983). The behavioral sequelae of head injury. *Journal of Clinical Neuropsychology, 5,* 361-376.

Miller, H., and Stern, G. (1965). The long-term prognosis of severe head injury. *Lancet, 1,* 225-229.

Miller, J. D. (1983). Early evaluation and management. In M. Rosenthall, E. R. Griffith, M.R. Bond, and J. D. Miller, (Eds.) *Rehabilitation of the Head-injured Adult.* Philadelphia: Davis, F. A. 37-58.

Moses, J. A., Jr., and Golden, C. J. (1979). Cross validation of the discriminative effectiveness of the standardized Luria Neuropsychological Battery. *International Journal of Neuroscience, 9,* 149-155.

Newcombe, F. (1969). *Missile Wounds of the Brain.* London: Oxford Press.

Oddy, M., Humphrey, M., and Uttley, D. (1978). Stresses upon relatives of head-injured patients. *British Journal of Psychiatry, 133,* 507.

Osterrieth, P. A. (1944). Le test de copie d'une figure complexe. *Archives de Psychologie, 30,* 206-356.

Panting, A., and Merry, P. H. (1972). The long-term rehabilitation of severe head injuries with particular reference to need for social and medial support for the patient's family. *Rehabilitation*, *38*, 33.

Pascal, G. R., and Suttell, B. J. (1951). *The Bender-Gestalt Test: Quantification for Validity and Adults*. New York: Grune and Stratton.

Plaisted, J. R., and Golden, C. J. (1982). Test-retest reliability of the clinical, factor, and localization scales of the Luria-Nebraska Neuropsychological Battery. *International Journal of Neuroscience*, *17*, 163-167.

Purisch, A. D., and Sbordone, R. J. (1986). The Luria-Nebraska Neuropsychological Battery. In G. Goldstein and R. A. Tarter (Eds.) *Advances in Clinical Neuropsychology Volume 3*. New Jersey: Plenum. 291-316.

Purisch, A. D., and Sbordone, R. J. (1987). Clinical neuropsychology: Medico-legal applications. Part 2. *Trauma*, *6*, 61-94.

Putnam, S. T., and DeLuca, J. W. (1990). The TCN Professional Practice Survey: Part 1: General practices of neuropsychologists in primary employment and private practice settings. *The Clinical Neuropsychologist*, *4 (3)*, 199-244.

Reitan, R. M. (1955). Investigation of the validity of Halstead's measure of biological intelligence. *AMA Archives of Neurology and Psychiatry*, *73*, 28-35.

Reitan, R. M. (1955). The distribution according to age of a psychologic measure dependent upon organic brain functions. *Journal of Gerontology*, *10*, 338.

Reitan, R. M. (1974). Methodological problems in clinical neuropsychology. In R. A. Reitan and L. A. Davison (Eds.) *Clinical Neuropsychology: Current Status and Applications*. New York: Hemisphere Publishing Group.

Rimel, R. W., Giordani, B., Barth, J. T., Boll, T. J., and Jane, J. A. (1981). Disability caused by minor head injury. *Neurosurgery*, *9*, 221-228.

Rimmele, C. T., and Hester, R. K. (1987). Cognitive rehabilitation after traumatic head injury. *Archives of Clinical Neuropsychology*, *2 (4)*, 353-384.

Romano, M. D. (1974). Family response to traumatic head injury. *Scandinavian Journal of Rehabilitation Medicine*, *6 (1)*.

Rosenthall, M., Griffith, E. R., Bond, M. R., and Miller, J. D. (1983). *Rehabilitation of the Head-injured Adult*. Philadelphia: F. A. Davis.

Russell, E. W., Neuringer, C., and Goldstein, G. (1970). *Assessment of Brain Damage: A Neuropsychological Key Approach*. New York: Wiley-Interscience.

Sbordone, R. J. (1984). A rehabilitation neuropsychological approach for severe traumatic brain-injured patients within a private practice setting. *Professional Psychology*, *15*, 165-175.

Sbordone, R. J. (1985). Minor head trauma: A changing perspective. *Trauma*, *2*, 1-14.

Sbordone, R. J. (1986). Does cognitive rehabilitation work? A case study. *Psychotherapy in Private Practice*, *4*, 51-62.

Sbordone, R. J. (1987). A conceptual model of neuropsychological based cognitive rehabilitation. In C. J. Long and J. M. Williams (Eds.) *The Rehabilitation of Cognitive Disabilities*. New York: Plenum. 1-25.

Sbordone, R. J. (1987). A neuropsychological approach to cognitive rehabilitation within a private practice setting. In B. Caplan (Ed.) *Handbook of Contemporary Rehabilitation Psychology*. New York: Thomas. 323-342.

Sbordone, R. J. (1987). Neuropsychological indicators of a subcortical disorder. *Proceedings of AMEDD Conference on Clinical and Health Psychology*, (March) *3*, 101-111.

Sbordone, R. J. (1988). Assessment and treatment of cognitive- communicative impairments in the closed head injury: A neurobehavioral-systems approach. *Journal of Head Trauma Rehabilitation*, *3 (2)*, 55-62.

Sbordone, R. J. (1989). Overcoming roadblocks: Rehabilitation of the traumatic brain-injured patient. *JMA Bulletin*, *1 (1)*, 6-7.

Sbordone, R. J. (1989). Relationship between location of brain injury and emotional problems. *JMA Bulletin*, *1 (2)*, 20-21.

Sbordone, R. J. (1990). Psychotherapeutic treatment of the client with traumatic brain injury: A conceptual model. In J. S. Kreutzer and P. Wehman (Eds.) *Community Integration Following Traumatic Brain Injury*. Baltimore: Brookes. 139-156.

Sbordone, R. J. (In press). Epilepsy and violence. In H. V. Hall and R. J. Sbordone (Eds.) *Forensic Neuropsychology of Executive Dysfunction: Civil and Criminal Law Applications*.

Sbordone, R. J. (In press). Neurobehavioral assessment of brain- injured patients. *Psychotherapy in Private Practice*.

Sbordone, R. J. (In press). Overcoming roadblocks in cognitive rehabilitation of brain-injured patients. In J. S. Kreutzer and P. Wehman (Eds.) *Cognitive Rehabilitation*.

Sbordone, R. J., and Caldwell, A. B. (1979). The OBD-168: Assessing the emotional adjustment to cognitive impairment. *Clinical Neuropsychology*, *1 (4)*, 36-41.

Sbordone, R. J., and Caldwell, A. B. (1984). The OBD-168. Reproduced in *The MMPI Review*.

Sbordone, R. J., and Eames, P. (1985). Atypical bipolar depressive disorder following right diencephalic brain injury. *Presentation given at the International Conference on Traumatic Head Injury*, San Jose, California, March 2, 1985.

Sbordone, R. J., and Hall, S. J. *The Reliability and Validity of the Sbordone-Hall Memory Battery*. Unpublished Manuscript.

Sbordone, R. J., and Jennison, J. H. (1984). A comparison of the OBD-168 and MMPI to assess the emotional adjustment to their cognitive deficits. *The MMPI Review*.

Sbordone, R. J., and Purisch, A. D. (1987). Clinical neuropsychology: Medico-legal applications. Part 1. *Trauma*, *1*, 17-102.

Sbordone, R. J., and Purisch, A. D. (1987). Clinical neuropsychology: Medico-legal applications. Part 2. *Trauma*, *6*, 61-94.

Sbordone, R. J., and Purisch, A. D. (1987). Clinical neuropsychology: Medico-legal applications. Part 3. *Trauma*, *1*, 17-102.

Sbordone, R. J., and Rudd, M. (1986). Can psychologists recognize neurologic disorders? *Journal of Experimental and Clinical Neuropsychology*, *8 (3)*, 285-291.

Sbordone, R. J., Gerrard, M. L., Kral, M. J., and Katz, J. (1984). The command performance syndrome: Emotional behavior of significant others of head trauma victims. *Clinical Neuropsychology*, *6*, 183-185.

Sekino, H., Nakamura, N., Yuki, K., Saton, J., Kikuchi, K., and Sanada, S. (1981). Brain lesions detected by CT scans in cases of minor head injuries. *Neurologica Medico Chirurgica*, *21*, 677-683.

Shelley, C., and Goldstein, G. (1982). Psychometric relations between the Luria-Nebraska and Halstead-Reitan Neuropsychological Battery in a neuropsychiatric setting. *Clinical Neuropsychology*, *4*, 128-133.

Shukla, S., Cook, B. L., Mukherjee, S., Goodwin, C., and Miller, M. G. (1987). Mania following head trauma. *American Journal of Psychiatry*, *144 (1)*, 93-96.

Siegal, A. W., Schechter, M. D., and Diamond, S. P. (1980). Neurobehavioral assessment format. Unpublished Manuscript.

Smith, A. (1968). The Symbol Digit Modalities Test: A neuropsychologic test for economic screening of the learning and other cerebral disorders. *Learning Disorders*, *3*, 83-91.

Smith, A. (1973). *A Symbol Digit Modalities Test Manual*. Los Angeles: Western Psychological Services.

Sperry, R. W. (1974). Lateral specialization in the surgically separated hemispheres. In F. O. Schmidtt and F. G. Worden (Eds.) *The Neurosciences: Third Study Program*. Cambridge, Massachusetts: MIT Press. 5-19.

Spruill, J. (1984). Wechsler Adult Intelligence Scale-Revised. In D. J. Keyser and R. C. Sweetland (Eds.) *Test Critiques: Volume I*. Kansas City: Test Corporation. 728-739.

Story, T. B., and Sbordone, R. J. (1988). The use of microcomputers in the treatment of cognitive-communicative impairments. *Journal of Head Trauma Rehabilitation*, *3 (2)*, 45-54.

Stuss, D. T., and Benson, D. F. (1986). *The Frontal Lobes*. New York: Raven Press.

Sweet, J. J., and Moberg, P. J. (1990). A survey of practices and beliefs among ABPP and Non-ABPP clinical neuropsychologists. *The Clinical Neuropsychologists*, *4 (2)*, 101-120.

Taylor, E. M. (1969). Localization of cerebral lesions by psychological testing. *Clinical Neurosurgery*, *16*, 216-287.

Teaseale, G., and Jennett, B. (1974). Assessment of coma and impaired consciousness: A practical scale. *Lancet*, *2*, 81-84.

Teuber, H. L. (1972). Unity and diversity of frontal lobe functions. *ACTA Nuerobiologica Experimentalis*, *32*, 615-656.

Teuber, H. L., and Mishkin, M. (1954). Judgement of visual and postural vertical after brain injury. *Journal of Psychology*, *38*, 161-175.

Teuber, H. L., Battersby, W. S., and Bender, M. B. (1960). *Visual Field Defects After Penetrating Missile Wounds of the Brain*. Cambridge: Harvard University Press.

Thomsen, I. V. (1981). Neuropsychological treatment and long-time follow-up in an aphasic patient with very severe head trauma. *Journal of Clinical Neuropsychology*, *3 (1)*, 43-51.

Trimble, M. R., and Thompson, P. J. (1986). Neuropsychological aspects of epilepsy. In I. Grant and K. M. Adams (Eds.) *Neuropsychological Assessment of Neuropsychiatric Disorders*. New York: Oxford Press. 321-346.

Vega, A., Jr., and Parsons, O. A. (1967). Cross validation of the Halstead-Reitan tests for brain damage. *Journal of Consulting Psychology*, *31*, 619-623.

Walker, A. E. (1972). Long-term evaluation of the social and family adjustment of head injuries. *Scandinavian Journal of Rehabilitation Medicine*, *4 (5)*.

Walsh, K. W. (1978). *Neuropsychology: A Clinical Approach*. New York: Churchill Livingstone.

Wechsler, D. (1981). *WAIS-R Manual*. New York: Psychological Corporation.

Wellman, M. M. (1985). Benton Revised Visual Retention Test. In D. J. Keyser and R. C. Sweetland (Eds.) *Test Critiques: Volume III*. Kansas City: Test Corporation. 58-67.

Wernicke, C. (1970). The aphasic symptom complex. *Archives of Neurology*, *22*, 280.

Wheeler, L., Burke, C. H., and Reitan, R. M. (1963). An application of discriminant functions to the problems of predicting brain damage using behavioral variables. *Perceptual and Motor Skills*, *16*, 417.

Whitworth, R. H. (1984). Bender Visual Motor Gestalt Test. In D. J. Keyser and R. C. Sweetland (Eds.) *Test Critiques: Volume I*. Kansas City: Test Corporation. 90-98.

Whitworth, R. H. (1984). The Halstead-Reitan Neuropsychological Battery and allied procedures. In D. J. Keyser and R. C. Sweetland (Eds.) *Test Critiques: Volume I*. Kansas City: Test Corporation. 305-314.

Wood, R. (1988). Management of behavior disorders in a day treatment setting. *Journal of Head Trauma Rehabilitation*, *3 (3)*, 53-61.

Index

A

Abstract thinking, tests of, 146-147
    strengths and limitations of, 169-170
Academic records, review of, in neuropsychological assessment, 100
Academic skills, tests of, 152-153
    strengths and limitations of, 173
Adjustment disorder, neuropathological aspects of, 57
American Board of Clinical Neuropsychology (ABCN)
    certification by, 20-21
    Diplomates of, 297
American Board of Professional Neuropsychology (ABPN), certification by, 20
Amnesia, neuropathological aspects of, 60-61
Aphasia Screening Test, 122, 153
    strengths and limitations of, 174
Arachnoid membrane, 31
Arterial hypoxemia, neuropathological aspects of, 51
Assessment in practice of neuropsychology, 2-4
Association cortices, 35
Attention-concentration skills
    Digit Span Test of, 132-133
    Paced Auditory Serial Addition Test of, 134
    Sbordone Attention Battery for, 134-135
    Symbol-Digit Modalities Test of, 135-136
    tests of, 132-136
        results of, in neuropsychological report, 236-237, 256
        strengths and limitations of, 161-163
    Trail Making Test of, 136
Attorney
    education of, about effects of brain damage, utilizing neuropsychologists in, 269-270
    sense of frustration for, related to clinical neuropsychology, 2

B

Background
    in neuropsychological report, 244-245
    of neuropsychologist, determining, in deposition, 271-273

Behavior
  alterations in, due to brain injury, 5
    determination of, 3
  neuropsychological test data and, integrating information about, importance of, 203-214
Behavior modification, determining need of brain-damaged patient for, 222
Behavioral observations
  in neuropsychological assessment, 97-99
  in neuropsychological report, 235-236, 245-246
  in reaching conclusions on brain damage/cognitive impairment, 208
  use of, determining, in deposition, 284-286
Bender-Gestalt Test in neuropsychological testing, 112-113
Benton Facial Recognition Test, 143-144
  strengths and limitations of, 168
Benton Judgement of Line Orientation Test, 144
Benton Visual Retention Test (BVRT), 137-138
  strengths and limitations of, 163
Bibliography, 347
Block Design Test, 150-151
  strengths and limitations of, 172
Blood flow, cerebral, reduction of, neuropathological aspects of, 51
Boston Diagnostic Aphasia Examination, 153
  strengths and limitations of, 174
Boston Naming Test, 153-154
  strengths and limitations of, 175
Brain
  anatomy of, 31-36
  cerebral lobes of, 31-33
  cortical lobes of, 33-35
  frontal lobes of, 35-36
  swelling of, neuropathological aspects of, 49
Brain-behavior relationship, knowledge of, determining, in deposition, 273
Brain damage
  assessment of, 3
  behavior of patient related to, in neuropsychological test scoring and analysis, 182-183
  behavioral alterations due to, determination of, 3
  behavioral and cognitive problems due to, 5
  caused by hydrocephalus, 43
  conditions during neuropsychological testing masking, 108-109
  cortical versus subcortical, 203
  diffuse
    axonal, neuropathological aspects of, 48-49
    patients with, neuropsychological test performance of, 199-200
  effects of
    educating attorneys about, utilizing neuropsychologists in, 269-270
    on family/significant others, determining, 225
  focal, patients with, neuropsychological test performance of, 199
  hypoxic, neuropathological aspects of, 50

patient with
referral of, to brain injury rehabilitation program, 219-220
treating/examining, experience in, determining, in deposition, 273-274
treatment and/or rehabilitation services needed by, determining, 221-227. *See also* Treatment/rehabilitation services
post-traumatic stress disorder vs., 65
prognosis of impairments following, determining, 215-220
psychiatric symptoms caused by, 58
psychological treatment after, types of, 5-6
reaching conclusions regarding, 197-214
recovery stages following, 215-216
secondary, neuropathological aspects of, 49-52
severity of, establishing, methods of, determining, in deposition, 286-287
site of, symptoms related to, 58-59
subcortical
versus cortical, 203
patients with, neuropsychological test performance of, 202-202
Brain stem, anatomy and function of, 39

C

Category test, 147
strengths and limitations of, 170
Cerebellum, anatomy and function of, 39
Cerebral blood flow, reduction of, neuropathological aspects of, 51
Cerebral concussion, neuropathological aspects of, 46-47
Cerebral contusions, neuropathological aspects of, 47-48
Cerebral edema, neuropathological aspects of, 49
Cerebral lobes of brain, 31-33
Cerebral spinal fluid (CSF) in cerebroventricular system, 42
Cerebrovascular system of brain, 38-42
damage to, 42
Cerebroventricular system, 42
Childhood, background on, in neuropsychological report, 244
Children in patient's background in neuropsychological report, 245
Clinical interview, 68-77
background history in
importance of, 75-76
of malingerers, typical, 72-73
from patient, obtaining, 71-72
case study on, 68-69
clinical history from
to detect malingering, 72
importance of, schools of thought about, 73
complaints of patient during, 70
estimating severity of brain injury in, index to, 74-75
information obtained from, 76-77

patient's description of accident in, 69
of significant others, 73-74
Cognitive functions, higher, tests of, in neuropsychological report, 257
Cognitive impairment
in brain-damaged patients, 5
reaching conclusions regarding, 197-214
relative severity of, determining, in neuropsychological test scoring and analysis, 178
Cognitive rehabilitation
for brain-damaged patient, 5-6
determining need of brain-damaged patient for, 222-223
in practice of neuropsychology, 5-7
Cognitive skills and abilities, pre-existing, determining, 84
Comment in neuropsychological report, 261-262
Comparison groups, representativeness of, in neuropsychological test scoring and analysis, 179-180
Competence of neuropsychologists, 20-21
Complaints, chief, in neuropsychological report, 230, 241-242
Conceptual thinking/problem solving, tests of, 147-149
strengths and limitations of, 170-171
Concussion, cerebral, neuropathological aspects of, 46-47
Constructional skills, tests of, 150-152
strengths and limitations of, 172-173
Consultation with other professionals in practice of neuropsychology, 7-8
Controlled Oral Word Association Test, 154-155
strengths and limitations of, 175
Contusions, cerebral, neuropathological aspects of, 47-48
Cortical brain damage versus subcortical brain damage, 203
Cortical lobes of brain, 33-35
Counseling
determining need of brain-damaged patient for, 222
family, 225-226
Cultural background in neuropsychological assessment, 86-87

D

Dementia, neuropathological aspects of, 61-63
Deposing a neuropsychologist, 271-287
determining background in, 271-273
determining consistency of conclusions with other sources of data/information in, 278-281
determining experience in, 271-273
with treating/examining brain-damaged patients, 273-274
determining how severity of brain damage established in, 286-287
determining if behavioral observations used in, 284-286
determining if psychologist interviewed family or significant others in, 283-284
determining inconsistencies between plaintiff's past history and psychologist's conclusions in, 281-283

determining knowledge of brain-behavior relationships in, 273
determining rationale for arriving at particular interpretations in, 276-278
determining training in, 271-273
determining use of quantitative/qualitative analysis of test data in, 284-286
exploring reasons for accepting particular case in, 274-276
Development, background on, in neuropsychological report, 244
Developmental assessment, 78-79
Deviation, mean and standard, in neuropsychological test scoring and analysis, 177-178
Diagnosis
in neuropsychological report, 240, 261
in practice of neuropsychology, 2-4
Diencephalon, anatomy and function of, 39
Diffuse brain damage
axonal, neuropathological aspects of, 48-49
patients with, neuropsychological test performance of, 199-200
Digit-Span Test, strengths and limitations of, 161
Diplomates of The American Board of Clinical Neuropsychology, 297
Discrimination, prior history of, in neuropsychological assessment, 86-87
Dominance in neuropsychological assessment, 79
Dorsal lateral damage, neuropathological aspects of, 54
Dura mater, 31

E

Ecological validity of neuropsychological testing, 107-108
Edema, cerebral, neuropathological aspects of, 49
Education
of attorneys about effects of brain damage, utilizing neuropsychologist in, 269-270
in neuropsychological assessment, 80-81
of neuropsychologist, 15-21
Emotional adjustment tests, 156-158
results of, in neuropsychological report, 238-239, 257-258
strengths and limitations of, 176
Encephalopathy
hypoxic, neuropathological aspects of, 59
toxic-metabolic, neuropathological aspects of, 63
Environmental modification for brain-damaged patient, 5
determining need for, 221-223
Epilepsy, post-traumatic, neuropathological aspects of, 52, 55-57
Equipotentialist school of neuropsychologic thought, 9
Executive functions, tests of, results of, in neuropsychological report, 238
Experience of neuropsychologist, determining, in deposition, 271-273
Expert, neuropsychological, selection of, 263-265

F

Falx cerebri, 31
Family
of brain-damaged patients, effects on, 5
counseling and psychiatric treatment for, 225-226
effect of brain damage on, determining, 225
interview of, use of, determining, in deposition, 283-284
in neuropsychological assessment, 94-96
Family therapy for brain-damaged patient, 6
Figures, list of, xv
Finger Oscillation (Tapping) Test, 118, 142
strengths and limitations of, 166
Fingertip Number Writing Perception Test, 121
Flexible neuropsychological test batteries, 127-130
Focal brain damage, patients with, neuropsychological test performance of, 199
Frontal lobes of brain, 35-36
damage to
causes of, 55
neuropathological aspects of, 52-55
orbital, neuropathological aspects of, 47, 53

G

Glossary, 313
Grip Strength Test, 119, 142
strengths and limitations of, 167
Grooved Pegboard Test, 142-143
strengths and limitations of, 167

H

Halstead, Ward C., neuropsychological assessment battery of, 11
Halstead Category test, 115-116
Halstead-Reitan Neuropsychological Test Battery (HRNB), 11, 115
limitations of, 124-125, 160
strengths of, 123, 160
validity and reliability of, 123
Head trauma, minor, neuropathological aspects of, 45-46
Hematoma
intracranial, neuropathological aspects of, 49-50
subdural, 42

History
of injury from patient in neuropsychological report, 230-231, 242-243
medical, in neuropsychological report, 245
Hooper Visual Organization test, 144-145
Hydrocephalus
brain damage caused by, 43
neuropathological aspects of, 51
post-traumatic, neuropathological aspects of, 59
Hypoxemia, arterial, neuropathological aspects of, 51
Hypoxic brain damage, neuropathological aspects of, 50
Hypoxic encephalopathy, neuropathological aspects of, 59

I

Impression in neuropsychological report, 258-261
Infections, intracranial, neuropathological aspects of, 51
Integrative school of neuropsychologic thought, 9-10
Intelligence tests
results of, in neuropsychological report, 236
strengths and limitations of, 159
Internal carotid artery system, 40
Inteviewing clients, utilizing neuropsychologist in, 267-268
Intracranial hematoma, neuropathological aspects of, 49-50
Intracranial infections, neuropathological aspects of, 51
Intracranial pressure, elevated, neuropathological aspects of, 50

L

Language
in neuropsychological assessment, 79-80
tests of, 153-155
results of, in neuropsychological report, 237
strengths and limitations of, 174-175
Legal history in neuropsychological assessment, 84-86
Limbic system, anatomy and function of, 36-39
Localizationist school of neuropsychologic thought, 9
Luria, Alexander, tests and neuropsychological assessment method of, 12-13
Luria-Nebraska Neuropsychological Battery (LNNB), 125-127
strengths and limitations of, 161

M

Malingering, 289-293
  case study on, 290-293
  characteristics associated with, 289-290
  definition of, 289
Marital background in neuropsychological report, 244
Marital status and history in neuropsychological assessment, 88-89
Medial frontal lobe damage, neuropathological aspects of, 54
Medical disorders in neuropsychological assessment, 90-91
Medical history in neuropsychological report, 245
Medical records, review of
  in neuropsychological assessment, 100-101
  in neuropsychological report, 231-233, 246-255
  in reaching conclusions on brain damage/cognitive impairment, 207-208
Memory
  Benton Visual Retention Test of, 137-138
  disorders of, neuropathological aspects of, 60-61
  Rey Auditory Verbal Learning Test of, 138-139
  Rey-Osterrieth Complex Figure Test of, 139-140
  Sbordone-Hall Memory Battery for, 140-141
  Selective Reminding Test of, 140
  tests of, 137-142
    results of, in neuropsychological report, 237, 256
    strengths and limitations of, 163-166
  Wechsler Memory Scale for, 141-142
Military records, review of, in neuropsychological assessment, 102
Military service in neuropsychological assessment, 81-82
Millon Clinical Multiaxial Inventory (MCMI), 157-158
  strengths and limitations of, 176
Minnesota Multiphasic Personality Inventory (MMPI), 122-123, 156-157
  strengths and limitations of, 176
Motor skills, tests of, 142-143
  results of, in neuropsychological report, 237-238, 257
  strengths and limitations of, 166-167

N

Neuroanatomy, 31-43
Neurobehavioral disorders, neuropathological aspects of, 45-65. *See also* Neuropathological aspects
Neurological examination, 29
Neurologists, clinical neuropsychologists compared to, 29-30
Neuropathological aspects
  of cerebral concussion, 46-47
  of cerebral contusions, 47-48

of dementia, 61-63
of diffuse axonal brain damage, 48-49
of frontal lobe damage, 52-55
of hypoxic encephalopathy, 59
of memory disorders, 60-61
of minor head trauma, 45-46
of neurobehavioral disorders, 45-65
of post-traumatic epilepsy, 55-57
of post-traumatic hydrocephalus, 59
of post-traumatic psychiatric disorders, 57-59
of post-traumatic stress disorder, 63-65
of secondary brain damage, 49-52
of toxic-metabolic encephalopathy, 63
Neuropsychological assessment, 10-13, 67-102
behavioral observations in, 97-98, 99
clinical interview in, 68-77. *See also* Clinical interview
cultural background in, 86-87
current stressors in, 93-94
developmental in, 78-79
dominance in, 79
education in, 80-81
family in, 94-96
language in, 79-80
legal in, 84-86
marital status and history in, 88-89
medical in, 90-91
military service in, 81-82
occupational in, 83-84
performing, utilizing neuropsychologist in, 269
psychiatric in, 92-93
religious in, 87-88
review of records in, 98, 100-102
sexual in, 89-90
siblings in, 96-97
Neuropsychological expert, selection of, 263-265
Neuropsychological reports, samples of, 229-262
Neuropsychological testing, 103-176. *See also* Testing, neuropsychological
Neuropsychologist(s)
clinical, 24
clinical psychologists compared to, 25
neurologists compared to, 29-30
psychiatrists compared to, 26-28
competence of, 20-21
deposing, 271-287. *See also* Deposing a neuropsychologist
education and training of, 15-21
experience of, in clinical neuropsychology, 16-19
services of, how to utilize, 267-270
in educating attorneys about effects of brain damage, 269-270

in interviewing clients, 267-268
in performing neuropsychological assessments, 269
in reviewing records, 268-269
Neuropsychology, clinical
definition of, 1-13
experience in, in training of neuropsychologist, 16-19
historical development of, 8-10
misconceptions of, 1-2
practice of, 2-8
assessment/diagnosis in, 2-4
consultation with other professionals in, 7-8
psychological treatment/cognitive rehabilitation in, 5-7
research in, 8
teaching in, 7
purpose of, 1
sense of frustration for attorney related to, 2
Normative data, fit of, in neuropsychological test scoring and analysis, 181-182

O

Object Assembly test, 151
Occupational history in neuropsychological assessment, 83-84
Orbital frontal lobe damage, neuropathological aspects of, 47, 53

P

Paced Auditory Serial Addition Test (PASAT), strengths and limitations of, 162
Personality tests, 156-158
results of, in neuropsychological report, 238-239, 257-258
strengths and limitations of, 176
Pia mater, 31
Pons, anatomy and function of, 39
Post-concussive syndrome, 47
Post-traumatic epilepsy, neuropathological aspects of, 52, 55-57
Post-traumatic hydrocephalus, neuropathological aspects of, 59
Post-traumatic psychiatric disorders, neuropathological aspects of, 57-59
Post-traumatic stress disorder (PTSD)
fictitious, criteria to detect individuals with, 64-65
neuropathological aspects of, 58, 63-65
vs. brain damage, 65
Pre-existing difficulties according to patient in neuropsychological report, 243-249
Precentral gyrus, 36
Problem solving, tests of
results of, in neuropsychological report, 238
strengths and limitations of, 170-171

Proverbs Test, 146-147
    strengths and limitations of, 169
Pseudodementia, neuropathological aspects of, 61-63
Psychiatric disorders
    in neuropsychological assessment, 92-93
    post-traumatic, neuropathological aspects of, 57-59
Psychiatric records, review of, in neuropsychological assessment, 102
Psychiatric treatment for family of brain-injured patient, 225-226
Psychiatrists, clinical neuropsychologists compared to, 26-28
Psychological assistants, use of, in neuropsychological testing, 107
Psychological manifestations of temporal lobe seizures, 57
Psychological records, review of, in neuropsychological assessment, 102
Psychological treatment
    for brain-damaged patient, types of, 5-6
    in practice of neuropsychology, 5-7
Psychologists, clinical, 23-24
    clinical neuropsychologists compared to, 25
Psychotherapy
    determining need of brain-damaged patient for, 222
    individual, for brain-damaged patient, 6

R

Raven Progressive Matrices, 147-148
    strengths and limitations of, 171
Records
    medical, review of, in neuropsychological report, 231-233, 246-255
    review of
        in neuropsychological assessment, 98, 100-102
        utilizing neuropsychologist in, 268-269
Rehabilitation. *See also* Treatment/rehabilitation services
    cognitive
        for brain-damaged patient, 5-6
        determining need of brain-damaged patient for, 222-223
        in practice of neuropsychology, 5-7
Rehabilitation program, brain-injury, referring brain-injured client to, 219-220
Reitan-Klove Sensory-Perceptual Examination, 145
    strengths and limitations of, 168
Reliability
    of Bender-Gestalt Test, 113
    of Halstead-Reitan Neuropsychological Test Battery, 123
    of Luria-Nebraska Neuropsychological Battery, 126
    of neuropsychological tests, 105-107
    of Wechsler Adult Intelligence Scale-Revised, 111
Religious background in neuropsychological assessment, 87-88
Research in practice of neuropsychology, 8

Rey Auditory Verbal Learning Test (RAVLT), 138-139
  strengths and limitations of, 164
Rey-Osterrieth Complex Visual Figure Test, 139-140, 152
  strengths and limitations of, 164, 172

S

Sbordone Attention Battery (SAB), strengths and limitations of, 162
Sbordone-Hall Memory Battery (SHMB), 113, 140-141
  strengths and limitations of, 165
Seashore Rhythm test, 117
Seizures in post-traumatic epilepsy, 56-57
Selective Reminding Test (SRT), 140
  strengths and limitations of, 165
Sensory-Perceptual Examination, 120
Sensory-perceptual tests, 143-146
  Benton Facial Recognition, 143-144
  Benton Judgement of Line Orientation, 144
  Hooper Visual Organization, 144-145
  Reitan-Klove Sensory-Perceptual Examination as, 145
  strengths and limitations of, 168-169
  Visual Form Discrimination, 145-146
Sexual background
  in neuropsychological assessment, 89-90
  in neuropsychological report, 245
Siblings in neuropsychological assessment, 96-97
Similarities test, 147
  strengths and limitations of, 170
Spatial-perceptual skills, tests of, 150-152
  strengths and limitations of, 172-173
Speech Sounds Perception Test, 117
Stress disorder, post-traumatic, neuropathological aspects of, 58, 63-65
Stressor(s)
  current, in neuropsychological assessment, 93-94
  type of disorder related to, 58
Stroke, 42
Subcortical brain damage
  versus cortical brain damage, 203
  patients with, neuropsychological test performance of, 200-202
Subdural hematoma, 42

T

Tables, list of, xv
Tactile Finger Localization test, 121
Tactile Form Recognition test, 121-122
Tactual perceptual examination in neuropsychological testing, 121-123
Tactual Performance test, 116-117, 152
  strengths and limitations of, 173
Teaching in practice of neuropsychology, 7
Temporal lobe damage, neuropathological aspects of, 48
Test(s), neuropsychological
  data from, quantitative/qualitative analysis of, determining, in deposition, 284-286
  interpretation of, 185-195
  poor performances on, 179
  scoring and analysis of, 177-183
    behavior of patient and, 182-183
    comparison groups in, representativeness of, 179-180
    in determining relative severity of cognitive impairments, 178
    mean and standard deviation in, 177-178
    normative data in, 181-182
Test batteries, neuropsychological, standardized, 113-120
  Finger Oscillation, 118
  Grip Strength, 119
  Halstead Category, 115-116
  Halstead-Reitan, 115
  Seashore Rhythm, 117
  Sensory-Perceptual, 120
  Speech Sounds Perception, 117
  strengths and limitations of, 160-161
  Tactual Performance, 116-117
  Trail Making, 118-119
Testing, neuropsychological, 103-176
  for attention-concentration skills, 132-136
  batteries of, standardized, 113-120
  conditions during, that may mask brain damage, 108-109
  data from, patient's behavior and, integrating information about, importance of, 203-214
  ecological validity of, 107-108
  "hit rates" in, 104-105
  in neuropsychological report, 236, 255-256
  in reaching conclusions on brain damage/cognitive impairment, 208-211
    results of, 209-211
  reliability of, 105-107
  results of, in neuropsychological report, 236-239, 256-258
  scoring and interpretation methods in, 123-127
  specific, 131-168
  Tactual Perceptual examination in, 121-123
  test validity in, 103-104

tests used in, 109-113
for abstract thinking, 146-147
for academic skills, 152-153
batteries of, flexible, 127-130
for conceptual thinking/problem solving, 147-149
for language, 153-155
for memory, 137-142
for motor skills, 142-143
for personality/emotional adjustment, 156-158
sensory-perceptual, 143-146
for spatial-perceptual and constructional skills, 150-152
use of psychological assistants in, 107
Token test, 155
Toxic-metabolic encephalopathy, neuropathological aspects of, 63
Trail Making test (TMT), 118-119
strengths and limitations of, 163
Training of neuropsychologist, 15-21
determining, in deposition, 271-273
Trauma, head, minor, neuropathological aspects of, 45-46
Treatment/rehabilitation services
behavior modification as, 222
cognitive rehabilitation as, 222-223
determining need for, 221-227
environmental modification as, 221-222
family counseling and psychiatric treatment as, 225-226
potential of, predictors of, 223-224
psychotherapy/counseling as, 222

V

Validity
of Bender-Gestalt Test, 113
of Halstead-Reitan Neuropsychological Test Battery, 123
of Luria-Nebraska Neuropsychological Battery, 126
of Wechsler Adult Intelligence Scale-Revised, 111
Vertebral artery system, 41
Visual Form Discrimination Test, 145-146
strengths and limitations of, 169
Vocational records, review of, in neuropsychological assessment, 100

W

Wechsler Adult Intelligence Scale (WAIS), 122
Wechsler Adult Intelligence Scale-Revised (WAIS-R)
in neuropsychological testing, 109-112
strengths and limitations of, 159
Wechsler Memory Scale, 141-142
Wechsler Memory Scale-Revised (WMS-R), strengths and limitations of, 166
Wide Range Achievement Test (WRAT), 152-153
strengths and limitations of, 173
Wisconsin Card Sorting Test, 149
strengths and limitations of, 171
Work histories, poor, patients with, 83